Logic, Truth and Meaning

Writings by G.E.M. Anscombe

D1452792

**ST ANDREWS STUDIES
IN PHILOSOPHY AND PUBLIC AFFAIRS**
Founding and General Editor:
John Haldane, University of St Andrews

Values, Education and the Human World
edited by John Haldane

Philosophy and its Public Role
edited by William Aiken and John Haldane

Relativism and the Foundations of Liberalism
by Graham Long

Human Life, Action and Ethics: Essays by G.E.M. Anscombe
edited by Mary Geach and Luke Gormally

*The Institution of Intellectual Values:
Realism and Idealism in Higher Education*
by Gordon Graham

Life, Liberty and the Pursuit of Utility
by Anthony Kenny and Charles Kenny

Distributing Healthcare: Principles, Practices and Politics
edited by Niall Maclean

Liberalism, Education and Schooling: Essays by T.M. Mclaughlin
edited by David Carr, Mark Halstead and Richard Pring

The Landscape of Humanity: Art, Culture & Society
by Anthony O'Hear

*Faith in a Hard Ground:
Essays on Religion, Philosophy and Ethics by G.E.M. Anscombe*
edited by Mary Geach and Luke Gormally

Subjectivity and Being Somebody
by Grant Gillett

Understanding Faith: Religious Belief and Its Place in Society
by Stephen R.L. Clark

*Profit, Prudence and Virtue:
Essays in Ethics, Business & Management*
edited by Samuel Gregg and James Stoner

Logic, Truth and Meaning

Writings by G.E.M. Anscombe

Edited by
Mary Geach and Luke Gormally

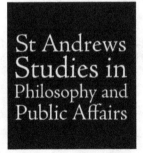

St Andrews
Studies in
Philosophy and
Public Affairs

imprint-academic.com

Published in the UK by Imprint Academic
PO Box 200, Exeter EX5 5YX, UK

Distributed in the USA by
Ingram Book Company,
One Ingram Blvd., La Vergne, TN 37086, USA

ISBN 9781845408800 paperback
ISBN 9781845408817 cloth

A CIP catalogue record for this book is available from the
British Library and US Library of Congress

Cover Photograph:
St Salvator's Quadrangle, St Andrews by Peter Adamson
from the University of St Andrews collection

For
More Geach

Contents

Part 2: Thought and Belief

Part 3: Meaning, Truth and Existence

Luke Gormally

Preface

The present volume is the fourth and final one in a series[1] designed to publish in book form hitherto uncollected and unpublished papers by the late Professor Elizabeth Anscombe. She herself had published in 1981 three volumes of *Collected Philosophical Papers*[2] but in the subsequent 20 years (she died in 2001) went on to publish more than 50 further papers. Work I have done as opportunity afforded in organising Professor Anscombe's *Nachlass* revealed additional papers worth publishing. That is the background to the present series of four further volumes of collected papers.

This fourth volume differs from the previous three in the series in reprinting in Part I a book — not a paper — which Anscombe had published in 1959, *An Introduction to Wittgenstein's* Tractatus. (The text is that of the revised Third Edition published in 1971.) The decision to do so was prompted by the advice of Professor John Haldane, the General Editor of the *St Andrews Studies in Philosophy and Public Affairs*, the series in which the new set of Anscombe volumes appear. The *Introduction* to the *Tractatus* has long been out of print in the UK and reprinting it sits well with a number of papers in the present volume which engage with 'Tractarian' themes.

---

[1]   The previous volumes in the series are: *Human Life, Action and Ethics. Essays by G E M Anscombe*, edited by Mary Geach and Luke Gormally (Exeter, UK & Charlottesville, VA, USA: Imprint Academic, 2005); *Faith in a Hard Ground. Essays on Religion, Philosophy and Ethics by G E M Anscombe*, edited by Mary Geach and Luke Gormally (Exeter, UK & Charlottesville, VA, USA: Imprint Academic, 2008); *From Plato to Wittgenstein. Essays by G E M Anscombe*, edited by Mary Geach and Luke Gormally (Exeter, UK & Charlottesville, VA, USA: Imprint Academic, 2011).

[2]   G E M Anscombe, *Collected Philosophical Papers*. Volume 1: *From Parmenides to Wittgenstein*. Volume 2: *Metaphysics and the Philosophy of Mind*. Volume 3: *Ethics, Religion and Politics* (Oxford: Basil Blackwell, 1981).

John Haldane also urged a reprinting of the second review that Elizabeth Anscombe published in 1985 of Saul Kripke's *Wittgenstein: On Rules and Private Language*. The first of those reviews we reprinted in *From Plato to Wittgenstein. Essays by G E M Anscombe* (pp. 231–246). Each review is quite distinctive in its approach to the critique of Kripke's book, so there seemed some justification for including the second review in this volume.

Of the remaining twelve papers in the volume six have not previously appeared in print. They are drawn from the Interim Archive of Anscombe's papers which I have gradually assembled in recent years. Four of the six previously published papers originally appeared in publications which are not easily accessible.

Apart from the initial editorial footnote to each paper indicating its provenance, other editorial footnotes in the present volume are preceded by the abbreviation *Ed*. Remaining footnotes are the author's though the bibliographical information they supply has often been supplemented.

In the case of previously published papers I have sought reprint permissions where appropriate but have not always succeeded in eliciting replies.

Thanks to Jared Brandt for his work in proofreading and indexing.

Gratitude is owing to John Haldane, the General Editor of the series in which this and its predecessor volumes appear, for his very active interest in their publication. In the case of this volume that interest has extended to taking responsibility for producing an electronic version of *An Introduction to Wittgenstein's* Tractatus and preparing final versions for printing of the typescripts which I produced in 2013. That amounts to a very generous contribution undertaken in the midst of the many other tasks which engage him. Beyond that contribution, John Haldane has exhibited in other ways an admirable commitment to promoting knowledge and appreciation of the work of Elizabeth Anscombe.

It remains, finally, to thank Imprint Academic, and in particular Anthony Freeman and Graham Horswell, former and present managing editors, for the excellent support they have given to our editorial undertaking.

My wife and I are pleased to be able to dedicate this volume to her youngest brother More Geach. We are moved to do so out of admiration and gratitude for the care he gave over many years to his parents, Elizabeth Anscombe and Peter Geach, in their old age.

July 2015

Mary Geach

Introduction

Fifty years back, my mother would teach me about the syllogism as I sat on the hearthrug in her study in Oxford. Over the hearth there was a mirror, inherited from her parents. Its frame was decorated with beaded grills and mother-of-pearl stars and low reliefs of formal flowers, and among the carvings of the triangle at the top there was an Arabic inscription. A friend, probably Norman Daniel, had told her what it meant, and she had noted that it was a truth. She had then forgotten what this truth was. It was an interesting example to her: that she knew that a piece of language was true, but had forgotten what true thing it said.

That mirror is the explanation of an example she uses in one of the papers in this book, a collection which, where it is not exegetical, is largely about truth in the way that logic is: any science is concerned with truth, but as Frege said, logic is concerned about truth as physics is about heat and light, and it is in this way that truth is studied here. There is work here about belief, which has this in common with assertion: that both a belief and an assertion are wrong if not true; if the proposition believed or asserted is not a true one. This means that belief as well as assertion should come within the purview of logic, though there are also problems of epistemology etc. connected with it. Moore's paradox is a problem in the field of logic, and so she deals with it.

She was commended by Bernard Williams for the seriousness of her philosophy. That seriousness was an attachment to truth, which she had learned from Wittgenstein to pursue in what he had called 'the bloody hard way', following its outlines and not trying to force it into some mould, so that where she found a serious exception she would take in the shape of it before returning to the generality which she was setting forth. Her interest in the example of the Arabic truth, which she discusses in the paper 'Making True', is an instance of this.

She slightly alters it to invent the case where to know something to be true is different from knowing the truth of any proposition besides '"Q" is true', where 'Q' is an Arabic noise one has learned to make. Saying this is like pointing to the inscription and saying 'That is true'. In most cases she would not for her purposes think there was an important difference between what makes 'p' true and what makes it true to say that 'p' is true, but here what makes it true to say that 'Q' is true is that 'Q' stands for some proposition which is true, and what makes that true depends on what sort of proposition it is.

Wittgenstein as she quotes him thought that there was a difference between proofs in logic, and proof of a significant proposition: the proof of a significant proposition shows that things are as it says. But what makes it true, when things are as it says, varies in ways which Anscombe investigates in this paper. What makes the proposition true is a proposition not logically equivalent to it. She had invented a name for a fallacy, which she called the Fallacy of Being Guided by the Truth, which is committed by one who gives an account of the meaning of a proposition or of a term within a proposition which relies on the proposition's being true, whereas a proposition has a meaning which is independent of its truth. According to the *Tractatus*, this meaning is a truth function of atomic facts: but even then, a disjunction is made true by something not logically equivalent to it.

Anscombe's approach to the *Tractatus* in her *Introduction* to it (Part 1 of this volume) is that of a sympathizer—who understands why the things said are said, though she never swallowed the thing whole. It is not a credible philosophy, which can be seen from its inability to accommodate historical propositions. The reason why shows what the interest is in the concept of making true. If historical propositions are made true by atomic facts, facts logically independent of one another, as they would have to be according to the *Tractatus*' metaphysic, this would not mean that these atomic facts were what was signified by these propositions, for in the cases where the historical propositions were not true, huge numbers of alternative sets of atomic facts could have made them so: the disjunction would be immensely long. Consider 'England was successfully invaded by the Dutch in 1688'—that is made true by the invading force of Dutchmen having landed at Tor Bay and their chief having ascended to the English throne. But the proposition does not mean that set of facts, does not logically imply it, and could have been made true in many other ways. It could have been made true by different common-or-garden facts, let alone atomic ones. These facts would not be of a kind to be the case or not the case and everything else remain the same, and since they are not really facts, nothing determines in what atomic facts the whole different situation would consist. Historical truths do not go very well with this metaphysic.

It is interesting that in discussing the question of making true she does not bring up the subject of the relation between more and less brute facts, especially as one of the examples she gives of a proposition being made true is that of the fact of one having paid having been made true by money having been paid. She did not apply this important discovery of hers (of the relation between more or less brute facts[1]) to the question of assertion, either, though I suppose that it was obvious to her that the fact that one is asserting *p* cannot be analysed in terms either of the circumstances or of the intentions which might be regarded as making it true that one is asserting. Though asserting *p* may consist in one's saying '*p*' under circumstances xyz, or with the intentions xyz, it is always possible to think of some further circumstance which would make the circumstances or intentions in question fail to give to the man's utterance the significance of an assertion. One might intend that one's hearer believe a line in a song one is singing, but that does not have to mean that one is asserting that line. So intention to produce belief that *p* is not enough to make it the case that one is asserting *p* in uttering it: this special context shows that definition in terms of this intention is an inadequate one. Further attempts to define the act of assertion in terms of the intentions or circumstances which make it the case that a proposition is being asserted are inevitably tiresome. Writing about the impossibility of defining concepts like 'owes' in terms of the range of circumstances under which they apply, Anscombe says 'no theoretically adequate provision can be made for exceptional circumstances, since a further special context can theoretically be imagined which would reinterpret any special context.'[2] The concept 'asserts', I think, is like this.

Perhaps realizing this, Anscombe makes no attempt to define the human act of assertion, what Russell calls 'psychological assertion', even though in her *Introduction* to the *Tractatus* she says on page 95 that 'assertion has *only* a psychological sense'. She appears here to follow Wittgenstein in his contempt for the Fregean assertion sign, and

---

1   See 'On Brute Facts' in G E M Anscombe, *Collected Philosophical Papers*, Volume III: *Ethics, Religion and Politics* (Oxford: Basil Blackwell, 1981), pp. 22–25.
2   'Modern Moral Philosophy' in *Human Life, Action, and Ethics. Essays by G E M Anscombe*, edited by Mary Geach and Luke Gormally (Exeter, UK & Charlottesville, VA, USA: Imprint Academic, 2005) at p. 173.

especially says that it can be no part of the sense of the technical term 'logically asserted', were such a term to be given a definition, that the proposition be true, as Frege and Russell thought it must be.

An example of a technical meaning being given to 'logically asserted' is an idea defined by Julianne Jack (referred to in the paper 'Belief and Thought' by her maiden name of Rountree). She defines when in a context the occurrence of a proposition is an asserted occurrence. For Anscombe, the purpose achieved by this definition is to save us from a dilemma: that we seem obliged to say either that there is a (defeasible) presumption that 'p' asserts that p, or that assertion adds some mysterious thing to a proposition. 'p' on its own turns out to be its own context. I was initially put off Jack's account of an asserted occurrence of p by the fact that on this account the occurrence of 'p' in the assertion '- - p' is not an asserted occurrence.

There are parallels between the question of what it is to assent to a proposition (as opposed to merely understanding it) and what it is to assert a proposition (as opposed to merely uttering it). Just as we can see that there is no additional content to the thought that something is so, which is there when we assent as opposed to merely entertaining the thought, so there is nothing added to a proposition when we assert it as opposed to merely uttering it. In her *Introduction* to the *Tractatus* Anscombe is dismissive of one of Frege's reasons for introducing the assertion sign, which has to do with this difference, the difference between entertaining and assenting, the difference between asserting and, say, uttering on the stage. The reason which she takes seriously is that 'p' occurs in contexts like 'p or q', and that the content of the proposition is the same in such a context as when 'p' is asserted on its own. It was thus important that Julianne Rountree was able to define what it was for 'p' to be asserted in a propositional context: that is, for an occurrence of 'p' in such a context to be an asserted occurrence. But if we follow what Anscombe said before, and think that assertion is only a psychological concept, what relation does this logical assertedness have to assertion considered as a human act? Anscombe says in 'Belief and Thought' that the tools of assertion lie ready to hand, that we do not make a mysterious addition to a proposition by asserting it, and deals with the case of fiction by saying that we make assertions which are not meant to be believed, and for this reason say that they are not assertions. The propositions in a fiction are logically asserted in the Rountree sense.

For myself, I think the relation of assertion to truth is the important one: that the reason why a fiction is not a lie is that it is not meant to be true, and that I think that to lie is quite simply to make an assertion which one does not believe. To make an assertion is to say something which is meant to be true. A problem arises about this 'meant', but a similar problem arises about Anscombe's saying that fictions are not *meant* to be believed. In both cases, the word 'meant' does not refer to the intention of the speaker or writer. He intends to be making an assertion, or to relate a fiction, but one can make an assertion which one knows to be false, and one might tell a fairy tale and hope that the hearer (who perhaps has some mad theory about these tales) will believe some propositions contained within it. So what is this 'meant'? Insofar as the speaker 'means' something, he means to play the language game of reciting fiction, or of making assertion, and the 'meant' in 'This is meant to be true' or 'This is not meant to be believed' belongs to the teleology of the tool rather than of the tool user. Fiction, like assertion, is a tool lying ready to hand.

Anscombe turns to the consideration of assertion from the consideration of belief, and of the assent which makes believing a proposition different from understanding it. Her reflections on belief are interesting not only because of the problem raised by assent, but because of the ways in which a belief sentence is, but need not be, about a disposition. We see her here following the unexpected outlines of truth in the way of which I have spoken.

Anscombe's apparent change of front about assertion is not the only case of a difference between what she says in her *Introduction* to the *Tractatus* and what she says in the papers published here. For instance, in the former she says that names are absolutely simple signs, whereas in the paper 'Grammar, Structure, and Essence' she says that Wittgenstein agreed with Proclus' saying that a name was a logical picture of its object, remarking to her, when she read a passage to him, how often he had had that thought. This, of course, was Wittgenstein in his later years, after the formation of his second philosophy, so when Anscombe wrote the *Introduction* she did not apply this memory to her account of the *Tractatus'* 'objects'. So this paper is of particular interest, in that it reflects a development in her thoughts on Wittgenstein. She saw his thought as being the same in various respects in the earlier and the later philosophy: the part played by grammar in the latter takes over from the part played in the *Tractatus* by the structure of propositions.

About Wittgenstein on grammar, Anscombe said to me, a thing she also says in the paper 'Grammar, Structure and Essence', that he did not mean anything peculiar by the word grammar. It was just that he did not confine the meaning to the grammar we learn in school. She mentioned to me in this connection the grammarian Jespersen as an example of one whose study of grammar went into the regions with which Wittgenstein dealt. People who are only thinking of school grammar are apt to think in terms of grammatical mistakes, and the rules which say when one is making them. But the difference between an imperative and an indicative is obviously a grammatical difference, which has to do with the fact that imperatives are answered by actions which make true the proposition which one would obtain by changing the mood of the verb. This is part of the grammar of an order, but this does not mean that to disobey an order would be a grammatical mistake. Some points are best made by pointing out that something would be a grammatical mistake: I was taught at school that cardinal numbers were adjectives, and it is a grammatical point that though each of three blind mice is a blind mouse, we should not conclude that each is a three mouse.[3]

The complexity of names, which she brings out in the paper 'Grammar, Structure and Essence', is also relevant to the notion of private ostensive definition, which she deals with in the paper 'On Private Ostensive Definition', where she attacks the modern mindset as represented by Locke by showing how, without even entering into the question of the privacy of the act of naming some private object, Wittgenstein had in the *Blue Book* dealt 'hammer blows' to the notion that naming was a simple act of attaching a name to a thing, or indeed that there could be any such act. What *about* the thing is one pointing to in giving an ostensive definition by means of it? (Anscombe uses Locke to represent the mindset attacked by Wittgenstein, though she had no reason to think that the latter philosopher had read the former. She thought that people in a culture were unconsciously influenced by philosophers, as she had been as a girl.)

She disagreed with Kripke in his interpretation of Wittgenstein on the topic of following a rule: she did not see Wittgenstein's arguments about language and private language as introducing a serious sceptical possibility; for Wittgenstein had said that the fact that we can imagine a doubt does not mean that we are in doubt.

She once said to me that no one understood Wittgenstein, but one does not have to have an overall comprehension of his philosophy in order to get much truth out of it. He did not try to make a system and

---

[3]   Further observations by Anscombe on grammar and numerals in 'A Theory of Language?' in *From Plato to Wittgenstein. Essays by G E M Anscombe*, edited by Mary Geach and Luke Gormally (Exeter, UK & Charlottesville, VA, USA: Imprint Academic, 2011), at pp. 200–201.

then apply it, and one does not need to learn a lot of technical apparatus apart from ordinary logic and mathematics in order to get something from his later philosophy.

The same is true of Anscombe. When she considers some philosophical subject, she does not do so by applying some method other than meeting the requirements of logic: she is sometimes making a path in a trackless waste. To appreciate her is to follow her closely, for often with each sentence she makes a new philosophical point. Even when she is doing very plain logic, though, Anscombe is able to surprise. She described to me the sight of her distinguished audience in America scribbling away as they worked out the validity of her 'queer pattern of argument'. What she does here is display a plain logical argument, which people not accustomed to truth-functional logic may find hard to follow. This book is really only suitable reading for such as have been logically trained.

July 2015

Part 1

Wittgenstein and the *Tractatus*

An Introduction to
Wittgenstein's *Tractatus*

Acknowledgments

Most of what appears here was originally delivered in the form of lectures at Oxford in the Michaelmas and Hilary Terms, 1957–8. I am indebted, first, to the Oxford audiences ... ; and, secondly, to Professor Paton [editor of the series in which the book first appeared], who made many useful criticisms of my exposition. I am also much indebted to Peter Geach for help afforded in frequent discussions and in revising the book. In particular, I obtained some logical information and references from him; for example, he supplied me with the explanations given in Chapter 9 of Wittgenstein's criticisms of *Principia Mathematica*, concerning the 'ancestral relation' and the unacknowledged use of 'formal series' made by Russell and Whitehead. Finally, I have had the advantage of reading through Professor Erik Stenius' highly interesting book on the *Tractatus* before its publication. It presents a very different account from my own of some important points, and enabled me to sharpen my own ideas by contrast.

I am grateful to the Rockefeller Foundation, which has supported me during six years' work on Wittgenstein's MSS.; this book was written during my tenure of a Research Fellowship sponsored by the Foundation.

Oxford   G.E.M. ANSCOMBE

Introduction

Ludwig Wittgenstein was born in Vienna in 1889, the eighth child of a family largely Jewish by extraction, though not by persuasion. His father had started the modern iron and steel industry in Austria; he was a man of forcible character who was generally both much feared and much respected. The children were brought up in an atmosphere of extreme contempt for most kinds of low standard. The whole generation had an unusual fire about them. All were aesthetically and, in particular, musically talented to a high degree; the father, however, though sharing such interests up to a point, regarded them as suited only to be a side-line for his sons: the only fit career for them was civil engineering. (It had to be concealed from him that one of them as a child played the violin in St. Peter's Church in Vienna.) The combination of family temperament and the attitude of the parents—who could not conceive that their children might suffer miseries worth taking account of—led to at least one suicide among the sons. Of himself, Ludwig said: 'I had an unhappy childhood and a most miserable youth'; but again, in connection with the work that a man was content to publish: 'I had luck: I was very well brought up'—i.e. as far as concerned critical standards.

Ludwig came to Manchester at the age of about nineteen to study engineering; but by 1911 his interest had been caught by the philosophy of mathematics, and he went to Cambridge to study under Russell. From 1912 to 1917 he was engaged in writing the work which is the subject of this book. The greater part of the writing was done while he was on active service in the Austrian army.

As a boy of sixteen Wittgenstein had read Schopenhauer and had been greatly impressed by Schopenhauer's theory of the 'world as idea' (though not of the 'world as will'); Schopenhauer then struck him as fundamentally right, if only a few adjustments and clarifications were made. It is very much a popular notion of Wittgenstein that he was a latter-day Hume; but any connections between them are indirect, and he never read more than a few pages of Hume. If we look for Wittgenstein's philosophical ancestry, we should rather look to Schopenhauer; specifically, his 'solipsism', his conception of 'the limit' and his ideas on value will be better understood in the light of Schopenhauer than of any other philosopher. It is one of the oddities of the present day that Schopenhauer is often vaguely associated with Nietzsche and even with Nazism, and is thought to be some kind of immoralist, worshipper of power and praiser of suicide; it is not the mythical Schopenhauer of popular repute, but the actual Schopenhauer, that we should remember in connection with Wittgenstein.

For the rest, Wittgenstein's philosophical influences are pretty well confined to Frege and to Russell, who introduced him to Frege's writings. His relative estimate of them comes out in the acknowledgment he makes in the Preface to the *Tractatus*: 'I owe a great part of the stimulation of my thoughts to the great works of Frege and to the writings of my friend Mr. Bertrand Russell.'

Frege, whose first important work was published in 1879 and who died in 1925, was a philosopher whose greatness, up to the present day, was acknowledged only by a very few. Russell and Wittgenstein were the most eminent of those who recognized it. He was not a general philosopher and had no concern with either ethics or theory of knowledge, but purely with logic and the foundations of mathematics; here however his considerations, being always concerned with fundamentals, are of the greatest general philosophical importance. I devote a good deal of space to Frege in this book for the following reason: Wittgenstein's *Tractatus* has captured the interest and excited the admiration of many, yet almost all that has been published about it has been wildly irrelevant. If this has had any one cause, that cause has been the neglect of Frege and of the new direction that he gave to philosophy. In the *Tractatus* Wittgenstein assumes, and does not try to stimulate, an interest in the kind of questions that Frege wrote about; he also takes it for granted that his readers will have read Frege.

Now, empiricist or idealist preconceptions, such as have been most common in philosophy for a long time, are a thorough impediment to the understanding of either Frege or the *Tractatus*. It is best, indeed, if one wants to understand these authors, not to have any philosophical preconceptions at all, but to be capable of being naively struck by such questions as the following ones: If I say that Russell is a clever philosopher, I mention Russell, and say something about him: now, is what I say about him something that I *mention*, just as I *mention* him? If so, what is the connection between these two mentioned things? If not, what account are we to give of the words expressing what I say about him? Have they any reference to reality? Further, suppose we try to explain the reference to reality by adverting to the *truth* of what is said, then what about false statements? These *say that* such and such is the case just as much as true statements do — so that the *saying-that* done by true statements cannot be explained by their truth. The investigations prompted by these questions are more akin to ancient, than to more modern, philosophy.[1]

Again, if I say that the evening star is the same as the morning star, is this statement about the object mentioned, or about the signs used in speaking of it? If it is about the object, then why is it informative to say this, but not informative to say that the evening star is the same as the evening star? If it is about the signs, then, once more, how can it be informative since we can make signs stand for what we like by arbitrary definition?

This latter problem led Frege to formulate his famous distinction between the *sense* (*Sinn*) and the *reference* (*Bedeutung*) of words: The expressions 'the morning star' and 'the evening star', he said, have the same reference — for they refer to the same object, namely the planet Venus. But they have different senses, and that is why the statement of identity can be informative. This distinction between 'sense' and 'reference', once formulated, was used by Frege throughout his accounts of truth and falsehood, of objects and concepts, of propositions and thoughts.

Above all, Frege's enquiries were in no way psychological; nor had he any interest in private mental contents. If people speak of the number 100, they may have quite different images: one may have a mental picture of the letter C, another of ten rows of ten dots, another of a collection of hens in a yard; and the same man may have different images at different times, or again one may have no image. None of this has the slightest bearing on what is meant when we speak of the number 100. Nor can the history of the race or of language, nor again the mental processes by which a man grasps that 10 x 10 = 100, be relevant to the question what it is that he grasps.

Russell, who discusses many of the same questions as Frege, differs from him by introducing the notion of immediate experience, and

---

[1]   cf. Plato's *Theaetetus* 189A: 'In judging, one judges something; in judging something, one judges something real; so in judging something unreal one judges nothing; but judging nothing, one is not judging at all.' Wittgenstein returned to the problem presented by this argument again and again throughout his life.

hence that of private mental contents, into his explanations of meaning and his theory of judgment. For Russell was thoroughly imbued with the traditions of British empiricism. Wittgenstein's admirers have generally been like Russell in this, and have assumed that Wittgenstein was too; therefore they have had assumptions about what is fundamental in philosophical analysis which were quite out of tune with the *Tractatus*.

We owe to Frege the notion of a 'truth-value' which is current at the present day. The truth-value of a proposition is its truth or false-hood as the case may be. Frege says: its truth-value is *the true* if it is true and *the false* if it is false. This term is now very familiar to any student of elementary logic, and may easily seem to be no more than a conveniently short expression by means of which circumlocution is avoided. In Frege, however, we find it arrived at through hard work on the theory of meaning and truth: work which also produced other allied and fruitful conceptions.

One of the most important of these is the profound comparison[2] between a predicate and the expression of an arithmetical function, e.g. $'(x)^2'$. The notion of what is termed a 'propositional function', e.g. 'x is bald', is directly based on this comparison: here we get a propo-sition if we replace the 'x' by a (real) proper name, just as from $'(x)^2'$ we get an expression of definite value by replacing the 'x' by a definite number. This comparison is fundamental to all modern logic.

Frege also gave us the modern conception of 'quantification', which is so useful and in such general use in logic that we regard it as we regard the wheel, forgetting its inventor. Quantification essentially consists in reformulating 'Everything is heavy' as: 'For all x, x is heavy'; and 'Something is heavy' as: 'For some x, x is heavy' or 'There is an x such that x is heavy'. These are written in a symbolic notation.[3] The general reader may wonder at first whether the interest of such a device is not purely technical. It is easy to bring out that this is not so; it is of great general interest in philosophy.

For example, this formulation supplies us with a perspicuous refutation of the celebrated Ontological Argument of Descartes: people have been generally agreed that, but not how, it is to be refuted. According to the Ontological Argument the notion of God involves that of existence, as that of a triangle involves the various properties of a triangle; therefore, God exists. Let us concede the

---

[2]   *See* Chapter 7.
[3]   *See* Glossary and Chapter 11.

premise. (There is even good ground for it in the fact that e.g. 'There used to be a God, but isn't any more' seems to conflict with the concept 'God'.) The premise should be stated as follows: Just as, *if* anything is a triangle, it has those properties, so *if* anything is God, it must possess eternal existence. This is fair; we must be permitted to take seriously the argument about triangles which Descartes relies on. But in the sense in which the conclusion 'God exists' is intended, it means that *there* is a God. And that by no means follows from the premise. For, quite generally, from: 'For all x, if ϕx, then ψx', we cannot infer: 'There is an x such that ϕx.' That is, interpreting 'ϕx' as 'x is God' and 'ψx' as 'x has eternal existence', we cannot infer '*There is* a God' from 'For all x, if x is God, x has eternal existence'. We can very well grant that and still ask 'But *is* there such a being?' We may well say: 'It belongs to the concept of a phoenix never to die, but eternally to renew its life in the flames'; but we cannot infer from the concept that there lives such a creature.

Again, the following fallacious piece of reasoning is found in Aristotle: 'All chains of means to ends[4] must terminate in a final end. This final end will be the supreme good.' The first statement is reasonable; the second assumes that the first has shewn that there is some one end, the same for all chains of means to ends, in which they all terminate: the fallacy is immediately avoided by writing:

For all x, if x is a chain of means to ends, there is a y such that y is a final end and x terminates in y,

which is quite different from:

There is a y such that y is a final end, and for all x, if x is a chain of means to ends, x terminates in y.

It is of general usefulness to be armed against all fallacies of this type.

Again, a possible limitation on the sense in which a man is free can be brought out by considering that:

At all times there is a possibility of my abstaining from smoking, is quite different from and unluckily does not imply:

There is a possibility of my abstaining from smoking at all times. The difference here is quite easily made out in ordinary language; but it is also easily missed. In symbolic notation it cannot be missed, for there is no ambiguous way of writing down what we are saying.

Thus this device of modern logic at least is an instrument for the clarification of thought which is of use to anyone who engages in

---

4   i.e. every case of doing a in order that b in order that c ...

reasoning. And without the development of this part of logic by Frege and Russell, it is inconceivable that Wittgenstein should have written the *Tractatus*.

Russell, studying the same range of topics as Frege, criticized and rejected one of Frege's (at first sight) most plausible devices: the distinction between the sense and the reference of phrases. At the same time he used the new way of representing 'all' and 'some' in analysing sentences containing definite descriptions (singular descriptions preceded by the definite article).[5] Frege had treated such descriptions as proper names which, while they always had a sense, might or might not have a reference. According to him sentences containing definite descriptions without reference were neither true nor false. This view is dependent on the validity of the distinction between sense and reference, not merely as he first introduced it in connection with identity, but in the very extended application that he made of it; if that has to be rejected, a new account of such sentences has to be found. This was given by Russell in his Theory of Descriptions. Wittgenstein embraced the logical analysis afforded by Russell's theory with admiration, and, as we shall see, it exercised a great influence on the thought of the *Tractatus*.

The notions of 'sense', 'reference' and 'meaning' as they occur in these three authors, Frege, Russell and Wittgenstein, perhaps need a summary account. Frege's 'sense' corresponds roughly to the ordinary English 'meaning'. When we ask for the meaning of a phrase, we are not asking to have an object indicated to us: we want a paraphrase with the same meaning—or, as Frege would say, the same sense. On the other hand, if I say 'When I spoke of "that fat charlatan", I *meant* Smith', what I 'meant' is a man; Frege's 'reference' (*Bedeutung*) corresponds to what is 'meant' in this use of of the word.

Wittgenstein follows Frege in this use of the words '*Bedeutung*', '*bedeuten*'. Generally, in the *Tractatus*, they ought not to be rendered, as C.K. Ogden[6] rendered them, by 'meaning' and 'mean', but rather by 'reference' and 'stand for'. Wittgenstein's conception of 'sense' may be called the same as Frege's, if we are careful to add that Wittgenstein

---

5   *See* Chapter 2.
6   At least, if we use 'reference' etc. for Frege's *'Bedeutung'* —Ogden's translation of the *Tractatus* has mistakes which Wittgenstein did not detect. He later said (wrongly) that he did not work on the translation: he only remembered answering a list of questions. E.g., as we now know, he suggested the free but excellent rendering of the first sentence of 4.023.

had different *theses* about it: for he held that names had no sense but only reference, and propositions no reference but only sense; and also that a proposition could not have a sense without being either true or false. Further, he uses the suggestion of 'direction' that is contained in the word 'sense' when he speaks of positive and negative as opposite senses: we shall see that he considered significant negatability to be of the essence of a significant proposition, and a proposition and its negation as like arrows pointing in opposite directions. ('*Sinn*' is not ordinary German for 'direction', but, like 'sense' in English usage, it occurs with that meaning in mathematics.)

Russell uses only one notion 'meaning' and holds that the meanings of words must always be objects that one is directly acquainted with. He also speaks of 'denoting': a 'denoting' expression is such an expression as 'Some ambassador', 'Any horse', 'The (one and only) earth satellite'. It was the object of the Theory of Descriptions to analyse such expressions away, and so 'denoting' has no part in Russell's final explanation.

This, then, is the historical background of the *Tractatus*. It is a book which is apt to captivate people's minds, while at the same time seeming in many parts excessively obscure. Some people, once they have looked into it, are prevented from throwing it away in despair of penetrating its meaning by the impression they receive of great light in certain areas. This *Introduction* is addressed primarily to such readers as these. It is certainly not meant to be of any value to someone who does not read or propose to read the *Tractatus* itself.

The *Tractatus* is not presented in an order of demonstration from premises; if we want to find the grounds for its contentions, we must look in the middle and not at the beginning. It is divided into a set of numbered remarks in a decimal notation shewing what is of greater and what of subsidiary importance: the more decimal places in a number, the more subsidiary the remark it is attached to. The main propositions are the ones numbered with the whole numbers 1–7. These run:

1. The world is everything that is the case.
2. What is the case — the fact — is the existence of atomic facts.[7]
3. The logical picture[8] of the facts is the thought.
4. The thought is the significant proposition.

---

[7] *See* Chapters 1 and 4.
[8] *See* Chapter 4.

5. The proposition is a truth-function[9] of elementary propositions.[10]
   (The elementary proposition is a truth-function of itself.)
6. The general form of truth-function is $[\bar{p}, \bar{\xi}, N(\bar{\xi})]$.[11] This is the
   general form of proposition.
7. What we cannot speak of, we must be silent about.[12]

It is clear enough from this that the principal theme of the book is the connection between language, or thought, and reality. The main thesis about this is that sentences, or their mental counterparts, are pictures of facts. Only we must not suppose that what is pictured by a proposition has to exist: as Wittgenstein wrote in explaining himself to Russell in 1919, a fact is what corresponds to a proposition *if* it is true. The proposition is the same picture whether it is true or false — i.e. whether the fact it is a picture of *is* a fact, is the case, or not. This should not make us ask 'How, then, can a fact not be a fact?' For, following Wittgenstein's explanation, it means: The proposition is the same picture whether what corresponds to it *if* it is true is the case or not: it is a picture of that. And what corresponds to it if it is true is the same, whether it is true or false. The world is the totality of facts — i.e. of the counterparts in reality of *true* propositions. And nothing but picturable situations can be stated in propositions. There is indeed much that is inexpressible — which we must not try to state, but must contemplate without words.

In his Introduction Wittgenstein suggests that he may be understood only by people who have had the same thoughts as he; certainly he can only be understood by people who have been perplexed by the same problems. His own writing is extraordinarily compressed, and it is necessary to ponder each word in order to understand his sentences. When one does this, they often turn out to be quite straightforward, and by no means so oracular or aphoristic as they have been taken to be. But few authors make such demands on the close attention and active co-operation of their readers.

In my account, I have not followed the arrangement of the *Tractatus* at all. That, I think, is something to do when one reads the book for enjoyment *after* one has come to understand its main ideas. I have chosen what seem to me to be the most important themes and

---

9   *See* Glossary and Chapter 3.
10 *See* Chapter 1.
11 *See* Chapter 10.
12 *See* Chapters 5 and 13.

problems of the book. My first six chapters aim at giving the reader some idea of the 'picture theory' of the proposition. I devote a great deal of space to the topic of negation, for 'not', which is so simple to use, is utterly mystifying to think about; no theory of thought or judgment which does not give an account of it can hope to be adequate. It is thus one of the central topics of the *Tractatus*.

Chapter 7 is mainly concerned with what becomes of the great problem of Universals in Wittgenstein's theory, and Chapter 8 with certain aspects of 'not', 'and', 'or', etc., which are not covered in my account of the picture theory. Chapters 9 and 10 deal with important technical notions which are rather special to the *Tractatus*, and could be omitted by a beginner who wanted first to familiarize himself with its foundations: these chapters, we may say, treat of the upper storeys of the edifice. But with Chapter 11, on the theory of generality, we are once more working on the foundations. The last two chapters are about some general philosophical consequences which Wittgenstein drew from his investigations into the philosophy of logic.

The logic, a knowledge of which is necessary for an understanding of the *Tractatus*, is very elementary; my own aim has been to write in such a way that someone who was not already familiar with it could pick it up as he went along. In case the symbols and technical terms of elementary modern logic should be unfamiliar to a reader, I append a short glossary.

Glossary

p, q, r	These small letters are used to represent propositions. (By Wittgenstein, only for elementary propositions.)
a, b, c	These small letters (from the beginning of the alphabet) are used to represent proper names of objects.
fa, ga, ϕa, ψa	represent propositions containing the name 'a'. Similarly
f(a,b), ϕ(a,b)	represent a proposition containing the names 'a' and 'b': 'f' and 'ϕ' are here shewn to be 'two-place' predicates, or 'dyadic relational expressions'.
R, S	These large letters are used to represent relations, e.g. 'to the right of', 'larger than', 'father of'. And
aRb	symbolizes a proposition asserting a relation between a and b.
x, y, z	These small letters (from the end of the alphabet) mark (different) empty places in propositions written in the forms 'fa' or 'f(a,b)', or 'aRb', from which a proper name or names have been removed; e.g. if we remove 'a' and 'b' from 'aRb' we have '–R–', which yields a proposition if we put names in the blanks. To differentiate blanks, we put 'xRy'; to shew

they are to be filled up the same way, we put 'xRx'.

Variable	Such a small letter as x, y, z, in the role just described. Variables are chiefly used in the construction of
Quantified propositions	Propositions containing the notions 'all', 'some'. When we are speaking of 'all' so-and-so, and any example of so-and-so would be an object which could have a proper name, the proposition is written in the form:
$(x)\phi x$	For all x, ϕx; i.e. 'Everything is ϕ'.
$(Ex)\phi x$	For some x, ϕx; i.e. 'Something is ϕ' or 'There is an x such that ϕx'.
Truth-value	The truth or falsehood (as the case may be) of a proposition.
Function (Value, Argument)	Cannot be defined, but only illustrated: a *function*, say ( )², takes different *values* for different *arguments*: e.g. the value of the function ( )² for the argument 3 is 9, since $(3)^2 = 9$. The value of the power function ( )⁽ ⁾ for arguments 2 and 3 in that order is 8: since 2 to the power 3 (2^3) is 8.
Truth-function	A function (e.g. '– and –' whose argument(s) (e.g. 'p' and 'q') and values (e.g. 'p and q') are propositions, such that the truth-value of its value is determined by the truth-value(s) of its argument(s).
Truth-functional connectives (one kind of 'logical constants')	Signs used to express truth-functions, e.g. 'not', 'and', 'or'. For the truth-value of 'not-p' is determined by the truth-value of p, and the truth-value of 'p and q' and 'p or q' is determined by the truth-values of p and of q.
~	not.

.	and.

∨   or; non-exclusive, i.e. 'p ∨ q' is true when both 'p' and 'q' are true, as well as when only one of them is.

⊃   if . . . then . . ., defined as 'either not . . . or . . .'. Thus 'p⊃q' is true if 'p' is false or 'q' true, regardless of any real connection in their subject-matters. This (minimum) sense of 'if . . . then' occurs in 'If that is so, I'm a Dutchman', which if I am known not to be a Dutchman is a way of saying that 'that' is *not* so.

Material implication   the 'if . . . then' expressed by '⊃'.

Truth-table[1] (or: Matrix)   A table designed to show the relation between the truth-value of a truth-function and the truth-value(s) of its argument(s). Thus the truth-tables for 'p and q' and 'p or q' are:

p	q	p and q	p or q
T(rue)	T	T	T
T	F	F	T
F(alse)	T	F	T
F	F	F	F

Tautology   Any truth-function such that whatever the truth-values of its arguments, its value for those arguments is always true. Examples: p ∨ ~p; (p.p⊃q)⊃q.

Logical product   Conjunction of all the propositions of a given set, e.g. p. q. r.

Logical sum   Disjunction of all the propositions of a given set, e.g. p ∨ q ∨ r.

=   In the logical contexts this is used as the sign of identity, not of equality in quantity; 'a=b' means that a *is* b.

---

[1]   Invented (independently) by Wittgenstein and Post.

N( )	Joint negation of the propositions put between the brackets; used only by Wittgenstein (*see* Chapter 10).
O, Ω	variable signs for an operation in Wittgenstein's sense; these symbols are peculiar to the *Tractatus* (*see* Chapter 9).
ξ, η	variables for expressions, not tied to any one kind, as is x, which is a name variable, or again n, which is a numerical variable: used in informal exposition by Frege and Wittgenstein.
ﬧ	sign for a special operation, used only in the present book (*see* Chapter 10). Read as 'Resh'.

1

Elementary Propositions

Karl Popper has described the *Tractatus* in the following way:

'Wittgenstein tried to shew that all so-called philosophical or meta-physical propositions were in fact non-propositions or pseudo-propositions: that they were senseless or meaningless. All genuine (or meaningful) propositions were truth-functions of the elementary or atomic propositions which described "atomic facts", i.e. facts which can in principle be ascertained by observation. In other words, they were fully reducible to elementary or atomic propositions which were simple statements describing possible states of affairs, and which could be in principle established or rejected by observation. If we call a state-ment an "observation statement" not only if it states an actual observa-tion but also if it states anything that may be observed, we shall have to say that every genuine proposition must be a truth-function of and therefore deducible from, observation statements. All other apparent propositions will be, in fact, nonsense; they will be meaningless pseudo-propositions.'[1]

I cite this passage because it expresses the most common view of the *Tractatus*. It only needs a small supplement to express that view com-pletely. For it is sufficiently well known that the *Tractatus* contains a 'picture theory' of language, of which Popper here makes no mention. The whole theory of propositions is, then, on this view, a merely external combination of two theories: a 'picture theory' of elementary propositions (viz. that they have meaning by being 'logical pictures' of elementary states of affairs), and the theory of truth-functions as an account of non-elementary propositions; this latter theory breaks down rather easily, because it is impossible to regard generalized propositions that relate to an infinitely numerous universe as truth-functions of elementary propositions.

---

[1] *British Philosophy in Mid-Century*, Allen and Unwin, 1957: pp. 163–4.

Someone who, having read the *Tractatus*, reads Popper's account of it, must be struck by one thing: namely that there is a great deal about 'observation' in Popper's account, and very little about it in the *Tractatus*. According to Popper, the elementary propositions of the *Tractatus* are simple observation statements. Now can we find any support for this view in the *Tractatus* itself? I think that the strongest support that we can find is at 3.263: 'The references of primitive signs can be made clear by elucidations. Elucidations are propositions containing the primitive signs. Thus they can only be understood, if one is acquainted with the references of these signs.' I think we can take it that 'primitive signs' are the same thing as 'names', from the passage above, 3.261: 'Two signs, one a primitive sign, and the other defined by means of primitive signs, cannot signify in the same way. *Names* cannot be expounded by means of definitions.' Here it is clear enough that 'names' are 'primitive signs'; and as we know from elsewhere that Wittgenstein did not regard logical signs as primitive signs, or as having anything that they stand for, we can also say that the only primitive signs for him are what he calls 'names'. Names, then, can be made clear by elucidations, by sentences containing them spoken to someone who is acquainted with the objects that they stand for.

An obvious example of a name might seem to be the word 'red' uttered in a sentence, perhaps 'Red patch here' in the presence of someone who is contemplating the red patch and who may be supposed to have acquaintance with the object designated by the word 'red'. And 'red patch here' would seem to be a candidate for being a simple or elementary observation statement such as Popper refers to. This suggests that the elementary propositions are not merely observation statements, but sense-datum statements; as, indeed, they were taken to be both by many members of the Vienna Circle and for many years in Cambridge discussions. And I think it is quite possible that Wittgenstein had roughly this sort of thing rather vaguely in mind. His speaking of 'acquaintance' (for that certainly seems the best rendering of '*kennen*' and its compounds where they occur in the *Tractatus*) very strongly suggests this; we immediately think of Russell's distinction between 'knowledge by acquaintance' and 'knowledge by description'.

I do not believe that any other support for Popper's view of elementary propositions is to be found in the *Tractatus*. And this passage is a rather slender support.

In the first place, Wittgenstein does not state, or even suggest, that the proposition which contains an elementary name and 'elucidates' that name for a person acquainted with its reference must be an elementary proposition.

In the second place, the kind of example that comes most readily to mind, 'This is a red patch', can be proved not to be an elementary proposition according to the *Tractatus*. For at 6.3751 we find in parenthesis: 'It is clear that the logical product of two elementary propositions can be neither a tautology nor a contradiction. The assertion that a point in the visual field is two different colours at the same time is a contradiction.' It follows directly from this that 'This is a red patch' cannot be an elementary proposition.

Indeed, quite generally, if elementary propositions are simple observation statements, it is very difficult to see how what Wittgenstein says here can possibly hold good of them; for, for any proposition which could reasonably be called a 'simple observation statement', one could find another that would be incompatible with it and be precisely analogous to it logically. Therefore, whatever elementary propositions may be, they are not simple observation statements; and this accounts for the lack of reference to observation in all the remarks concerning elementary propositions; which would surely be very strange if Popper's interpretation were the correct one.

With this is connected the fact that there is hardly any epistemology in the *Tractatus*; and that Wittgenstein evidently did not think that epistemology had any bearing on his subject-matter. We find epistemology put in its place at 4.1121: 'Psychology is no nearer related to philosophy than is any other natural science. The theory of knowledge is the philosophy of psychology.'

A letter to Russell in 1919, written from the prison camp at Monte Cassino, throws further light on this. Russell had asked: '... But a *Gedanke* [thought] is a *Tatsache* [fact]: what are its constituents and components, and what is their relation to those of the pictured *Tatsache*?' To this Wittgenstein replies: 'I don't know *what* the constituents of a thought are but I know *that* it must have constituents which correspond to the words of language. Again the kind of relation of the constituents of the thought and of the pictured fact is irrelevant. It would be a matter of psychology to find out.' That is to say, it would be a matter of empirical investigation to find out, both what the constituents of a thought are and how they are related to the 'objects' occurring in facts, that is to say, to the objects designated by the 'names' in language.

That this is fantastically untrue is shewn by any serious investigation into epistemology, such as Wittgenstein made in *Philosophical Investigations*. But it is fair to say that at the time when he wrote the

Tractatus, Wittgenstein pretended that epistemology had nothing to do with the foundations of logic and the theory of meaning, with which he was concerned. The passage about the 'elucidation' of names, where he says that one must be 'acquainted' with their objects, gives him the lie.

More positively, the grounds on which Wittgenstein holds that there are elementary propositions and simple names shew that the elementary propositions have not the role of simple observation statements. At 5.5562 we find: 'If we know, on purely logical grounds, that there must be elementary propositions, then this must be known by anyone who understands propositions in their unanalysed form.' But it is clear that he thought we did know this on purely logical grounds. That is to say, the character of inference, and of meaning itself, *demands* that there should be elementary propositions. And that there should be simple names and simple objects is equally presented as a *demand* at 3.23: 'The demand for the possibility of the simple signs is the demand for definiteness of sense.' We shall see that he holds that an indefinite sense would not be a sense at all; indeed in the Preface he put this forward, not just as one of the most important contentions of the book, but as an epitome of its whole meaning: 'Whatever can be said at all, can be said clearly; and what we cannot speak of, we must be silent on.'

Again, the simple objects are presented as something demanded by the nature of language at 2.021, 2.0211: 'The objects form the substance of the world. That is why they cannot be complex. If the world had no substance, then one proposition's making sense would depend on another one's being true.' But this is not the case: we can *devise* propositions at will and know what they mean, without ascertaining any facts. If one proposition's making sense always depended on another one's being true, then it would be impossible to do this — impossible, as Wittgenstein puts it, to *devise* a picture of the world (true or false) (2.0212); he means by this no more than devising a proposition.

We get further (though, I should judge, unnecessary) confirmation from an entry in the notebooks out of which he composed the *Tractatus*, in which he remarks (23.5.15): 'It also seems certain that we do not infer the existence of simple objects from the existence of particular simple objects, but rather know them — by description, as it were — as the end product of analysis, by means of a process leading to them.' The thought of this entry in the notebooks is in fact echoed in the *Tractatus* text at 4.221: 'It is obvious that in analysing propositions we must arrive at elementary propositions consisting of names in immediate combination.' This view of names, and hence of our knowledge of objects, is a more truthful one than is suggested by the remark about 'elucidations'. And in the notebooks he exclaims at the fact that he is absolutely certain that there are elementary propositions, atomic facts, and simple objects, even though he cannot produce one single example.

If the elementary propositions of the *Tractatus* are not simple observation statements, it seems necessary to find some other account of them before we can grasp the doctrines of the book even in vague outline. For an understanding of the notion of an elementary proposition will help us with its correlate, an atomic fact, or elementary situation.

Wittgenstein opens the *Tractatus* by saying that the world is the totality of facts (*Tatsachen*). He quickly introduces a new term (translated 'atomic fact'): '*Sachverhalt*'. Literally this word simply means 'situation'. Etymologically it suggests 'hold of things' – i.e. a way things stand in relation to one another. Wittgenstein plays heavily on this suggestion. It rapidly becomes clear that by a 'situation' he means an arrangement of objects, which objects, he says, are 'simple'. The 'situation' is a concatenation of simple objects, which 'hang in one another like the links of a chain' (2.03). Hence the word was translated 'atomic fact'; for 'situation', not carrying with it the special suggestion of '*Sachverhalt*', would have been obscure; and 'atomic fact' had been Russell's term for the correlate of a true 'atomic' proposition.

Writing to Russell from Monte Cassino in 1919, Wittgenstein explained *Sachverhalt* as what corresponds to an elementary proposition if it is true, and a *Tatsache* as what corresponds to the logical product (i.e. the conjunction) of elementary propositions when this product is true.[2] This explanation concerns the first introduction of

---

2   Some critics have objected to the translation 'atomic fact' because an atomic fact is presumably a fact, and it is awkward to speak of 'non-existent facts'; but Wittgenstein does speak of non-existent *Sachverhalte* (2.06). This objection does not amount to much. But it is added that Wittgenstein never speaks of 'possible facts' (*Tatsachen*). For what he speaks of as possible, he uses another German word, *Sachlage*, which means 'state of affairs'. Prof. Stenius suggests that this is the real non-atomic parallel to *Sachverhalt*, and that Wittgenstein was simply wrong in giving Russell parallel accounts of *Sachverhalt* and *Tatsache*. I find suggestions that Wittgenstein gave an incorrect account of the *Tractatus* in 1919 quite unacceptable. In German a 'possible fact' (*mögliche Tatsache*) would be something that is *perhaps* a fact – i.e. for all we know to the contrary; this irrelevant reference to our knowledge would surely be what ruled the phrase out. The difficulties we encounter here are really those of the subject-matter itself, and not of Wittgenstein's terminology. Wittgenstein accepted the translation 'atomic fact'.

'*Tatsache*' or 'fact'. At 2.06 he introduced the further expression 'a negative fact': 'We also call the non-existence of atomic facts a negative fact.'

That is to say, to the question 'What is a fact?' we must answer: 'It is nothing but the existence of atomic facts.' This is a thesis about facts; not the assignment of a technical meaning to the word in Wittgenstein's system. And to the question: 'Is there such a thing as a negative fact?' we must answer: 'That is only the non-existence of atomic facts.' Thus the notion of a fact is supposed to be explained to us by means of that of an atomic fact, or elementary situation. And that in turn is simply what corresponds to a true elementary proposition. Thus an exploration of this notion is indispensable.

The following appear to be theses which hold for elementary propositions:

(1) They are a class of mutually independent propositions.

(2) They are essentially positive.

(3) They are such that for each of them there are no two ways of being true or false, but only one.

(4) They are such that there is in them no distinction between an internal and an external negation.

(5) They are concatenations of names, which are absolutely simple signs.

As for the reasons for holding that there are such propositions as these, we know at least that, according to the *Tractatus*, they are 'purely logical'. About these purely logical grounds I will only say here that the main one is this: we can draw conclusions from a false proposition. This is the same fact as that we can invent or devise a proposition and know what it means, without first discovering the facts which hold in regard to its subject-matter. For to understand a proposition is to know what is the case *if* it is true.

The five theses which hold good of elementary propositions can be found at or inferred from several places in the *Tractatus*.

(1) *Elementary propositions are a class of mutually independent propositions*. This we have already seen stated in a restricted form at 6.3751: 'It is clear that the logical product of two elementary propositions can neither be a tautology nor a contradiction.'[3] Strictly, it may be said that this might be true and the general mutual independence false; but we need not delay over the suggestion. It is worth noticing that the

---

3   And also 4.211 and 5.134.

existence of a great class of mutually independent propositions is implicit in the common explanation of truth-functions and truth-functional tautologies. For we are told that a complex proposition is a truth-function of the proposition(s) contained in it if its truth-value is uniquely determined by the truth-value of the proposition(s) in question; and it is a tautology if it is true for all combinations of the truth-values of its components. If it is a function of several propositions, it is impossible that its tautological truth should consist in its truth for all the combinations unless its components have some mutual independence. To take an example, the syllogism 'If all Europeans are white and some Europeans are Mohammedans, then some white men are Mohammedans' is a logical truth in which three propositions occur; its being a logical truth is equivalent to the logical impossibility of the case in which the first two component propositions are true and the last false. A truth-table will thus not display the tautological character of the proposition; for if one constructs a truth-table for 'If p and q, then r', one has to show the truth-value (namely falsehood) of this conditional for the case where 'p' and 'q' are both true but 'r' is false; and it is not the truth-table but the interpretation of 'p', 'q', and 'r' which shows that in the syllogistic case the conditional cannot be false.

Nevertheless a truth-table containing inconsistent rows *may* display the tautological character of a proposition. e.g. Aristotle felt a difficulty about the following form of geometrical argument: 'All triangles are either isosceles[4] or scalene; all isosceles triangles have the property ϕ; all scalene triangles have the property ϕ; therefore all triangles have the property ϕ.' We can see that his difficulty consisted in the argument's not being formalizable in his syllogistic calculus. What he needed was the truth-functional calculus. Let x be a figure, then let 'p' = 'x is a triangle', 'q' = 'x is isosceles', 'r' = 'x is scalene', and 's' = 'x has the property ϕ'. Then the fact that $(p \supset q \lor r . q \supset s . r \supset s) \supset (p \supset s)$[5] is a tautology of the truth-functional calculus would have supplied the missing formalization. Now being a tautology means being true for all combinations of the possible truth-values of the elements (means being, as logicians say, a tautology *of* the given elements), and the truth-table setting forth these combinations will include a row in which both 'q' and 'r' are true, and another in which

---

4   i.e. possessed of at least two equal sides.
5   In English 'p implies that q or r, and q implies that s, and r implies that s, all implies that p implies that s'.

both 'q' and 'r' are false while 'p' is true. But if 'q' = 'x is isosceles', and 'r' = 'x is scalene', these combinations will be impossible.

We may conclude from this that a complex proposition can be shewn to be a logical truth from the fact that it is a tautology of its component propositions, even though some of these are mutually inconsistent; and from the syllogistic example, that it cannot be shewn *not* to be a logical truth from the fact that it is *not* a tautology of its component propositions.[6] Nevertheless, the type of tautology in which some of the combinations of truth-possibilities are inconsistent must be regarded as degenerate. The fact that by our calculus the complex proposition turns out 'true' if we assign an inconsistent set of truth-values to its components does not help to demonstrate its tautological character; we might rather strike out inconsistent rows of the truth-table as not counting. But if all cases were like this, with now one now another row of our truth-tables inconsistent, then the *formal* truth of the truth-functional tautology would vanish.

Thus either the theory of truth-functions has no application, or there is a class of mutually independent propositions. But we apply the calculus of truth-functions every time we reason e.g. 'If p, then q, but not q, therefore not p': a thing which we constantly do in the most diverse contexts of ordinary life. Here is the beginning of a justification for Wittgenstein's saying: 'We know on purely logical grounds that there must be elementary propositions' and 'everyone knows this who understands propositions in their unanalysed form'. At any rate everyone manifests an implicit knowledge that there is a (very large) class of mutually independent propositions.

(2) *Elementary propositions are essentially positive.* This we can infer from 4.25: 'If the elementary proposition is true, the atomic fact exists; if it is false the atomic fact does not exist' together with 2.06: 'We also call the existence of atomic facts a positive, and their non-existence a negative fact': the elementary proposition therefore is such as to express something *positive*, namely the holding of an elementary situation. This, of course, does not mean that the occurrence of the sign of negation in a propositional sign would prove that it did not state an

---

6   According to Wittgenstein, this logical truth can be exhibited as a tautology of a set of elementary propositions, though not as a tautology of the propositions explicitly occurring in it; *see* Chapter 11. Von Wright has shown a simple way of exhibiting it as a tautology if we assume men to have any given finite number; *see* *Logical Studies* (Routledge & Kegan Paul, 1957), Chapter I; it is exhibited as a tautology of singular propositions about men.

elementary proposition. Wittgenstein warns us at 4.0621: 'The occurrence of negation in a proposition is not *enough* to characterize its sense' — i.e. to characterize it as negative rather than positive in sense; as stating, if true, a negative fact.

Russell in his letters to Wittgenstein after receiving the text of the *Tractatus* once asked whether the negations of elementary propositions were themselves elementary propositions, and received the indignant-sounding rejoinder: 'Of course not.'

(3) *Elementary propositions are such that for them there are no two ways of being true or false but only one.*

This is clearest for falsehood. By 4.25 the falsehood of an elementary proposition is simply the non-existence of a single atomic situation.

At 3.24 Wittgenstein says: 'A complex can be given only by its description, which will hold or not hold. The proposition in which there is mention of a complex will not be meaningless when the complex does not exist, but merely false. That a propositional element designates a complex can be seen from an indefiniteness in the propositions in which it occurs.' One kind of indefiniteness in a proposition might be that there was more than one way of its being false: the complex might exist, but what was said of it might not hold; or the complex might not exist.

We could imagine a proposition in which there was mention of a complex, which had only one way of being true, though two ways of being false. Let us suppose a proposition 'ϕa' such that 'a' is a simple name, ϕ being such that there was only one way for ϕ to hold of anything. Then let us suppose a complex A, which exists if bRc. Then 'ϕA' will be false if A exists but ϕ does not hold of it, and also if not bRc, so there are two ways for it to be false; but only one way for it to be true, namely that bRc, so that A exists, and ϕA.

'We *know*,' Wittgenstein goes on, 'that not everything is settled by such a proposition' — that is to say, by a proposition in which there is mention of a complex. In the example that I have imagined, 'everything would be settled' by the *truth* of the proposition, but not everything by its falsehood. What he principally had in mind was the sort of proposition where there is a variety of ways for the proposition to be true. (This is in fact the most ordinary sort of proposition, of which alone one can give examples; to illustrate other sorts of proposition one has to use dummy names and dummy predicates and stipulate their characters.) Take for example 'My watch is lying on the table', which Wittgenstein considers in his notebooks. There are hundreds of different, more minutely statable, and incompatible states of affairs which would make that proposition true. The elementary proposition will have only one state of affairs that will make it true: 'everything' will be settled by it — i.e. nothing be left open.

(4) *Elementary propositions are such that there is in them no distinction between an internal and an external negation.* This is in part the same point as has already been made in connection with definiteness of sense. We can say: 'The King of France is bald' has as a negation 'The King of France is not bald'; I distinguish this *internal* negation of the proposition from the *external* negation: 'Not: The King of France is bald' — we have already seen how these differ in sense. To take another case: the proposition 'Everyone is wise' has an *internal* negation, 'Everyone is not wise' (or: 'is unwise'), and another, *external*, negation: 'Not everyone is wise.' Aristotle was rather puzzled by this difference between 'Socrates is wise' and 'Everyone is wise': if 'Socrates is wise' is untrue, then 'Socrates is not wise' is true; but if 'Everyone is wise' is untrue, still it does not follow that 'Everyone is not wise', or 'is unwise', is true; the contradictory is the different proposition that not everyone is wise.

It is true that we sometimes use 'Everyone is not …' in the sense 'Not everyone is …'; and hence it is convenient to use the term 'unwise' to make our point. But, to adapt what Frege says,[7] it should not be supposed from this attachment of the negation to 'wise' that 'what is negated is the content, not of the whole sentence, but just of this part … It is incorrect to say: "Because the negative syllable is combined with part of the sentence, the sense of the whole sentence is not negated." On the contrary; it is by combining the negative syllable with a part of the sentence that we do negate … the whole sentence.' That is to say, the sentence 'Everyone is wise' is certainly made out to be untrue by someone who says 'Everyone is unwise'; but this is still a different negation from that expressed by 'Not everyone is wise'.

I choose 'internal' and 'external' merely as convenient labels to attach to these negations. An elementary proposition will be one for which no such difference, between an internal and an external negation, can be found. The falsehood of the elementary proposition never consists in anything but the non-existence of a single atomic fact.

(5) *Elementary propositions are concatenations of names.* This we find stated explicitly at 4.22: 'The elementary proposition consists of

---

[7]   Negation, *Philosophical Writings of Gottlob Frege*, ed. Geach & Black (Blackwell, 1952), p. 131.

names. It is a connection, a concatenation, of names.' Names are simple signs; this is not merely asserted, but argued for, in the *Tractatus*, at 3.3411: 'So it could be said that the real name is what all symbols that designate the object have in common. Then we could get the result, in a number of steps, that no kind of composition was essential to the name.' That is to say, any name will of course have a certain physical complexity, but you could replace it by another, with a different complexity, without detriment to its doing the job of naming the object. Whereas you could not, for example, adequately symbolize a relation without using a symbol whose complexity enabled you to shew the difference between, say, aRb and bRa.

So far what is argued about names would seem to be perfectly applicable to ordinary names, such as 'Wittgenstein', which are not names in the sense of the *Tractatus*. 'Wittgenstein' is what he calls a 'simple symbol' at 3.24: 'The contraction of the symbol of a complex into a simple symbol can be expressed by means of a definition.' This 'definition' will be basically the same thing as the 'description' which he speaks of as 'giving' the complex.

Now the physical complexity of the name 'Wittgenstein' expresses nothing, as can be shewn in the way suggested. But if the 'real' name, or 'real' symbol, of the object called Wittgenstein, has something about it that implies complexity, then the name can be said not to be a logically simple sign, even though it appears as a simple sign in the sentence. For, as it is put at 3.262: 'What does not get expressed in the signs is shewn by their application. Their application declares what the signs fail to bring out.' And the application of the name 'Wittgenstein' brings out that a great many things, and a great variety of things, have to be true in order for there to be true statements in which the name occurs. The same would be true of any sign which had the same function as this sign 'Wittgenstein'. But what is common to all the symbols with this function is what is essential to the symbol, as has been said at 3.341: 'In general what is essential about a symbol is what all symbols capable of fulfilling the same function have in common.' Therefore a certain complexity, which only comes out in the application, is essential to the name 'Wittgenstein'.

Thus the true names of the *Tractatus* will be, not physically simple signs, but ones lacking the sort of complexity that the name 'Wittgenstein' has; and it is clear that elementary propositions can contain only such names, since if they contained names like 'Wittgenstein' they could not have only one way of being true or false.

So much here for the simplicity of names; we must now discuss 'concatenation'. The metaphor of a chain should suggest an essential feature of elementary propositions. As we have seen, what is expressed by calling an elementary proposition a concatenation is expressed for elementary situations ('atomic facts') at 2.03: 'In the atomic fact the objects hang in one another like the links of a chain.' In a literal chain consisting of links

$$A - B - C - D$$

there is no difference between A's being linked to the B end of the chain B − C − D, and D's being linked to the C end of the chain A − B − C. I think this element in the analogy should be taken seriously; in the elementary proposition there must be nothing corresponding to bracketing.

Let us look at what Wittgenstein says about bracketing at 5.461– 5.4611: 'The apparently unimportant fact that logical pseudo-relations like ∨ (or) and ⊃ (if ..., then ...) − as opposed to real relations − require brackets is significant.' This remark has been criticized on the ground that a bracketless notation, such as that invented by Łukasiewicz, is possible. In this notation we write

$$Cpq$$

instead of

$$p \supset q$$

and then the difference between

$$(p \supset q) \supset r$$

and

$$p \supset (q \supset r)$$

will be expressed by the difference between

$$C(Cpq)r$$

and

$$Cp(Cqr)$$

where, though I have put brackets in, these are only an aid to reading and are not needed to resolve any ambiguity. Now this is of course true; it is true because the collecting done by brackets is done by the rule for reading an expression containing 'C'. Some method of collecting is required, and that is the essential point. 'Logical operation signs are punctuation marks,' Wittgenstein says, and Łukasiewicz's notation, far from refuting Wittgenstein's remarks about brackets, brings out what Wittgenstein meant, for in it the collecting or punctuating normally done by brackets is done by the rule for reading the logical operation-signs. Now if the chain metaphor is to be taken seriously, this differentiation of meanings by punctuation or collection must somehow be inapplicable to the elementary proposition.

What I call 'collection' or 'punctuation' can occur in propositions other than those (overtly) containing truth-functional connectives. Consider the sentence 'Every man loves some girl.' We may regard this as splitting up into three 'expressions': 'Every man', 'loves' and 'some girl'. It is useful here to adopt the metaphor of structural formulae in chemistry for the structure of sentences. An expression will then sometimes correspond to what chemists call a 'radical': that is, a group of atoms which cannot by itself form a stable molecule, but which can in chemical transformations pass from one compound into another without the break-up of its own inner connection of atoms. And the fact that what compound you have depends, not only on what radicals you have, but also on how they are fitted together, would be a parallel to such a difference as that between 'Socrates loves Plato' and 'Plato loves Socrates', or again 'Every man loves some girl' and 'Some girl loves every man'. There is, however, a difference between two possible senses of 'Every man loves some girl' which *could* be brought out by a difference of bracketing. In

(Every man) (loves some girl)

we could take the bracketing as indicating that 'every man' is supplied as an argument in

—loves some girl

and the sense will be that the predicate 'loves some girl' is true of every man; whereas in

(Every man loves) (some girl)

'some girl' is supplied as an argument in

Every man loves—

and the sense will be that of some girl it is true that every man loves her. The difference is of course the one usually brought out by the order of quantifiers.[8] This difference is one that cannot be illustrated

---

[8] *See* Chapter 11, pp. 115–18.

by our chemical analogy. And it is a sort of possibility of difference that has to be absent from the elementary proposition.

Contrast with this case 'Socrates loves Plato'. We can indeed introduce two different bracketings: '(Socrates) (loves Plato)', which asserts of Socrates that he loves Plato, and '(Socrates loves) (Plato)', which asserts of Plato that Socrates loves him. But in this case Wittgenstein, following Frege, would say that there was absolutely no difference of sense.

Now it seems plausible to say that the reason why we have an ambiguity resoluble by brackets in the one case but not in the other is that, at any rate as compared with 'Every man' and 'some girl', the *expressions* 'Socrates' and 'Plato' are simple. This sort of consideration may lead us to divine behind our propositions a kind of proposition to which the chemical analogy of radicals will apply perfectly; unlike a proposition in which, though you have the same expressions combined in the same way, it makes a difference by what stages you conceive the proposition as built up. Such a proposition will be a concatenation of really simple signs, which have indeed an accidental complexity, but one irrelevant to their function as signs.

2

The Theory of Descriptions

Wittgenstein's 'picture theory' of the proposition is much influenced by Russell's Theory of Descriptions. According to that theory, definite descriptions such as 'the author of Waverley', and 'the present King of France', and again indefinite descriptions like 'a man' as this phrase occurs in 'I met a man', or 'A man has been here', are not the designating expressions they at first seem to be.

At first sight, one readily assumes that, if the sentences in which descriptions occur are true, each description stands for an object, and the rest of the sentence expresses what holds of the object. To say this is to compare descriptions with (real) proper names; but at the same time the way in which descriptions stand for objects must be different from the way in which proper names stand for objects; indeed, the consideration of this leads to a breakdown of the idea that descriptions 'stand-for' at all.

This is most obvious for indefinite descriptions; but is also true of definite descriptions. A proper name will stand for its object because that object is called by that name; but a description, if it stands for its object, does so because the object satisfies it, which is clearly quite a different relation.

Further: If a proper name (i.e. what has the superficial grammar of a proper name) has in fact no bearer in the use that is being made of it, then nothing has been ascribed to any object by sentences in which it occurs; and so nothing has been said, truly or falsely. But if it has a bearer (i.e. if it has the use, and not merely the superficial grammar, of a proper name) then the sentence is false if what is predicated in it does not hold of that bearer. Now if a sentence like 'Some man has been on the Moon' is false, this is not because 'has been on the Moon' is false of some man — though if it is true, it is true because 'has been on the Moon' is true of some man. So, if we persist in thinking that the sentence would be made true by the fact that something holds of what the grammatical subject stands for, it turns out that its falsehood would not consist in the same thing's *not* holding of what the grammatical subject stands for.

When we turn to definite descriptions, it is easier to retain the comparison with proper names; hence Frege called definite descriptions proper names. But the comparison breaks down in various ways. The predicate occurring as part of a definite description must be uniquely true of something, if the description is to be taken as standing for anything; whereas a proper name stands for a bearer to which it has been assigned, without its being guaranteed, concerning any given unique description, that the bearer satisfies it. Hence we can give truth-conditions for statements containing definite descriptions regardless of whether the descriptions are vacuous or not.

It has been said (in the first instance by Frege) that the occurrence of a vacuous definite description in a sentence disqualifies that sentence from making a true or false statement. But this is unplausible except when the sentence is a simple one. A vacuous definite description can occur in a clause within a sentence without so disqualifying the whole sentence, e.g. 'Either he has no children or his first child's name is Hilary.' All this shews that the object, if there is one, satisfying a definite description, is not so designated by it that nothing could be truly or falsely said by a sentence containing the description if that object did not exist; whereas if Scott had never existed, the use of the word 'Scott' as the name of that famous author never could have existed either.

As a logical doctrine, Russell's Theory of Descriptions makes the contrast between definite descriptions and (ordinary) proper names which these considerations seem to demand. When doing logic, Russell always treats e.g. 'Scott' as a proper name, by contrast with descriptions like 'the author of Waverley'. His theory of knowledge, on the other hand, leads him to propound the less convincing part of the theory: that ordinary proper names, like 'Scott', are not the real proper names at all. A genuine proper name must have a bearer; this is a harmless point of logic; it becomes less harmless if it is rendered as: What a proper name stands for must exist. For this may lead us to the idea that the bearers of the only genuine proper names are existents not subject to Cartesian doubt (Russell's objects of immediate acquaintance — sense-data, etc.); or are eternal and changeless simples (Wittgenstein's 'objects').

Russell says that a definite description has no meaning by itself, but the whole sentence in which it occurs has a meaning. He means simply that a definite description does not function like a name. He puts the point in that obscure way because of his idea of what it is for a word or phrase to 'have meaning', namely: a word has meaning if it is a word with which one means an object; to mean an object one must be acquainted with it; for a word or phrase to have meaning, then, it is necessary for what we mean by it to exist. In accordance with this theory of meaning Russell passes from the truism that in order to understand a sentence we must know what each word means, to the doctrine that in judging or supposing we must be acquainted with each of the objects that the judgment or supposition is *really* about.

Thus, on Russell's view, if a description had 'meaning by itself', it would follow that what it stood for had some sort of being. In the *Principles of Mathematics* Russell had actually thought that there were entities 'meant' by descriptions, and called these entities 'denoting concepts'; not only definite descriptions, but such phrases as 'any number' in 'Any number is either odd or even', had denoting concepts as their 'meanings'. But what a proposition containing a description asserted would ordinarily be asserted not of the corresponding denoting concept, but of a term or complex of terms somehow connected with the denoting concept: e.g. it is not the denoting concept answering to the phrase 'any number' that is said to be odd or even. Russell's Theory of Descriptions represents an escape from this position: he adopted Frege's way of handling 'some' and 'all', indefinite descriptions and phrases like 'any number',[1] and further applied it, as Frege never did, to definite descriptions as well.

Frege's enquiries had already given the notion of proper names an importance for logic and the theory of truth which it had never had before. In Russell's theory it retains that importance, and at the same time comprises only logically simple signs: 'A "simple" symbol is one which has no parts that are symbols. Thus "Scott" is a simple symbol because though it has parts (namely separate letters), these parts are not symbols. On the other hand "the author of Waverley" is not a simple symbol because the separate words that compose the symbol are parts which are symbols.'[2] This account of the simplicity of proper names is correct; as also it is correct to say that the way a proper name

---

[1]   *See* Chapter 11. cf. also *Philosophical Writings of Gottlob Frege* (Blackwell, 1952), pp. 13–14, 16–20, 35–8, 93.
[2]   *Introduction to Mathematical Philosophy*, p. 173.

contributes to the meaning of a sentence in which it occurs is simply that it stands for its bearer.

Russell analyses e.g. 'The author of Waverley drank port' as: 'For some x, x wrote Waverley and for all y, y wrote Waverley only if y = x, and x drank port'; such an analysis of sentences containing definite descriptions and other 'denoting phrases' excludes these from the class of signs that contribute to the meaning of sentences in which they occur by standing for their bearers. The denoting phrases disappear, and only the predicates (and proper names, if any) used in their construction play a part in the result of the analysis. In consequence, 'standing-for' is shewn to be attributable *only* to simple signs. 'Where,' Wittgenstein asked in a later writing, 'does language hook on to the world?' One place will be here, where the proper name stands for its bearer.

In Russell's doctrine, a simple sign's having a meaning consists in its standing for something; its meaning simply is the thing for which it stands; and 'simple signs' will include not only proper names of 'individuals', but also signs for 'universals' — i.e. for relations, and for non-relational properties (if there are any) — and perhaps signs for logical forms as well; and these other simple signs will equally have as their meanings the non-individual 'things' they are signs for. Now, after *Philosophical Investigations*, it is easy to distinguish between the two different elements of this doctrine which we have mentioned: (a) the doctrine of the simplicity of the proper name, and of its contributing to the meaning of the sentence precisely by standing for its bearer; and (b) the idea that the meaning of a name just is its bearer, or the meaning of a simple sign like 'red' just *is* the quality with which we have immediate acquaintance. At the time when Russell wrote, these elements were inextricably conflated into one theory.

One of the most noteworthy features of Russell's doctrine is his rejection of the Fregean distinction between sense and reference.[3] This distinction is highly plausible and tempting; but as an instrument in the theory of truth it leads to great difficulties, and not to the solution of our problems. Frege held that all symbols — i.e. both 'proper names' and predicates — had 'sense', that some 'proper names' had reference as well, and that all predicates had reference, the reference of a predicate being what he termed a concept. (But he does not explain the

---

3   His detailed criticisms were, however, partly based on misunderstanding : he wrongly assimilated Frege's views to what he had held in the *Principles of Mathematics*.

distinction of sense from reference for simple predicates.[4]) An unasserted sentence (e.g. one occurring as a clause in another sentence) is for him a proper name; if it has reference, its reference is a truth-value. This raises the problem how it comes about that certain senses — namely those of sentences containing no vacuous proper names — are guaranteed to have reference.

On Russell's theory this problem does not arise; in any fully analysed sentence there will occur nothing but words whose meanings are present to us and are real things; for those meanings will just *be* the 'things' (including relations, properties, and logical forms signified by logical words and logical schemata) for which the words stand. In his theory, we may say, 'language reaches right up to reality', which is something we want to shew it doing.

But there are great defects in the theory as Russell states it, even if for the moment we allow him to identify the meaning of a name with its bearer. For Russell held that judgment and supposing are (different) relations in which the mind stands to a set of objects including a relation R; if R relates the objects other than R in this set, then the judgment or supposition is true, and if not it is false.

This theory (a) 'does not make it impossible to judge a nonsense', as Wittgenstein complains at 5.5422; (b) fails to distinguish effectively between judging (or supposing) that aRb and that bRa; and (c) fails to explain negative judgments. For if when I judge that A is to the right of B I stand in the judging relation to A, B, and the relation *to the right of*, what happens when I judge that A is *not* to the right of B? Do I stand in the judging relation to A, B, *to the right of*, and *not*? Similar questions arise for the other logical constants, 'if', 'and', and 'or'.

This difficulty lies behind Wittgenstein's remark (3.42): 'Although the proposition can only determine a single region of logical space, still the whole of logical space must be given by it. Otherwise negation, the logical sum,[5] the logical product,[6] etc. would keep on introducing new elements — in co-ordination' (sc. with those previously introduced).

Wittgenstein avoids these difficulties, while retaining the idea that the meaning of a simple sign is its bearer, by giving a different account

---

[4]   For at least some complex predicates the distinction is easily made out: the two predicates 'killed Socrates' and 'killed the philosopher who was executed by a draught of hemlock' have different senses but the same reference.

[5]   *p* or *q*.

[6]   *p* and *q*.

of propositions, judgments, and logical constants. On the other hand he accepts Russell's Theory of Descriptions in its purely logical aspect —in so far as it shews how the analysis of propositions into the complete statement of their truth-conditions is to be carried out for propositions containing definite descriptions. The statement of truth-conditions for a proposition containing a definite description thus includes a statement that there is one and only one object satisfying the description, i.e. a statement that for some x, ϕx, and, for all y, ϕy only if y = x.

Let us now suppose that we have a proposition 'A is corrupt'. Here 'A' appears in the argument place in the function 'x is corrupt'. Now let us consider the negation: 'A is not corrupt.' Can we distinguish between an external and an internal negation here—i.e. between taking this as the negation of the result of substituting 'A' for 'x' in 'x is corrupt' (external negation), and taking it as the result of substituting 'A' for 'x' in 'x is not corrupt' (internal negation)? If we cannot, then 'A' is a proper name: if we can, it is not. One sort of case where we can is where 'A' is, e.g. 'Some committee' or 'Any institution'. For these cases the point is readily seen (cf. Chapter 1, p. 25). But where 'A' is a definite description, the distinction between the internal and external negation still holds.

The question whether there must be simple signs in Russell's sense thus leads us on to the question whether there must be substitutions in 'x is corrupt' for which there is *no* distinction between internal and external negation. Now if 'A' is an ostensibly singular term, the distinction could arise only because the expression 'A' itself indicated certain truth-conditions.

A proper name never does this; either one has to be told *ad hoc* what, and what kind of thing, it is a proper name of; or one may glean this latter information from the predicates associated with the name, or guess it from custom: for example 'John' is customarily a masculine human name in English-speaking countries—though this does not mean that a man makes a mistake if he calls his sow 'John'.

Our question is: *Must* there be (at least the possibility of) proper names? And this question can be reformulated thus: Is it impossible that, for any given f, *every* proposition which is a value of fx should indicate truth-conditions C distinct from the conditions for the holding of the property f? Now the statement of the truth-conditions C will run: 'There is an x such that ϕx, and, for all y, ϕy only if y = x'. But this could not be true, unless *some* singular proposition of the form 'ϕb' were true. It might indeed be known, without our knowing any singular proposition of the form 'ϕb'; but if we claimed to know it we should be postulating, even if we did not know, a proposition of the form 'ϕb'.

Thus we have

   (1) fA, where 'A' is of the form "The ϕ.
   (2) There is an x such that ϕx, and, for all y, ϕy only if y = x.
   (3) ϕb.

Now what do we postulate about the sign 'b' in this postulated proposition? Necessarily, that there is for it no distinction between $(\sim\phi)b$ and $\sim(\phi b)$. For if there were such a distinction, the proposition 'There is not an x such that ϕx' would in turn be ambiguous in its truth-conditions: it might require that every proposition got by substituting an expression of the kind 'b' in '$(\sim\phi)x$' shall be true, or that every proposition got by substituting an expression of the kind 'b' in 'ϕx' shall be false. There would thus be two quite different ways in which '(Ex)ϕx' might be false, if the only substitutions for x in 'ϕx' were expressions 'b' such that 'ϕb' had different possible negations.

So much follows from the *logical* part of the Theory of Descriptions. This, however, does not lead us to 'simples'; for the theory in its logical aspect has nothing to do with any theory of reduction to simples. It only demands that such simple symbols as 'Parliament' shall be possible if such propositions as 'The body making laws for Great Britain is corrupt' are to make sense. The type of name that is postulated here is the type: *name of a body corporate*. A truth-condition for 'The British legislative body is corrupt' is 'There is an x such that x corporately makes laws for Great Britain'. The variable 'x' here ranges over bodies corporate.

If there were no such things as bodies corporate, there would be no proper names of them either; so it looks as if in that case 'There is an x such that x corporately makes laws for Great Britain' would lose its meaning. But in a world where there were no such things, it might still be possible to imagine them. For a body corporate, e.g., to *pass a measure by a large majority* means that men stand in certain relations to one another and do certain things. If there were no bodies corporate, someone might yet imagine certain men standing in these relations to one another, might give an imaginary proper name to the complex so formed, and might construct predicates that were to hold of the complex when the individuals standing in these relations did certain things. The proposition 'There is an x such that x corporately makes laws' would then after all not fail to have meaning.

Let us suppose that someone in a world without bodies corporate has imagined there being such things, and has constructed this proposition; there are now two quite different ways in which it can be false, though not the same two ways as we considered before. It is false in his world, because there are no bodies corporate at all there. But in a possible world where there were bodies corporate, there would be no distinction between 'All substitutions for "x" in "x corporately makes laws" are false' and 'All substitutions in "x does not corporately make laws" are true'; these propositions would both be true or both false together, and if they were true then 'There is an x such that x corporately makes laws' would be false.

Let us call the falsehood of this proposition in the world where there are no bodies corporate 'radical falsehood': the proposition is radically false because certain propositions about men are false — they do not stand in such relations or do such things.

The question arises: could there always be the possibility of radical, as opposed to ordinary, falsehood? It is clear that a 'radical falsehood' always depends on the possibility of an ordinary falsehood. Wittgenstein's starting-point is: We can construct propositions at will, without enquiry into any facts at all, and know what is the case *if* they are true. On the supposition that the question of 'radical falsehood' can always be raised, we should always have to distinguish between possible kinds of falsehood of our statements.

But then we could never determine the sense of the falsehood of a proposition, except on the supposition of the *truth* of some prior proposition; for otherwise we should each time have to consider the possibility of a radical falsehood, which must be explained in terms of the ordinary falsehood of a prior proposition. Then we might indeed start from the *truth* of certain propositions; but without this we could never know the sense of any. 'Whether one proposition made sense would depend on whether another one was true; so we should not be able to invent a picture of the world (true or false)' (2.0211–2).

Thus if we can construct propositions at will and know what is the case if they are true, without knowing what is true and what is false, it follows that there must be propositions incapable of what I have called 'radical' falsehood. That is to say, there must be names of simples which can only be named, and not *defined* by a description as Parliament is, and whose existence is guaranteed. 'The demand for the possibility of the simple signs is the demand that sense shall be determinate' (3.23).

Here the 'simple signs' are not the 'simple symbols' of the Theory of Descriptions, in its purely logical aspect as presented by Russell.

Wittgenstein shares with Russell the idea that the meaning of a name is its bearer: but in him this is not noticeably based on the British empiricist epistemology that influences Russell. We have, rather, a Frege-like argument: Unless names have bearers, there is no truth or falsehood. But if you *always* distinguish a sense and a reference in names, as you must for a name like 'Parliament', the connection between sense and truth-value becomes obscure. For then the sense of a name will present a reference if something satisfies the description in which that sense might be set forth, i.e. if something is *true*; now this truth must be expressible by combining a name and a predicate; and unless names are somewhere nailed to reality without the mediation of senses which hold true of objects, that relation between sentences and reality which constitutes their truth will in no way have been explained.

3

Negation: (1) The Logician's Definition of 'not p'

'Everyone is unwise' is a negation of 'everyone is wise', but it is not what logicians call *the* negation of it; in logic books, when the sign for 'not' is introduced, we are told that 'not p' is '*the* proposition that is true when p is false and false when p is true'. 'Everyone is unwise' is not certainly true if 'Everyone is wise' is false; hence it is not *the* negation of 'Everyone is wise'. This was the point already noticed by Aristotle in the *De Interpretation*.

Such a definition of 'not p' as is found in many logic books may make us ask (rather in the manner of Frege) what right anyone has to give such a definition. I can define something as *the* so-and-so, only if I am justified in being sure, first that there is a so-and-so, and second that there is only one. If I have no such assurance, it is not certain that I am succeeding in defining anything. How, then, am I assured that there is one, and only one, proposition that is true when p is false, and false when p is true?

It might seem that we could say: It is evident that a proposition has two truth-values, as a coin has two sides; and we might think of truth-functions as like bets on the results of tossing coins. Thus if one coin is tossed once, there are two possible bets, which can be represented as follows:

Coin	Bet 1	Bet 2
H	W	L
T	L	W

in a table in which H and T stand for heads and tails, and W and L for win and lose. This could be considered to correspond to the following truth-table:

p	p	~p
T	T	F
F	F	T

The analogy of course holds for the whole range of truth-functions. For example, if we have two coins, A and B, we could set forth one possible bet as follows:

A	B	
H	H	W
H	T	L
T	H	W
T	T	W

Here the bet that the coins, in a single toss of both together, will fall so that either A is tails or B is heads, corresponds to the truth-function

p	q	or alternatively	
T	T	T	T
T	F	F	T
F	T	T	F
F	F	T	T

that is to say: to ~p ∨ q, or alternatively, to ~q ∨ p; which, depends on whether we assimilate 'Heads' or 'Tails' to 'True'.

The most striking thing about this analogy is that when we set forth the table of bets on the toss of a coin, we put different symbols in the columns that display the bets from those we put in the columns of possible results of the toss, whereas in the truth-table we used the same signs in all three columns. The question arises with what right, or on what grounds, or again, with a view to expressing what, we use the same symbols in all the columns of the truth-table, which we should not think of doing in all the columns of the betting tables.

Consider the explanations of propositions and truth-functions, or logical constants, which are commonly found in logic books. It is usual for us to be told: first, propositions are whatever can be either true or false; second, propositions can be combined in certain ways to form

further propositions; and third, in examining these combinations, i.e.
in developing the truth-functional calculus, we are not interested in
the internal structure of the combined propositions.[1]

Such explanations raise certain questions: e.g. has the internal
structure of the propositions, which does not concern us when we
study truth-functions, anything to do with the property of being true
or false? Again, is the property of being true or false, which belongs to
the truth-functions, the very same property as the property of being
true or false that belongs to the propositions whose internal structure
does not interest us? And, finally, if that is so, is it to be regarded as an
ultimate fact that propositions combine to form further propositions,
much as metals combine to form alloys which still display a good
many of the properties of metals?

In short, is there not an impression as it were of logical chemistry
about these explanations? It is this conception that Wittgenstein
opposes in the *Tractatus* at 6.111: 'Theories that make a proposition of
logic appear substantial are always wrong. It might be thought, for
example, that the words "true" and "false" denote two properties
among other properties, and then it would look like a remarkable fact
that every proposition possesses one of these properties. This now
looks no more a matter of course than the proposition "all roses are
either red or yellow" would sound, even if it were true.'

Logical calculi are sometimes described as essentially sets of marks
with rules for manipulating them. For example Lewis and Langford
(*Symbolic Logic*, p. 227) say: 'Whatever more it may be, the matrix
method at least is a kind of game which we play with recognizable
marks, according to certain rules.' They then make some remarks concerning an extract for a table for pIq (which might have the *logical*
interpretation $p \supset q$, but of course need not):

p	q	pIq
1	1	1
1	0	0

They rightly assert that such a table need not have 'any "logical"
significance'; p and q may be 'any kind of things'. What is required on
their view is that in some game or other there should be 'an operation
or move, pIq, which according to the rules can be taken when p has
the property A, only if q also has the property A'; and in that case the

---

1   *See* e.g. Hilbert and Ackermann, *Mathematical Logic*, p. 3.

table will tell us that if p has the property A, and pIq is an allowable move, then q must have A. The logical interpretation will then consist in taking the property A, expressed by the figure '1', to be truth, and the property expressed by the figure '0' to be falsehood, and reading 'pIq' as 'p ⊃ q'.

The animus behind such a view as this is a desire to get rid of the notion of 'logical truth' in the mysterious character that it assumes to someone with an empiricist outlook. But the argument presented by Lewis and Langford fails, and, by the way in which it fails, helps us to see the importance of the fact that we use the same signs, 'T' and 'F', or '1' and '0', in all the columns of a truth-table. For—as has been remarked by Geach[2]—there is an inconsistency here in the interpretation of the figure 1, if p and q may be 'any kind of things'. As regards p and q, the figure '1' is taken to stand for some property A, but as regards pIq it is taken to stand for the property of being an allowable move in a certain game. This is inconsistent unless A *is* the property of being an allowable move—and that is not necessary.

That it is not necessary is clearly seen if we take a simple non-logical interpretation of the table. Let the figures '1' and '0' connote the presence and the absence of an hereditary property A, and let 'pIq' mean 'offspring by p out of q'. Then the table will have no reference to moves in any game. It will state that the trait A is present in the off-spring, when it is present in the sire, if and only if it is also present in the dam: a good example of what Wittgenstein would call a 'sub-stantial' piece of information. Note that here pIq is not a 'move in a game' at all—any more than p and q are; pIq is an animal.

Now though, as this example shows, you need not interpret the figures '1' and '0' to mean that moves in a game are respectively allowed and forbidden, it is of course perfectly permissible to do so. But in that case p and q cannot be 'any kind of things' but must be moves in the game, like pIq. The table will then be equivalent to the following sentence: 'If p is an allowable move, then q is an allowable move if and only if pIq is also an allowable move.' And here the sign 'I' does not belong to the terminology of any special game, like 'Kt' in chess; it expresses what we may fittingly call a logical relation of the move pIq to the moves p and q, so that the significance of the notation 'pIq' is after all 'logical'.

---

[2]   *Ifs and Ands*, Analysis, Vol. 9, 1948-9. This and the succeeding two paragraphs are adapted from this article.

Now 'If p is an allowable move, then q is an allowable move if and only if pIq is an allowable move' at least sounds like a substantial piece of information about a game; at any rate if one can specify p, q, and pIq independently as moves: p might be a diagonal move of a certain piece on a squared board, q a move of another piece parallel with an edge of the board, and 'pIq' the name given (we won't ask why, for the moment) to a move by yet another piece along one of the edges of the board. Then the information 'If you can move this piece diagonally you can move this piece along the edge of the board if, and only if, you can move this piece parallel with one of the edges' might either be a rule of the game, or inferable from the rules of the game.

If, however, we now do ask why moving this piece along the edge of the board should be symbolized by a sign mentioning those two other moves, then we can answer by saying that

p	q	
1	1	1
1	0	0

defines a possible allowability in terms of given allowabilities, and 'pIq' is a notation in which this allowability is set forth: that, and that alone, is the meaning of this notation. Then the substantial information as far as this game is concerned is that there do exist some moves whose allowability is so conditioned, and that the move along the edge of the board is in fact one of them; but that any move describable as pIq is allowable, if p is allowable, if and only if q is also allowable, is not a 'substantial' piece of information.[3]

Similarly, if we revert to the analogy of tossing coins, we set forth part of the betting table we have already considered:

Coin A	Coin B	Bet: A tails or B heads
H	H	W
H	T	L

and it is not a substantial piece of information that this is a possible bet on the result of a toss of two coins, each with two possible sides to come uppermost. Nor is it informative to say that this *is* the bet 'A tails or B heads'; that is simply another way of writing what is already

---

3   The reader must be careful, in reading this passage, to distinguish between 'pIq' and pIq. pIq is a move in the game, 'pIq' a notation for the move.

written down in the WL column; one could simply point to the column and say: That's my bet.

And so Wittgenstein says that such a sign as

p	q	
T	T	T
T	F	F
F	T	F
F	F	F

or, assuming a standard convention for the p and q columns, '(TFFF) (p,q)' *is* a propositional sign: we find this statement at 4.442. '(TFFF) (p,q)' is just another way of writing 'p.q'.

This is the explanation of the symbolism introduced at 5.5:

$$(- - - - - - T) \ (\xi, \ldots \ldots)$$

The Greek letter ξ is a variable whose value is a proposition; the dots after it indicate a set of such variables of unspecified length. The dashes in the left-hand bracket indicate an absence of T's in the truth-table, however long this may be: its length in any given case will depend on how many propositions are indicated in the right-hand bracket. The point is that only the bottom row of the matrix has T set against it: this is the case in which *all* the propositions indicated in the right-hand bracket are false; this combination is to stand at the bottom, whichever of various possible conventions is adopted for arranging the other possible combinations of truth-values in the matrix. Thus Wittgenstein's formula'$(- - - - - - T) \ (\xi^4 \ldots \ldots)$' is the negation of all the propositions in the right-hand bracket.

Now in the coin-tossing case, the 'substantial' information is that the toss of a coin has two possibilities, heads and tails. And as we have seen, this substantial fact has an analogue in the opening explanations of logic books: that propositions are what can be true or false. We might say that for coin-tossing purposes a coin has only two possibilities of falling: if a coin e.g. stood on its edge when it reached the floor, that wouldn't count as a toss. And similarly if (for whatever reason) a sentence hasn't got a truth-value, it doesn't count for making statements with or for operating the truth-functional calculus with.

---

4   This is used rather than 'p' because 'p' is generally used for an elementary proposition, and there is no requirement here that the value of ξ be elementary.

Frege allows such sentences: if a sentence is a fiction, it has not got a truth-value; and it is a fiction if it contains empty names. It can still have a perfectly good 'sense', but not have a truth-value. In our day, Mr. P.F. Strawson has also introduced a concept of a sentence's having a sense, which is not sufficient to guarantee that if it is uttered a statement is thereby made. We know its sense, if we know in what circumstances it *could* be used to make a statement. Now, apart from sentences containing fictitious proper names, Frege found his view inconvenient; he regarded the possibility of constructing such sentences as a defect in the language of (*a priori*) science.[5] So when in developing the foundations of mathematics he needed to use a descriptive phrase which as ordinarily interpreted might have no reference, he used an artificial reinterpretation to guarantee that it had a reference;[6] and this artificiality, as Russell remarks, is an objection to his procedure. Mr. Strawson's own suggestion has not been sufficiently worked out for us to estimate its value.

It is well known that Russell and Wittgenstein were on the other side of this fence; for Wittgenstein 'having a sense' was one and the same thing with being true-or-false. We have already seen this at 3.24: 'The proposition in which a complex is mentioned does not become nonsensical if the complex does not exist, but simply false.' And we see it again at 4.063, where he develops an illustration of the concept of truth by a black spot on white paper: black corresponds to true and white to false. If you indicate a point on the surface, that is like pointing to what Frege calls a 'thought', or the sense of a sentence; and you are, of course, pointing to something that is in fact either black or white. But, Wittgenstein says, the point at which the illustration goes lame is this: you can indicate a point on a sheet of paper without so much as having a notion of black and white; what would correspond to this would be indicating a thought without so much as having a notion of true and false: 'but to a proposition without a sense there corresponds nothing, for a proposition doesn't designate an object

---

5   In an empirical science, such as astronomy, the possibility cannot be regarded as a defect of language, or legislated away, e.g. at one time it was thought that there was an extra planet, which was called 'Vulcan'. On Frege's view propositions about Vulcan could not have a truth-value.

6   In school mathematics one is told that '$\frac{x}{y}$' does not mean any number when $y = 0$; a reinterpretation in Frege's style might stipulate that when $y \neq 0$, $\frac{x}{y}$ is the number z such that $zy = x$, and when $y = 0$, $\frac{x}{y} = x$.

with the properties called "true" and "false":' as, say, the description of a point designates an object with the properties called 'black' and 'white'. That is to say, unless the proposition is already something true or false, he calls it something 'without sense'.

Again, at 4.064, we find Wittgenstein saying: 'Every proposition must *already* have a sense; assertion cannot give it one.' Since this is an attack upon Frege, it may well confuse a reader; for of course Frege would agree that every (well-formed) sentence must already have a sense! But Wittgenstein holds that what already has a sense must already be true or false; he is attacking Frege's idea that in judging we 'advance from a thought to a truth-value'.[7]

Wittgenstein remained on this side of the fence all his life; for in the very passage of *Philosophical Investigations* in which he attacked the ideas about complexes which he expounded in the *Tractatus*, he asked: 'Am I really prepared in advance to say what, and how much, has got to turn out untrue before I give up my proposition about Moses as *false*?' The kind of thing he has been considering has been facts that, taken together, would tend to shew that there was no such person as Moses; and he spoke of giving up the proposition about Moses, not as neither true nor false, but as false.

It will be worth while to say a few things about the Frege-Strawson side of the fence. First, Frege was sure that a well-formed sentence whose names were not empty had a truth-value. But is it not strange to be sure of that? Is it not as if there were a great metal wall with holes in it, and we had some way of casting metal objects, and were absolutely certain that each object that was properly cast would fit into a hole in the wall one way up or the other (the well-formed proposition or its negation is true) although no connection had been shewn between the principles of casting objects and the character of the metal wall? The fact that Frege's account makes things look like this is a sure sign that he has gone wrong, like the accounts of 'true' and 'false' which make 'Every proposition is either true or false' like 'Every rose is either red or yellow'. Frege's reply to this would be that a sentence is only well-formed if the concepts it employs are sharply defined, and a concept is sharply defined if it is determined for every object whether it falls under that concept or not. The problem now assumes the form: how does it come about that we can form concepts for which this is determined, without any reference to the facts?

---

[7] *See* 'Sense and Reference', in *Philosophical Writings of Gottlob Frege*, p. 65.

Secondly, Frege actually said that the truth-conditions determine the sense of a proposition. He specifies the truth-conditions, and therefore (since he is working in an *a priori* discipline) the truth-value, which on his theory is also the reference, of any well-formed formula in his system; he then adds, as if to anticipate the objection that he has only specified the reference and not the sense, that the sense of such a formula is the sense of this: that its truth-conditions are fulfilled. And to this, *mutatis mutandis*, we may see a correspondence in Mr. Strawson's 'knowing in what circumstances the sentence could be used to make a statement'. The propositions embodying the truth-conditions, or describing the circumstances in which a sentence could be used to make a statement, must themselves be either true or false, or require explanation in terms of further truth-conditions, or further circumstances. In view of this, the Frege-Strawson position on the possibility of sentences without truth-value appears to be a waste of time: in such an account the concept of 'sense' is not divorced from those of truth and falsehood; it is merely determined that when certain of the truth-conditions of a proposition are false we are to say that 'nothing either true or false has been said'.

We have observed that the most striking difference between the coin-tossing tables and the truth-tables is that in the former we use different symbols in setting out the possible results of coin-tossing and the possible bets on these results. Now let us suppose that we have a coin with 'win' written on one side and 'lose' on the other, so that we said that we bet on the coin's coming up 'win' or 'lose' rather than 'heads' and 'tails'. Then a bet that the coin would 'win' — a bet, so to speak, in agreement with the coin — on the one hand, and a bet that the coin would lose, would be exactly comparable to the two truth-functions of a single proposition:

$$
\begin{array}{ccc}
p & & \\
T & T & -F \\
F & F & T \\
\end{array}
$$

The objection immediately arises that while we have a good sense for 'winning' and 'losing' in connection with a *bet* on whether the coin will fall one side up or the other, there really is no sense in these terms as applied to the sides of the coin themselves, except that we *happen* to write this sign on one side and that on the other. The signs are not really the same; any more than 'jam' is the same word in English and in Latin. Now that may be so: but we have in fact already encountered a parallel difficulty in connection with using the word 'true' for the elementary propositions and for the truth-functions. It may be intuitively obvious that there is no equivocation; and it is certainly extremely natural to give the explanations found in the logic books and then simply get on with the calculus. But our questions were reasonable ones; if there is no way of answering them, and we have just to rely on our intuition, that is of itself an important fact—at any rate, it is important for philosophy.

The *Tractatus*, however, does attempt to give an answer to these questions other than that the correctness of these two uses of the words 'true' and 'false' is intuitively obvious. I opened by raising the question: If we offer a definition of 'not p' as 'that proposition which is true when p is false and false when p is true' how can this be justified if we are not assured that there is such a proposition, and only one? Now grounds are given for saying that there is only one such proposition at 5.513: 'It could be said that what is common to all symbols that assert p as well as q, is the proposition "p.q." What is common to all symbols that either assert p or assert q, is the proposition "p ∨ q".

'And in this way it can be said: Two propositions are opposed to one another, if they have nothing in common, and: Every proposition has only one negative, because there is only one proposition which is wholly outside it.'

In the first of these paragraphs, we must understand that it is the propositions 'p.q' and 'p ∨ q' that are being explained in terms of what is common to a class of symbols. We have already seen Wittgenstein saying (3.341) that the essential thing about a symbol, or the *real symbol*, is what all symbols that do the same job have in common. If then there is anything that a set of propositions all say, then what is common to that set of propositions he calls the *real symbol* for the thing that they all say. So you might say that a set of propositions, 'A is red', 'A is green', 'A is blue', etc., have something they *all* say, namely: 'A is coloured.' And the 'real symbol' for 'A is coloured' will be what is common to the propositions 'A is red', 'A is green', 'A is blue', etc.

Now any set of independent propositions has something that they all say; what this is is brought out by writing out a truth-table where all places but the bottom are marked 'T', the bottom place having F in it opposite the row of F's of the matrix. This truth-table specifies a proposition, which is made true by the truth of any one of the components; hence I call it something that they *all* say. And according to Wittgenstein's dictum, the 'real symbol' for this will be what is common to them all. But the proposition in question is of course the disjunction of them all: and hence the 'real symbol' for e.g. p ∨ q is what is common to all propositions that either assert p or assert q.

How the common thing about a set of symbols, and hence the 'real symbol', is to be described is a matter of which the *Tractatus* gives an account in the range of entries under 3.31, that is to say, 3.31–3.318, and there is further matter relevant to the specification of *sets of propositions* at 5.501. Let us assume that the account is satisfactory. For our present purpose is to shew how Wittgenstein proposes to justify our assurance that every proposition has only one negative.

'Two propositions are opposed to one another if they have nothing in common.' That is to say, if there is nothing that they both say. In this sense 'The King of France is bald' and 'The King of France is not bald' are not opposed to one another (if the latter is the result of substituting 'The King of France' for 'x' in 'x is not bald'), for there is something that they both say. This comes out in the fact that 'The King of France is bald or the King of France is not bald' may not hold, namely if there is no King of France; the proposition therefore asserts something, viz. that some one of the situations in which it would hold is actual; it asserts something because these situations are not an exhaustive list of all possible situations; it excludes the situation in which it would not hold.

He goes on to say: 'Every proposition has only one negative, because there is only one proposition that lies wholly outside it.' Let us test this by supposing that there might be two *Ex hypothesi*, these two must have different senses, i.e. it must be possible for one to hold and the other not. Let us write them as not-p (1) and not-p (2). Then the disjunction of p and not-p (1) could be false, if what held were not-p (2). So the disjunction of p and not-p (1) does assert something, and there is something asserted by both p and not-p (1), namely that some one of the situations in which the disjunction would hold is actual. It follows that there can be at most *one* proposition that has 'nothing in common' with any given proposition. There can of course be many propositional *signs* for this proposition, but their sense will all be the same.

That there can be at most one proposition of this character for any given proposition does not shew that there is one; and we must next shew how this is made out in the *Tractatus*.

4

Negation:
(2) The Picture Theory

We have been troubled by the procedure of the logic books in e.g. placing the same signs, T and F, under the signs of the elementary proposition in the truth-table and in the final column, and by the justifications of this procedure, which consist in quasi-factual pronouncements. Let us now consider remedying this procedure. I adopt two new signs, P and N, which mean 'Positive' and 'Negative', which I put under the signs for the elementary propositions:

	p	
P	T	F
N	F	T

The proposition which is an element in a truth-function is thus introduced as having two senses, the positive and the negative, rather than two truth-values, true and false.

Now there is actually some foundation for looking at it like this, in the *Tractatus* itself. At 4.463 Wittgenstein writes: 'The proposition, the picture, the model, in the negative sense are like a solid body, which restricts the free movements of another; in the positive sense, like the space limited by solid substance, in which a body may be placed.' Here at any rate a proposition, as well as a picture or model, is conceived as something that can have both a positive and a negative sense.

As far as concerns a picture, this is quite reasonable. It is in fact connected with one of the objections that it is most natural to feel to Wittgenstein's 'picture' theory of the proposition. A picture is not like a proposition: it doesn't say anything. A picture is not an assertion that something like it is to be found somewhere in the world, whereas in a proposition something is *said to be the case*. If we accept Wittgenstein's dictum at 4.022 that 'A proposition *shews* how things are *if* it is true. And it *says* that they are so', we might say: 'Just this shews the difference between a proposition and a picture; for while a picture may be said to *shew* how things are, *if* there is something it is a correct representation of, it certainly does not *say* that that is how things are; the most that one could grant would be that we could *use* the picture *in* saying how things are: we could hold the picture up and ourselves say: "This is how things are."'

Now in fact this is Wittgenstein's point. For in order to be able to do this in a quite straightforward sense, it is necessary that the elements of the picture should be correlated with objects.

For example, here is a picture:

and if I have correlated the right-hand figure with a man A, and the left-hand figure with a man B, then I can hold the picture up and say: 'This is how things are.' But I can just as well hold the picture up and say: 'This is how things aren't.'

If you could not do this with, say, the figures drawn or painted on a piece of paper, once they had been correlated with actual people or objects, then what was on the paper would not be a picture, but a set of figures each of which was correlated with some object.

I may for example draw a figure here

and call it 'Plato'; and then draw another figure here

and call it 'Socrates'; the two figures do not together constitute a picture, because although of course there is a relation between them — they are, say, a certain distance apart on a single leaf — this relation is non-significant. Whereas in the drawing of the two men fencing, the relation of the ink strokes constituting the drawing of the first man and those constituting the drawing of the second man was significant.

The isolated figures labelled 'Plato' and 'Socrates' each consist of strokes in significant relationship, and hence it seems reasonable to speak of correlating such figures, one with one person, another with another. But if I just put a single stroke

/

and then another stroke

/

the sense that there was in saying 'correlate the first mark with one person and the second with another' would vanish. If someone said this, we should wait for something to be done with the strokes; we might think that this announcement was a preparation for something; unless it is that it is not anything at all. Suppose I said: 'That door stands for Dante and that table for Bertrand Russell.' My audience would, if anything, look at me enquiringly and say: 'Well?' And here 'Well?' means 'Do something to shew the point of this'; and *that* means 'Let something else come into such a relationship with this door, or again with this table, that the terms in relation represent something.' We could say: 'Only in the connections that make up the picture can the elements of the picture stand for objects.'

The picture-theory of the proposition is that the proposition in the positive sense says: 'This is how things are' and in the negative sense says: 'This is how things aren't' — the '*this*' in both cases being the same: the comparison is a comparison with a picture of the '*this*' in question. It is because of the character of the '*this*' that there is the *possibility* of saying 'it's how things are' or 'it's how things aren't'. And this character is in pictures, ordinary pictures, themselves — all that is required for the possibility to be actualized is that their figures be correlated with objects. This begins to tell us why Wittgenstein says at 2.182 that 'Every picture is *also* a logical picture'; and at 2.1514 that 'the picturing relation consists of the co-ordinations of the elements of the picture and of the things'.

The quite straightforward possibility of doing this depends on the correlations' having been made; now this correlation is in one way quite external. The picture of two men fencing was intelligible as a picture, without our making any correlations of the figures with individual men. We might compare to this picture, without individual correlations, what Wittgenstein at 3.24 calls the 'proto-picture' occurring in the generality notation: the 'xRy', for example, in '(Ex)(y)xRy'.

What I have called the externality of the correlations between the elements of a picture and actual objects is an important feature of Wittgenstein's account. Giancarlo Colombo, S.J., the Italian translator of the *Tractatus*, commented on Wittgenstein's theory of the 'isomorphism', as it is called, between language and the world, that it was difficult to see why a described fact should not be regarded as itself a description of the proposition that would normally be said to describe it, rather than the other way round. And as far as concerns the internal features of proposition and fact, this is a strong point; for all the internal features are supposed to be identical in the proposition (or describing fact) and the described fact.

But after having stated at 2.15 that the way the elements are connected in the picture is the same as the way it sets forth the things as being connected, Wittgenstein goes on to compare it to a ruler which you set up against an object (2.1512–2.15121) and then says: (2.1513) 'According to this conception, the picture must have in addition the depicting relation which makes it into a picture';[1] and, as we have already seen, this depicting relation consists of the correlations with objects (2.1514).

Thus there are two distinct features belonging to a picture (in the ordinary sense of 'picture'): first, the relation between the elements of the picture; and second, the correlations of the elements in the picture with things outside the picture; and as we have seen, the first feature must belong to a picture before the second one can; only if significant relations hold among the elements of the picture *can* they be correlated with objects outside so as to stand for them. The correlating is not something that the picture itself does; it is something *we* do.

---

[1] Ogden's rendering of this sentence: 'the representing relation ... also belongs to the picture' can be misleading. There is evidence in Ramsey's review of the *Tractatus* (since Ramsey helped with the translation) that it was intended in an incorrect sense. Ramsey says that the elements 'are co-ordinated with the objects by the representing relation which belongs to the picture' (*Foundations of Mathematics*, p. 271). This interpretation throws Wittgenstein's quite straightforward idea into obscurity; the sentence has no such obscurity for educated native speakers of German.

We see this at 5.4733, where Wittgenstein says: 'Frege says: Every well-formed proposition must have a sense; and I say: Every possible proposition is well-formed, and if it doesn't make sense, this can only come of our not having supplied any reference for some of its component parts.' What Wittgenstein means by 'Every possible proposition is well-formed' is that the relations that must hold between the elements if a sentence is to be a sentence at all must be there also in any nonsensical sentence, if you could make this have a perfectly good sense just by changing the kind of reference that some part of the sentence had. Here it is 'we' who 'give' a sign its reference.

This is why at 3.13 Wittgenstein says that 'A proposition has in it everything that a projection has; but it hasn't got the projected thing in it; so it has the possibility of the projected thing in it, but not the very thing itself: And so the proposition does not yet contain its sense; what it does contain is the possibility of expressing that sense ... It contains the *form* of its sense, but not its content.'[2] The reason why the proposition doesn't 'contain its sense' is that the correlations are made by us; we mean the objects by the components of the proposition in 'thinking its sense': this is part of what is meant at 3.11: 'The method of projection is the thinking of the sense of the proposition.' It is we who 'use the sensibly perceptible signs as a projection of a possible state of affairs'; we do this by using the elements of the proposition to stand for the objects whose possible configuration we are reproducing in the arrangement of the elements of the proposition. This is what Wittgenstein means by calling the proposition a picture. It is at any rate clear enough that we could use a picture in this way.

Now, confining ourselves to pictures, it is also clear that if we 'think[3] the sense of the picture' by correlating its elements with actual objects, we can in fact think it in either of *two* ways: namely either as depicting what is the case, or as depicting what isn't the case. That is to say, there are two senses which we can 'think' in connection with the picture. For it is the very same picture we hold up if we wish to say that *it* holds or that *it* doesn't hold. Or again, if I hold up a picture and say 'If I correlate the elements of this picture with things, I can *say*

---

2   Wittgenstein's use of 'projection' is a metaphorical extension of the mathematical use, which may be explained thus: 'The drawing of straight lines through every point of a given figure, so as to produce a new figure each point of which corresponds to a point of the original figure.' The new figure is also said to be a *projection* of the original one, which is *projected into* it (cf. *The Shorter Oxford Dictionary*).

3   This is a Germanism which it seems necessary to retain in English.

something by holding it up', someone might reply: There are two things you could assert in holding the picture up: first the existence, and second the non-existence, of that situation which is represented by the picture so soon as its elements are correlated with objects. And the difference between the two is not that the relations between the elements are taken to be different; on the contrary, they are exactly the same.

It is clear that one must convey *what* situation one is saying does not exist, and this will be conveyed precisely by the picture depicting that situation. No other *picture* could be involved: you could not for example make a *picture* of the situation's *not* existing. We must be careful not to confuse what is not the case with what is the case instead of it; if you tried to make a picture of a situation's *not* existing you would only make a picture of what did exist instead of it. The only exception to this is when we have the convention that not shewing something shews that the thing does not exist: as when a map shews that no large river passes through Birmingham by *not* shewing a river passing through Birmingham.

These, then, are the reasons for speaking of a picture as having — or rather being capable of being given — a positive and a negative sense. The two senses are integral to the picture, once the correlations have been established. Certainly a picture whose 'sense' is 'thought' one way or the other, as I have described, *is* a propositional sign.

What is mysterious about negation is that something's *not* being the case should be capable of being something that *is* the case;[4] and it is a peculiarity of a picture of something's being the case that it can be taken as presenting us with something that is the case by being a *picture of what is not the case*. In his notebooks, Wittgenstein speaks of logical constants as giving the method of projection of the proto-picture in the proposition. I think this conception is not discarded in the *Tractatus*.

In the course of his researches prior to writing the *Tractatus*, Wittgenstein invented what he called the a-b notation. He proposed to write a proposition like this:

a p b

---

4   cf. *Philosophical Investigations*, §429: 'The agreement, the harmony, of thought and reality consists in this: if I say falsely that something is *red*, then, for all that, it isn't *red*.' The problem is the ancient one of how a false proposition makes sense.

the a and b being what he called the 'two poles' of the proposition. This notation has survived in the *Tractatus* at 6.1203, except that he writes T and F instead of a and b. But we could represent the propositional sign that is a picture (of the most ordinary kind) in the same way:

T 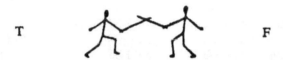 F

This rendering of the picture become proposition would stress the fact that it has acquired two 'poles', or senses in which it can be thought, by having the drawn figures correlated with actual men.

Now the question is: does this conception give us what is essential to propositions, so that it is at all plausible to say that all propositions have this character?

I believe that the most that we can say is that the bi-polarity of the picture, of the occurrence of *one* picture in two senses, has a very striking analogy in the fact that if we have a proposition, and insert a 'not' into it, then *what* is being denied is exactly *what* the original proposition said. In negating a proposition we use the propositional sign to form another, and we tend to feel that both *say* something: and hence want an account that would justify this feeling. Both propositions *mention* exactly the same things in the same relation to one another. The picture-proposition we have imagined gives us a very clear idea of structures for which these points hold. And it is also true that the non-existence of a configuration of things is a clear and intelligible idea. What constitutes the truth and falsehood of the picture-proposition; its opposed positive and negative senses; its possession of these senses independently of whether it is true or false (i.e. of *which* truth-value it has) — all this is extremely intelligible: and what is intelligible here is precisely the *logical* character of the picture-proposition. But is it not the logical character that marks a proposition as such and that we want clarified? Something that seems to make this really clear might rather convincingly be taken to shew the essential character of a proposition.

So far as I can see, these are the real grounds for being struck even to the point of conviction by this account. It adds to its persuasiveness that it was capable of being further, and beautifully, thought out, and that it seemed to offer a solution to many problems, and finally even give a 'way of seeing the world rightly'. There are indeed serious difficulties about it; nevertheless, we shall understand the *Tractatus* best if we let ourselves succumb to the attractiveness of this idea, assume its correctness, and follow up its consequences throughout the *Tractatus*.

Every picture-proposition has two senses, in one of which it is a description of the existence, in the other of the non-existence, of a configuration of objects; and it is that by being a projection. It is the peculiarity of a projection that from it and the method of projection you can tell what is projected; the latter need not physically exist, though the points in space that it would occupy must. The idea of a projection is therefore peculiarly apt for explaining the character of a proposition as making sense independently of the facts: as intelligible before you know whether it is true; as something concerning which you can ask *whether* it is true, and know what you are asking before you know the answer.

If this explanation can be made to stick it will make the character of a proposition completely clear. For supposing TpF and TqF to be picture-propositions, then someone who says 'TpF' will be saying (let us suppose) that the situation pictured by 'p' exists; he can say it does not exist by reversing the T and F poles of 'TpF' — a procedure represented by Wittgenstein with: 'F-TpF-T'. The diagram

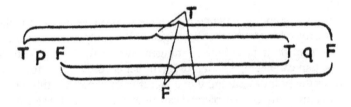

gives a picture-proposition, whose T pole is joined to a line joining the two T poles, and also to a line joining the two F poles, of 'TpF' and 'TqF', and whose F pole is joined to a line joining the T pole of 'TpF' with the F pole of 'TqF', and again to a line joining the F pole of 'TpF' with the T pole of 'TqF'. This proposition is true if the situations pictured by 'p' and 'q' both exist, or again if neither exists; otherwise false. This way of writing the propositional sign brings it out that nothing is mentioned but the objects correlated with the elements of 'p' and 'q' and no configurations introduced except those set forth in 'p' and 'q'.

The propositional sign written here in diagram form is the same proposition as what we would most commonly write (p.q) ∨ (~p.~q).

This brings out why Wittgenstein says: 'The structure of the fact consists of the structures of the elementary situations' (2.034); 'The picture presents ... the existence and non-existence of elementary situations' (2.11); 'The truth-conditions determine the play left to the facts by the proposition' (4.463); 'A proposition may be an incomplete picture of a particular state of affairs' (in this case, say, the state of affairs that neither p nor q) 'but it is always *a* complete picture' (5.156). For his idea was that definiteness of sense consists in this: a proposition may indeed leave a great deal open, but it is clear *what* it leaves open.

We must now return to the fact that a picture (in the ordinary sense) becomes a proposition the moment we correlate its elements with actual things. To shew this, I draw it shewing the T-F poles that it gets directly the correlation is made:

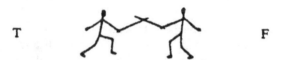

T   F

We must always remember the condition for the possibility of the correlation: namely that the arrangement of the ink strokes themselves is significant, is capable of picturing a situation *if* the correlations are made.[5]

Now, that some arrangement of shapes on a surface is capable of being a projection of another arrangement of shapes on a surface is obvious from their both being arrangements of shapes on a surface. Wittgenstein calls being spatial (or again being coloured) a 'form', and expresses the point by saying that a picture can depict anything whose form it shares: the spatial picture can depict the spatial, the coloured picture anything coloured, etc.

By analogy with this conception he erects one of 'logical form'. As children we sometimes amuse ourselves by drawing imaginary maps. Given the method of projection a person could say what the imaginary country's coasts would be like. But that is not to say that the imaginary map is already a true or false map of any actual coastline. But we

---

[5]   There is something that I slur over here for purposes of a first rough exposition: and that is the difference between the significant relations of the mere ink strokes, and the relations of the drawn members of the drawn figures and of the drawn figures among themselves. This corresponds to the difference between the significant relations between the sensibly perceptible signs, and the relations between the *symbols. See* 3.326.

might say it becomes a true or false map of the world — given the method of projection — the moment we pin it to any actual place by correlating some of its points with places on the globe.

This is to suppose that we call it a true map if, correlating one point on the drawn coastline with one point on the globe, and another with another, the projection of the drawn coastline coincides with an actually existent coastline; and otherwise we call it a false map of that part of the globe. These facts, however, do not imply that, supposing it to be a false map in the sense I have defined, there is another method of projection for that map which will make it a true map of a coastline, the same points on the map and on the globe being correlated. After all, the originally selected points might be in the middle of a great ocean, in which case no method of projection would make the imaginary map a true map of a coastline.

Thus we can consider the T and F poles of the picture-proposition as giving two senses, positive and negative (as it were, the different methods of projection), in which the picture-proposition can be thought. Now although a map is a picture-proposition once a method of projection and correlations have been established, it is not so simply in virtue of its *spatial* form. For saying 'It's *not* like this' is using the map to say something true; but it is not giving a correct *map*. If then the positive and negative senses are compared to different methods of projection, then it is not the spatial form, but something comparable to spatial form, that makes the map into a picture-proposition when correlations are established. This Wittgenstein calls 'logical form'.

It is obvious enough that a proposition divides up into parts. It is also obvious that the division is not arbitrary. You cannot divide 'The cat is often drunk' into 'The cat is of' and 'ten drunk', although each part could be significant: as Wittgenstein would say, the first expression's standing to the left of the second is not what signifies in our sentence, and (3.314) 'An expression has reference only in the context of a proposition'. (It was of course on this pronouncement, and on that of Frege, repeated by Wittgenstein, that 'A name has reference only in the context of a proposition' that I modelled my statement about pictures: 'It is only in the connections that make up the picture that its elements stand for objects.')

Propositions thus have a feature that is very comparable to a feature of pictures. We call the possibility of the kind of connection that sets up a proposition 'logical form', as the possibility of any particular spatial arrangement can be called spatial form. And since logical form is that through which a structure can have T and F poles, and for something to be true or false is the very same thing as for reality to be thus or otherwise, Wittgenstein calls 'logical form' also 'the form of reality'. Thus he provides a distinctive new solution to the old old problem of shewing the connection between thought and reality. That the logical form is common to reality and the propositions is a further analogue to the way the spatial form is common to the spatial object and its spatial picture: 'A picture can depict any object whose form it has.'

The notion of logical form leads straight to that of logical space. We can construct a spatial illustration a bit like Wittgenstein's black spot on white paper, but one which 'goes lame' at a different point. If you consider an island marked on the surface of a sphere, it is clear that it defines not merely its own shape but the shape of the rest of the surface. A proposition is to be compared to such an island, its negation to the rest of the surface.

Let us say that you illustrate the concept of truth by painting the island white and the rest of the surface black, to correspond to calling a proposition true and its negation false; if on the other hand it is the negation that is true, the island is black and the rest of the surface white. Obviously you could do this with a real globe; and *any* map, real or imaginary, would divide the globe. Only as we saw, the divisions would not necessarily correspond to any actual coastlines. But the division made by the two senses of any proposition is a division of truth from falsehood; each coastline partitions the whole earth's surface, so each proposition 'reaches through the whole of the logical space'. But it *is* a proposition precisely by making a division of true from false. Now let us represent the proposition saying that *either* this *or* that is true, by a new globe with *both* the corresponding areas white; what corresponds to saying that either a proposition or its negation is true is painting the *whole* surface of the globe white—in which case you have no map. And similarly for painting the whole surface black, which would correspond to 'not (p or not p)'. But it is clear than an all-white or all-black globe is not a map.

So when—as sometimes happens in old-fashioned philosophical textbooks—the laws of contradiction and excluded middle are laid down as truth with which reason starts, this may be compared to the admiration of the sailors for the Bellman's map in the *Hunting of the Snark*:

> 'Other maps are such shapes, with their islands and capes!
> But we've got our brave captain to thank'
> (So the crew would protest) 'that he's bought us the best—
> A perfect and absolute blank!'

At 4.463 Wittgenstein uses a similar but double analogy. He says that the proposition in the positive sense is like the space in which a body can be placed; in the negative sense it is like a solid body which prevents any body from being placed in the space it occupies. Now since any proposition p divides the whole space, then the positive proposition 'p or not p' leaves the whole space empty, both the island indicated by p and the rest of the space; and its negative 'not (p or not p)' blocks the whole space.

The point at which such analogies go lame is that e.g. a globe shewing Australia as land and the rest as sea, and one shewing the rest as land and what is now Australia as sea, have the shape of a coastline in common; so that one *is* saying something about the globe if one says that either this or that representation of it is true.

On the other hand, each of these two globes could be used to depict what the other depicts, by changing the conventions for shewing sea and land. This feature does illustrate what holds for propositions: 'p' could be used to say what '~p' says and *vice versa*. A code by which one always meant the negative of what one said need not break down. Hence, Wittgenstein says, 'though "p" and "~p" have opposite senses, one and the same reality corresponds to them' (4.0621): the reality is the coastline itself. It is important to remember that if 'p' and 'not p' were so substituted for one another, 'not' would still mean 'not': and this is enough to shew that 'not' itself has nothing corresponding to it in reality: its presence does not determine the sense of the proposition.

We can now understand some of what Wittgenstein says about tautology and contradiction. They are not 'pictures' (4.462), just as all-white or all-black globes are not maps. And so they are not 'logical connections of signs' (4.466): the relations between them are non-significant—i.e. depict nothing: the representing relations, like two projections which between them fill a space, cancel one another out.

The all-white globe, though, might be said to be a representation of the whole world. It is because of the shape of the whole that the two shapes, p together with not-p, combine to make the shape of the whole. And this throws light on what Wittgenstein means when he says that the logical propositions describe, or rather represent, the framework of the world. 'It must shew something, that certain combinations of symbols are tautologies.' But what is represented here is not something that '*we* express by means of the signs', but that 'speaks out on its own account' (6.124).

It seems sure that the *Tractatus* account is wrong. This is partly because one cannot believe in the simple objects required by the theory; partly because it leads to dogmatic and plainly false conclusions about the will, about modality and about generalizations in infinite cases. But it is a powerful and beautiful theory: and there is surely something right about it — if one could dispense with 'simples' and draw the limits of its applicability.

It represents a high point of development of an historic line of thought. The idea that the proposition is an interweaving of simple names representing an interweaving of simple elements is to be found in Plato's *Theaetetus*; Aristotle thought about it a great deal, and rejected it largely because something more than the elements was required, something connecting them. And the idea that the complexity of a proposition reflects a complexity in its object has everywhere been influential: it is part of what is expressed, for example, in the idea of natural theologians that God, being 'simple', is not really describable or knowable — however many propositions they might construct about him.

Here it is worth remarking that the truth of the *Tractatus* theory would be death to natural theology; not because of any jejune positivism or any 'verificationism', but simply because of the picture theory of the 'significant proposition'. For it is essential to this that the picturing proposition has two poles, and in each sense it represents what may perfectly well be true. Which of them is true is just what *happens* to be the case. But in natural theology this is an impermissible notion; its propositions are not supposed to be the ones that happen to be true out of pairs of possibilities; nor are they supposed to be logical or mathematical propositions either.

Wittgenstein used to say that the *Tractatus* was not *all* wrong: it was not like a bag of junk professing to be a clock, but like a clock that did not tell you the right time. It is noticeable that he sounds like himself in the *Tractatus* whenever he writes about negation in the *Philosophical Investigations*. And at one place the voice of the author of the *Tractatus* is heard, like that of the drowned ghost in the song: 'A description is a projection of a distribution in a space.'[6]

---

6   *Philosophical Investigations*, p. 187.

5

Consequences of the Picture Theory

Convinced that he had penetrated the essential nature of truth, false-hood and negation with his picture theory, Wittgenstein now had a great programme to carry out. He had to shew how the vast number of propositions that do not immediately appear to fit in with his theory do in fact fit in with it. There was a residue that would never fit in with it; these he dismissed as nonsensical: perhaps simply nonsensi-cal, perhaps attempts to say the inexpressible. The following list gives us some idea of the greatness of the task. He had to deal with:

Laws of inference, and, generally, logical truths.

Statements that one proposition implies another.

Generality — i.e. propositions containing 'all' and 'some'.

Propositions giving logical classifications of terms and expressions —e.g. '"to the right of" is a relation', '"a is to the right of b" is a proposition'.

Propositions that are important in the foundation of mathematics such as 'a is the successor of b'.

Statements about the possibility, impossibility, necessity, and certainty of particular states of affairs.

Statements of identity.

Propositions apparently expressing functions of propositions, such as 'it is good that p', or 'p is possible', 'p is necessary' or again 'A believes p' or 'A conceives p'; and perhaps even statements about e.g. the beauty of pictures.

Propositions stating probabilities.

Propositions of mathematics.

Propositions stating laws of nature.

Propositions about space and time.

Egocentric propositions.

Propositions about the world as a whole, about God and the meaning of life.[1]

It would be wrong to suggest that Wittgenstein formed his views on all these topics simply so as to fit in with the picture-theory. It was rather in most cases that his views on them all did fit in with the picture-theory; the fact that what seemed to him true views on them did so fit in would seem an extra confirmation of the picture theory.

There is, however, one exception to this; his view, expressed at 6.37, that 'there is only *logical* necessity', and at 5.525, that the possibility of a state of affairs is simply expressed by an expression's being a significant proposition, appears to be a pure exigency of the picture theory of the proposition. It is a very common dogma at the present day that there is no sense of 'necessity' and 'possibility' except 'logical necessity' and 'logical possibility'. It is possible that this dogma, which is in part an effect of the influence of Hume, is also a hangover from the time of the overwhelming influence of the *Tractatus*.

With this is connected Wittgenstein's inference from the fact that there is no logical connection between the will and the world (6.374) (since what I intend does not *have* to come about), to the view that 'the world is independent of my will' (6.373): the connection *must* be a purely accidental one. This means that 'all happening and being this way or that', and 'everything that is the case' is independent of my will. If one should object to this that it is obvious that what people intend has some bearing on what happens, he would reply that that is just 'a phenomenon, only of interest to psychology' (6.423).

Even here, though, the view has a connection with his ideas about ethics. For the will as it appears in the world, the 'mere phenomenon, only of interest to psychology', is what is spoken of at 5.631: 'If I were to write a book: "The world as I found it", I should also have to give an account of my body in it, and to say which members are subject to my will and which not.' Now that such-and-such members are subject to my will is a *mere* fact; if I were suddenly so paralysed that nothing happened, the will would remain—I should still have willed; but this will is not merely an impotent thought of the thing's happening, but is of good or evil; and that, apart from the mere vulgar facts of what happens, is the interest of the will. But of that 'we cannot speak'

---

[1]   I am not able to discuss Wittgenstein's treatment of all of these topics in the compass of this book.

because value lies outside the world and we can only express what is in the world. Now that value lies outside the world is not a mere consequence of Wittgenstein's picture theory of language; had he only been concerned with the fact that 'good' and 'evil' could not fit into the picture theory, he might have done as many positivists did, and debunked value altogether.

Thus the part of his views which seems to be nothing but a dogmatic consequence of the 'picture theory' is in fact his rejection of modality. Any sense of 'may', 'can', 'possible', other than that of 'logically possible', would be unamenable to explanation in terms of the picture theory. And the assertion that something is logically possible itself requires explanation. For the picture theory does not permit any functions of propositions other than truth-functions. Indeed, we should not regard Wittgenstein's theory of the proposition as a *synthesis* of a picture theory and the theory of truth-functions; his picture theory and theory of truth-functions are one and the same. Every genuine proposition picks out certain existences and non-existences of states of affairs, as a range within which the actual existences and non-existences of states of affairs are to fall. Something with the appearance of a proposition, but which does not do this, cannot really be saying anything: it is *not* a description of any reality.

Possibility of a state of affairs is said at 5.525 to be expressed not in a proposition ('p is possible' is not a picture of a state of affairs) but in an expression's being a significant proposition: thus the logical possibility of p is one of those things that cannot be asserted, according to the *Tractatus*, but that 'shew'. This explanation does not get us much further forward. For an expression's being a significant proposition cannot be a 'fact' either: at 5.5351 we find Wittgenstein criticizing Russell for trying to symbolize the 'nonsense' '"p" is a proposition' by the senseless tautology 'p ⊃ p' so as to guarantee that only propositions should be put in the argument-places of the succeeding propositions. This, he says reasonably enough, is absurd, because if that were not already assured, it could not possibly be assured by the extra premise that p ⊃ p, which would become not false but nonsensical with the wrong sort of substitution for 'p'.

The objection to '"p" is a proposition' is a case of a quite general objection to a whole range of similar formations: 'n is a number'; 'ϕ is a function'; 'it is a (possible) fact that p'; '"the king of France" is a complex'; 'a is an object'. 'Object', 'fact', 'proposition', 'number', 'function', 'complex': all these Wittgenstein called 'formal concepts', saying (4.126): 'That anything falls under a formal concept as its object cannot be expressed by a proposition, but is shewn in the sign for the object itself. (The name shews that it designates an object, the numeral that it designates a number, etc.) Formal concepts cannot, like proper concepts, be presented by a function.' Now at least for the examples '2 is a number', 'red is a colour' the point is easily made that these propositions cannot express anything that might be false; there are not two possibilities, that 2 is, and that it is not, a number; that red is, and that it is not, a colour; of which the first happens to be actual in each case.

Carnap strongly objected to Wittgenstein's doctrine with its corollary of the 'unsayables' that are 'shewn', which seemed to lead on to the 'mysticism' of the *Tractatus*.[2] In order to avoid it, he proposed to use the 'formal mode of speech'; instead of saying 'red is a property', '2 is a number', '*to the right of* is a relation' we are to say '"red" is a predicate', '"2" is a numeral', '"to the right of" is a relational expression', which were held not to involve the same difficulties.

This (perhaps deliberately) failed to take account of Wittgenstein's doctrine that the real symbol is what is common to all the symbols that can do the same job. To say of the 'real symbol' for 'to the right of' — the common feature that enables all expressions for this in all languages to have this meaning — that *it* is a relational expression is *not* to say something that has the true-false poles. It is clear that Wittgenstein's objection to propositions in which an object is said to fall under a formal concept is not limited to the ones like 'red is a property' which are in the 'material mode of speech', and so would not be removed by translation into the 'formal mode'. 'Predicate' would be just as much a 'formal concept' for him as 'property'.

Carnap was well aware of this, and flatly denied that there was any difficulty about propositions in which an object was stated to fall under a formal concept, so long as these propositions were translated into the formal mode. At first sight this seems reasonable enough. In '"red" is a predicate' we are saying something about the object named by the first word of the sentence; that object is itself a word. What is said about it might not have been true: the sentence therefore has the true-false poles, and Wittgenstein's supposed difficulties about it are illusory.

It is an essential part of Carnap's view that the convention of forming the name of a word by writing it in quotes is *wholly* arbitrary; there

---

[2]   I once had occasion to remark to Wittgenstein that he was supposed to have a mystical streak. 'Like a yellow streak,' he replied; and that is pretty well how the Vienna Circle felt about certain things in the *Tractatus*.

is no necessity for *any* systematic relation, any more than the names of shapes like 'square' and 'round' need have shapes corresponding to the shapes named; and 'red' *as a word* no more occurs in its name '"red"' than it does in 'predatory'.

Carnap's view is, however, radically defective. This was made clear by a Czech logician, K. Reach.[3] He gives a table, of which I reproduce a part here:

;	Semicolon	Secol
Semicolon	Secol	Sco

remarking that really, instead of 'table' one should say 'museum', for a table correlates names of things, whereas in a museum things and their names are exhibited together. The table consists of two rows. In the upper row there are samples of various single symbols of a language; beneath each is a word arbitrarily chosen as a name of the given symbol. Carnap calls such a correlation of simple symbols with their arbitrary names a '*syntaktische Zuordnung*'. When we say 'red' is a colour-word, our first word is the name of an object (as it so happens, of a word); but there is no essential connection between this object and its name, other than that this *is* its name, any more than there is any other connection between, say, a man and his name; and so we may (as here) use as names of symbols, symbols that have no systematic connection with them.

Reach demonstrates the defects of Carnap's *syntaktische Zuordnung* by taking it quite seriously, as follows: 'The purpose of the sentence "Secol is the name of Semicolon" is to give information about the meaning of Secol (i.e. [the word] "Semicolon"). Does this sentence serve its purpose? Suppose somebody asks "What is the meaning of Secol?" and he receives the answer "Secol is the name of Semicolon." If the answer is to convey anything to the questioner, it must be understood; i.e. the questioner must know what Sco and Secol [i.e. what the words "Secol" and "Semicolon"] stand for in the sentence. That he knows the former [knows what Sco, i.e. the word "Secol", stands for] is shewn by the *form* of his question; but the meaning of his question is that he does not know the latter [he does not know what

---

[3] *Journal of Symbolic Logic*, September 1938: 'The Name Relation and the Logical Antinomies.'

the word "Semicolon", i.e. Secol, stands for]. Hence the answer is incomprehensible to the questioner.'

Reach's work suggests the formulation of a very simple paradox, which takes Carnap's view of the use of quotation marks seriously: It is impossible to be told anyone's name by being told 'That man's name is "Smith"'; for then his name is named, not used as a name, in that statement, and so what I hear is the name of his name and not his name; and I can only learn his name if I know what name this name-of-a-name is a name of, just as I can only obey the order 'Fetch a red one' if I know what colour the colour-word 'red' is a name of. But from Reach's argument it is clear that I cannot *informatively* be told that this name-of-a-name, i.e. '"Smith"', is the name of the name 'Smith'; if I do not already understand this, I shall not understand the statement that it is so. This, then, seems to be a rather clear case of 'what can be shewn' but 'cannot be [informatively] said'.

Nevertheless, 'what shews' in this sense can be *illuminatingly* said. We have an (admittedly rather trivial) example of a proposition lacking the true-false poles in '"Someone" is not the name of someone'. This is obviously true. But it does not have the bipolarity of Wittgenstein's 'significant propositions'. For what is it that it denies to be the case? Evidently, that 'someone' is the name of someone. But what would it be for 'someone' to be the name of someone? Someone might christen his child 'Someone'. But when we say '"Someone" is not the name of someone', we are not intending to deny that anyone in the world has the odd name 'Someone'.

What then are we intending to deny? Only a piece of confusion. But this *sort* of denial may well need emphasizing. Students, for example, may believe what Professor Flew tells us in the Introduction to his collection *Logic and Language*, 1st Series, pp. 7–8: namely that 'somebody' refers to a person, that it is part of the 'logic' of 'somebody', unlike 'nobody', to refer to somebody. If this were so, then on being told that everybody hates somebody, we could ask to be introduced to this universally hated person. When we say '"Somebody" does not refer to somebody', what we are intending to deny is what Professor Flew meant. But he did not really mean anything (even if he felt as if he did).

Here a statement which appears quite correct is not a statement with true-false poles. Its contradictory, when examined, peters out into nothingness. We may infer from this that Wittgenstein's account of propositions is inadequate, correct only within a restricted area. For it hardly seems reasonable to prohibit the formula: '"Somebody" does not refer to somebody' or '"Someone" is not the name of someone';

nor, of course, is this logical truth in any sharp sense of 'logical truth'. It is, rather, an insight; the opposite of it is only confusion and muddle (not contradiction).

The example of '"Someone" is not the name of someone' is particularly clear, because the true proposition is negative. According to Wittgenstein, however, since what our proposition denies does not turn out to be anything, it itself is *not* a truth; for there isn't anything which it says is not the case, as opposed to the equally possible situation of its being the case. Therefore Wittgenstein would either have looked for a more acceptable formulation (which I think is impossible) or have said it was something which *shewed* — stared you in the face, at any rate once you had taken a good look — but could not be *said*. This partly accounts for the comical frequency with which, in expounding the *Tractatus*, one is tempted to say things and then say that they cannot be said.

At 4.1121 Wittgenstein says: 'Does not my study of sign-language correspond to the study of thought processes which philosophers have held to be so essential to the philosophy of logic? Only they got involved for the most part in inessential psychological investigations, and there is an analogous danger with my method.' The development represented by Carnap and his school seems to be a fulfilment of this expectation.

6

Sign and Symbol

As we have seen, if the possibility of a state of affairs is expressed, not in a proposition, but in an expression's being a significant proposition, then according to the *Tractatus* the very thing that it is expressed in again cannot be expressed by a proposition. But we are not yet in the realm of the 'inexpressible' according to the *Tractatus*: for instead of speaking of an expression's being a significant proposition, we could speak of the fact that '"p" says that p'. And we shall find out that this, taken one way, is a genuine fact. To understand this we must examine two reputedly obscure passages. The first is 5.541–5.5421:

'At first sight it appears as if there were another way [other than as a truth-argument] in which one proposition could occur in another. Especially in certain psychological forms of proposition, like "A believes that p is the case" or "A conceives p" etc.[1] Here it appears superficially as if the proposition p stood in some kind of relation to an object A. And these propositions have actually been so taken in modern theory of knowledge (Russell, Moore, etc.). It is clear, however, that "A believes that p", "A conceives p", "A says p" are of the form "'p' says p". And here what is in question is not a correlation of a fact to an object, but a correlation between facts by means of a correlation between the objects in them. This also shews that the mind—the subject etc.—as it is conceived in the superficial psychology of the present day, is a chimera. For a composite mind would no longer be a mind.'

The statement that 'A believes that p' etc. are of the form '"p" says p' has been variously taken to mean that Wittgenstein held it was impossible to have a thought without uttering a sentence; or that he held that a person was to be analysed as a complex.

---

[1]   Russell mentions such forms of proposition (*Principia Mathematica*, 1st Edition, Vol. 1, p. 8) in order to explain truth-functions by contrast.

For the first interpretation I can see no reason at all. Against the second it seems to be an objection that it takes a theory that a person is a complex as Wittgenstein's *ground* for saying that 'A believes p' is of the form '"p" says that p'. Whereas it is evident that he is arguing: You can't explain the mind as 'the judging subject' in 'A judges p', *because* 'A judges p' is of the form '"p" says p'; so that way you will only reach a complex, and a composite mind would not be a mind. Therefore Wittgenstein's statement that 'A believes p' is of the form '"p" says p' cannot be based on any Humean theory that a person is a complex.

'It is clear,' he says; and of course what was clear to him was that for anything to be capable of representating the fact that p, it must be as complex as the fact that p; but a thought that p, or a belief or statement that p, must be potentially a representation of the fact that p (and of course actually a representation of it, if it *is* a fact that p). It is perhaps not quite right to say that 'A judges p' is of the form '"p" says that p'; what he should have said was that the business part of 'A judges that p', the part that relates to something's having as its content a potential representation of the fact that p, was of the form '"p" says that p': 'A believes p' or 'conceives p' or 'says p' must mean 'There occurs in A or is produced by A something which is (capable of being) a picture of p'. We should here remember the letter to Russell in which he said he did not know what the constituents of thoughts were, but he was certain that a thought must have constituents corresponding to the words of language.

Here, then, we are given '"p" says that p' as a possible form of proposition. If Wittgenstein has not been careless, it must fit his general account of propositions—that is, it must have true-false poles. Now if a sentence is an arrangement of words, it would seem to follow in accordance with the general principles of the *Tractatus* that a way of designating a sentence must be (or be defined by) a description of its arrangement of words; though it is a reasonable complaint for a reader to make that Wittgenstein might have been more explicit than he is on this important point. The passage which comes nearest to stating it is as well known, and has been found as obscure, as the one we have just considered. It comes at 3.1432, and runs:

'"The complex sign 'aRb' says that a stands in the relation R to b." No, not that, but rather "*That* 'a' stands in a certain relation to 'b' says *that* aRb".'

This statement is really not particularly obscure. Consider what relation the sign 'a' does actually stand in to the sign 'b' in virtue of which the whole sign so composed says that aRb. There are all sorts of possibilities. For example, if I happened to write the 'a' in blue and the 'b' in red, the question could arise whether it is in virtue of the fact that 'a', 'b', and 'R' are written side by side (the order being immaterial), with the 'a' blue and the 'b' red, that the sign so composed says that aRb. In fact, we know that even if I do this, this is not the expressive feature of the sign, though of course it might be. The expressive feature is that the 'a' stands to the left and the 'b' to the right of the 'R'; for if I reversed that, putting 'b' to the left and 'a' to the right, then, according to our present conventions, a different sense would be expressed. From this we can see how we should take '"p" says that p'. The expression schematically represented by '"p"', which in a concrete case would consist of an actual proposition in quotation marks, is to be taken as a way of describing the arrangement of signs that constitutes the proposition. '"p" says that p' thus admits of various interpretations; e.g.:

'That in "aRb" "a" is written in italics and "b" in Roman says that aRb' might be the way that we *interpreted* '"aRb" says that aRb'. And although it contains a true description of the propositional sign as here occurring, it is a false statement (though it could be a true one); for it is not, as it happens, this fact, but the fact that 'a' stands to the left and 'b' to the right of 'R', that says that aRb. The use of italic and Roman letters is immaterial as far as concerns the expression of a relation.

If this is the sort of thing we are to understand, then the proposition '"p" says that p' is a genuine proposition, with true-false poles, according to the conceptions of the *Tractatus*; for its truth or falsity depends on how the propositional sign 'p' is understood to be described. Of course, in order to be false, the description has got to be of some feature of the propositional sign that *might* have been used to express p. So while some interpretation or other of '"p" says that p' *must* be true, its exact interpretation is something that can be true or false.

If a man says — perhaps wonderingly — something of the form '"p" says p', he need not be thinking of the interpretation of the part of his expression which is a quoted expression, but that does not matter: for as Wittgenstein says at 4.002: 'Man possesses the capacity of constructing languages in which any sense can be expressed without having an inkling what each word stands for, and how. Just as we speak without knowing how the individual sounds are produced ... The tacit conventions for understanding ordinary language are enormously complicated.' Someone who had given no thought to *how* 'aRb' says that aRb would immediately know that someone else had gone wrong who thought that it was the italics that mattered, and that one could say that bRa by writing 'aRb'.

That is to say, in '"p" says that p' what is being considered is the propositional *sign*, mental or physical; and it was of course primarily of the physical sign that Wittgenstein was thinking. Signs are after all what we actually hear or see; it is from them that we gather the meaning of what is said or written; and *some* of the variations in them embody variations of meaning. That is to say, the kind of sensibly perceived difference that there is between 'aRb' and 'bRa' is that from which we gather, and by means of which we express, *a* difference of sense.

Now if we consider the difference between

A and B are poetical

and

A and B are identical

we shall have gone far wrong if we think that the difference in sense between the two propositions is expressed purely by the difference of four letters, that in the one one thing is asserted of A and B, and in the other another thing, the difference of words expressing a difference just in *what* is asserted. For that difference of two words signifies much more than that; as comes out in the fact that if A and B are poetical, A is poetical; whereas if A and B are identical, we can't go on from this to say 'A is identical'. Thus Wittgenstein says: 'What does not get expressed in the signs, comes out in their application; What the signs fail to express, their application declares.' By 'application' he did not mean 'role in life', 'use', 'practice of the use' in the sense of *Philosophical Investigations*; he meant 'logico-syntactic application' (i.e. that kind of difference between the syntactical roles of words which concerns a logician). 'Only together with its logico-syntactic application does a sign determine a logical form' (3.327). And it was by the possession of a logical form that a proposition was capable of expressing a sense.

But it is pretty well impossible to discern logical form in everyday language. As an example of the difficulty, consider the difference between Roman and Arabic numeration. MCMXLVIII is the same number as 1948, but reading it is more complicated. For example, the way of reading MCM is different from the way of reading VII, though each is composed of three of the elements placed side by side. This does not mean that the Roman system fails to express the same number as the Arabic. It expresses it perfectly.

This illustrates Wittgenstein's view of the difference between ordinary language and a good symbolic notation. In his Introduction (p. 9) Russell said that Wittgenstein was 'concerned with the conditions for a logically perfect language—not that any language is logically perfect, or that we believe ourselves capable, here and now, of constructing a logically perfect language, but that the whole function of language is to have meaning, and it only fulfils this function in proportion as it approaches to the ideal language which we postulate.' This statement of Russell's was plainly contrary to the intentions of the *Tractatus*, as is very easily shewn. At 5.5563 Wittgenstein says: 'All the sentences of our everyday language, just as they are, are logically in perfect order.' Language could not *approximate* to having meaning; any language, just *qua* language, fulfils its purpose perfectly.

It is a mistake to suppose that the dictum 'Ordinary language is all right' is an expression only of Wittgenstein's later views. He was dialectically expounding, not opposing, his point of view at the time of writing the *Tractatus*, in the following passage of *Philosophical Investigations*:

> 'On the one hand it is clear that every sentence in our language "is all right as it is". That is, that we are not *striving* after an ideal: as if our ordinary vague sentences had not yet got an irreproachable sense, and a perfect language had yet to be constructed by us. On the other hand this seems clear: Where there is sense, there must be perfect order. And so there must be perfect order even in the vaguest sentence.'[2]

That is to say, the sentences of ordinary language no more fail to express a sense than our Roman numeral fails to express a number. The one expresses a sense, the other a number, perfectly. And so the ideal order that characterizes language is there in every sentence of ordinary language. But: 'Everyday language is a part of the human organism and is just as complicated. It is humanly impossible to gather the logic of language from it directly' (4.002). This, then, is why, according to Wittgenstein, we study logic and construct logical symbolisms: in order to understand the 'logic of language', so as to see how language mirrors reality.

We want in pursuit of the picture-theory to be able to say that the expressive feature of language is that *signs* are *combined in certain ways*. We compared 'aRb', and 'bRa', saying that we have here a sensible difference in which a difference of sense is expressed. That is to say, this is a particular instance of a *kind* of difference which is essential to *any* relational expression in any language: we have here an example of 'what is common to all symbols that can do the job'. But of course

---

2   *Philosophical Investigations*, Part I, §95.

'aRb' expresses something, as e.g. 'X-O' does not, because the elements in 'aRb' are not just *signs* in the sense of 'marks', but are *symbols*, as those in 'X-O' are not. So the expressive feature of 'aRb' is not just an order of elements, but is the fact that a *sign* 'a', which is a *symbol*, stands to the left, and the *sign* 'b', which is also a symbol, to the right, of the *sign* — again a symbol — 'R'.

On the other hand, we have to remember the central point of the picture theory which we have already explained: 'Only in the context of a proposition has a name reference'; 'Only in the context of a proposition has an expression reference.' This prohibits us from thinking that we can *first* somehow characterize 'a', 'R' and 'b' as symbolic signs, and *then* lay it down how we can build propositions out of them. If 'a' is a symbolic sign only in the context of a proposition, then the symbol 'a' will be properly presented, not by putting it down and saying it is a symbol of such and such a kind, but by representing the whole class of the propositions in which it can occur.

This we may do provisionally by taking a proposition in which 'a' occurs, and retaining 'a', while we substitute a variable (I will use 'ξ') for all the rest of the proposition. Then the symbol 'a' is rightly presented, not just by putting it down and saying it is a sign of an object, but by a variable proposition

$$(\xi)a$$

This Wittgenstein says quite generally for symbols, or 'expressions', at 3.311–3.313: 'The expression presupposes the forms of all propositions in which it can occur. It is the common characteristic mark of a class of propositions. It is therefore presented by the general form of the propositions of which it is characteristic. And in this form the expression will be *constant* and everything else *variable*. Thus the expression is presented by a variable: the propositions which contain the expressions are values of this variable ... I call such a variable a "propositional variable".' Equally, of course, it would have been possible, considering a proposition such as 'aRb' in which 'a' occurs, to take 'Rb' as the expression to be presented, and to substitute a variable (I will use 'η') for the 'a'; then the expression will be presented by the variable proposition

$$(\eta)Rb$$

This account is perhaps inspired by Frege's *Concept and Object*. Frege said:

'Language has means of presenting now one, now another part of the sentence as the subject; one of the most familiar is the distinction of active and passive forms ... It need not then surprise us that the same sentence may be conceived as an assertion about a concept and also as an assertion about an object; only we must observe that what is asserted is different.'[3]

Frege was thinking at first of the fact that we can re-form propositions, as is shewn by his reference to active and passive forms. Language shews now one, now another, part of the sentence as the subject, by altering the sentence, so that now one part, now another, appears as the grammatical subject. e.g. 'John murdered James', 'James was murdered by John'. And, also, 'The sun is red', 'Red is a property of the sun'.

But when Frege says: 'The same sentence can be conceived as an assertion about a concept and also about an object; only we must observe that what is asserted is different', he has passed from considering a reformulation of 'The sun is red', like 'Redness is a property of the sun', to considering the one sentence 'The sun is red' in two ways. And these two ways are very well explained by Wittgenstein. Adopting his explanations we can take them as the alternatives of regarding it as a value of a variable sentence:

$$\text{'} - - - - - \text{red'}$$

which takes 'The sun' as an argument, and

$$\text{'The sun} - - - - - \text{'}$$

which takes 'red' as argument. In the first, we shall therefore be regarding the sentence as 'about' the sun; in the second as 'about' red —for what we are 'taking as the subject' is what fills the argument-place. Only, as Frege says, if we so regard the sentence as now an assertion about a concept, now about an object, what is asserted is different, though the sense of the whole analysis is in each case the same.

This last point was missed by Ramsey in his essay *Universals*. He speaks of a theory—which he rejects—that in a proposition 'aRb' we can discern 'three closely related propositions; one asserts that the relation R holds between the terms a and b, the second asserts the possession by a of the complex property of "having R to b", while the third asserts that b has the complex property that a has R to it. These

---

3   *Philosophical Writings of Gottlob Frege*, ed. Geach and Black, p. 49.

must be three different propositions because they have three different sets of constituents, and yet they are not three propositions, but one proposition, for they all say the same thing, namely that a has R to b. So the theory of complex universals is responsible for an incomprehensible trinity ...' Ramsey's thought is bedevilled at this point by the idea that you cannot analyse a proposition in a variety of ways: that if you say that 'Socrates taught Plato' ascribes something to Socrates, you cannot also say that it ascribes something to Plato without making it out a different proposition.

Ramsey's essay, however, quite apart from its intrinsic interest, is also very helpful for exegesis of the *Tractatus* theory of 'expressions'. For Wittgenstein tells us at 3.314 that every variable can be conceived as a propositional variable — even the variable name. But how can this be? The variable proposition

$$x \text{ loves Socrates}$$

has as values only those propositions in which a name is substituted for x; but the propositional variable

$$\xi \text{ loves Socrates}$$

indicated by Wittgenstein has as values *all* the propositions in which 'loves Socrates' occurs, e.g. 'Everyone loves Socrates', 'Anyone who loves Plato loves Socrates', 'No one loves Socrates', 'Plato does not love Socrates'. And similarly for all other variables, as variables are usually understood. 'Plato has n sons' is a variable proposition whose values are e.g. 'Plato has 6 sons', 'Plato has 100 sons', 'Plato has no sons', but not 'Plato has stupid sons', or 'Plato has as good sons as Socrates'. That is to say, its values are *not* all the propositions in which the expression 'Plato has ... sons' can occur.

Here, following Ramsey, we may draw a distinction between a wider and a narrower range of propositions which an expression can be used to collect. Only there is no need to follow Ramsey in holding that the expression 'Socrates' cannot be used to collect a range including e.g. 'Socrates is wise and Plato is not'. For this opinion of Ramsey's was based on his rejection of 'complex universals'; and this in turn is based on his conviction that if you define e.g. 'ϕx' as 'aRx', and then treat 'ϕ' as a predicate of b in 'ϕb', you must be denying that 'ϕb' is a relational proposition — which of course is absurd, if you have defined 'ϕx' as 'aRx'.

Now it may be that proponents of 'complex universals' were confutable by this argument; but it does not follow that anyone who, like

Frege, picks a name out of a proposition and calls the rest of the proposition a predicate can be dealt with in this way. Only Ramsey's belief that one analysis of a proposition excludes all others enabled him, just on the strength of this argument, to deny that 'Socrates' could be used to collect just as varied a range of propositions as e.g. 'wise'. For he thinks that 'wise' *can* be used to collect such propositions as e.g. 'Neither Socrates nor Plato is wise' or 'Someone is wise'. And he goes on to distinguish between a wider and a narrower range of such propositions: one, *all* the propositions in which 'wise' occurs, and the other a narrower collection of simpler propositions, of the form 'x is wise'. We can adopt this distinction, just as he intends it for 'wise', for 'Socrates' also.

Now the question arises: why is there no hint of this in Wittgenstein's text? It would certainly seem from what Wittgenstein says that the 'class of propositions' of which an expression was 'the common characteristic mark' was the *whole* class of propositions in which the expression could occur. But 'x loves Socrates' can only be completed into a proposition by substituting a *name* for 'x'; therefore 'x loves Socrates' *cannot* give us the general form of the whole class of propositions, in which the expression 'loves Socrates' occurs. We seem to be forced to call Ramsey's distinction to our aid, and say that the 'class of propositions' presented by 'x loves Socrates' is a narrower class that can be discerned within the wider class of all the propositions in which 'loves Socrates' can occur.

The answer to this puzzle lies in the theory — which is integral to the picture theory of the proposition — that all propositions are truth-functions of the elementary propositions.[4] On this theory, the 'wider class' that we have been considering will be the class of all the truth-functions of any set of propositions among which are propositions containing the expression in question. It immediately follows from this that any expression presupposes the most general form of all propositions, as well as the special form of the proposition in which it immediately occurs. But unless — which is very possible — I have missed some essential feature of Wittgenstein's idea,[5] it must be admitted that his account is sketchy, unsatisfactory and obscure.

---

[4]   In particular, general propositions such as 'Everyone loves Socrates'. *See* Chapter 11.

[5]   It is possible that Wittgenstein was satisfied with 'the great works of Frege' as far as concerns the general form of all propositions in which a given predicate (such as 'loves Socrates' or 'is clever') occurs. Frege's general form is '$M_\beta \phi(\beta)$': this is the

general form of second-level functions, such as 'Everything is ϕ', 'Something is ϕ', 'ϕ is what James is and John is not'. The 'β' shews that ϕ is a concept or first-level function, being the mark of an argument-place.

7

Wittgenstein, Frege and Ramsey

We have inferred from Wittgenstein's remarks on 'expressions' — which must include names — that a name 'a' can be represented by a propositional variable '(ξ)a' which is an informal — and somewhat uninformative — version of the most general form of propositions in which 'a' occurs. Thus Wittgenstein would not accept Frege's way of distinguishing between object and concept — that an object is something complete in itself, whereas a concept is in need of completion — is, as it were, something with a hole in it. For it looks as if Wittgenstein will make out both that expression in a sentence which designates an object, and that expression which remains over in the sentence when we have picked out the expression designating the object, to be something with, so to speak, a hole in it. And this conception is the same as the picture theory, in terms of which we have explained what Wittgenstein meant by Frege's dictum: 'Only in the context of the proposition has a name reference.'

Ramsey, in his essay on 'Universals', took Wittgenstein to mean that there was no difference between qualities and objects.

> 'Against Mr. Russell it might be asked how there can be such objects as his universals, which contain the form of a proposition and are incomplete. In a sense, it might be urged, all objects are incomplete; they cannot occur in facts except in conjunction with other objects, and they contain the form of propositions of which they are constituents. In what way do universals do this more than anything else?'

Ramsey therefore suggests that it is mere prejudice to distinguish between individuals and qualities; there is no reason why we should not speak of Socrates' attaching to ϕ as well as of ϕ's attaching to Socrates in a proposition 'ϕ Socrates'.

The distinction has a practical point, he says, in that if 'ϕ' stands for e.g. 'either having R to a or having S to b', we cannot put $\phi = $ Ra $\vee$ Sb because we should not know whether the blanks in ( )Ra and ( )Sb were to be filled with the same or different arguments. Instead we must put $\phi x = $ xRa $\vee$ xSb; which explains not what is meant by ϕ by itself, but that followed by any symbol x it is short for 'xRa $\vee$ xSb'. But if ϕ were a simple property, there would be no reason to say that 'ϕ' is asserted of Socrates rather than that 'Socrates' is asserted of the reference of 'ϕ'. And he takes this to be Wittgenstein's doctrine, chiefly because he observed quite correctly that Wittgenstein holds that both a name, and the remainder of a sentence from which a name has been removed, are represented by 'propositional variables'; moreover, Wittgenstein does not speak of 'concepts' or 'universals' as a kind of thing that is to be found in the world: it is quite clear that for him there is nothing but objects in configuration.

That Ramsey has mistaken Wittgenstein's intention is fairly clear from Wittgenstein's calling 'function', like 'object', a formal concept (*see* Chapter 9) and from his explanation at 4.24: 'Names are simple symbols, I indicate them by single letters ("x", "y", "z"). The elementary proposition I write as a function of names in the form "f(x)", "ϕ(x,y)".' Now it must not be supposed from this that Wittgenstein intends 'ϕ(x,y)' to represent an atomic fact consisting of three objects. He has only just remarked (4.2211): 'Even if the world is infinitely complex, so that every fact consists of infinitely many atomic facts and every atomic fact is composed of infinitely many objects, even so there must be objects and atomic facts.' So when he writes 'ϕ(x,y)', nothing whatever is indicated about how many names may be covered by the sign of the function; there might, on the hypothesis that he has just mentioned, be an infinite number.

Wittgenstein's doctrine, however, is not at all easy to understand; for on the one hand he speaks of the elementary proposition as a concatenation of names, as consisting of names in immediate combination; and on the other hand he says at 5.47: 'Where there is complexity, there is argument and function': therefore the elementary proposition too consists of argument and function.

These remarks considered together raise the problem: if the elementary proposition consists of names in immediate connection — if it is just a concatenation of names — then it is not *reproduced*, even if it can be faithfully represented, by a formula consisting of some letters for names and some letters for functions. And this is borne out by many passages. Notably for example 3.143: 'The nature of the propositional sign becomes very clear, if we imagine it as composed of three-dimensional objects (say tables, chairs, books) instead of written signs. Here the spatial lay-out of those things expresses the sense of the proposition.' We are reminded of the models of cars, buses and buildings set out in a law court to shew how an accident took place, which made Wittgenstein say: 'That's what a proposition is!' And in the succeeding entry, which we have already considered, he says: 'That "a" stands in a certain relation to "b" says *that* aRb.' Now the actual relation in which, in the propositional sign 'aRb' 'a' stands to 'b' was, as we remarked, that 'a' stands to the left, and 'b' to the right, of a further sign 'R'. Now let 'R' be 'to the left of'. In a waxwork display shewing the way people stood, the fact that a man A stood to the left of a man B will be shewn by having the wax figure that goes proxy for A in the display standing to the left of the wax figure that goes proxy for B, and there will be no need for any third object to signify the relation. At 4.0311 Wittgenstein makes the comparison with the *tableau vivant*: 'One name stands for one thing, another for another, they are connected together: that is how the whole images the atomic fact — like a *tableau vivant*.'

It is natural — and reasonable — to say of this idea: This is all very well; but it is possible only when the picture-proposition shares a 'form' as Wittgenstein calls it, *other* than what he calls 'logical form', with what it depicts. The waxwork show and the *tableau vivant* need no figures going proxy for the spatial relations just because, being three-dimensional models of three-dimensional situations, they can reproduce the spatial relations instead of having something standing for them. And the coloured picture can represent that a cloak is red without having the cloak in one place and the redness in another, just because it is a coloured picture representing something coloured, so that it can simply shew the cloak as red. Further, even if the picture were in black and white, and represented the colour of objects by some conventionally agreed shading — still, it has the advantage of being able to shew the shading that means red, on the cloak and not somewhere else.

This is exactly what does not happen in a proposition. In a sentence saying that the man wore a red cloak the word for the cloak is not printed in red to shew this. Even if we had some such conventions — and perhaps we can admit we have something of the sort in the difference between 'aRb' and 'bRa' — they do not take us very far. Even in this very favourable case, we need a special sign for the relation itself.[1] And rightly so, because there is some material content to relations like 'to the right of' or 'bigger than'; that is why signs between which the same kind of relations hold can reproduce them; but if you were quite generally to express relations between things by relations between their signs, then you would need to have as many different relations between signs as we in practice have words to express relations.

This is in fact Wittgenstein's requirement for the fully analysed sentences of a language. For the fully analysed elementary proposition is a concatenation of simple names; though not a mere list, because the way they are combined is expressive.

This does not mean that function and argument would disappear in the final analysis. If for the moment we may give 'a-b-c-d' as an elementary proposition, then 'a-b-c-( )' and 'a-(')-(")-d' would be two different functions; which might be represented as 'fx', '$\phi(x,y)$' respectively; and the representations of 'a-b-c-d' as a value of these two functions would be 'fd', '$\phi(b,c)$'. I write primes in the second function to shew that it can be completed with different names in the two empty argument-places. (')-(")-(''')-('''') would be a formula, 'a logical form—a logical proto-picture', of an elementary proposition.

Now we just do not know the composition of any elementary proposition; that is why Wittgenstein never gives any such example. But Ramsey writes as if, say, 'a-b' were a specifiable elementary proposition, which Wittgenstein *chooses* to write as, say, 'f(b)'. That is quite to misunderstand Wittgenstein's use of the sign 'f' in 'f(b)': 'f(b)' symbolizes an elementary proposition, but not necessarily one in whose sense (the atomic fact) *only* two objects occur. The point can be put most briefly like this: to represent a name 'a' by '(ξ)a', i.e. by the most general way for that name to occur in a proposition, is not to represent a name as a function, but only to stress that the name has reference only in the context of a proposition.

The idea of conceiving a proposition as a function of the expressions contained in it comes from Frege, and to understand it we have to go back to his great essay *Function and Concept* and follow the steps by which he formulated this conception.

First we introduce the notion of a numerical *function*—i.e. what is expressed by a numerical formula containing one or more 'indefinitely indicating' letters; if the letter or letters are replaced by signs for a

---

definite number or numbers, the expression so obtained has a definite numerical value: e.g. x^2, $x+y$. The function could be fittingly expressed by a formula with an empty place in it: $(\ )^2$. By an 'argument' we mean what is signified by the sign we put into the empty place. 'We give the name "the value of a function for an argument" to the result of completing the function with the argument.' Thus e.g. 4 is the value of the function $(\ )^2$ for the argument 2. But it is necessary, if there is more than one empty place, to distinguish between cases where the function can be completed by putting different things, and cases where it must be completed by putting the same thing, into the empty places. That is why we use letters instead of empty places.

There are functions whose value is always the same, whatever the argument, such as $2 + x - x$; and there are pairs of functions whose values are always the same for the same argument: for example $x^2 - 4x$ and $x(x - 4)$.[2]

Following Frege, we now add to the signs +, -, etc., which serve for constructing a functional expression, such signs as =, >, <, which occur in arithmetical statements. So we speak of the function $x^2 = 1$. The value of the function for a given argument is signified by the result of substituting a definite numeral for the letter x. But the result of substituting a definite numeral for x here has not a numerical value, but is something true or false; hence the now familiar idea of a 'truth-value' is derived from this conception of Frege's.

The 'value' of $x^2 = 1$ is 'true' for a definite argument, e.g. for –1; to say this is the same thing as to say that –1 is a square root of 1, or that –1 has the property that its square is 1, or that –1 falls under the concept 'square root of 1'. 'We thus see,' Frege says, 'how closely what is called a concept in logic is connected with what we call a function.' This suggests an interesting definition of a proposition as 'the result of completing a sign of a function by filling up an argument-place, when the value of the result is a truth-value'. And so far, Wittgenstein is in agreement with Frege, and expresses his agreement at 3.318: 'I conceive the proposition — like Frege and Russell — as a function of the expressions it contains.'

To speak of conceiving the proposition as a function *of* the expressions it contains is of course not inconsistent with denying, as Frege does, that a proposition is a function; it is like speaking of 8 as a function of 2, say its cube. It is important to grasp this point, that what is a function *of* something is not a function *tout court*; confusion on this

---

2   I follow Frege in speaking of two functions here. It is not usual.

point is often found. A function for example is sometimes explained as a variable magnitude. Now it is true that, say, the volume of a gas is a variable magnitude (i.e. variable in time) and is also a function of the pressure and temperature. But the volume of a gas is not a function *tout court*, and therefore we do not get here an example of a function that is a variable magnitude. To say that the volume is a function of pressure and temperature is to say that there is a function f such that $V = f(p,t)$. For the volume to be a function *tout court* would be represented by the nonsense $V = f(\ )$.

We must now consider Frege's next step. He has defined a function as what is signified by an expression with an empty place; and he says: 'An object is anything that is not a function, so that the expression for it does not contain an empty place.' It follows that (unasserted) propositions designate objects, since they have no empty places; and since Frege regards a proposition as one kind of completed functional expression, and considers that a completed functional expression (e.g. '2^3') is a designation of a value of the function, it becomes natural to say that propositions designate values. This might be a matter of terminology, to which it would be unreasonable to object, granted that the conception of a proposition as a completed functional expression recommends itself.

Frege now proceeds to construct a function

$$—x$$

whose value is 'the true' when 'the true' is its argument, and in *all* other cases is the false. By taking 'the true' as argument Frege means putting a true proposition in place of the 'x'; you can put a designation of anything there instead — a false proposition or a definite description of a numeral or an ordinary proper name: anything, in short, that stands for anything, without having any empty places in it. For example

$$—2$$

is a possible result of completing this function, and the value of the function when so completed is: false, or, as Frege puts it, —2 *is* the false. This way of speaking is of course a consequence of the distinction between sense and reference. If I use an expression which stands for something, then in using it I am speaking of what it stands for; and if I have another name, 'B', for that thing, I can use the first name, 'A', and say that A *is* B. So since '—2' is a designation of the truth-value: false, Frege can say that —2 is the false. We must accept this sort of consequence if we accept the *prima facie* plausible distinction between the sense and reference of expressions; this constitutes an objection to the distinction.

The reason why Frege wished to construct such a function is that he has no truck with attempts to stipulate ranges of significance in the manner of Russell.[3] If a truth-value is an object, it can be an argument; but he is not willing to specify 'propositions' as the range of significant substitutions for 'x' in functions taking truth-values as arguments; and indeed the specification of ranges of significance is a very dubious business.

Ordinarily, if we write down '5 > 4' we wish to assert something; but according to Frege's view, '5 > 4' is just an expression for a truth-value, without any assertion. Therefore, he says, we need a special sign in order to be able to assert something, as opposed to expressing a *mere assumption*[4]—the putting of a case without a simultaneous

---

[3]   *See* Chapter 9, pp. 102–3.

[4]   It has sometimes perplexed readers of Wittgenstein that he refers, both in the *Tractatus* (4.063), and in *Philosophical Investigations*, to 'the Fregean *Annahme*', as if '*Annahme*' (assumption) had been a technical term in Frege, as it was in Meinong. His reference is to this passage; and it is evident that his attention was especially fixed on it by a passage in Russell's account of Frege in the *Principles of Mathematics*, Appendix A, §477. Russell says: 'There are, we are told, three elements in judgment: (1) the recognition of truth, (2) the *Gedanke* (the thought), (3) the truth-value. Here the *Gedanke* is what I have called an unasserted proposition—or rather, what I have called by this name covers both the *Gedanke* alone and the *Gedanke* together with its truth-value. It will be well to have names for these two distinct notions; I shall call the *Gedanke* alone a *propositional concept*; the truth-value of a *Gedanke* I shall call an *assumption*.' And here Russell has a footnote referring to the passage in *Function and Concept*, and, saying: 'Frege, like Meinong, calls this an *Annahme*.' 'Formally, at least,' he goes on, 'an assumption does not require that its content should be a propositional concept; whatever x may be, "the truth of x" is a definite notion. This means the true if x is true, and if x is false or not a proposition it means the false.'

What Russell refers to as 'the truth of x' is of course Frege's function ——x. Frege introduces a second function

$$\overline{}\mathsf{T}\text{—x}$$

whose value is the false for just those arguments for which the value of ——x is the true. Thus, as Russell says, we do not have assertions and negations—there is not a negation sign, corresponding to the assertion sign—but we have assertions of the truth and falsity of 'thoughts', or, as Russell calls them, 'propositional concepts'.

It is a peculiarity of Russell's account that he takes

$$\text{——}5 > 4$$

to be something different from

$$5 > 4$$

judgment as to whether it holds or not. So he puts a vertical stroke at the left of the horizontal, e.g.

$$\vdash 2 + 3 = 5$$

and *this* expresses the *assertion* that 2 + 3 = 5.

We must now examine Wittgenstein's main criticism of Frege. At 4.431, he says: 'The proposition is the expression of its truth-conditions', and then remarks: 'Hence Frege was quite right to premise the truth-conditions as defining the signs of his symbolism.' The reference is presumably to the passage in the *Grundgesetze* where Frege says that he has specified the reference, i.e. the truth-value, of any

---

and calls '5 > 4' the 'thought' and '——5 > 4' the 'assumption'; thus turning Frege's quite innocent and untechnical expression 'a mere assumption' into a technicality.

What Russell failed to notice was that if a proposition is substituted for x in '——x' there is no difference at all, for Frege, either in sense or in reference, between the proposition by itself and the proposition with the horizontal stroke attached; moreover a 'thought' is not a proposition, not even an unasserted proposition, but is the sense of a proposition, and hence there is the same *Gedanke* when we have a proposition and when we have a proposition with the stroke attached. It is only when we substitute the designation of something *other* than a truth-value for 'x' in '——x' that there is any difference, either in sense or in reference, between the designation by itself and the designation with the stroke attached. In that case, the designation designates whatever it does designate—the Moon or the number 3 for example; and the designation with the stroke attached designates a truth-value, in these cases the false.

Russell's remarks, which mistakenly give special prominence to Frege's use of the word 'assumption', must be the source of Wittgenstein's references to it. Further, it appears that Wittgenstein actually accepted Russell's interpretation; for his comment on Frege at the end of 4.063 is not otherwise intelligible: 'The proposition does not stand for any object (truth-value) whose properties are called "true" or "false"; the verb of the proposition is not "is true" or "is false"—as Frege thought—but what "is true" must already contain the verb.' Although in *Begriffsschrift* Frege said that the verb of the proposition was 'is true'—a view which he rejected in *Sense and Reference*—he never thought this of 'is false'. But if we were to adopt Russell's interpretation of the passage in *Function and Concept*, we should say that according to Frege there are three stages

(1)   x
(2)   the truth of x
                    or: the falsehood of x

and then (3) the final stage of assertion, which we might think of as a tick put against whichever is right, the truth of x or the falsehood of x; and *such* a view might easily be rendered as a view that the real verb in the proposition that gets asserted—i.e. in the 'assumption'—is 'is true' or 'is false'.

well-formed proposition in his symbolism by specifying the truth-conditions, and that the sense of the proposition is the sense of: such-and-such truth-conditions are fulfilled. 'Only,' Wittgenstein continues, 'the explanation of the concept of truth is wrong: if "the true" and "the false" were really objects, and were the arguments in ~p etc., then according to Frege's own specifications the sense of ~p would by no means be specified.'

Frege has specified the truth-*values* of his propositions by specifying the truth-*conditions*, because his propositions are logical truths: it is the characteristic feature of logical truths (or again of logical falsehoods) that their truth-values are determined by determining their truth-conditions. But he has also said that the sense of his propositions is the sense of this: that their truth-conditions are fulfilled; and in this way he has ensured that his propositions are scientifically perfect; he has guaranteed a sense and a reference for them, and determined which truth-value they have.

Thus, if Frege has a negative proposition, '~p', its sense must also be the sense of the fulfilment of its truth-conditions. But his explanation of negation is this: he introduces a new function ──┬─x, whose value is the false for just those arguments for which the value of ──x is the true, and conversely; and so in '~p' we have a proposition determined as expressing the result of completing with the argument 'p' a function whose value for given arguments is given; but where is the *sense* of '~p'? '~p' appears to be defined in effect as that proposition whose reference is the true in certain circumstances and the false in others. But on Frege's own principles you do not specify a sense by specifying a reference; and so, Wittgenstein says, according to Frege's own principles, the sense of '~p' is not determined.[5]

The problems involved here are at bottom the same as those I discussed in Chapter 3. As a criticism of Frege the point can be summarized by saying: 'If truth-values are the references of propositions, then you do not specify a sense by specifying a truth-value.' Now this objection is quite decisive; but the essential difficulty about negation, although it receives a special form in connection with Frege's theory, is, as we have already seen, not generated just by Frege's conceptions. We encountered it at the very outset, when we examined the customary definition of '~p' as *the* proposition that is true when p is false and false when p is true; and we have seen how

---

[5]   This criticism is quite independent of the misinterpretation of Frege's theory (taken over by Wittgenstein from Russell) which was discussed in the last footnote.

Wittgenstein's picture theory of the proposition guaranteed the legitimacy of the customary definition by supplying the conditions required for offering such a definition: namely that there is not more than one such proposition and that there always is such a proposition.

Furthermore, negation gives us good grounds for rejecting Ramsey's suggestions, not just as interpretations of the *Tractatus*, but in themselves. For you can negate a function, but not an object: this shews that even the simplest possible sign of a function is not the same thing as a name. It may be asked why, in analysing 'Socrates is not wise', we should not take the negation with 'Socrates' rather than with 'wise' —'Socrates-is-not wise'. We can certainly speak of 'all the things that *Socrates is not*'; and Frege would have said that this phrase stood for a second-level concept, its role being to say, concerning the reference of a predicate, that this is one of the things Socrates is not. But though it can be treated as an 'expression', the common characteristic mark of a class of propositions, 'Socrates is not' is not on an equal footing with 'Socrates' —they cannot be treated as one another's contradictories, like 'red' and 'not red'. The result of attaching 'Socrates is not' to the conjunction of predicates 'wise and just' is quite different from the conjunction of the results of attaching it to 'wise' and 'just'; for the name 'Socrates' no such difference can arise. Accordingly, 'Socrates is not' is not an allowable interpretation of a name variable, in the way that a negative predicate is always an allowable interpretation of a predicate variable.

It should be apparent, however, that Wittgenstein's views are extremely Fregean. What, then, has become of Frege's 'concepts' in Wittgenstein's theory? They seem to have disappeared entirely; actually, however, instead of making concepts or universals into a kind of objects, as Ramsey wished to, Wittgenstein made the gulf between concepts and objects much greater than Frege ever made it. So far as concerns the content of a functional expression, that will consist in the objects covered by it. But in respect of having argument-places, concepts go over entirely into logical forms. In the 'completely analysed proposition', which is 'a logical network sprinkled with names',[6] the

---

6   I take this expression from a late notebook of Wittgenstein's in which he makes some comments on the theories of the *Tractatus*. In his pre-*Tractatus* notebooks Wittgenstein says 'Properties and relations are objects too' (16.6.15). On my view, he no longer holds this in the *Tractatus*. I think my view necessary (a) to reconcile the various passages I have cited about functions and elementary propositions and (b) because if Wittgenstein held that objects fell into such radically distinct categories as functions and individuals, it is an incredible omission not to have made this clear.

Fregean 'concept', the thing with holes in it, has become simply the logical form. Thus there is no question of two kinds of *reference* for expressions; one which is incomplete, having a hole in it that awaits, say, an object to complete it; and another, complete and capable of completing the incomplete, itself requiring no completion.

An interesting consequence follows about, say, two propositions expressing (completely) different facts: A is red, and: B is red. If these propositions were 'completely analysed', so that we had elementary propositions consisting of names in immediate connection, then the question arises whether the *objects* that would be named, in place of our using the colour-word 'red' in the two cases, would be different. I think Ramsey would have supposed that they would be the same. And no doubt he would have pooh-poohed the feeling that in that case these objects would have the character of universals rather than 'individuals'; we don't think A is a 'universal' because it can enter into a variety of facts, so why should we think this of red — or if red is composite, of the objects into which 'red' is 'analysed'? This is perhaps a proper reply; yet it is difficult not to feel that an object that can exist all over the world in different facts has rather the character of a universal. It takes a little mental habituation to think that existence in several facts is the only feature that counts, so that since both A and red can exist in several facts, we should not be impressed by A's at least existing in only one place at a time, while red can exist in so many.

Anyhow, whatever the merit of Ramsey's view, we cannot *certainly* ascribe it to Wittgenstein. Let us pretend once more that we can make an actual model of an elementary proposition 'with the names in immediate connection'; then for Wittgenstein the two facts: A is red, and: B is red, would be analysed into (1) facts corresponding to the descriptions of the complexes A and B, and (2) facts about the elements of the complex A along with certain further elements, say a, b, c, for A's redness, and exactly corresponding facts about the elements of the complex B along with certain other elements, say d, e, f, for B's redness. There is no need for a, b, c, to be the same as d, e, f, respectively; for it is only the 'logical network' that is 'universal'.

We normally tend to assume that different occurrences (at least of the same shade) of red differ only in that there are different *things that are* red — that no real difference other than this answers to the two predications of the predicate 'red'. This has helped to form the belief in universals; though there have been philosophers, e.g. among the medievals, who have wished to speak of 'individualized forms' — 'this whiteness' for example. The problem of 'universals' can in fact be given the form: was Frege right to introduce two wholly different kinds of 'reference' for words, namely 'objects' and 'concepts'? A 'concept' was the 'reference' of a predicate; now the characteristic mark of a predicate is its possession of an argument-place or -places, which could be filled with the names of now one, now another object; hence a 'concept' is a 'universal'. In Wittgenstein's fully analysed proposition, we have nothing but a set of argument-places filled with names of objects; there remains no kind of expression that could be regarded as standing for a concept.

The objects 'behind' a true predication of 'red' would indeed be of the same logical form in every case. We must remember that the original seat of form is the objects themselves: 'If things can occur in atomic facts, this must be something that is in things themselves ... If I can imagine an object in the nexus of an atomic fact, I cannot imagine it outside the *possibility* of this nexus.' (2.0121): And that is why Wittgenstein says: 'The possibility of its occurrence in atomic facts is the form of the object' (2.0141), and: 'The objects form the substance of the world' (2.021); and so they are *'form and content'* (2.025). Thus at 2.0231 we learn that the substance of the world—i.e. the objects—*can* determine only a form, not any material properties. For it needs propositions (as opposed to names) to represent material properties; such properties are 'only formed by the configuration of the objects'. Red is a material property, and therefore formed by a configuration of objects —and, as I suggest, by the *same configuration* of *different* objects in the different facts that exist when different things are red. These different objects, having the capacity to enter into configurations forming the material property red, will be of the same logical form: that of objects whose configurations yield colours. (Hence colour is a 'form of objects': 2.0251.)

This, then, will be why he immediately goes on to say: 'Two objects of the same logical form—apart from their external properties—are only distinct from one another in that they are different' (2.0233). The only 'external properties' his simple objects can have, of course, are those of actually occurring in certain facts.

Here Wittgenstein adds a remark, which may seem at first sight to contradict the previous one: 'Either a thing has properties that no other has, in which case one can mark it out from the others through a description without more ado, and point to it; or on the other hand there are several things with all their properties in common, and then it is absolutely impossible to point to one of them. For if nothing marks a thing out, I cannot mark it out—if I did, it would be marked out.' It is possible that he is here thinking of what is involved in e.g.

distinguishing between and identifying particles of matter. It would be wrong to infer from this passage that he thinks that there cannot be two things with all their properties in common: at 5.5302 he is explicit that it makes *sense* to say that two objects have all their properties in common.

Frege's notion of concepts led him to the awkwardness of saying: 'The concept *horse* is not a concept'; for, in statements about 'the concept *horse*', the concept *horse* is not the reference of these words since they are not words being used predicatively as words that stand for a concept must be. Frege came to think[7] that any such statement was ill-formed; a concept must not occur except predicatively. That is, we can speak of 'the animal that both the Derby winner for 1888 and the Derby winner for 1889 are', but this expression, like 'a horse' itself, can occur only predicatively; we cannot say: 'the reference of this expression is the concept *horse.*'

Wittgenstein would say the sign for a function *shewed* itself to be the sign for a function; that something falls under a formal concept like 'function' is for him something that cannot be said; and Frege's difficulties about 'the concept *horse*' explain the point of this. If you say that your expression 'the animal that both the Derby winners are' has a concept as its reference, you at once lay yourself open to the question 'what concept?', with only one possible answer: 'the concept *horse*' — yet this 'is not a concept'. But the formal concept is rightly represented by the type of variable used in: 'There is a ϕ such that both the Derby winners are ϕ' : the variable employed expresses what Frege wanted to express by the phrase 'the concept', and yet saw he could not properly express in this way.

8

Operations

We must now consider Wittgenstein's remarks on operations. They have a special interest in connection with his rejection of the Frege-Russell assertion sign, and Wittgenstein arrived at them in grappling with the problem of the assertion sign as introduced by Frege.

Although this sign, '⊢', is still in use in symbolic logic, it has not now the same meaning as it had for Russell and Frege; it now means 'is a theorem', and so can occur (as it could not in Russell and Frege) hypothetically: 'if ⊢p', i.e. 'if p is a theorem ...'. Russell's use of the sign explicitly follows Frege's; for Frege, the assertion sign symbolizes the difference between the thought of something's being the case and the judgment that it *is* the case—it can thus never occur in an *if*-clause. Frege has two arguments for its necessity, one weak and the other strong.

The weak argument is from the necessity of a distinction between entertaining an hypothesis (formulating the content of a judgment, having a 'sense' before one's mind) and asserting a proposition. He says that an actor on the stage, for example, is not asserting. At that rate, it would be an inexcusable *faux pas* to make an actor write the assertion sign before a proposition on a blackboard in a play! This argument need not delay us.

The strong argument—in the light of which we can understand Wittgenstein on operations—is that we must distinguish between the occurrence of a proposition in a conditional: 'if p, then q', or a disjunction: 'either p, or q', and its occurrence when we simply say that p. The distinction is an obvious one, but quite difficult to express; it is natural to say that we are distinguishing between the occurrence of the proposition, unasserted, as a component of an assertion, and its occurrence when it is itself asserted: and here the distinction we are trying to make is certainly not a psychological one. But we cannot say that 'p', when it occurs by itself and when it occurs in a disjunction, 'p ∨ q', has a different sense; for from 'p ∨ q' and '~q' we can infer 'p', and the proposition that stands by itself as the conclusion must be the very same proposition as occurred as a disjunct.

Russell[1] uses this point in his explanation of the 'non-psychological' sense of *'being asserted'*, which is what according to him must accrue to a proposition (besides what it has just *qua* proposition) when it is used as a premise to prove something, or is (rightly) inferred as a conclusion from a premise. 'When we say *therefore*, we state a relation which can only hold between asserted propositions, and which thus differs from implication.'

Being asserted (in this 'logical' sense) is, for both Russell and Frege, something that cannot possibly attach to a proposition unless it is true. But it is more than its being true; for in the disjunction 'p or q' it may be that one or the other proposition is true, but neither is being asserted. In Frege's terminology, we might say that if an unasserted proposition is true, it is (in fact) a designation of the true; but in the asserted proposition the true is actually being presented to us as such, it is not just that some designation of it occurs in our discourse.

Wittgenstein says curtly: 'Frege's assertion sign "⊢" is logically quite meaningless: in Frege (and in Russell) it only indicates that these authors hold the propositions so marked to be true' (4.442). We must therefore enquire how he deals with the problem raised by Russell, about *therefore*; and also with the difference between 'p' and 'q' by themselves and in 'p ∨ q' or 'p ⊃ q'.

The first point, about *therefore*, is dealt with at 6.1263–4: 'It is clear in advance that the logical proof of a significant proposition and proof in logic [i.e. proof of a proposition of logic from another proposition of logic] must be quite different things. The significant proposition says something, and its proof shews that things are as it says; in logic every proposition is the form of a proof. Every proposition of logic is a symbolic representation of a *modus ponens*. (And the *modus ponens* cannot be expressed by a proposition.)'

That is to say, Wittgenstein takes the tautology

$$(p.p \supset q) \supset q$$

to be just another symbolic representation of the form of argument called *modus ponens*, viz.:

---

[1]   *Principles of Mathematics*, §38.

$$* \quad p$$
$$p \supset q$$
$$\therefore \quad q$$

Now 'representation' is the term Wittgenstein uses of a picture: what a picture represents is its sense. So here he is saying that the implication '(p, and p implies q) implies q', is *as it were* a picture or proposition with the *modus ponens* as its sense.

Russell says: 'When we say *therefore*, we state a relation that can only hold between asserted propositions.' He means, among other things, that *therefore* is something we are wrong to say, unless the premises are true and the conclusion too. This idea finds an echo in a statement by Frege in his essay on negation: 'One cannot infer anything from a false thought.' But that is not true. What is true — and, of course, what Frege was referring to — is that one cannot *prove* anything from false premises; one can criticize a proof by saying that the premises are false or doubtful. But it is wrong to say that 'therefore' is being misused in a correct argument from false premises. To be sure, 'therefore' is the utterance of someone who is asserting one or more propositions that precede it, and one that follows it, and he is in error if he asserts what is false; he is not however committing a *further* error in using 'therefore' just because his premises are false and his conclusion, accordingly, perhaps false. If these are his errors, they do not import a further mistake into his 'therefore'.

We must of course distinguish between the way a proposition occurs when used to assert what it means, and the way it occurs when e.g. it is merely a subordinate clause in a proposition that is asserted (a clause, moreover, that may be false, though the whole proposition is true); it is a mistake, though it is natural, to describe this difference as a difference between a 'logically asserted' and a 'logically unasserted' proposition. We have here a necessary distinction, wrongly made. 'Assertion' has *only* a psychological sense. We might indeed perhaps accept 'logically asserted' and 'logically unasserted' as technical descriptions of different ways in which propositions may occur; but it can be no part of the requirements for being 'logically asserted' that a 'logically asserted' proposition be true, as both Frege and Russell thought; and once that feature of 'logically asserted' propositions is removed, the terms become a mere pair of labels, and cease even to have an air of being explanatory. 'Logical assertion' is no longer an extra feature attaching to a proposition, or added to its sense; we have no idea what it is; we only know when to *call* propositions 'asserted' in this sense.

But this is not the end of the matter: the difference, if it has only been labelled, demands both to be made clearer and to be explained. First, although you cannot prove anything unless you know something, you can construct the *modus ponens* that *would* be a proof *if* you found out that its premises are true. '*If* these premises are true, this conclusion is true' is then a description of this *modus ponens*; which I suppose is what Wittgenstein meant by his remark (6.1264). The premises that you construct may be quite hypothetical; or again, you may know one premise and make an hypothesis of the other. This is the reason why Aristotle rightly says a conclusion is reached in just the same way in a 'demonstrative' and a 'dialectical' syllogism: if you say 'suppose p, and suppose q, then r'; or if, being given 'p', you say: 'suppose q, then r'; you are just as much inferring, and in essentially the same way, as if you are given 'p' and 'q' as true and say '*therefore* r'.

This, Wittgenstein would say, is because 'the structures of (the) propositions stand in internal relations to one another' (5.2). For at 5.131 he has said: 'If the truth of one proposition follows from the truth of others, this is expressed by relations in which the forms of those propositions stand to one another ... These relations are internal and exist simultaneously with, and through, the existence of the propositions.'

Wittgenstein goes on (at 5.21) to say that we can 'emphasize these internal relations in our form of expression, by representing one proposition as the result of an operation that produces it out of others (the bases of the operation)'. This is perhaps best explained in a simple, but not quite familiar, example. Take a relation and its converse, e.g. 'husband of' and 'wife of', and consider the two propositions: 'a is husband of b', 'a is wife of b'. We now introduce an operation, called 'conversion', the sign of which is 'Cnv' placed before a relative term; thus, instead of writing e.g. 'bRa', we write 'aCnvRb'. Then 'aCnv(husband of)b' emphasizes the internal relations of two propositions 'a is husband of b' and 'a is wife of b' by exhibiting the second proposition as the result of an operation upon the first (of course, an operation that could only be performed on propositions of this relational form).

An operation must not be assumed to be necessarily an inferential operation. In our present case, indeed, since 'husband of' is an asymmetrical relation, the two propositions are incompatible. An operation upon a given proposition as base may produce one that is compatible or incompatible with the proposition operated on; the only thing it does not produce is something equivalent to the proposition operated on. An operation is what has to happen to a proposition in order to turn it into a *different* one (cf. 5.23). And 'the operation is the expression of a relation between the structures of its result and of its base' (5.22).

In this example we can also understand clearly enough what is meant by saying: 'The occurrence of an operation does not characterize the sense of a proposition. For the operation does not assert anything, only its result does, and this depends on the bases of the operation' (5.25). It is very clear in this instance that 'Cnv' is not a distinguishing mark of the sense of a proposition, as 'not' might easily be thought to be; for you might think you can pick out a special class of *negative propositions*, but you would not be tempted to think that you can pick out a special class of *relations that are converses; every* relation has a converse, and is thus the converse of its converse, and can be written 'CnvR' for some suitable interpretation of 'R'.

Having grasped the general notion of an 'operation', we can now proceed to the next step, which is taken at 5.234: 'The truth-functions of the elementary propositions are the results of operations with the elementary propositions as bases. (I call these operations truth-operations).'

To say this is to make a radical distinction between a truth-function and an ordinary function like 'ϕx'. For as we have seen, Wittgenstein says that 'the occurrence of an operation is not a distinguishing mark of the sense of a proposition: for the operation does not assert anything, only its result does'. Now a function of names is certainly a distinguishing mark of the proposition in which it occurs: such a function certainly expresses something, marks out a form and a content. But the sign of an operation not merely stands for nothing—has no reference—it does not even mark out a form: it only marks the difference between forms.

Consider the following propositions which have 'p' and 'q' as bases of truth-functional operations:

$$p \lor q$$
$$p \cdot q$$

Each of these can be written differently, e.g. we have the same pair of propositions in

$$\sim(\sim p \cdot \sim q)$$
$$\sim(\sim p \lor \sim q)$$

For the first of the pair, we have here two versions: in one the proposition reached is shewn as the result of disjunction performed on 'p'
and 'q'; in the other as the result of negation performed on the result
of conjoining the results of negation performed on 'p' and 'q'; this is
sufficient to shew that the mere occurrence of disjunction, or conjunction, or negation, is not a distinguishing mark of a proposition. On
the other hand, if you perform a different operation on the very same
base, you get a difference of sense.

Let us now compare Wittgenstein's position with those taken up
by Frege and Russell. For Russell, a truth-function is one kind among
the functions that take propositions as arguments. Frege places no
such restrictions on what can be an argument; as we have seen, he
constructs a function whose value is the true if a designation of the
true occupies the argument-place, and is otherwise the false; and
another function whose value is the false for those arguments for
which the value of the previous function is the true, and *vice versa*. He
finally constructs a third function:

whose value is to be the false if we put a true proposition into the 'y'
argument-place, and any designation which is *not* of the true (i.e.
either a false proposition, or any designation other than a proposition)
into the 'x' argument-place; in all other cases the value of the function
is to be the true. This is material implication: 'either not p or q.'

Thus both for Frege and for Russell a truth-function is the same
kind of thing as a function with an empty place for a name; but there
is still a certain difference between Frege and Russell. For Frege, the
empty place is a place for a *name*; propositions are counted among
names, for he takes propositions (whose components all have reference) as names of truth-values. For Russell, propositions are just the
range of significant substitutions for the variable in this kind of function; and he would not call a proposition a name. Further, he does not
construct a function and stipulate what its values are to be for various
arguments; he simply defines each of the truth-functions as 'that
function which with argument p or arguments p and q (these being
propositions) is the proposition that …', filling up the *that* clause with
some statement about the truth or falsehood of the argument(s) like 'p
is not true' or 'p and q are both true'.

Both Frege and Russell, however, would hold that the truth-
functional connectives themselves express functions. For Wittgenstein
it is otherwise. We saw earlier that to say: 'A proposition is a function

of the expressions it contains' is not incompatible with saying: 'A proposition is not a function.' To say that a proposition is a function of the expressions it contains is to say that it is the result of completing them with one another. To say it is not a function is to say that it is not itself something with an empty place awaiting completion. In this sense of course a proposition that is a truth-function *of* others is not a function, on any view. But on Wittgenstein's view we must go further: a truth-function of propositions is not a function *of those propositions*; for it is the result of an *operation*, not a result of completing one expression with another; and a truth-argument is not the argument of a function, but the base on which an operation is performed. At 5.25–5.251 it is said explicitly: 'Operation and function must not be confused. A function cannot be its own argument, but the result of an operation can be the base of that very operation.' For example, we cannot put 'x is a man' into the argument-place in 'x is a man' itself — we get the nonsense 'x is a man is a man'; but we can write '~p' for 'p' in '~p' itself, and the result '~ ~p' makes perfect sense. Similarly, any operation may be iterated, any number of times. Sometimes an operation cancels out when it is iterated: '~ ~p' reduces to 'p', and 'aCnv(CnvR)b' to 'aRb' (*see* 5.254). A genuine function never behaves in this way.

With this we come to the question: What is the 'occurrence' of a proposition 'in' a complex proposition, which we have seen to be wrongly characterized as the occurrence of an unasserted in an asserted proposition? Wittgenstein's answer is that in the complex proposition its component proposition has the role *only of a truth-argument*: i.e. it is the base of a truth-operation.

We were inclined to argue: 'In "~p" the *sense* of "p" must occur, but it is not being asserted, so we must distinguish between the sense of "p" and the assertion; here "assertion" has a non-psychological import, and signifies something that we add to the sense of "p" when we assert *that* p.' But Wittgenstein says: 'the sense of a truth-function of p is a function of the sense of p' (5.2341); here he is certainly making an arithmetical comparison: as 2 is a function of 4, namely its square root, so the sense of '~p' is a certain function of the sense of 'p', and the sense of 'p' only occurs in that of '~p' in the way in which 4 occurs in 2.

The difference, then, that we first wanted to call the difference between an asserted and an unasserted proposition — because we wished to say that the *sense* of 'p' must occur in '~p' or in 'p ∨ q' — is rightly described as a difference between the occurrence of the sense, and the occurrence, not of the sense, but of a certain function of the sense.

The argument by which we reached the view that 'assertion' was an extra feature which somehow gets added to the sense – '"p" must mean p, in "~p" and "p ∨ q", which nevertheless do not assert that p' – could be compared to arguing: '"7" must mean 7 in "I had 7–3 apples"; so we must distinguish, even in empirical propositions where numerals occur, between the use of a numeral to designate a number of things, which we will call its positive use, and uses where it has the same sense but does not designate a number of things. Some extra feature therefore attaches to the use of the numeral in "I had 7 apples", but not in "I had 7–3 apples".' By this argument, we might propose to symbolize that 'extra feature' by prefixing the sign 'P' for 'positive' to certain occurrences of numerals, and think it necessary to write: 'I had P7 apples' and 'I had P (7–3) apples'.

9

Formal Concepts and Formal Series

At the end of his life, as we saw, Frege came to think that if something is a concept, we cannot correctly *say* that it is a concept — i.e. predicate the term 'concept' of it — because an expression for a concept can significantly occur only in the place of a predicate, not as a subject of the predicate 'concept'. This doctrine was what Wittgenstein expressed by saying: 'Something's falling under a formal concept, as an object[1] belonging to it, cannot be expressed by a proposition, but is rather shewn by the sign for that object' (4.126); e.g. if something falls under the 'formal' concept *concept* or *property*, this is shown by the predicative character of the sign we use for that 'something'; and again, a variable relating to properties will have to be one that we take as having one or more argument-places.

---

[1] This use of the term 'object' must not mislead us into thinking we have some evidence for Wittgenstein's counting properties and relations as objects, of different 'type' from the objects they attach to (contrary to the view stated in Chapter 7). It is the same use as Wittgenstein adopts, but apologizes for, at 4.123: 'A property is internal if its not belonging to its object is inconceivable. (This blue and that blue *eo ipso* stand in the internal relation of brighter and darker. It is inconceivable for *these* objects not to stand in this relation.) (To the shift in the use of the words "property" and "relation" there answers here a shift in the use of the word "object").' Just as internal properties and relations are not properly speaking properties and relations, so neither are shades of blue objects in the proper sense.

It may be asked: Why then did Wittgenstein resort to this misleading terminology? The answer, I think, is that the terminology of objects' falling under concepts is less loaded with philosophical doctrine, and more of a familiar way of speaking, in German than in English. Mr. Michael Dummett tells me that at Münster railway station he saw a notice beginning: 'All objects that fall under the concept *hand-luggage*' (*Alle Gegenstände, die unter den Begriff Handgepäck fallen*).

In Wittgenstein, as we saw (Chapter 5, pp. 65–7), the notion of a 'formal' concept, a concept that cannot be properly expressed by a predicate or general term, but only by the way we apply the corresponding sort of sign, is extended much more widely than this. Not only 'concept', 'function', 'object', but also 'number', 'fact', 'complex', are formal concepts; and, in opposition to Carnap, Wittgenstein would maintain that such linguistic concepts as 'name', 'predicate', 'proposition', 'relational expression' are also formal concepts. In none of these cases can it be informatively said of something that it falls under the concept; the only proper way of expressing a formal concept is (as Frege held for the concepts 'object', 'concept', 'function') the use of a special style of variable; and what makes a style of variable special is not (say) belonging to a special alphabet, but something that comes out in the use of the variable. If any proposition 'ϕA' contains a symbol 'A' for something falling under a formal concept, then we may always introduce the appropriate style of variable into the two blanks of '$(E-)\phi-$' or 'For some$-,\phi-$'. Thus: 'Socrates is snubnosed and bald' – 'For some x, x is snubnosed and x is bald.' 'Socrates is bald and Plato is not' – 'For some f, Socrates is f and Plato is not f.' 'Ten men mowed the meadow' – 'For some *n*, *n* men mowed the meadow.' Thus: 'Along with an object falling under a formal concept, that concept is itself already given' (4.12721); the concept *object* is given by using 'Socrates', the concept *property* by using 'bald', the concept *number* by using 'ten'; and in each case the formal concept is to be symbolically expressed by a style of variable (4.1272).

As regards the formal concepts that he himself recognized, Frege so constructed his logical notation that inappropriate substitutions for the corresponding variables gave a visibly ill-formed expression; he had no need to appeal to what the signs were supposed to stand for, but only to formal rules. Russell abandoned this ideal for a symbolic language, and his system requires at critical points that he should tell us in English how the interpretation of his signs is to restrict their use; Wittgenstein sharply criticizes him for this at 3.33–.331 and again at 5.452. But Frege's own system does not, on Wittgenstein's view, satisfy the ideal; if '$\phi(\ )$' is a predicate, the empty place in it can according to Frege be filled up with *any* 'proper name', and for Frege 'proper names' include ordinary proper names, clauses in sentences, definite descriptions, and numerals. The fact that we should not ordinarily attach any sense at all to '(a rose is a rose) is white' or '7 is white' did not worry Frege; the concept *white*, he says, can be handled in logic only if we can stipulate, as regards any possible subject for the predicate 'white', what would be the condition for the predicate's holding; and *any* 'proper name' is such a possible subject. It was this sort of paradox that Russell sought to avoid by appealing to 'ranges of significance'; but Wittgenstein thought this remedy worse than the disease, because logic cannot rest on vague intuitions expressed in the vernacular about what is 'significant', but 'must take care of itself' (5.473).

Wittgenstein's own remedy was to give a wholly new account of the formal concepts 'proposition' and 'number', which should of itself show the mistake of treating clauses and numerals as proper names of objects. This account brings in the notion of a *formal series*. The doctrine underlying this notion is that operations, in the sense of the word explained in the last chapter, can be iterated — 'the result of an operation can be the base of that very operation' (5.251). For example if we double a number, we can double the result. If we take 'O' to be an arbitrary operation, then starting from a base 'a' we get the formal series 'a, Oa, OOa, OOOa, ...'[2]; and Wittgenstein represents an arbitrary term of this series by '[a, x, Ox]', where the first of the three expressions within the square brackets represents the first term of the series, and the other two represent the way of getting from each term on to the next. In important cases, the variable expressing a formal concept will relate to the terms of a formal series; Wittgenstein holds that this is so for the formal concept 'number' and (as we shall see in the next chapter) for the formal concept 'proposition' also.

One might thus well think that for the concept 'number' it would have been enough for Wittgenstein to say as he does at 6.022–.03: 'The concept "number" is the variable number ... The general form of the whole number is $[0, \xi, \xi +1]$' — so long as this was supplemented by some account of '0' and of the special operation '+1'. In fact Wittgenstein goes about it in quite a different way. At 6.02 he gives the following definitions:

$$\Omega^0 x = x; \; \Omega^{n+1} x = \Omega\Omega^n x$$

---

[2]   I omit the apostrophe that Wittgenstein puts after symbols of operation to indicate that he is speaking of *the result of the operation*: this is a vestige of the apostrophe used by Russell, who writes 'R'a' for 'the R of a'. In Russell this is significant, because '-Ra' is the predicate 'is an R of a', whereas 'R'a' is a definite description. In Wittgenstein it is superfluous and therefore meaningless, since operations are in any case sharply distinguished from relations. Nor is it used very consistently in the printed version of the *Tractatus*.

This explains the meaning of a zero exponent of the operator 'Ω' and also the meaning of an exponent of the form 'n + 1' given the meaning of the exponent 'n'.[3] He then defines the ordinary numerals in terms of 0 and +1, as follows:

$$1 = 0+1; 2 = 0+1+1; 3 = 0+1+1+1; \text{etc.}$$

This enables us to interpret the use of any ordinary numeral as an exponent; e.g. $\Omega^3 x = \Omega\Omega\Omega x$. And a number is always 'the exponent of an operation' (6.021); sentences where numerals appear to have other uses must be translatable into sentences where they occur as exponents—e.g. '2+2 = 4' into '$\Omega^2\Omega^2 x = \Omega^4 x$' (cf. 6.241). The formal concept 'term of such-and-such a formal series' just is the concept 'result of applying such-and-such an operation *an arbitrary number of times* to such-and-such a base', and a number is an exponent of *any* such operation; it would thus involve a vicious circle to treat numbers as just one special case of formal series. The informal way of writing the general term of a formal series, '$[x,\xi,\Omega\xi]$', (whose informal character is shown by the use of 'ξ', just as in Frege), is thus replaced by:

$$[\Omega^0 x, \Omega^n x, \Omega^{n+1} x] \quad (6.02)^3.$$

Wittgenstein's reason for introducing numbers only here, when he has already often used the conception of a formal series, is that you can explain what is meant by 'an arbitrary term of a formal series' quite clearly without explicit mention of numbers: 'First we have a; then Oa—the result of performing a certain operation on a; then OOa—the result of performing it on Oa; then OOOa; *and so on*; "an arbitrary term" means "some term or other reached in this way".'

To give a concrete example: We might explain 'ancestor in the male line' by saying: 'There's my father, and my father's father, and my father's father's father, and so on.' 'The concept of the successive application of an operation is equivalent to the concept *and so on*' (5.2523). We have the concept of an arbitrary term of a formal series when we understand 'and so on' in connection with the series; e.g. for the series of relations: father, father's father, father's father's father ...,[4]

---

3   He uses here a capital omega, instead of a Roman O as in other places, because 'O^0', where the big O is the sign of the operation and the exponent is 0, is disagreeably unperspicuous. The use of a Greek v, by assimilation to the use of 'Ω', is pointless.

4   The series of ancestors is not a formal series, of course; but the series of relations thus involved is one.

we know what its general term is when we know what 'and so on' (or the row of dots I have just written) means in connection with the series. But if we ask, as regards some term of such a series, *which* term it is, *which* performance of the generating operation the term results from, the interrogative 'which?' is really an ordinal interrogative (Latin *quotus?*) requiring an ordinal numeral as an answer.

For Frege and Russell, *(natural) number* was not a formal concept, but a genuine concept that applied to some but not all objects (Frege) or to some but not all classes of classes (Russell); those objects, or classes, to which the concept *number* applied were picked out from others of their logical type as being 0 and the successors of 0. The relation *successor of* was in turn defined by means of the relation *immediate successor of;* plainly these two are related in the same way as *ancestor (in the male line) of* and *father of*—the one relation is, as Russell says, the ancestral of the other in each case. This brings us to the Frege-Russell account (independently devised by each of them in essentially the same form) of what it is for one relation to be the ancestral of another.[5] For simplicity's sake, I shall merely explain how *ancestor* would be defined in terms of *parent*; the generalization of this account can readily be supplied.

We first define the notion of a *hereditary* property: viz, a property which, if it belongs to one of a man's parents, belongs also to him. We then define 'a is an Ancestor of b' to mean:

'a is a parent of some human being, say x, all of whose hereditary properties belong to b.'

Let us for the moment treat this as an arbitrary verbal stipulation of what the defined term 'Ancestor' is to mean; we must now enquire whether it is true that, on this definition, a is an Ancestor of b if and only if a is in the ordinary sense an ancestor of b; if so, we have an adequate definition of ordinary ancestorship which does not introduce the 'and so on' brought into our ordinary explanations of the term (cf. the last paragraph but two). And it is quite easy to show intuitively that this equivalence between 'Ancestor' and 'ancestor' does hold.

A. Suppose a is an ancestor of b. Then either (1) a is a parent of b, or (2) a is a parent of an ancestor of b.

(1) If 3 is a parent of b, then b himself fulfils the conditions of being a human being, x, whose parent is a and whose hereditary properties all belong to b. So a is an Ancestor of b by our definition.

---

5   The relevant passages can be found in Frege's *Foundations of Arithmetic*, §§79–80, and in Russell and Whitehead's *Principia Mathematica*, Vol. I, Part II, Section E.

(2) If a is a parent of some human being x, who is b's ancestor, then the hereditary properties of x will all descend, through a finite number of generations, to b; so once again a will be a parent of some human being x whose hereditary properties all belong to b—i.e. will be an Ancestor of b.

Hence, if a is an ancestor of b, a is an Ancestor of b.

B. Suppose a is an Ancestor of b. Then there is some human being, x, whose parent is a and whose hereditary properties all belong to b. But *the property of having* a *as an ancestor is itself a hereditary property,* since any human being, one of whose parents has a as an ancestor, himself has a as an ancestor; hence, since this hereditary property belongs to x, and all hereditary properties of x belong to b, this property belongs to b—i.e. b has a as an ancestor.

Hence, if a is an Ancestor of b, a is an ancestor of b.

The italicized assertion in proof B may well make the reader suspect a vicious circle; if we are attempting a definition of ancestorship, how can we without circularity, in a proof that the definition is adequate, bring in properties that are themselves defined in terms of ancestorship? In an informal argument to show that a formal definition fits our ordinary idea of ancestorship, this might, to be sure, not seem to matter very much; for we are anyhow supposed to know informally what 'ancestor' means, and it is 'ancestor', not 'Ancestor' the formally defined term, that is the word used in specifying the questionable 'hereditary property'. This threat of circularity is, however, not found only in informal arguments; in *Principia Mathematica* some of the theorems and proofs formally and explicitly assume that the properties that are hereditary with respect to a relation R include some that are themselves defined in terms of that ancestral relation which corresponds to R as *Ancestor* corresponds to *parent.*[6] Wittgenstein's accusation of having run into a vicious circle about the ancestral relation (4.1273) was a peculiarly vicious blow against Russell, who had elaborately contrived the system of *Principia* in order to avoid circles of this sort (*see op. cit.,* Vol. I, Introduction, Ch. II). Russell came to be seriously worried by the accusation, and in the second edition of *Principia* he added as an appendix a new chapter of proofs designed to avoid the vicious circle.

---

[6]   *op. cit.,* Vol. I, *90.163, *90.164, and proof of *90.31. (To make this strictly correct, one would have to modify slightly the definition of 'Ancestor' so as to count also as his own Ancestor anyone who either was or had a parent.)

Wittgenstein himself did not need the analysis of ancestral relations in order to give an account of the number-concept; but such relations are logically important in their own right, and supplied him with an application for his notion of a formal series. It is clear that the series of propositions

$$aRb; (Ex)\ aRx.xRb; (Ey)\ (Ex)\ aRx.xRy.yRb;$$
and so on

is a formal series in Wittgenstein's sense, as he says (4.1273). He does not, however, tell us what operation must be applied to each term to yield the next one; and if we use 'x', 'y', etc. as variables, the operation is not perspicuously displayed. For here 'what the signs conceal, their use reveals'; it is the case, though the style of variables here used conceals it, that we have to think of variables as *themselves* forming an indefinitely long series, a *formal* series, in which each variable is derived from its predecessor; otherwise our capacities of expression would run out as soon as we had used all the letters of the alphabet. 'The same operation turns the variable "p" into the variable "q", "q" into "r", and so on. This can only be explained by these variables' giving general expression to certain formal relations' (5.242). Wittgenstein's idea of an unlimited stock of variables, given once for all by a formal rule, is taken for granted in modern discussions of logical syntax.

The series may be exhibited more clearly as a formal series by using 'x, x', x'', x''', ...' instead of 'x, y, z, ...' as variables, and writing the terms of the series as follows:

$$(Ex')\ (Ex)\ a = x.xRx'.x' = b$$
$$(Ex'')\ (Ex')\ (Ex)\ a = x.xRx'.x'Rx''.x'' = b$$
$$(Ex''')\ (Ex'')\ (Ex')\ (Ex)\ a = x.xRx'.x'Rx''.x''Rx'''.x''' = b$$
and so on.[7]

Indeed, it would be quite easy to put into words a formal rule for deriving each successive line from the last line. If we use ר (Hebrew Resh) as a symbol of the operation successively applied, the general term of this formal series will be written in Wittgenstein's style as:

$$[\text{ר}^{0}p, \text{ר}^{n}p, \text{ר}^{n+1}p]$$

---

[7]   Remember that 'a = x' means that a is the same thing as x; and 'x' = b', that x' is the same thing as b.

where 'p' is '(Ex') (Ex) a = x.xRx'.x' = b'. And to say that b is a successor of a with respect to the relation R will be to assert the logical sum of this formal series of propositions—i.e. to assert that some proposition or other in the series is true.[8]

Wittgenstein used his doctrine of formal series to make a further important criticism of Russell and Whitehead: that they kept on making tacit use of formal series whose component propositions were, on their own theory, propositions of different 'logical type' and as such could not form a single series (5.252). One example of this fallacy occurs in their use of the Axiom of Reducibility. This axiom may be stated as follows: *For any property of individuals that is specified in terms of quantification over properties of individuals,*[9] *there is another property that applies to the same individuals and is not specified in terms of such quantification.*[10]

Now at *20.112 Russell requires, not this axiom, but a parallel axiom got by substituting '*properties of individuals*' throughout for '*individuals*'; yet he simply refers back to the Axiom of Reducibility for individuals (in fact he merely gives its number, *12.1). Clearly he would in strictness need a new Axiom for properties of individuals, and another for properties of properties of individuals, *and so on*—i.e. a formal series of axioms, each constructed in a uniform way from its predecessor; and the only legitimate way of supplying what is required would be to give the generating operation of this series. But Russell's Theory of Types explicitly rules out the possibility of such an operation, since each successive proposition in the series would be of higher 'type' than its predecessor, and not groupable with it in a single

---

[8]   In his paper 'On Derivability', *Journal of Symbolic Logic*, Vol. II, No. 3 (September 1937), Quine shews that a certain notion, practically the same as that of a formal series of expressions, enables us to define ancestral relations without any such quantifications as 'every property that …' or 'some one of the relations …' at all. This definition, which may be called a fulfilment of Wittgenstein's intentions, accordingly avoids any risk of a vicious circle, such as might arise if some of the properties or relations covered by the quantifications employed had themselves to be specified in terms of the ancestral relation.

[9]   e.g. the property of having *all* the properties of a great general; or again, the property of having *all* the vices of Charles I and *none* of his virtues.

[10]   The property of *being* a great general applies to the same individuals as the property of *having all the properties of* a great general; but is not itself specified, as that property is, in terms of quantification over properties of individuals.

series.[11] Unlike the criticism about ancestral relations, this criticism was ignored by Russell in preparing the second edition of *Principia Mathematica*.

---

[11] Wittgenstein's objection that the Axiom of Reducibility would not be a *logical* truth anyhow (6.1233) is independent, and not here relevant. For a clear modern account of *this* problem, see Quine's *From a Logical Point of View*, Chapter VI, §6.

10

'The General Form of Proposition'

It is now possible to explain the formula [$\bar{p}$, $\bar{\xi}$, $N(\bar{\xi})$], which Wittgenstein gives as 'the general form of truth-functions'. (Russell's Introduction gives an attempted explanation, which unfortunately is not much use.) On the face of it, this formula exemplifies 'the general term of a formal series' (5.2522), which we have just been discussing. The variable 'p' ranges over the elementary propositions, of which all others are truth-functions. The stroke indicates that we are using a sign that goes proxy for writing down all the propositions of a given range, between a pair of brackets (5.501); thus '$\bar{p}$' goes proxy for a complete list of elementary propositions. As in Frege, 'ξ' marks informal exposition; $\bar{\xi}$ will be any set of propositions reached as a term of the formal series, and by applying the operation $N(\bar{\xi})$ we are to reach the next term of the series.

$N(\bar{\xi})$ is explained as the joint negation of all the propositions in the set $\bar{\xi}$ (5.502). At this point we get into difficulties. The joint negation of a set of propositions will itself be just a single proposition; and though Wittgenstein explains the result of applying $N(\bar{\xi})$ to a single proposition, as simply equivalent to ordinary negation (5.51), even so we cannot get all the truth-functions of a set of propositions into a single formal series with repeated applications of $N(\bar{\xi})$. Suppose we start with the list p, q, as the first term of our series; we then get $N(p, q)$, $N(N(p, q))$, $N(N(N(p, q)))$, and so on; the first, third, etc., of these are all equivalent to ~p.~q, the second, forth, etc., are all equivalent to p∨q, and no other truth-functions ever make their appearance in the series.

What we need is a formal series of *sets* of propositions (though *some* of these may be unit sets), such that each possible truth-function of the set we start with makes its appearance as the result of applying

N($\bar{\xi}$) to *some* term of this formal series. And this requirement can be met; I shall describe one method of meeting it. In this way Wittgenstein will have been right in regarding all the truth-functions as generable in a formal series; though the method is more complicated than his own schematic formula suggests.

Suppose for simplicity that there are two elementary propositions p, q: this set will be the first term of our series; and our first truth-function will be the joint negation ~p.~q. The unit set whose sole member is this result (as logicians say the unit set *of* this proposition) is our second set; and by applying N($\bar{\xi}$) to it we get p∨q. Our third set has our last two propositions as members; since they are contradictories, their joint denial is the contradictory truth-function of p and q. Our fourth set is the unit set of this last result; applying N($\bar{\xi}$) to it, we get tautology.

We shall get nothing new by applying N($\bar{\xi}$) either to the unit set of the last result, or to the last pair of results, or to both or either of them in any combination with the first result. We form a fifth set by combining the first of our original bases, p, with our first truth-function, ~p.~q; the joint negation of these two works out as ~p. (p∨q), i.e. as q.~p. The sixth set is the unit set of q.~p; and by applying N($\bar{\xi}$) we get q ⊃ p. If we form a set out of p and our second truth-function p∨q, we find that joint negation gives us only our first truth-function ~p.~q over again. So we form our seventh set by combining p with our third truth-function, which was contradiction; joint negation of this set gives us (tautology.~p), which reduces to plain ~p. Our eighth set is the unit set of ~p; and applying (N$\bar{\xi}$) we get p, our eighth truth-function of p and q.

When we cease to get new truth-functions with our first base p, we form sets containing our second base q along with propositions already obtained. And we go on in this way until we have generated all possible truth-functions of our original set; with two elementary propositions to start with, we get a series of sixteen sets, and the joint negations of these are the sixteen truth-functions of two elementary propositions.

It is clear that we can have here a series with a definite order, no matter how many elementary propositions there may be, provided that the elementary propositions themselves are given at the first in a definite order. (If the elementary propositions were given in a different order, we should still get all their truth-functions, but not in the same order.) This of course is why Wittgenstein speaks at 5.242 of propositional variables as having to 'give general expression to certain formal relations'; the symbolism must enable us to show a definite order for an arbitrary number of bases—'p, p', p'', p''', ...' would do this more perspicuously than 'p,q,r,s, ...'.

We also see why Wittgenstein claims to give us 'the general form of a way that one proposition can be generated by an operation upon another' (6.002). Assuming we have a fixed set of elementary propositions in a definite order, each truth-function of this set—i.e., for Wittgenstein, each proposition, elementary or not—will make its appearance somewhere along the series; and thus all propositions are generated from one another, as terms of a single formal series.

That Wittgenstein's account makes sense for any finite set of bases is clear enough. What was needed was that the description 'the result of the nth application of the operation $N(\bar{\xi})$ to these bases' should be an absolutely precise determination of a proposition for any number n up to the total number of truth-functions that there are for this set of bases. It is clear that it is such a precise determination of a proposition.

Here we come to the defect in the *Tractatus* which Wittgenstein described, later, as a failure to distinguish between the 'dots of laziness', as when we represent the alphabet by writing just 'A,B,C, ...', and the indispensable dots used to represent an infinite series, as in '1,2,3,4, ...'. It is easy to see how he came not to make this distinction, if we consider the diagram opposite.

This table represents a quite definite truth-function of a set of propositions of unspecified number; this truth-function has the truth-value *false* for all combinations of truth-values except the final one; it does not matter how many propositions there are, because the bottom line of arguments is all F's anyway. This truth-table defines, for an arbitrary number of bases, our operation $N(\bar{\xi})$—joint negation of all the propositions in the set; and the liberal use of dots in it may well seem not to matter—the rule for constructing the table is plain. If, therefore, the repeated application of this operation to the given bases will in any finite case generate all their truth-functions, and if it is possible to specify a set of propositions otherwise than by enumeration, then it is very natural to say: what does it matter that the number in the set is not known, what does it matter even if it is infinite?

p	q	r	s	t	v								
T	T	T	T	T	T	T	T	T	T	T	T	.	F
F	T	T	T	T	T	T	T	T	T	T	T	.	F
T	F	T	T	T	T	T	T	T	T	T	T	.	F
F	F	T	T	T	T	T	T	T	.	.	.	.	F
T	T	F	T	T	T	.	.	.	.	.	.	.	F
F	T	F	T	T	T	.	.	.	.	.	.	.	F
T	F	F	T	T	T	.	.	.	.	.	.	.	F
F	F	F	T	T	T	.	.	.	.	.	.	.	F
T	T	T	F	T	T	.	.	.	.	.	.	.	F
F	T	T	F	T	T	.	.	.	.	.	.	.	F
.	.	.	$(^8{}_{F's})$	$(^{16}{}_{T's})$	$(^{32}{}_{T's})$								.
.	.	.	.	.	.								.
.	.	.	.	.	.								.
.	.	.	.	.	.								.
.	.	.	.	.	.								.
.	.	.	.	.	.								.
.	.	.	.	.	.								.
.	.	.	$(^8{}_{F's})$	$(^{16}{}_{F's})$	$(^{32}{}_{F's})$								.
T	T	F	F	F	F	F	F	.	.	.	.	.	F
F	T	F	F	F	F	F	F	.	.	.	.	.	F
T	F	F	F	F	F	F	F	.	.	.	.	.	F
F	F	F	F	F	F	F	F	.	.	.	.	.	T

(In the left-hand column, the T's and F's alternate; in the second column they alternate in pairs, in the third in fours; and so on.)

There would indeed be a serious objection if operating thus upon the set of propositions did not generate a simple infinite series (a progression) but one that was e.g. like the set of odd numbers in natural order followed by the set of even numbers in natural order. That series can of course be rearranged as the progression 1,2,3,4, ...; but it might be that without ceasing to be a formal series our series could not so be rearranged. In that case the expression 'the nth term of the series' would never, for any finite n, get you into the part of the series that began after you had started on a second infinite series. Hence, if in the generation of a series of truth-functions by repeatedly performing the operation $N(\bar{\xi})$ upon the set of elementary propositions (in the way I have described) there would have to be a series of generations which you could only begin *after* you had gone through the process of bringing down each new member of the set in turn, right to the end of the infinite set; then Wittgenstein's idea would be worthless.

But this difficulty can in fact never arise. You can perform the new operations on the terms up to the nth term, which are made possible by the introduction of the $n + 1^{st}$ term, as soon as you have introduced the $n + 1^{st}$ term; and there is never an infinity that you have to finish before you can get on, because you quickly generate propositions that either are tautologies or contradictions, or are identical with propositions you have already generated, and you do not have to proceed further with those. You clear up as you go along.

On the other hand, the claim that is being made, in offering this as the general term of the series of truth-functions of an infinite set of elementary propositions, is apparently in conflict with the well-known theorem that the truth-functions of an infinite set of elementary propositions form a non-denumerable set. This is so, because the number of different assignments of truth-values to n propositions is 2^n. The number of different assignments of truth-values to $\aleph_0$ propositions (i.e. to a denumerably infinite set of propositions) is therefore $2^{\aleph_0}$. But this has been proved by Cantor to be greater than $\aleph_0$; that is to say, you could not find a one–one correlation between a set whose number was $2^{\aleph_0}$ and a set whose number was $\aleph_0$. And the truth-functions of $\aleph_0$ propositions must be *at least* as many as the possible ways of assigning truth-values to them. Therefore an account which correlates the series of truth-functions of an infinite set of elementary propositions with the series of natural numbers, as Wittgenstein's does, must be wrong if Cantor is right.

It seems likely enough, indeed, that Wittgenstein objected to Cantor's result even at this date, and would not have accepted a Cantorian device for specifying an infinite subset of the elementary propositions such that a truth-function of it could not be generated by his formula. For though he came to think his idea wrong, it was certainly not through any conversion to Cantor that this happened. On the contrary: whether or no he already objected to Cantor at the time when he wrote the *Tractatus*, he certainly did so later.

However, the theory of the *Tractatus*, promising though it looked at the time, has been clearly and cogently refuted in another way. If all truths of logic are tautological truth-functions of elementary propositions, then there is in principle a decision procedure for them all. But it was proved by Church in the 1930's that multiple quantification theory has no decision procedure; that is, that there cannot be a method by which one could settle, concerning any well-formed formula of that theory, whether it was a theorem or not.

11

Generality

Frege's invention of the quantifier-notation must be reckoned among the greatest benefits conferred on philosophy by logic. The fallacies which are excluded by the insight it gives have been committed over and over again by the greatest philosophers. No one should now be able to get away with transitions like that from 'Every boy loves some girl' to 'Some girl is loved by every boy'. In this down-to-earth example, the fallacy sounds silly and impossible to commit; in abstract contexts, it and similar fallacies (involving the notions, not just of 'some' and 'all', but of one of these combined with 'necessary', or 'possible') have proved very difficult to avoid.

A recent example of this sort of fallacy is afforded by Professor Ayer;[1] he argues from the fact that it is not possible, and *a fortiori* not necessary, that every identification or recognition (of a person, shape, quality, etc.) should in fact be checked, to the innocuousness of the notion of an uncheckable identification. An argument running 'It is not necessary that every identification is checkable; *ergo*, it is possible that some identification is uncheckable' has all the appearance of formal validity — 'Not necessarily (every S is P); *ergo*, possibly (some S is not P).' But in fact it is an illicit transition from:

(I) It is possible that it is not possible that every identification should be checked

to

(2) It is possible that there should be some identification that it is not possible to check.

---

[1] *The problem of knowledge*, pp. 60–1. The passage concerns Wittgenstein's objection (in *Philosophical Investigations*) to 'private' ostensive definition. Professor Ayer seems to accept a kind of checkability as necessary to the notion of an identification; but in reply to the objection that 'private' checks are not checks, he retorts that in any case checks always have to come to an end somewhere.

It is one of the uses of the quantifier-notation to make this clear. Let 'M' represent 'possibly'; (1) and (2) then come out as:

(1) M~M(x) (x is an identification ⊃ x is checked)

(2) M(Ex) (x is an identification. ~M (x is checked))

or (equivalently): M~(x) (x is an identification ⊃ M (x is checked))

The quantifier-signs now in use, '(x)ϕx' for 'Everything is ϕ' and '(Ex)ϕx'[2] for 'Something is ϕ', were given us by Russell and Whitehead; but the former is a variation of Frege's generality notation, and the latter can be defined in terms of it, so the real inventor was Frege.

Often enough a logical symbolism simply puts some new sign in place of a word or phrase; this may be helpful. But what the quantifier-notation does is quite different. At first sight 'Everyone is clever' looks to be just such a sentence as 'Socrates is clever'. It becomes clear that it is not, as soon as we consider negation: if 'Socrates is clever' is untrue, then 'Socrates is not clever' is true; but, as Aristotle remarked, the same does not hold for 'Everyone is clever'. Frege's genius consisted in inventing a notation in which a formula of a different layout is employed for universal propositions; and not just of a different layout, but of the right layout.

This was surely partly what prompted Wittgenstein to say at 3.323: 'In ordinary language it is enormously common for ... two words, which signify in different ways, to be applied in the sentence in ways that are outwardly the same. ... In this way there easily arise the most fundamental confusions (with which the whole of philosophy is filled).

'In order to avoid these errors, we must use a symbolism which excludes them — A symbolism, then, that follows *logical* grammar — logical syntax'. And again, it will have been this that inspired the 'feeling' that he speaks of at 4.1213, the 'feeling that we are in possession of the right logical conception if only all is right in our symbolism'.

At 4.0411 Wittgenstein dilates on the excellence of the symbolism '(x)fx'. He brings this out by considering alternative ways of expressing what we use this symbolism to express. We might try putting 'Gen.fx'; but 'this would not tell us what was generalized'. That is, it would be ambiguous as between what we should now write as '(x)fx' and '(f)fx'. If we try to make good this defect by writing the sign for generality as a subscript to the x, thus: 'f(x_g)', it still would not do: 'we should not know the scope of the generality-sign': That is, '$\phi x_g \lor \psi x_g$'

---

would be ambiguous as between '$(x)\phi x \vee (x) \ \psi x$' and '$(x) \ \phi x \vee \psi x$'. Finally, if we thought of writing the generality sign itself in the argument-place: $(G,G)f(G,G)$ 'we should not be able to determine the identity of the variables'. That is to say, the expression

$$(G,G)\phi(G,G) \vee \psi(G,G)$$

would be ambiguous as between what we should now write as

$$(x,y)\phi(x,y) \vee \psi(x,y)$$

and

$$(x,y)\phi(x,y) \vee \psi(y,x).$$

In particular, we could not distinguish between these cases:

$$(x,y)\phi(x,y) \vee \sim\phi(x,y)$$

which holds for any relation ϕ, and

$$(x,y)\phi(x,y) \vee \sim\phi(y,x)$$

which means that the relation ϕ is symmetrical.

These difficulties could of course be got over by supplementary conventions, corresponding to the 'enormously complicated tacit conventions' which Wittgenstein mentions at 4.002 as needed for the understanding of ordinary language. Think of the English sentence 'If you can eat any fish, you can eat any fish', which sounds like a tautology, but is, on the contrary, a false judgment. Any native English-speaker will understand that sentence: few could explain how it works. And again e.g. 'You can fool some of the people all of the time' is ambiguous; the ambiguity is resolved, in some complicated way, by the context. It is clear that the Fregean quantifier-notation is far more perspicuous than any that has to be backed up with complicated conventions.

Turning now to Wittgenstein's special treatment of generality, we shall find it helpful to place the opening entry, 5.52, in juxtaposition with 5.51, the immediately preceding entry of the same numerical level in the book:

5.51: 'If ξ has only one value, then $N(\bar{\xi}) = \sim p$ (not p); if it has two values, then $N(\bar{\xi}) = \sim p.\sim q$ (neither p nor q).'

5.52: 'If the values of ξ are all the values of a given function fx for all values of x, then $N(\bar{\xi})$ will be the same as $\sim(Ex)fx$.'

Russell's account in the Introduction, then, is quite correct: 'Wittgenstein's method of dealing with general propositions [i.e.

"(x)fx" and "(Ex)fx"] differs from previous methods by the fact that the generality comes only in specifying the set of propositions concerned, and when this has been done the building up of truth-functions proceeds exactly as it would in the case of a finite number of enumerated arguments p, q, r, ...' Wittgenstein emphasizes the difference by saying: '*I* separate the concept *all* from the truth-function' and goes on to accuse Frege and Russell of not having done this: 'Frege and Russell introduced generality in connection with the logical product [p.q.r.——] or the logical sum [p ∨ q ∨ r ∨——). This made it difficult to understand the propositions "(Ex)fx" and "(x)fx", which cover both ideas.'

Now there is no ground in their texts for a direct accusation that either Frege or Russell 'introduced generality in connection with the logical product or the logical sum'. We must therefore see in this remark Wittgenstein's comment on their way of introducing generality: a claim that this is what it amounts to. So we must examine how they actually introduce generality.

Frege introduced his generality notation in this way in *Function and Concept*: he constructs the sign

$$\underset{a}{\text{᷼}} f(a)$$

in which what he has done is (to quote from his *Begriffsschrift*) to *replace an argument*, say 'London' in 'London is a capital city', '*with a German letter, and insert a concavity in the content stroke, and make this same German letter stand over the concavity*'.

The sign so constructed signifies the thought that 'The function is a fact whatever we take its argument to be.' Or, as he puts it in *Function and Concept*, the sign

$$\underset{a}{\text{᷼}} f(a)$$

is 'to mean the true when the function $f(x)$ always has the true as its value, whatever the argument may be'. Certainly there is nothing here about a logical product. So what is Wittgenstein's argument?

It is based on his own view: the truth of such a proposition as '(x)fx' (to use the signs now usual) is the truth of the logical product: 'fa.fb.fc.fd——' where the dots cover up our failure to write down all the names there are as arguments in the function fx. Therefore when Frege explains his symbol, by stating *what* is judged to be the case in the judgment that it symbolizes, he is in fact introducing 'all' in connection with the logical product.

Frege does not employ an existential quantifier like '(Ex)' in constructing the symbol for judgments of the form 'Some——'; he simply uses negation together with his universal quantifier, just as we can define '(Ex)fx' as '~(x)~fx'; but the same point would hold for the explanation of particular judgments: their truth—according to Wittgenstein—consists in the truth of a logical sum (fa ∨ fb ∨ fc ∨ fd——) and hence what they say is that that logical sum is true. So someone who explains them by explaining what they say is 'introducing generality in connection with the logical sum'.

Russell's explanations are not relevantly different from Frege's.

'This,' Wittgenstein says, 'made it difficult to understand "(x)fx" and "(Ex)fx", which cover both ideas.' By 'both ideas' he means both the idea of generality on the one hand, and that of the logical product (in the case of universal propositions), or the logical sum (in the case of particular propositions), on the other. The reason why 'it became difficult to understand' these propositions was that their pictorial character was obscured. Their pictorial character consists in their being truth-functions of a set of propositions. But the notation also covers the way of *specifying* the set a truth-function of which is being asserted, viz. giving a function *all* of whose values are the set in question. 'The function's being a fact whatever we take the argument to be' explains generality in terms of the truth of the generalized proposition. With such an explanation, how are we to understand the inference from $(x)\phi x$ to ϕa; i.e. from something's holding of a function, to something's holding of an object? As Ramsey says, Wittgenstein's view 'explains how "fa" can be inferred from "For all x, fx", and "There is an x such that fx" from "fa". The alternative theory that "There is an x such that fx" should be regarded as an atomic proposition of the form "F(f)" ("f has application") leaves this entirely obscure; it gives no intelligible connection between *a* being red and red having application, but abandoning any hope of explaining this relation is content merely to label it "necessary".'[3]

Wittgenstein goes on to make further comments on the generality notation. It has, he says, two peculiarities: it points to a logical protopicture, and it emphasizes constants. Ramsey explains the second point to us. 'Let us consider when and why an expression occurs, as it were, as an isolated unit. "aRb" does not naturally divide into "a" and "Rb", and we want to know why anyone should so divide it and isolate the expression "Rb". The answer is that if it were a matter of

---

3   *The Foundations of Mathematics*, pp. 153–4.

this proposition alone, there would be no point in dividing it in this way, but that the importance of expressions arises, as Wittgenstein points out, just in connection with generalization. It is not "aRb" but "(x)xRb" which makes "Rb" prominent. In writing (x)xRb we use the expression "Rb" to collect together the set of propositions xRb which we want to assert to be true; and it is here that the expression "Rb" is really essential because it is this which is common to this set of propositions.'[4]

Wittgenstein does not explicitly say that the importance of 'expressions' arises in connection with generalization: rather he uses the notion of an expression to form his theory of generality. For him expressions explain generality: an expression, by being 'the common characteristic mark of a class of propositions', gives us that class — the class of them all. But the class in question is clearly that narrower range of propositions in which an expression occurs, which Ramsey found it necessary to distinguish.

At 4.12721 Wittgenstein tells us: 'The formal concept is already given with an object that falls under it.' That is, if we have been given fa, the formal concept presented by the name-variable x is already given: the 'proto-picture' 'fx' is given. Here I assume that 'f' is a constant; thus this proto-picture is not the 'logical proto-picture' that is obtained by turning all the constants, into which a proposition divides up, into variables, as was described at 3.315: 'If we change one component of a proposition into a variable, then there is a class of propositions which are all values of the resulting variable proposition. This class in general still depends on what we, by arbitrary convention, mean by parts of that proposition. But if we change all those signs whose reference has been arbitrarily determined into variables, there is still always such a class. This, however, now no longer depends on convention; it depends only on the nature of the proposition. It corresponds to a logical form — a logical proto-picture': '(x)x moves slower than light', for example, *lays emphasis on* 'moves slower than light' as an expression which collects together a class of propositions, and *points to* a 'logical proto-picture' xRy, where (taking R as variable) all the constants have been turned into variables.

This paves the way for Wittgenstein's next remarks: 'The sign of generality appears as an argument. Once objects are given, that of itself gives us *all* objects. Once elementary propositions are given, that is enough for *all* elementary propositions to be given' (5.523–4). When

---

4   Ramsey, *ibid.*, pp. 123–4.

he says 'the sign of generality occurs as an argument' he is referring to the 'x' in '(x)ϕx': we have passed from the form 'ϕa' to the construction of the form 'ϕ everything' which we can do because the expression '$\phi($)' collects all propositions of the same form as 'ϕa': it determines a certain range of propositions. '(x)ϕx' is then just the proposition which is a certain truth-function of those propositions: we saw just why this should be so good a notation at the opening of the present chapter. Thus it is that we are formally given 'all objects' — and therewith the possibility of all their connections, which form the elementary situations—; and thus it is that we are given 'all elementary propositions', and therewith all possible propositions, i.e. all possibilities of being the case or not the case.

Wittgenstein's view has the following strong advantage. If we introduce '$\vee$' as a truth-functional connective, then unless we adopt Wittgenstein's view we need a new account of it in such propositions as '(x)ϕx $\vee$ ψx' — e.g. 'All roses are either red or yellow', for here it does not conjoin clauses to which a truth-value can be assigned. 'If logic has primitive notions,' he says at 5.451, 'they must be independent of one another. If a primitive notion is introduced, it must be introduced for all the contexts in which it occurs at all. Thus we cannot introduce it first for *one* context, and then introduce it all over again for another. For example: If negation has been introduced, we must understand it in propositions of the form "~p" just as in propositions like "~(p $\vee$ q)", "(Ex)~fx", etc. We cannot introduce it first for the one class of cases, and then for the other, for then it would be doubtful whether it meant the same in both cases, and there would be no ground for using the same kind of connective in both cases. In a word, what Frege said (in the *Grundgesetze der Arithmetik*) about the introduction of signs by means of definitions holds, *mutatis mutandis*, for primitive signs.' Russell and Whitehead did introduce '~' and '$\vee$' all over again for uses with quantifiers (*see* Sections *9 and *10 of *Principia Mathematica*). Modern logicians mostly introduce them with a merely truth-functional explanation, and then go on using them 'with innocent faces'[5] in the predicate calculus.

The concept 'all' is all-pervasive in the *Tractatus*. 'The world is *everything* that is the case—the *totality* of facts—determined by the facts and by their being *all* the facts' (1–1.11). And at 4.51–2 we find: 'Suppose *all* elementary propositions were given me: then we can

---

cf. *Tractatus*, 5.452. For an example, *see* Quine, *Methods of Logic*, Section 16.

simply ask what propositions I can form from them. And these are *all*
propositions: *that* is how they are limited. Propositions are: All that
follows from the totality of elementary propositions (and of course
from its being the *totality of them* all). Thus it might be said that in a
certain sense *all* propositions are generalizations of the elementary
propositions.'

We have to think of the case in which the world is finite, remem-
bering that Wittgenstein did not think there was any essential difference between the finite and the infinite case. If we want to say not
merely that such-and-such things are green, but that everything (in a
box, for example) is green, this can be expressed by saying: 'There are
an x and a y in the box, x and y are green, and there are not an x and a
y and a z in the box.' (Here I am using Wittgenstein's proposed convention about identity: 'Identity of the object I express by identity of
the sign, not by a sign of identity: difference of the object by difference
of the sign'⁶ (5.53).) It is clear that 'Everything in the box is green' does
not follow just from 'The objects a and b, which are in the box, are
green': it must also be the case that a and b *are all the objects in the box*.

Similarly, that such-and-such an independent possibility is not the
case follows from all the facts, together with the fact that these are all
the facts. (As Professor Stenius has pointed out to me, at this stage
(1.11) Wittgenstein means by 'the facts' only 'positive facts': he has not
yet introduced the expression 'a negative fact' for the 'non-existence of
atomic facts', but has only brought in 'facts' which are stated to consist
in the existence of atomic facts.) And so Wittgenstein says: 'the totality
of facts determines both what is the case and also all that is not the
case' (1.12); and this is so whether the world is finite or infinite.

How this is so is seen clearly in the finite case; yet in the finite case
Wittgenstein's doctrine appears to have a rather inconvenient consequence which Ramsey drew. Ramsey argues that 'There are an x and
a y such that x ≠ y' is the logical sum of the propositions x ≠ y, which
are tautologies if x and y have different values, contradictions if they
have the same value. Hence it is itself a tautology if any one of the set
is a tautology, but otherwise a contradiction. That is, it is a tautology if

---

⁶   He has sometimes been taken to *demand* this convention. This is a misunderstanding; he merely puts it forward as a possible one. The fact that (however
inconvenient) it is possible shews that identity is not a genuine function. His view,
then, does not require the abandonment of the sign of identity if it should be
convenient to use it. But it does exclude uses of it which make a genuine function of
it: as for example, in the attempt to express 'a exists' by 'For some x, x is identical
with a'.

x and y can take different values (i.e. if there are two individuals), but otherwise a contradiction.[7] He concludes that the series 'There is one individual ... There are at least 2 individuals ... There are at least n individuals ...' begins by being tautologous; but somewhere it begins to be contradictory, and the position of the last tautologous term shews the number of individuals.

Now Wittgenstein rejected propositions of the form 'There is not an x such that x ≠ x', jeering at it with the remark: 'Would this not be true if "there were things" but these were not identical with themselves?' (5.5352). He did not regard identity as a genuine function. But the point can be made without using identity. Let us suppose, for the sake of simplicity, that there are only two objects, a and b, and one function, f. Then the possibilities fa, ~fa, fb, ~fb, will be all the possibilities that there are. Suppose that we write these possibilities down as follows:

(1) There are an x and a y and a ϕ such that ϕx and ϕy
(2) There are an x and a y and a ϕ such that ϕx and ~ϕy
(3) There are an x and a y and a ϕ such that ~ϕx and ϕy
(4) There are an x and a y and a ϕ such that ~ϕx and ~ϕy.

These are *all* the possibilities; therefore, the 'complete description of the world in a completely generalized proposition', of which Wittgenstein speaks at 5.526, will be given by one of them.

Here we have 'described the world' without any preliminary correlation of a name with a particular object. And then, in order to arrive at the usual way of putting it, in which names are used, we need only add e.g. 'x is a, and y is b, and ϕ is f'. But *that* this is a complete description, i.e. is all the facts there are, can only be expressed if we can add such propositions as 'and there are not an x and a y and a z, and there are not a ϕ and a ψ such that ...'. Hence it is required at 5.526 that we should have propositions stating: 'There is one and only one x such that ...', which would have to be of the form: 'There is an x and there are not an x and a y, such that ...'.

This surely means that the 'complete description in completely generalized propositions' would, in the finite case, consist partly of existential propositions employing *more* variables than there are names of distinct objects. But if what *is* false *can be* true, then the completely generalized propositions will allow more play to the facts

---

7   Ramsey, *The Foundations of Mathematics*, pp. 59–60.

than the totality of elementary propositions. Yet at 5.5262 Wittgenstein denies this: 'The truth or falsehood of *every* proposition alters something about the general structure of the world. And the play which is allowed to its structure by the totality of elementary propositions is just that which is limited by the completely general propositions.'

This conclusion can only be avoided by adopting Ramsey's suggestion and saying that the series of propositions

$$(Ex, \phi)\phi x \vee \sim \phi x$$
$$(Ex, y, \phi)\phi x \vee \sim \phi x . \phi y \vee \sim \phi y$$
$$(Ex, y, z, \phi)\phi x \vee \sim \phi x . \phi y \vee \sim \phi y . \phi z \vee \sim \phi z$$

etc., would go over, in the finite case, from being tautologies to being contradictions at the point at which the number of different name variables employed exceeded the number of different names. And it is really only in the finite case that Wittgenstein's theory can be expounded with much clarity.

I find this conclusion unsatisfactory: in the infinite case, Wittgenstein's theory can hardly be explained at all: we have to take the finite case and say that he saw no important difference between it and the infinite case; while in the finite case the view seems to lead to a sudden transition of an *existential* proposition from tautology to contradiction.

Did not Wittgenstein resist any attempt to symbolize 'The universe is not empty' in 'There are things', regarding these as 'pseudo-propositions' attempting to *say* what *shews*? At 5.535 he says that what the 'Axiom of Infinity' (which says that there is an infinite number of objects) is supposed to mean 'would be expressed in language by there being infinitely many names with different references'.

If $(Ex)fx$ is the logical sum: 'fa $\vee$ fb $\vee$ fc ...' then $(Ex)fx \vee \sim fx$ is the logical sum of the singular tautologies: fa $\vee$ ~fa $\vee$ fb $\vee$ ~fb $\vee$ fc $\vee$ ~fc ...; and so $(Ex, \phi)\phi x \vee \sim \phi x$ will be the logical sum of all the singular tautologies: fa $\vee$ ~fa $\vee$ fb $\vee$ ~fb ... ga $\vee$ ~ga $\vee$ gb $\vee$ ~gb ... etc. In these propositions, then, we can see how 'the existence of things' is something 'shewn' and not said. But if Wittgenstein allows $(Ex)\phi x.\sim(Ex, y)\phi x.\phi y$ as a way of saying that *only* one thing has ϕ, as he does at 5.5321, it is difficult to see how he could avoid a way of admitting formulae which say 'There are *only* n things and m functions' without using either 'thing' or 'function' as a function.

12

Knowledge
and Certainty

Probably the best-known thesis of the *Tractatus* is that 'metaphysical' statements are nonsensical, and that the only sayable things are propositions of natural science (6.53). Now natural science is surely the sphere of the empirically discoverable; and the 'empirically discoverable' is the same as 'what can be verified by the senses'. The passage therefore suggests the following quick and easy way of dealing with 'metaphysical' propositions: what *sense-observations* would verify and what falsify them? If none, then they are senseless. This was the method of criticism adopted by the Vienna Circle and in this country by Professor A.J. Ayer.

There are certain difficulties about ascribing this doctrine to the *Tractatus*. There is nothing about sensible verification there. If Wittgenstein means to suggest that we can test a proposition for significance by seeing if we can state the sense-observations that would verify it, then it is surprising that he does not say so. Nor is a reference to sensible verifiability immediately implicit in the identification of 'what can be said' with 'the propositions of natural science'; for the totality of natural science has been defined earlier in the book (4.11) as the totality of true propositions. Nowhere have we any suggestion of a general method for criticizing sentences, according to which we may say: 'What observations would verify (or falsify) that? If none, then it does not mean anything.' Such a general method for criticizing sentences would obviously need a preliminary justification; and it is difficult to see how the *Tractatus*, for example, can be taken as such a preliminary justification, when it says nothing about sensible observation.

The general method that Wittgenstein does suggest is that of 'shewing that a man has supplied no meaning [or perhaps: "no reference"] for certain signs in his sentences'. I can illustrate the method from Wittgenstein's later way of discussing problems. He once greeted me with the question: 'Why do people say that it was natural to think that the sun went round the earth rather than that the earth turned on its axis?' I replied: 'I suppose, because it looked as if the sun went round the earth.' 'Well,' he asked, 'what would it have looked like if it had *looked* as if the earth turned on its axis?' This question brought it out that I had hitherto given no relevant meaning to 'it looks as if' in 'it looks as if the sun goes round the earth'. My reply was to hold out my hands with the palms upward, and raise them from my knees in a circular sweep, at the same time leaning backwards and assuming a dizzy expression. 'Exactly!' he said. In another case, I might have found that I could not supply any meaning other than that suggested by a naive conception, which could be destroyed by a question. The naive conception is really thoughtlessness, but it may take the power of a Copernicus effectively to call it in question.

Different philosophers have meant different things by 'metaphysical'. Kant also attacked metaphysics: but Kant would not have called 'Every rod has a length', or 'Time is one-dimensional and has only one direction', metaphysical in the sense in which he attacked metaphysics; whereas for Wittgenstein they are so.

The criticism of sentences as expressing no real thought, according to the principles of the *Tractatus*, could never be of any very simple general form; each criticism would be *ad hoc*, and fall within the subject-matter with which the sentence professed to deal. For example, if someone says that time moves only in one direction, we investigate this by asking him what processes he is comparing.

One frequently used tool in such enquiries is: 'What would it be for it to be otherwise?' — when, e.g. someone has said: 'Time has only one direction.' Here we are asked for an intelligible description of a state of affairs in which the asserted proposition — let it be, say, 'the future comes *after* the past' — does *not* hold. As far as sensible verification is concerned, the asserted proposition and the alternative to it that is being asked for are, or may be, on the same level; the relation of actual sense-experiences to each is not necessarily being investigated. What is operative here is evidently not a sensible-verification theory, but the picture theory of the significant description: both the proposition and its negation are supposed to describe a possibility, otherwise the status of the proposition is other than that of a significant description.

'Psychology is no more akin to philosophy than any other natural science. Theory of knowledge is the philosophy of psychology'

(4.1121). In this passage Wittgenstein is trying to break the dictatorial control over the rest of philosophy that had long been exercised by what is called theory of knowledge—that is, by the philosophy of sensation, perception, imagination, and, generally, of 'experience'. He did not succeed. He and Frege avoided making theory of knowledge the cardinal theory of philosophy simply by cutting it dead; by doing none, and concentrating on the philosophy of logic. But the influence of the *Tractatus* produced logical positivism, whose main doctrine is 'verificationism'; and in that doctrine theory of knowledge once more reigned supreme, and a prominent position was given to the test for significance by asking for the observations that would verify a statement. (Further, in the period between the *Tractatus* and the time when he began to write *Philosophical Investigations*, Wittgenstein's own ideas were more closely akin to those of the logical positivists than before or after.)

We can see how the *Tractatus* generated logical positivism, although the two philosophies are incompatible, by studying Moritz Schlick's essay, *Meaning and Verification*: 'Whenever we ask about a sentence, "What does it mean?" what we expect is instruction as to the circumstances in which the sentence is to be used; we want a description of the conditions under which the sentence will form a *true* proposition, and of those which will make it *false*.' Here Schlick seems to follow the *Tractatus*, except in the last clause of his statement: the *Tractatus* says that I 'determine the sense' of a proposition by 'determining in what circumstances I call it true' (4.063). (It is implicit in this that the 'circumstances' in question may hold or not hold; for it is an essential part of the picture theory that a proposition which held in *all* circumstances would not have 'sense': it would lack TF poles.)

Schlick calls the 'description of the conditions' under which a word has application, or a sentence is true, the 'rules for the use' of the word or sentence. These 'rules' will consist partly of 'ostensive definitions', of which the simplest form will be a pointing gesture combined with the pronouncing of the word; this can be done with words like 'blue'. For words like 'immediate', 'chance', 'because', 'again', Schlick says, the ostensive definition is of a more complicated kind: 'in these cases we require the presence of certain complex situations, and the meaning of the words is defined by the way we use them in these different situations.' All rules for use 'ultimately point to ostensive definitions'. 'This,' Schlick says, 'is the situation, and nothing seems to me simpler or less questionable. It is this situation and nothing else that we describe when we affirm that the meaning of a proposition can be given only by giving the rules of its verification in experience. (The addition "in experience" is really superfluous, as no other kind of verification has been defined.)'[1]

This shews us the transition from the *Tractatus* to 'verificationism' very clearly. What Schlick says leads immediately (a) to the quick test for significance: 'What experience would verify this?' and (b) to the maintenance of theory of knowledge as the cardinal theory of philosophy.

In the *Tractatus*, the 'determination of the circumstances in which I call a proposition true' must be a statement of its truth-conditions. This is a completely different thing from a 'rule for the use' of a sentence, if this takes the form of an 'ostensive definition'. There could be no statement of the truth-conditions of an elementary proposition, other than a restatement of it; and for all non-elementary propositions there can always be statements of truth-conditions. If, then, Schlick is following the *Tractatus*, 'ostensive definition' can only be relevant to the elementary proposition.

Further, Schlick insists that our 'rules for use' are 'arbitrary'; we give what rules we like; all that is essential is that we give some. The only arbitrariness in the *Tractatus* is in the assignment of names. There is no arbitrariness about the fact that a certain type of arrangement of names is capable of representing such-and-such a situation; it can do that only by reproducing in its own structure the arrangement of objects in the situation, and we cannot *make* it do so at will. Therefore, on the *Tractatus* view, there is no room for criticizing a sentence on the ground that we have not stipulated what situation it describes; but only on the ground that we have not assigned a reference to some of the words in it. The utterance of a sentence in a context in which it is true does not take the place of a stipulation of truth-conditions; the most that it can do is to shew someone the reference of the words; he will then understand the propositional sign, in its positive or negative sense, by meaning the objects named in it. Then 'you have said something meaningless' could only mean 'you have not assigned a reference to *this* expression', and never 'you have not shewn what observations would establish the truth of this'.

On the *Tractatus* view, then, one could not ask what observations would establish the truth of a proposition unless the 'structures' of possible observation statements already stood in certain internal relations to the 'structure' of the proposition. In the presence of these

---

[1]   Moritz Schlick, *Meaning and Verification*, reprinted in Feigl and Sellars, *Readings in Philosophical Analysis*.

internal relations, the question of meaningfulness cannot arise, except in the form of a question about the reference of the individual signs; if these signs are not given a reference, the proposition could not be 'given' a sense, even by stipulating that its truth would be established if and only if such-and-such observation statements were verified. An alleged 'proposition' that was so 'given a sense' would necessarily be, not a proposition, but the simple sign of a complex; and then the sentences in which the 'proposition' occurred would have to stand in internal relations to the 'observation statements'; these internal relations would then supply us with the description of a complex, and the definition of a simple sign for that complex; and the 'observation statements' would give the truth-conditions of propositions in which that sign occurred. This doctrine is quite different from Schlick's.

In *Philosophical Investigations*, where Wittgenstein makes an extensive investigation of psychological concepts, his object was to shew that it is not necessary to introduce the problems of epistemology of—i.e. of perception, imagination, and generally of 'experiencing'—into the discussion of other problems of philosophy. That is to say, we can discuss e.g. the problems implicit in the expression 'the process of time', without laying foundations by giving an account of the ways in which we apprehend time—memory, expectation, experience of succession, and so on.

Knowledge and certainty, however, *are* topics for the philosophy of logic. In doing logic we are not indeed interested in what is the case, or in what things are certainly known, or in the conditions for certainty in practice. But logical theory must allow for the certainty of propositions which are not logically necessary. Otherwise logic would have no application. For 'It is clear in advance that the logical proof of a significant proposition and proof *in* logic (i.e. proof of a logical proposition) must be two quite different things. The significant proposition asserts something, and its proof shows that it is so' (6.1263, 6.1264). Thus the proof of a significant proposition is not hypothetical. If its proof proves that it is the case, it is presupposed that those propositions from which it is proved are known to be true; for if they were uncertain, the conclusions would be equally uncertain. The only 'certainty' would then be hypothetical—that if the premises are true the conclusion is; but that is not what Wittgenstein calls a significant proposition; it is a proposition of logic, and proof of it nothing but a 'mechanical expedient to facilitate the recognition of it as a tautology' (6.1262). Thus, if we are to speak of proving significant propositions, 'A knows p' cannot be an ideal form of description without specifiable instances, nor one exemplified only in 'knowledge' of tautologies.

It is easy to misunderstand certain remarks in the *Tractatus* which have to do with this question and to suppose that Wittgenstein calls *only* tautologies certain. At 4.464 he says: 'The truth of tautology is certain, that of a proposition is possible, and of contradiction impossible. (Certain, possible, impossible: here we have a hint of that gradation which we need in probability theory.)' And at 5.525: 'Certainty, possibility or impossibility of a state of affairs are expressed, not by a proposition, but by an expression's being a tautology, a significant proposition or a contradiction.' It would be natural at first sight to take these remarks as implying that certainty belongs only to tautology. But the 'state of affairs' *whose certainty is expressed by an expression's being* a tautology cannot be a state of affairs *described by* a tautology; for Wittgenstein is insistent that tautology describes no state of affairs — is true for every possible state of affairs (4.466). Again the 'significant proposition asserts something, and its proof shows that it is so'; but there will be no such proof if certainty belongs only to a tautology.

Now if we take the hint given by the parenthetical remark at 4.464 and examine the theory of probability as it is described by the *Tractatus*, we find that the first impression perhaps conveyed by these propositions is mistaken, as it must be if Wittgenstein is consistent.

The account of probability is closely connected with the view that all the propositions are truth-functions of elementary propositions. At 5.15 we are told: 'If T_r is the number of truth-grounds of the proposition "r", T_{rs} the number of the truth-grounds of the proposition "s" which are at the same time truth-grounds of "r", then we call the ratio $T_{rs}:T_r$ the measure of the *probability* given by the proposition "r" to the proposition "s"' (5.15). That is, if we assume 'p' and 'q' to be elementary, since 'p or q' has 3 possible combinations of the truth-values of 'p' and 'q' which make it true, and only 1 in common with 'p and q', the measure of the probability given by 'p or q' to 'p and q' is $1:3$.

This account of probability has been criticized as resting upon the arbitrary dogma that all elementary propositions are equally probable. 'Two elementary propositions give one another the probability ½' (5.152). Now Wittgenstein also says: 'Propositions which have no truth-arguments in common with one another, we call independent of one another' (5.152). This is not an author's 'we'. Turning it round we might say: 'When we speak of propositions as independent of one another, what this really means is that they have no truth-arguments in common, i.e. are truth-functions of quite separate sets of elementary propositions.' With this we get some light on what is meant by saying 'the *application* of logic decides what elementary propositions there are' (5.557). That is to say: if in the *application* of logic — i.e. reasoning not 'in logic' but from facts — we (rightly) say 'even if *this* is so, *that* would not have to be so, it is not even made probable, they have nothing to do with one another': then we have found propositions that are truth-functions of quite separate sets of elementary propositions. But he goes on to say at this place: 'Logic cannot anticipate what resides in its application' and 'Logic and its application must not overlap.' Thus the question what are the elementary propositions does not belong to logic at all.

These passages shew the doubtfulness of part of Wittgenstein's criticism of the *Tractatus* in *Philosophical Investigations*. He jeers at the idea that when I say 'The broom is in the corner' I really mean 'The broomstick is in the corner and so is the brush and the broomstick is stuck in the brush.' But I shall recognize the negation of any of those propositions as constituting an objection to 'The broom is in the corner'; and that is all that the *Tractatus* theory requires. If I understand a proposition, I shall know what more detailed statements are inconsistent with it; these will then be more elementary than it is.

To return to the probability theory: 'If p follows from q, then the proposition "q" gives the proposition "p" the probability 1. The certainty of the logical conclusion is a limiting case of probability' (5.162). This can readily be seen from the *Tractatus* account of probability together with its account of inference, according to which what follows from a proposition is already stated by it (5.14–.141).

Now, however, we are in a position to understand the proposition: 'Certainty, possibility, or impossibility of a state of affairs is expressed not by a proposition, but by an expression's being a tautology, a significant proposition, or a contradiction.' Since an expression that is a tautology (or contradiction) does not answer to any 'state of affairs', what expresses the certain (or impossible) 'state of affairs' *itself*, as opposed to expressing its certainty (or impossibility), will not be the tautologous (or contradictory) expression, but rather one of the propositions that occur as components of this tautology (or contradiction). Moreover, in order to get 'a hint of that gradation which we need in probability theory', 'possibility' must here be taken as excluding *both* certainty *and* impossibility. Take a case where 's' is a significant proposition and 'r' expresses something we know. Then the 'state of affairs' expressed by 's' will be certain if 'r.~s' is a contradiction (i.e. if 'r ⊃ s' is a tautology); it will be impossible if 'r.s' is a contradiction (i.e. if 'r ⊃ ~s' is a tautology); it will be, relative to our knowledge, merely 'possible' if 'r.s' and 'r.~s' are *both* significant propositions (*each* of them must be *either* a significant proposition *or* a contradiction, if 'r' and 's' are both significant propositions).

This raises the question how we know that r; does the same account apply as would apply to 's' if it were 'certain' that s, and does this go on indefinitely, or do we come to a stop somewhere? Wittgenstein's view is at this point obscure; but he refers to 'being completely acquainted with a fact' (5.156), and presumably held that here we do come to a stop.

Thus Wittgenstein offers an extraordinarily over-simplified account of knowledge, which would presumably have to be filled out with an account of 'acquaintance with facts'. 'A knows p', he remarks at 5.1362, 'is senseless if p is a tautology.' (We should notice that the word is 'senseless', not 'nonsensical'; that is to say, the knowledge that p, when 'p' is a tautology, is treated as he treats the truth of 'p'.) But he has just said that the connection between knowledge and what is known is that of logical necessity. He is not referring to the mere fact that 'A knows p, but p is not true' is a contradiction; but to his theory, which would be the foundation for that fact, that the certainty of a state of affairs comes out in an expression's being a tautology. That is to say, if A knows p, then, for some q, the fact that q is a fact that A is 'acquainted' with, and q ⊃ p is a tautology.

The remark: 'Certainty, possibility and impossibility of a state of affairs are expressed, not by the proposition but ...' stands as a comment on 'It is incorrect to give "fx is possible" as the verbal rendering of (Ex)(fx), as Russell does.' Russell held that necessity, possibility (contingency) and impossibility belong, not to propositions, but to propositional functions, such as 'fx'. '"fx" is necessary', he says, means that all values of fx are true.[2]

In the passage we have been considering, Wittgenstein discusses not necessity, possibility and impossibility, but certainty, possibility and impossibility. This might seem insignificant, from his saying 'the truth of tautology is certain'; but, as we have seen, he cannot hold that *only* the truth of tautology is certain. His objection to Russell's account of necessity (and hence of logical impossibility) is made elsewhere, at 6.1231: 'The mark of logical propositions is *not* general validity. For to be general only means: to be accidentally valid for all things. An ungeneralized proposition can be tautologous just as well as a generalized one.'

---

[2]   See e.g. the final paragraph of a chapter 'Propositional Functions' in Russell's *Introduction to Mathematical Philosophy*.

'That precedent,' Wittgenstein concludes 5.525, 'to which one would always like to appeal, must reside in the very symbol itself.' He evidently refers to a reason why it is especially tempting to equate '(Ex)(fx)' and 'fx is possible'. The most fundamental motive for adopting Russell's views is that it would be one way of getting rid of the puzzling character of 'necessary', 'possible' and 'impossible'; Wittgenstein has his own way of doing that. There remains, however, the feeling that a case will guarantee possibility, and thus give the assertion of possibility a sense, as nothing else could; this is like the lawyer's feeling that the best way of showing a procedure to be legal is to cite a precedent for it. So Russell thought that 'fx' is possible only if there is an *actual* case of an f.

Now Wittgenstein acknowledges this desire for 'a precedent', but says that this precedent resides in the symbol itself. The 'symbol itself' will be the significant proposition. For 'in the proposition a situation is as it were put together experimentally' (4.031). It is as if the construction of small models of mechanisms were used to make reports on what machines there were in some place, and one also constructed hypothetical models, say in order to ask whether there are any of these in that place. If the models are in clay and do not move, one might want to know what makes them express possible hypotheses. But if the models are themselves working mechanisms, the 'precedent' to which one would want to appeal would be in the models themselves. And so it is, Wittgenstein says, with *significant* propositions.

No 'precedent' is to be found in tautology and contradiction; Wittgenstein's remark has sole application to significant propositions. For 'sentences which are true for every state of affairs cannot be connections of signs at all, for otherwise only particular connections of objects will correspond to them. (And there isn't any logical combination to which there corresponds *no* combination of the objects.)' (4.466). To regard tautologies (logically necessary propositions) as descriptions is as if one were to regard the empty space where the mechanism was to go as itself a model — for all possible mechanisms. But the significant proposition is a *logical working model* of the situation it asserts to exist.

13

'Mysticism' and Solipsism

When Russell received the MS. of the *Tractatus* from Wittgenstein, then in an Italian prison-camp, after the First World War, he wrote some comments and questions. Presumably he laid great stress on the account of logical propositions as tautologies; his letter is not extant but we know he attached great importance to Wittgenstein's researches on this subject from a footnote in his *Introduction* to *Mathematical Philosophy*. In reply he received a letter from Wittgenstein saying:

> 'Now I'm afraid you haven't really got hold of my main contention, to which the whole business of logical propositions is only corollary. The main point is the theory of what can be expressed (*gesagt*) by propositions—i.e. by language (and, what comes to the same, what can be *thought*) and what cannot be expressed by propositions, but only shown (*gezeigt*); which, I believe, is the cardinal problem of philosophy ...'

We have seen what 'can be said' according to this theory: that, and that only, 'can be said' the negative of which is also a possibility, so that which of the two possibilities is actual has to be discovered by 'comparing the proposition with reality'. This notion is rather vague, but it is clearly implied that the comparison does not consist in mere thought: 'there is no picture that is true *a priori*'. That is to say, if a proposition has a negation which is a perfectly good possibility, then it cannot be settled whether the proposition is true or false just by considering what it means. The locus of direct 'comparison with reality' lies in the facts we are 'acquainted with'; if so, then, on Wittgenstein's theory of inference, we can have no knowledge of significant propositions that is not a restatement (or an 'abstract'—5.156) of propositions known by 'acquaintance' to be true. (This theory of knowledge has, to be sure, nothing but clarity and simplicity to recommend it.) As for tautologies and contradictions, they are devoid of 'sense' and 'say nothing'.

But an important part is played in the *Tractatus* by the things which, though they cannot be 'said', are yet 'shewn' or 'displayed'. That is to say: it would be right to call them 'true' if, *per impossibile*, they could be said; in fact they cannot be called true, since they cannot be said, but 'can be shewn', or 'are exhibited', in the propositions saying the various things that can be said.

Now the things that would be true if they could be said are obviously important. Can we then draw a distinction between things that are 'shewn', and things the opposite of which is 'shewn'; between the things that would be true if they could be said, and those that would be false if they could be said? It is impossible to speak like this of attempted contradictions of what 'is shewn', as we have already seen in a trivial case: whereas '"Someone" is *not* the name of someone' is intended to say something 'quite correct' (as Wittgenstein says of solipsism), we must say concerning '"Someone" *is* the name of some-one' that what such a proposition intends is not merely not correct, but quite incoherent and confused; the demonstration that this is so com-pletely destroys the idea that there is anything at all behind the would-be statement. Nevertheless there are utterances which at least sound like attempts to say the opposite of the things that are 'quite correct' in this sense; and there will be more error, or more darkness, in such attempts than in trying to say the things that are 'shewn', even if they are really unsayable.

It would presumably be because of this that Wittgenstein regards the sentences of the *Tractatus* as helpful, in spite of their being strictly nonsensical according to the very doctrine that they propound; some-one who had used them like steps 'to climb out beyond them' would be helped by them to 'see the world rightly'. That is to say, he would see what 'is shewn', instead of being down in a bog confusedly trying to propound and assert sometimes cases of what is 'shewn', some-times would-be contradictions of these.

This idea of philosophic truth would explain one feature of philosophy: what a philosopher declares to be philosophically false is supposed not to be possible or even really conceivable; the false ideas which he conceives himself to be attacking must be presented as chimaeras, as not really thinkable thoughts at all. Or, as Wittgenstein put it: An *impossible* thought is an impossible *thought* (5.61) – and that is why it is not possible to say what it is that cannot be thought; it can only be forms of words or suggestions of the imagination that are attacked. Aristotle rejecting separate forms, Hume rejecting substance, exemplify the difficulty: if you want to argue that something is a philosophical illusion, you cannot treat it as a false hypothesis. Even if for purposes of argument you bring it into contempt by treating it as an hypothesis, what you infer from it is not a contradiction but an incoherence.

We must distinguish in the theory of the *Tractatus* between logical truths and the things that are 'shewn'; logical truths, whose character we have already discussed, are the 'tautologies', and are '*sense-less*' propositions (lacking TF poles), their negations being 'contradictions': attempts to say what is 'shewn' produce '*nonsensical*' formations of words—i.e. sentence-like formations whose constituents turn out not to have any meaning in those forms of sentences—e.g. one uses a formal concept like 'concept' as if it were a proper concept (Chapter 7, pp. 91–2). Here the attempt to express what one sees breaks down.

The connection between the tautologies, or sense-less propositions of logic, and the unsayable things that are 'shewn', is that the tautologies shew the 'logic of the world'. But what they shew is not what they are an attempt to say: for Wittgenstein does not regard them as an attempt to say anything. They are, however, legitimate constructions, introduced into the system of propositions as 0 was introduced into the system of numerals. Nor are they the only propositions which 'shew' anything, or which shew 'the logic of the world': on the contrary, every proposition at least does that.

Of all the things that are unsayably 'shewn', the most prominent in the *Tractatus* is this 'logic of the world' or 'of the facts'. 'My most fundamental thought is this: logical constants are not proxies for anything. The logic of the facts cannot have anything going proxy for it' (4.0342). Here he is contrasting logical constants with names, which 'go proxy' for their objects: 'The possibility of sentences,' he has just said, 'rests upon the principle of signs as going proxy for objects'—and what this principle in turn amounts to is the possibility of logical picturing through one fact's having the same logical form as another— for only in the context of the proposition will a sign go proxy for an object.

Sentences thus cannot represent, and nothing in them can stand for, 'the logic of the facts': they can only reproduce it. An attempt to say what it is that they so reproduce leads to stammering.—This view does seem to be true. I once bought toffees with the names of the flavours, 'treacle', 'Devon cream' and so on printed on the papers, and was momentarily startled to find one labelled 'fruit or nut'. It cannot be 'fruit or nut', I said; it's fruit or it's nut! Any attempt to say what the truth-functional constants like 'or' mean must fail; we can only shew it.

Or again; if asked to explain the composition of the simplest statement, we say that this word means, or refers to, such-and-such, and this one means such-and-such, and together they mean that ... (or: someone who puts them together makes the statement that ...)—and there follows just such another composition of signs as we were trying to explain.

Again, if we try to explain the essence of a relational expression to ourselves, we reproduce the relational form in our explanation. For, as we have seen, we must make the distinction between 'aRb' and 'bRa'; and if we do this by e.g. saying that in one the relation goes from a to b, and in the other from b to a, we produce a sentence which employs the essential relational form; for it reproduces the distinction produced by exchanging the places of the terms.

All the logical devices—the detailed twiddles and manipulations of our language—combine, Wittgenstein tells us at 5.511, into an infinitely fine network, forming 'the great mirror'—that is to say, the mirror of language, whose logical character makes it reflect the world and makes its individual sentences say that such-and-such is the case. The simplest and most characteristic mark of this is that we do not have to learn the meanings of all the sentences of our language; given the understanding of the words, we understand and construct sentences, and know what they mean without having it explained to us.

It is essential to see that logic does not describe any facts: that there are no logical facts. It was at one time natural to think that the field of logic was the field of what was *a priori* true, i.e. true independently of all existence. On this Wittgenstein says at 5.552: 'The "experience" that we need to understand logic is not that something is thus or thus, but that something *is*: but that is not an experience. Logic precedes any experience—that something is *thus*. It comes before the *How*, not before the *What*.' According to the *Tractatus* the 'what' is conveyed by the simple names, which cannot be taken to pieces by definitions (3.261) and which name the 'substance of the world' (2.0211). Thus even when a simple name is replaced by a definite description, the description is merely 'about' the object, it could not 'express' it (3.221).

From this, it is clear that Wittgenstein held that what was given by experience was always facts; a grasp of the 'substance of the world', which we shew we have in being able to describe the facts we experience, is not given by any experience. For of any experience it can be asked what it shews as being the case; since this can be the case or not, indifferently, its being the case cannot possibly tell us anything about logic. For everything logical about a (significant) proposition is understood before it is known whether the proposition is true or not.

But logic cannot be thought of as something quite independent of the world either. For then 'How could we apply logic?' (5.5521). That is to say, if logical truth were there without any world, then when there was a world, how could it be said: such-and-such cannot be, because there is a logical fact that is inconsistent with it? 'It could be said: If there would be such a thing as logic, even if there were no world, then how can there be such a thing as logic, when there is a world?' (i.e.: if logic comprised facts that the facts in the world had to be consistent with, then logic would no longer be logic, for it is logic that judges of the consistency of facts.) 'It has been said that God can create everything but what is contrary to the laws of logic. — The point is, that we could not *say* what an "unlogical" world would be like' (3.031). So the medieval philosopher says that God, to whom no 'word' is impossible, yet cannot change the past, because 'change the past' is not a 'word'.

Thus when the *Tractatus* tells us that 'Logic is transcendental', it does not mean that the propositions of logic state transcendental truths; it means that they, like all other propositions, shew something that pervades everything sayable and is itself unsayable. If it were sayable, then failure to accord with it would have to be expressible too, and thus would be a possibility.

I will now consider the most notorious of the things that Wittgenstein says are 'shewn', but cannot be said: the truth of solipsism. I am a solipsist if I think: 'I am the only *I*: the world, including all the people in it, is essentially an object of experience, and therefore of *my* experience.' Wittgenstein says: what is intended here is right, but it can't be said. (5.62).

It is a fairly natural thought that 'where there is consciousness, there is an I'; but this raises immediate questions both about 'consciousness', and about the legitimacy of speaking of '*an* I'. If one considers examples of consciousness, as it is being approached here, one does not think of how e.g. one can see that someone is now *conscious* (he was, say, asleep before); but rather of contents of consciousness, such as pain, images, the visual field; and what is there *to* the consciousness except the pain, the image, or the visual field itself? The essential thing is that these are being considered 'from inside'; all that there is from outside corresponding to these words is manifestations of them in words and behaviour.

So it comes out that it is illegitimate to speak of '*an* I'. 'From inside' means only 'as *I* know things'; I describe those things — something, however, I cannot communicate or express: I try to, by saying I speak 'from an inside point of view'. But there is no other *point of view*. Suppose others too speak of the 'inside point of view'? That is *my* experience or *my* supposition of spoken words.

In a later writing Wittgenstein imagined a convention whereby some individual, A, is used as a centre for the language of experience and thought in the following way: Everyone says 'There is pain', or 'It thinks', when A is in pain, or is thinking; for other people the locution would be, say, 'X is behaving as A behaves when there is pain etc.' Now, he said, if I am the centre, this language has a peculiar but quite inexpressible advantage over the languages in which other people are taken as centres. It is inexpressible, because if I try to express it in the language with myself as centre naturally my statement, as coming from the person who is the centre, is specially related to the language that has me as centre; and if I try to express it in a language with someone else as centre, then the description, in that language, of the alternative possible language with me as centre gives it no special position in comparison with any other alternative language. But all these languages correspond, and one and the same reality corresponds to them all and to the 'physical language'.

This passage, though written some years after the *Tractatus*, appears very close to it in thought. For that 'advantage' was absolute. Thus I *am* the centre, but this is inexpressible.

In the *Tractatus* Wittgenstein speaks of 'my language' (5.6) and explains this as meaning 'the only language that I understand'[1] (5.62). Its limits 'stand for the limits of my world'. I cannot postulate a language for talking about the relation of language, the world, and the philosophical I, in which my world (the world given by the limits of my language) would be one particular thing to talk about. I can only say how things are in the world corresponding to my language. But this manifests the 'all-comprehending world-mirroring logic'.

That is why, having said at 5.6 'The limits of my language mean the limits of my world', Wittgenstein gives as the first comment on

---

1 The emphasized definite article shews that 'der Sprache' in 5.62 means '*that* language' making a back reference which must be to 'my language' in 5.6. — In the first edition of this book I translated the parenthesis in 5.62 'the language that only I understand'. But Dr. C. Lewy has found a copy of the first edition of the *Tractatus* with a correction by Wittgenstein giving 'the only language that I understand'.

this pronouncement a number of remarks on logic: 'Logic fills the world: the limits of the world are also its limits' (5.61). The argument is: 'The limits of my language mean the limits of my world; but all languages have one and the same logic, and its limits are those of the world; therefore the limits of my world and of the world are one and the same; therefore the world is my world.'

But the 'I' of this way of talking is not something that can be found as a mind or soul, a subject of consciousness, one among others; there is no such thing to be 'found' as the subject of consciousness in this sense. All that can be found is what consciousness is of, the contents of consciousness: 'I am my world' and 'The world and life are one'. Hence this 'I', whose language has the special position, is unique; the world described by this language is just the real world: 'Thoroughly thought out, solipsism coincides with pure realism' (5.64).

It is not possible to understand this passage unless one has a good deal of sympathy with solipsism. We should remember that Wittgenstein had been much impressed by Schopenhauer as a boy; many traces of this sympathy are to be found in the *Tractatus*. Probably no one who reads the opening of *The World as Will and Idea*: 'The world is my idea', without any responsiveness, will be able to enter into Wittgenstein's thought here.

Mrs. Ladd Franklin is reported to have written to Bertrand Russell saying that she was a solipsist and could not understand why everyone else was not too! It is possible that the comic effect was intentional, and the joke on her side. The necessity of solipsism is very arguable; why should a solipsist not argue it with everyone capable of arguing? Nothing would follow, even if two solipsists exchanged views with mutual congratulation, about any cession by either to the other of the unique position he conceives for himself. If two people discuss Descartes' 'Cogito', they can agree that 'This is an argument I can administer to myself alone,' and each can hold the other would be incorrect to have disputed that; if snow fell in appropriate sentences, one could dispute, agree and disagree with, those sentences.

Further, it is very difficult to think of ways out of solipsism. Indeed solipsism is often held to be irrefutable, but too absurd to concern oneself with. In Wittgenstein's version, it is clear that the 'I' of solipsism is not used to refer to anything, body or soul; for in respect of these it is plain that all men are alike. The 'I' refers to the centre of life, or the point from which everything is seen.

It is difficult to get rid of such a conception once one has it. One may well want to do so; e.g. one may feel that it makes the 'I' too godlike. 'What is history to me? Mine is the first and only world!'

Wittgenstein wrote in his notebooks on this theme, and: 'There are two godheads: God, and the I.' (He did not follow Schopenhauer in saying: 'The world is my will'; on the contrary: 'The world is independent of my will—and anything's being as I want it is a "grace of fate".' (6.373–4). 'Hence,' he wrote in his notebooks, 'the feeling of being dependent on an alien will.')

It is not altogether easy to understand Wittgenstein's idea of 'the limit'. It too is partly derivative from Schopenhauer, who wrote of it as follows:

> 'Any one percipient being, with the object, constitutes the whole world as idea just as fully as the existing millions would do; but if this one were to disappear then the whole world as idea would cease to be. These halves are therefore inseparable even for thought, for each of the two has meaning and existence only through and for the other, each appears with the other and vanishes with it. They limit each other immediately.'

Again, Schopenhauer remarks on the fear of death that it is really the fear of losing the present, and says that this is like being afraid of slipping down the sides of the globe, as someone might do who did not realize that the top is wherever he is.

The idea of the world as having *limits* which philosophy displays to us appears over and over again in the *Tractatus*. It is perhaps best known in the dictum of 6.45: 'The view of the world *sub specie aeterni* is the view of it as a—limited—whole. The feeling of the world as a limited whole is the mystical feeling.' The world 'as a limited whole' is not suddenly introduced here as a new topic. We encounter the world conceived as a whole—as *all* that is the case—and as limited—namely by being all that is the case—at the very outset of the book; the feeling of the world as a whole appears in the remark at 1.2: 'The world splits up into facts', for it is only of a whole that we can say it splits up.

'Mysticism' is a rather odd name for what Wittgenstein is speaking of; in popular language it suggests extraordinary and unusual experiences, thoughts and visions peculiar to an extraordinary type of individual; and no doubt it has been taken in that sense, and written off, the more easily because Wittgenstein was himself well known to be an extraordinary individual—the very man to have some mysticism about him. But Wittgenstein took the term over from Russell, who used it in a special way, with reference to an entirely ordinary feeling; one that is well expressed at 6.52: 'We feel that even if all *possible* scientific questions have been answered, still the problems of life have not been touched at all.' And his further comment on this is: 'Of course there then just is no question left, and just this is the answer.'

This comment can be taken in two ways: First, Wittgenstein might be saying—and this is what Professor Ayer, for example, would make of his remarks—that people who have wanted to say what the meaning of life consisted in have had nothing in them but a lot of nonsense. This cannot be the right interpretation; for he speaks of people 'to whom the meaning of life has become clear'. But he says of them that they have not been able to say it. Now such people have not failed for want of trying; they have usually said a great deal. He means that they have failed to state what they wished to state; that it was never possible to state it as it is possible to state indifferent truth. He probably had Tolstoy especially in mind, whose explanations of what he thought he understood are miserable failures; but whose understanding is manifested, and whose preaching comes through, in a story like *Hadji Murad*.

Wittgenstein's idea is probably made clearest at 6.41: 'The meaning of the world must lie outside the world. In the world everything is as it is, everything happens as it does happen; there is no value *in* it—if there were any, it would have no value. If there is a value that has value, it must lie outside all happening and outside being this way or that. For all happening and being this way or that is accidental. What makes it non-accidental cannot be found in the world, for otherwise this thing would in its turn be accidental.' And: 'God does not reveal himself *in* the world' (6.432)—i.e. it is not in things' being this way as opposed to that that God is revealed.

This follows from the picture theory; a proposition and its negation are both possible; which one is true is accidental. Why then, having said that whatever is the case is accidental, does Wittgenstein speak of 'what makes it non-accidental'? To understand this, we have to understand what he says about the will. The most important remark that he makes here is: 'The facts all belong to the task set, and not to the solution' (6.4321). '*Aufgabe*', which I translate 'task set', is the German for a child's school exercise, or piece of homework. Life is like a boy doing sums. (At the end of his life he used the analogy still.) Now the reason why the solution cannot bring in any facts is that it is concerned with good and evil; and the good or evil character of what is good or evil is non-accidental; it therefore cannot consist in this happening rather than that, for that is accidental.

In doing one's task, one receives certain laws, of the form 'Thou shalt ...' This, Wittgenstein says, prompts the question: And suppose I do not do it? 'But it is clear that ethics has nothing to do with punishment or reward in the ordinary sense.' Still 'there must be something right about that question. There must be a kind of ethical reward and ethical punishment, but these must reside in the action itself. (And it is also clear that the reward must be something pleasant and the punishment something unpleasant)' (6.422).

Now what is 'the action itself'? Wittgenstein insists that 'the world is independent of my will; there is no logical connection between will and world'—no logical connection between my will and what actually happens at all. In so far as an event in the world can be described as voluntary, and volition be studied, the will, and therefore action, is 'a phenomenon, of interest only to psychology'. Therefore 'action', in the ethical sense, is something independent of what happens; and this is the bearer of good and evil. Thus the 'will that is the bearer of the ethical' (6.423) belongs among the transcendentals of the *Tractatus*, along with the mystical and the meaning of life. The connection of will with the world is that 'the facts' belong to the task one is set. If one has reached a solution, this is made to be a solution, not by any alteration of the facts that may have taken place—any such alteration, even if one intended it, is accidental and merely a 'grace of fate'—but by an alteration 'in the limits of the world' (6.43).

It is this part of the *Tractatus* that seems to me most obviously wrong. As Wittgenstein asks in *Philosophical Investigations* (§644): 'Did not your intention [of which you are ashamed] reside also in what you *did*?' 'What happens' includes 'actions', in the sense of the word in which 'good' and 'bad' are predicated of actions. But the philosophy of the *Tractatus* could not allow this to be so; hence the chimerical 'will' which effects nothing in the world, but only alters the 'limits' of the world. In his notebooks Wittgenstein entertained some more reasonable considerations, which are closely akin to his thought in *Philosophical Investigations*; and then rejected them, in the following revealing passage:

> 'The consideration of willing makes it look as if one part of the world were closer to me than another (which would be intolerable). But, of course, it is undeniable that in the popular sense there are things that I do and other things not done by me. In this way, then, the will would not confront the world as its equivalent,[2] which must be impossible.'

---

[2]   The contrast with Schopenhauer, as well as the kinship, is interesting. Schopenhauer thought that 'the world is my will' and is bad; and that the only redemption for the will is 'to turn and freely deny itself'. Wittgenstein thought that the world is good and independent of my will; good and bad willing are attitudes

The true philosophical account of this matter has still to be found; saying that the *Tractatus* is obviously wrong here, I do not wish to suggest that I know what is right.

There is a strong impression made by the end of the *Tractatus*, as if Wittgenstein saw the world looking at him with a face; logic helped to reveal the face. Now a face can look at you with a sad or happy, grave or grim, good or evil expression, and with more or less expression. And so he speaks of the world 'waxing or waning as a whole', i.e., in terms of my analogy, as having more or less expression, or a good or evil expression. The world thought of, not as how things are, but as *however* they are—seen as a whole—is the matter of logic; thought of as my life, it is the matter of ethics; thought of as an object of contemplation, the matter of aesthetics: all these, then, are 'transcendental'. Many years later, in a 'lecture on Ethics', Wittgenstein wrote: 'If I want to fix my mind on what I mean by absolute or ethical value, it always happens that one particular experience presents itself to me which is therefore in a sense my experience *par excellence* ... the best way of describing it is to say that when I have it *I wonder at the existence of the world.*' The identification of ethics and aesthetics (6.421) comes about in this way: good and bad willing changes the world only as the object of contemplation as a whole.

The man, however, who having been helped by the *Tractatus* 'sees the world rightly', i.e. sees what logic reveals as 'shewn', will not attempt to say it, since he knows it is unsayable. As for how much advantage it is to him, Wittgenstein makes no great claim; in the Introduction he said: 'The whole meaning of the book could perhaps be summed up as follows: What can be said at all can be said clearly, and what cannot be spoken of we must be silent about.' But his final judgment on the value of the book was this: 'It shews how little has been done, when these problems have been solved.'

---

to the world as a whole. The goodness of the world, however, is not anything in *how* it is, but in its being at all; and lies outside all being-this-way-or-that. The good will therefore will not be concerned with how things are, and in that sense is like Schopenhauer's good will.

Further Reading

Wittgenstein, L. *Philosophical Investigations*; Blackwell, Oxford, especially
    Part I, §§1–116.
    Remarks on the Foundations of Mathematics; Blackwell, Oxford, Part I.
    Notebooks 1914–16; Blackwell, Oxford.
Frege, G. *Translations from the Philosophical Writings of Gottlob Frege*;
    Blackwell, Oxford.
    The Foundations of Arithmetic; Blackwell, Oxford.
Russell, B. *The Principles of Mathematics*; Allen & Unwin, London,
    especially Chapters III–V and VII.
    The Problems of Philosophy; Home University Library.
    Logic and Knowledge; Allen & Unwin, London, especially 'On Denoting'
    and 'The Philosophy of Logical Atomism'.
    Introduction to Mathematical Philosophy; Allen & Unwin, London.
Ramsey, F.P. *The Foundations of Mathematics*; Routledge, London.
Basson and O'Connor. *Introduction to Symbolic Logic* (2nd edition);
    University Tutorial Press, London.
Quine, W.V.O. *Methods of Logic*; Routledge, London.
Hilbert and Ackermann. *Mathematical Logic*; Chelsea Publishing Co., New
    York.
von Wright, G.H. *Logical Studies*; Routledge, London.

Part 2

Thought and Belief

1

Belief and Thought

I

Introduction

Often 'I think' and 'I believe', 'He thinks' and 'He believes', 'I thought', 'I believed', etc. are pretty well interchangeable. Among the *loci* where they are so, we find ones in which 'think' has a sense such that what one thinks is one's — long or short term — standing belief. We are not concerned with *nuances* — e.g. that what I think is appropriately *my own judgment*, whereas belief may be simply a matter of acceptance of the judgment of others. This is important, but not for us at present; and still less any other finer differences between 'believe' and 'think' in this sense of 'think'.

'Standing belief' (whether long or short term) is a grammatically dispositional concept. For 'A thinks that all conservatives are prosperous people chiefly interested in their own pockets and the wealth of their own class' or again 'A believes that John will borrow from the bank tomorrow' are not frequentative statements, and yet do not have as truth-conditions any contemporaneous acts or experiences on A's part, or happening to A, or characteristic of A — except whatever is requisite for A to be the kind of being, or to be in a position, to have a belief of the sort. In the second case, for example, A must have some acquaintance with the institution of money, know of the John in question, etc. But in neither case need A be awake, say, at the time at which we have a right to say that he thinks or believes that ...

---

* Sections I to V are from an undated typescript with written corrections in the author's hand. A footnote reference in section V refers to two further sections on 'Contradictory Beliefs' and 'Degrees of Assent'; there is no typescript of these. There are a number of manuscripts on both these topics in the Interim Archive of Professor Anscombe's papers but they are either incomplete or not obviously finalised. She lectured on the subject of 'Belief and Thought' twice a week in Cambridge in the Lent and Easter terms of 1970, just after taking up the Chair there.

But 'think' is used in another sense, i.e. a sense more akin to that of 'reflect'. To think anything in this sense is an *act* of mind, and thought in the corresponding sense is an event. 'I thought to myself...' is a report of such an event. Here the words 'to myself' show that the report is of an inner event. When I say something meaning it sincerely, without previously 'thinking it to myself', here too we have what I will call *occurrent thought*.

One may believe (and so in one sense think) various things without the thought that they are so ever coming into one's consciousness. For it is possible to discover, with surprise, that one has always thought something. Or again, to realise the falsity of something which one had always thought without ever bringing it to consciousness. E.g. 'Why! I have always thought that modern Greek was as different from ancient as Italian is from Latin.' Someone who truthfully said this might never have formulated this belief of his, until this moment when perhaps he learns it is untrue.

We might then suppose it an accidental equivocation by which the word 'thought' and the verb 'to think' have these two senses. On reflection, however, this does not seem true. For — to mention only one point — in yet another sense thoughts may be found written down in books; and both what one thinks when actively reflecting, and what one believes, is given in a proposition, a sentence, which expresses a thought in a non-psychological sense.

An occurrent thought that *p* may be the initiating act of the disposition which is the belief that *p*. For though it need not, a belief *may* have an initiating act. In this belief is like intention which also may but need not in general have an initiating act. If an intention does have an initiating act, that act is a decision.

The concept of a grammatically dispositional term must not be confused with the concept of a real disposition. A real disposition is a state of affairs which tends toward some definite result, like e.g. the organisation and present set of a clock mechanism. The clock is disposed to ring an alarm bell at noon, say. And this may be seen in two different ways. In one, we see that the alarm hand is pointing to that time, that the clock is functioning, is now telling the right time, etc., and we know that when this is so, the clock goes off accordingly. In the other, we see into the works themselves and understand *how* the clock is set so as to ring the bell. Sometimes we may label something — a seed, say — as being of a kind to produce such-and-such without being able to identify it by any external distinguishing character or by its inner organisation. (Here we have the prejudice that something about the seed will correspond to its being a seed of this and not that plant.) In all these cases we may speak of a disposition toward such-and-such specifiable effects. But a grammatically dispositional term does not imply that something of which such a term is true is somehow organised or qualified to do such-and-such. This sort of disposition is then not a disposition towards certain things. The assumption that belief was a disposition to do anything could only be expressed with great vagueness, and would have to be hedged about with many saving clauses.

What I call a real disposition—I might say a 'physical' or 'natural' disposition if it were not for certain misleading associations of these words—is a property D such that to say an object has D is to say that it is such as to do such-and-such under such-and-such conditions. The only saving clause we have to put in here is 'saving external interference'. By this criterion neither 'knowledge' nor 'belief' signify 'real' dispositions.

What we may reasonably speak of here are acts which are acts of these dispositions. This does not commit us to predictions of definite kinds of action and reaction, which may readily be falsified with no detriment to the ascription of the dispositional term.

But we must grant that 'believe' is not always dispositional. For example, I may suddenly believe someone's story—which up to that point I have heard with incredulity. Or I may suddenly believe that N. is the man who has been making trouble for me. The report of such a happening is not the ascription of a disposition. Or should we say it is the report of the onset of a disposition? At any rate when we hear of such sudden belief, and we ask how long it lasted, we aren't asking how long a state of consciousness lasted. If the belief lasted only for a moment, then I must have changed my mind a moment later. If it lasted for longer than its content was before my mind, then the report that I believed ... for that half hour, or for months, or up till now, uses the word 'believe' dispositionally. But if I suddenly believed the thing just for a moment, and then decided I was wrong, then *here* 'believe' is not being used dispositionally, for (something connected with) the matter must have been in my mind in the brief moment of belief. This makes it look as if 'belief' had at any rate *two* senses: we speak of it in one use as a state of consciousness, in the other as a disposition. But the question as to the *duration* of it shows that we are not after all speaking of it as a state of consciousness. What difference can it make to the *sense* of 'belief', as applied to so brief a space of time, that I changed my mind at once? I might not have done so, and then we would think of what happened, not as the belief, but as the onset of belief. We are not justified in speaking of different senses of 'believe';

nevertheless, according to context, the word may be used dispositionally *or* otherwise. So we should not say 'Belief is a dispositional concept', but rather that a great part of its application is *dispositional*.

In this, we may contrast 'believe' and 'know'. Yet don't we say 'I
suddenly know'? — We do: but sudden belief and sudden knowledge
are more dissimilar than they sound, and — strange as this may seem —
'sudden knowledge' is more akin to the concept of an inner experience
than is 'sudden belief'. If we say of someone else 'He suddenly knew
who had done it' we are referring to an experience of realisation — as
the haver of it will feel it to be — and *also* endorsing it. It is the endorse-
ment which means that knowledge, even here, is not a concept of an
inner experience. But the idea of 'sudden knowledge' does involve
such a concept. You *suddenly knew* — What was that like? we may ask,
and the question does not reveal a mistake in our conceptions. 'Like a
light coming on; like seeing; like the experience of clarity' — these are
appropriate answers.

By contrast, 'sudden belief' is not a concept of something experienced. 'I suddenly believed his story' — What was that like? Faced with
this question, one does not find something which was the experience,
but rather, if anything, one finds accompanying experiences — a feeling
of shock, a reorganisation of the facts in my mind, a feeling of being
impressed by a look or phrase. But none of these was the believing.

In non-dispositional uses of 'believe', we have further cases of the
inter-changeability of 'believe' and 'think'. For, if I suddenly come to
the conclusion that N. was the man who ... I may equally well say I
suddenly believed it was so, or that I suddenly thought it was so.

But when do we say 'I suddenly believed *p*'? Contrast this with 'I
suddenly *thought of* my child'. That may happen any time I am awake;
it needs no further facts about what I am doing or noticing or how my
mind is occupied. The contrast shows that even sudden belief is not an
act — for one may perform an act at any time if, so to speak, one has the
equipment. But someone might even feel perplexed whether there
could be such a thing as suddenly believing something. If so, he is
probably envisaging it like this: I am thinking of other things, and then
without anything else, I suddenly believe that N. is the man who ...
Just as I may be thinking of other things and suddenly the thought, or
memory, of N. comes into my head. This really is impossible for belief.
Not by any physical impossibilities: it is, rather, a misuse of language,
like answering the question 'What are you doing?' by saying
'Believing that ...'. At most, I may suddenly *find* that I believe ... What
is impossible is that there should be a sudden belief as it were naked,
just the believing, without something else. There is this amount of

truth in Hume's definition of belief as an idea associated with a present impression. Immediate belief is associated with the presentation of what is believed; sudden later belief with some new occurrence. This does not have to be an impression. But it may be one. E.g. I noticed an expression on N's face at a certain juncture, and I suddenly believed *he* was the man who ... However, the occurrence may be no impression of the senses, it may be that I merely think *of* what I have previously disbelieved, and it suddenly strikes me as convincing. (Bertrand Russell throwing his tobacco tin into the air and exclaiming 'By Jove! The ontological argument is valid!') This is not itself the sudden belief, but rather a sudden thought which may be an initiating act of the disposition. And the feeling of convincingness *can* be an 'experience'.

Another case where 'think', in the 'believe' sense, is not dispositional: I mistread, bringing my weight down on my foot unsuitably, and I say 'I thought there was a step there'. This was the case that led Russell to offer as a 'minimum' definition of belief: 'muscular preparedness for action'.

It is easy to see what prompts this. For *when* did I think there was a step? In the usual case of an episode of this kind, the answer simply is 'When I was taking a step—i.e. when I was treading'. That makes one look for what was going on at the time. But it is obvious that one may have had no thoughts, no conscious beliefs about the step at the time. (Nor would a *standing opinion* be what was involved here.) Nothing relevant was going on then, except that one was treading in that way. That is to say, one's muscles were in a certain state. So that was what the believing consisted in!

However, that same state of the muscles might have existed in quite different surroundings (treading on levers rather than steps, for example), and then one would not have 'thought there was a step'. This shows that the belief cannot consist in the state of the muscles. Perhaps it is said: 'Well, it consists in the state of the muscles in that situation, namely one in which one is going up or down steps'. But then one is granting that the question 'What does the belief consist in?' can't be answered without looking outside the time of the belief.

I exclaim: 'I thought there was a step!', and this tells my hearer that I was treading *to* step on a step. But—someone may say—doesn't it say something about my having *believed* something? Well, if one cannot φ by doing A unless *p*, then 'I thought *p*' may be an immediate response to the misfiring of A because ~*p*.

But ought it not to be a memory of a belief?—Whether one calls it a memory depends on how long after the mistreading it is said. If I switch on the light, saying at once 'I've switched on the light', that is not a memory. If the *thought of the mistreading* is occurring long enough after to be called a memory, then 'I thought there was a step' is a memory. A memory of the treading in order to tread on a step — which was not there. 'But then it was the memory of an action, not of a belief!' We have got it the wrong way round: the misfired action gives the report of the thought its meaning. The thought explains the action only by making it clear what sort of — misfired — action it was.

'Then the subsequent memory is a memory, not of having thought something, but of a response — or is itself a response, to the misfired action.' That is quite correct. — 'But doesn't that mean that the words of the memory are *false*? The words related to the time of the mistreading, but the response came after. If the subsequent memory is a memory of the response, it is a memory of the thought "I thought there was a step". If it is itself a response, it is just an invention. And whenever the response occurs, it is itself false, just an invention.' If one knows that one cannot φ by doing A unless *p* (mount or descend a step by treading a certain way unless there is a step there), then one cannot do A in order to φ unless one *believes p*. But the belief that *p* may not be a separate condition, but may exist *inasmuch* as, in suitable circumstances, one does A in order to φ. In those circumstances 'I thought *p*' interprets A for the outsider; for me, it does not interpret A; nor is it something I tell myself; it is a characteristic reaction. If the thought 'I thought there was a step there' or 'There wasn't a step there!' is my — immediate — reaction to the situation, then that is just what it is for my explanation or subsequent memory to be true. To think otherwise is to be misled by the superficial form of the language, which makes one look for something at the time that the belief consisted in.

In innumerable cases, I believe something I am told. When? Well, when I am told. That again makes it look as if 'I believed it' were the report of an act which took place at the time. But here once more the question of duration shows it is not so: for the duration of belief is not the duration of any action. Note that in the mis-stepping case, the question '*How long* did you believe there was a step there?' is quite inappropriate.

Another case: I have to signal when a distant moving object passes a point. I watch intently, and when I think — believe — it is passing, I give the signal. This is certainly non-dispositional! But what are we to make of the question of duration here? Once the thing has passed the point I no longer think it is passing; but that does not mean I have changed my mind. If I subsequently believe that it was passing when I originally thought it was, is that the continuation of the belief I had when that belief's expression would have been 'It's passing now!'? Well, we may say so if we like, but if we do, we must acknowledge that we are *determining a concept* of continuation of the same belief. For nothing about this is determined before we make this decision. If anything, the weights lie rather against deciding this way: at least if the form of the subsequent belief is 'It was passing when I thought it was'.

If I acquired information suddenly, would that mean I suddenly believed these new things? Not at all—we would only say that if at first I doubted it and then the change to belief was sudden.

These few examples of non-dispositional uses of 'believe' should make us aware what a curious concept belief is. Of course a concept is curious only from a certain point of view. The point of view here is something like this: psychological concepts are some of them dispositional, some 'episodic', and if one concept should appear to be both, it is surely a combination of at least two rather different ones. An 'episodic' psychological concept—according to the same point of view —will correspond to a mental event or a state of consciousness. Intention is a typical 'dispositional' concept, making up one's mind a typical 'episodic' one. A pain, an inner sensory image, an occurrent thought—all these are 'episodic'. Attitudes are dispositions, feelings are episodes, hence when thinking about fear or hope, we may want to distinguish the concept of fear as it occurs in 'He is afraid there will be a third world war within twenty years' and as it occurs in 'He is in a fright'—and similarly for hope.

But belief does not fall into these classifications. Once we have noticed that there are many uses of 'believe' which are not dispositional, we may be inclined to differentiate, to take it that we have here another *sense* of belief; and that here 'belief' will be the name of a mental episode. But it seems wrong either to think that 'believe' has another sense than that which informs it when it is applied dispositionally, or to think that when it is applied non-dispositionally it signifies a mental act or state of consciousness.

When I do suddenly believe something; or believe it when I am told it, my belief is not an act; but does it perhaps *begin* with an act? If I suddenly believe what I have previously doubted, perhaps the belief does begin with an act, namely the thought 'So it is true'. But if I believe what I am told straight away, I do not normally have that thought.

Here one is inclined to postulate an inner assent, or act of acceptance. For it is not like the mistreading case. There it was very obvious that there is *nothing* of the sort that a crude way of taking the surface grammar suggests, at the time referred to. But here we look back and remember *believing*. Yet belief itself is not an act! So surely there was in some way an acceptance. And not only when I believe what I am told, but also in this case: I have just heard and doubted a story, and now I notice an expression on someone's face, as a result of which I *believe* the story — though I do not frame the thought 'So it is true!'.

What happened here? Did I click into the state of belief? And was doing so *assenting*?

This suggests a parallel with intention. Intention may be initiated with an act of decision. So we have:

| Decision | Act of assent |
| Intention | Belief |

Then 'I suddenly believed' would mean 'I suddenly inwardly assented'. It would be an accident of language that we say 'I suddenly believed', but hardly 'I suddenly intended'.

But note: at this point we seem to have two candidates for the role of initiating act of a 'disposition' which is a belief that p. One is an *occurrent thought* that p or that 'p' is true; and the other, an inward assent. Of course, if both of these exist, there is no difficulty: sometimes one, sometimes the other, might perform this role. Accepting for the moment the concept of 'occurrent thought' — we shall probe it later — we will address ourselves to the question of assent.

II

On Assent: The Problem

Philosophers of former times have regularly treated of believing as if it were primarily a mental doing on the part of the believer, as *we* are taking thinking *of* something to be a mental act. For example, there is an old definition of belief as *cogitatio cum assensu* — thought plus assent. — What we *first* mean by 'assent' is the giving of some external sign, like nodding or saying 'yes'. But if we think of assent as an element which is added to a thought when the thought is believed, it is clear that we are no longer taking it as an external sign given by one person to another. We are supposing that there is a mental act: assenting.

In considering this we are driven two ways. Is there really any such thing? It seems to elude us when we look for it. Yet also, do we not need to postulate assent as added, when we believe, to that grasping of a sense which happens when we understand, but do not believe, a thought?

At least, however, everyone will agree that assent cannot be a separate mental act which could happen by itself, as one may make chewing movements without chewing anything. Assent must be *to* something which the assenter has in mind.

Assent from one person to a proposition formulated by another gives us the picture of two procedures: the formulation of something assertible — what Frege calls a 'judgeable content' — and the assent to, or inward assertion of, that content. When someone thinks within himself that such-and-such is the case, he has inwardly done both things.

With this picture in mind, it would seem natural to take a view somewhat as follows: 'to think' has two broadly distinct senses. In one, 'think' is roughly equivalent to 'believe' (or, in appropriate contexts, 'intend'), while in the other it means 'to have an intelligible content before one's mind'. Whenever a report of thinking implies that the thinker believed what he thought, 'think' is being used in the first sense. This is often dispositional in its application. Where it is not dispositional, but refers to an episode, as in 'I suddenly believed him', or 'Just for a moment I thought that …' we have a case of thinking in the second sense, accompanied by assent. The definition of belief as 'thought plus assent' does therefore have some application, but only to a restricted range of cases. It has to be rejected as a general definition because one does not need to be thinking of what one believes. To be sure, the older philosophers knew this, for they spoke of 'habitual' as opposed to 'actual' belief in such cases. But that betrayed that they thought belief was first and foremost an act of mind, and secondarily the habit of performing that act. There is however no such thing as an act of belief; in the 'episodic' case, the act is that of assent, conjoined to a thought which is either actively produced or passively received into the mind.

This gives us a neat dissection of assent out from occurrent thought, except where a report implies their combination and is equivalent to an 'episodic' report of belief. Not that assent is conceived as separable from a thought: but the thought can occur without 'assent'.

The account will not do, however, because it is false in its central contention, namely that wherever a report of thinking implies that the thinker believed what he thought, 'think' is being used in the 'belief' sense. The mistake is apparent for a case like this: 'As I increasingly often do nowadays, I was sitting and thinking that my daughter was getting remarkably attractive when …'.

If we think we understand the notion of 'assent' we surely will count this a case of 'cogitation plus assent'; but the report is not that I was sitting and believing ... The error of thinking that belief was an act of mind comes out most clearly if we consider the absurdity of saying that someone is engaged in believing something, as he may be engaged in thinking it or may be busy with his imagination.

But what is assent? 'I inwardly assented' — what took place? Well, for example, I *thought to myself* that it was as he was saying. So in this case the assent took the form of another thought. On the view we are considering, however, this thought in turn will be distinguishable from assent to it. But it could only play the part assigned to it if it was assented to. This will hardly do as an account — or analysis — of assenting to something.

If I inwardly said, or somehow thought, '*Yes!*' to what I heard, the same objection doesn't arise; but 'I inwardly thought "Yes!"' seems to be a quite particular report, special to some occasions and not retailing what is to be expected in connection with every acceptance of what one hears. An inward assent, then, seems to be either something which only occurs in *some* cases, or a chimera.

'Well, what we *mean* by assent is what distinguishes believing from merely formulating or grasping a thought.' — This will be why it was right to say 'We are inclined to *postulate* an inner acceptance'; for we do not find such a thing, only it seems to be required.

Let us consider two lines of argument, one suggesting that 'assertedness' is an extra which attaches to a thought and the other suggesting that it isn't an extra feature at all, but is intrinsic to the thought if the thought is susceptible of it at all. At most, on the second view, it will be a defeasible feature of such a thought; that is to say, such a thought will be an inward assertion in its own right, unless some special circumstance takes away that character.

For the one view:

1. First, a thought may be before my mind without my assenting to it, as when I read or hear something and merely take it in without adopting any attitude to it.
2. Again, I may say: 'I can't grasp that thought, can't think those words together as a thought', and then 'Ah, now I've got it!' So here there is a 'thinking of the sense' which does not imply acceptance.
3. And when I do accept the proposition, what I accept is what I previously grasped and weighed. So there is a thinking of the sense which is different from the judgment in which the sense is asserted.

In the judgment, however, the sense is certainly formulated and understood, so here there are two things, the thinking of the sense and the thinking of things *as so* — using the sense, which gives *how* things are if it is true. This is not a thought of an extra, but an extra thing done *in* 'thinking the sense'.

4. We may call it imagining and not thinking when the assertible content is before one's mind. But this 'imagining' is not just a mental picture: it is the thought *of a being so*, which is not yet nailed down in *assertive* thought *as so*. Spinoza, indeed, thought that even a mental picture — say of a winged horse — involves 'affirming wings of a horse', but he was surely wrong. And *we* say that even attaching the attribute 'winged' to a horse does not involve affirming, i.e. asserting, that attribute of a horse.

5. Again, the same thought occurs in e.g. an if-clause and asserted — so assertion is an extra.

6. Again, I can say to you: 'Frame a thought — anything, it can be false or absurd if you like.' You think within yourself 'She's got a tail'. But you aren't thinking that I have a tail — for that, something must be added.

7. Again, I may think a certain thought without meaning it seriously — e.g. I see my friend pouring gin (as I know it to be) from a bottle labelled 'nicotine' — and I think facetiously to myself 'He's poisoning us'.

8. Or again it 'crosses my mind that *p*' without my 'really believing it'.

9. Or again, I have an impression, or it strikes me, that something is the case, without my subsequently having any opinion at all, so I never *believed* it. (And in this case, though not in others, I would have had to dwell upon it, if I was to believe it.)

10. And, finally, what are we to say about stories? Russell's dictum, that a fiction is a class of lies, is surely absurd. In a story, we are not concerned with truth-values; we are not asserting our sentences, but using them simply to present their senses.

These seem to be the reasons for regarding assertion as an extra which attaches to thought. Against this view, however, we may argue: It is mere mythology so to introduce a mental analogue of Frege's assertion sign. For:

1°. Elocution and acting and reading: the utterance of '*p*' in these circumstances is not asserting *p* not for lack of an extra assertableness but because the sentences aren't occurring in their usual roles.

2°. It is as much one thing to think within myself that *p*, as to *merely frame the thought* that *p*.

3°. As we have already seen the 'inner assent' is merely postulated; we do not experience, cannot recall, and know nothing of, the quite general performance of any such act.

4°. What is before my mind when I understand something I hear or read is *what is being said*. We may call this a proposition, and grant that a proposition—a certain sort of sentence in its context—is, or contains, a thought. But that is a non-psychological sense of 'thought'. Understanding what I hear or read is not proved to be the activity of 'thinking a sense' by the fact that what I understand is in that non-psychological sense a thought. And don't I understand both the asserted and the unasserted proposition? So assertion can be *in* what I understand. And so, though there are characteristic mental procedures which I may call 'getting to think the sense' when I experience difficulty in understanding, there is no reason to say that there is always such a procedure when I understand.

5°. It is said: when one thinks that *p*, one not merely thinks the sense of *p*, but thinks *it is so*. But, *isn't that already the sense of p?* Here those who think of assertion as an extra feel an immense difficulty. To be sure the sense of 'The cat is on the mat' is that the cat is on the mat, that it is so that the cat is on the mat. And that sense is present even when e.g. the proposition is only a disjunct. But— they want to say—when it is judged, asserted, what is in question is not just the sense—but that the cat IS on the mat. One has advanced to reality itself. 'Judgment is incomparable', Frege says; and Hume speaks of the inexpressible character of the idea as believed. It is something *sui generis*! To be sure the sense is: that it is so, but it isn't; IT IS SO, and that reality of its being so is what we get at when we *assert* it.

Only, as a proposition may be false, there may not be that reality, so we have to say: is what we *mean* to get at.—This too is what Gilson was about in saying that existence can't be conceptualised. With the judgment you *mean* real existence, and the asserted character of the sense when it is meant in that way can't itself be formulated in a sense at all.—That is, roughly, how we are driven to talk; and is it not evident that we are banging our heads on a wall?

That things are thus, we say, is the sense of p; and perhaps that things are thus is very inconvenient. But the sense of p isn't inconvenient! So is 'that things are thus' ambiguous? Meaning in the one case just a possible state of affairs, but in the other the reality that assertion reaches or intends to reach through to? But this cannot be an ambiguity—it is p that is in question all the time, not some different proposition. *That p* is what is inconvenient, if it is inconvenient that p. Indeed, this simply means: 'p, and it is inconvenient if p'. So we may grant that in a way 'that p' is ambiguous. For if we give an account of 'that p is the sense of q', p will not appear as a conjunct, as it does in our explanation of 'It is inconvenient that p'.—Now is this to concede the point? For, it might be said, in appearing as a conjunct, p is here *asserted*: it's not as if the conjunction were a subordinate clause. But that is not true! If I say '"It is inconvenient that p" simply means "p and it is inconvenient if p"' I have not asserted p. Not at all.

A similar point holds against the argument that the same thought occurs in an if-clause and when asserted, so that assertion must be an addition to the thought. For the argument 'If p then q, but p, therefore q' is valid whether anyone asserts p and the conclusion or not. The difference that it makes for p to occur as antecedent and as it occurs in 'But p' is there whether or not p is being asserted by anyone. It is there for example when there is a genuine argument but this part of the argument is purely suppositious. Thus, even if there is a mental counterpart of whatever it is about p by itself that doesn't hold in 'If p then q', that mental counterpart won't be mentally assenting to p.

Thus one valid point in Frege's conception of the assertion sign—namely its distinction of the proposition as clause from the proposition standing by itself as a whole—should be separated from his use of it to mark that the proposition is, say, a theorem for him. —In that use, the assertion sign does not *say* that the proposition is, say, a theorem—otherwise the assertion sign could occur within an if-clause. If it marks theorems without being governable by 'if', then it is either merely a useful flagging of theorems, or signifies nothing but that the author believes the propositions so marked. But that fact is irrelevant both to the content and the argument—the book would convey the same to us even if the author did not believe what he wrote, like Saccheri constructing non-Euclidean geometry.

The fact that a proposition that is only part of another one may be unasserted does not tend to show that a proposition that is not part of another is unasserted until something extra accrues to it. Rather the contrary.

However, these are considerations about propositions, 'thoughts' in a non-psychological sense. Maybe they show the invalidity of some of the arguments for assertion as an extra element attaching to a thought that is *believed*; for these arguments (3–5 above) turn out to be really about 'thoughts' in this non-psychological sense themselves. But if Frege's actual use of the assertion sign signifies that the author believes the propositions he marks with it, then perhaps it does express what we are looking for: namely something added in the thinking of a thought when it is a thinking *that* ...

But is anything added to what was there when the same idea was 'merely entertained'? Certainly I sometimes merely 'frame a thought' or 'have it occur to me' without believing it. And certainly this *contrasts* with the case where I am thinking *that* it is so. In both cases 'thinking is going on', as William James puts it. But isn't the framing of a thought a different thought from the thinking that ... in relation to the same content? And so *not* a component of the latter? For the latter is as much one thing as the former.

That is to say, the idea that the thought is the same in the two cases arises from the fact that the 'thought' in the non-psychological sense is the same. For if asked *what* thought I framed, to myself, I come out with a proposition — the very one that I came out with if my thought was a thinking *that* ... instead of a mere framing of the thought that ...

Here belongs the idea, from the side of the defeasibility theory: my real thought, if I am not thinking to myself that *p*, but merely framing that thought that *p*, is 'possibly *p*' or '*p*?' or 'suppose *p*'. As, if I am invited to frame a false thought, and I come out with 'twice two is five' it may reasonably be said that my thought in doing so was 'It is false that twice two is five'.

But if the idea of 'one of them having let us down' crossed my mind, without my accepting it, does that mean that my thought was 'Possibly one of them has let us down'? No: I might say the thought crossed my mind, but I did not think it possible nor yet impossible; it was merely there as a mental picture might be. The thought is the 'thought of a possibility', then, only in *this* sense: the proposition giving its content is 'logically possible'. We know what it would be like for it to be true. But of course a thought which crosses my mind may also be an impossibility, and its impossibility may or may not be apparent to me.

It seems to make a difference whether the content of a thought is given by, say, 'N married' or rather by 'N is married'. But what is the explanation of the difference? It cannot just be the 'is' — if our language had no copula, what would the difference be then? One would use the same form of words to report the content in both cases, and perhaps, if the context did not make everything clear, add 'but I didn't believe it' or 'and I believed it'. But belief is not an act.

It appears that both the theory of the extra and the defeasibility theory fail. Each seems to involve a myth: the defeasibility theory, that of a sort of content which if it occurs in the mind at all must be being believed, or must be being believed unless there is some explanation why not—e.g. there is a background of reasons to doubt it; and the other, that of the indescribable addition, the act of assent. Both views must arise from failure to understand.

It is a particular example of a situation which often arises in philosophy—e.g. in the dispute between nominalism and realism, or behaviourism and Cartesianism. We are confronted with something intensely problematic—in this case the difference between the occurrent thought which is something that 'one thought', and the thought which is merely an idea. One party opted for mental assertion as an extra ingredient, the other for assertedness as an intrinsic, but nevertheless defeasible, character of what occurs. Yet neither view leaves us satisfied.

III

The Solution

We have so far been speaking of inward assent as if it were mere inward assertion—an act of mind corresponding to the Fregean assertion-sign. In doing so, we take seriously the more psychological explanations of assertedness: we invoke a mental act when we distinguish a proposition's being *sincerely* asserted from its being insincerely asserted or uttered as a piece of elocution or, again, as a mere supposition. 'Inward assertion' is then necessary for sincere assertion; insincere assertion will be the *pretence* that inward assertion is present. This has to be distinguished from the *intention* that is necessary for any assertion at all to be made, even insincere assertion.

The view of assertedness as an extra and the defeasibility theory seem to fail in different ways according as we look at the question logically or psychologically. We look at it logically when we contrast the proposition as a disjunct with the proposition as the whole of what is said. We look at it psychologically when we think of the proposition's being *meant as so.*

The defeasibility theory fails as a psychological theory: a theory, namely, that we must believe, affirm, any judgeable content that is present to our minds unless some special circumstance accounts for our not doing so, or nullifies the affirmation. (Such special circumstances were supposed to be: a background of knowledge which causes doubts or causes rejection; the thought's being embedded in a more complex thought. The case we imagined of facetiousness in one's thought and the story-telling situation, would nullify the assertoric character of the thought.)

The theory fails in making gratuitous claims as to what must be believed. Without good grounds, it denies the possibility of a 'mere idea' in which there is no belief, though nothing suggests scepticism either. The child, according to Spinoza, must believe *everything* that presents itself to its mind — for how can it distinguish? But we can say with more right: it can *believe* nothing; for how can it distinguish? For, granting for the sake of the argument that the baby has no power of *dis*senting: why should that mean that it must *assent*? Has it that power?

Where does negation come into the account? Suppose we present the defeasibility theory, in its psychological form, like this: if a 'judgeable content' is before the mind, the mind must *eo ipso* be assenting to it, unless something prevents this. Well, if a negative thought is before one's mind, then the thought which it negates is so equally, for the negative thought contains the thought which it negates! If one can form the negation of an idea, will not the corresponding negative idea be in the offing whenever an idea is? But if one cannot, then what can assent amount to?

'False and fictitious ideas have no positive feature', Spinoza says, 'by which they are called false or fictitious; but are considered as such only from the lack of knowledge' (*De Intellectus Emendatione*). The first [sentence] is surely right; falsity is not, for example, part of the *sense* of a proposition, and ideas do not as it were come in two colours, true and false, any more than accurate and inaccurate drawings do. But his second sentence betrays that he thinks the falsity of an idea to be the same thing as error or at least ignorance on the part of one who has it. But that is to take 'idea' in the sense of *belief*, not in the sense of *image* or *conception*. If there were a race of men which never lied and never made mistakes they might still formulate falsehood in formulating truth. At least they would do so if they had language in which yes-no questions were formulated and answered; and in which there were disjunctions and conditionals.

'But what we *mean* by your thought is your judgment! If something occurs, or is presented, to you, either you think it is so or you think it isn't so, or you suspend judgment — i.e. you think you can't tell. And it is this total result, which *must* follow on the presentations, and which always is a judgment to some effect or other, which is your thought. So a thought, where there is a judgeable content presented, includes assent to it unless there is some withholding action such as dissent or suspension.' Of course, if we don't call something a thought unless it is a judgment, then we settle the matter an easy way, by giving a definition. But there are many thoughts that are not judgments. E.g. such as are expressed by 'If only he would come!' And why should the expression of a thought not be 'It just crossed my mind that N. is in London'—without this implying that I actually think he is? Of course, this is just where we say 'as a possibility'. But that does not mean that a thought was in my mind in a modal form. The thought 'It just crossed my mind that possibly N. is in London' would be a different one.

What is right about the objection is this: if I express my thought simply by giving the proposition, that does imply that I thought that N. was in London. This fact may lead to the picture of a sort of content which must be being thought *to be so*, if it is before the mind at all. For the *proposition* was the expression of it.

Another point that is related to this one: when I hear or read something, and I believe it, what I believe is already an *asserted* sense. In spelling out the conception of assent as an extra we spoke of two procedures, one of setting up the assertible content and the other of assenting to it or asserting it, and observed that when someone 'is thinking something', then, by this Fregean account, he will have inwardly done both things. As if, when he believes what someone else says, the other had *merely* formulated the assertible content. But there is no such division of labour. What the other put before him will already have been an assertion, and that was what he believed.

Yet Frege might reply that one might *believe* the unasserted component clauses within the other's assertions, so what is believed does not have to be already an assertion. Wittgenstein observes that the assertion sign may serve to mark off the whole period, distinguishing it from the clause within the period, and he remarks that if I hear the words 'it is raining' and do not know whether they are the whole sentence, they do not serve to tell me anything. That is true enough; so, if what is in question is believing what I am told, I do not yet know what to believe. But even in this case I may believe something I hear— it may strike me as so—though no one is telling me it. And must not what I believe be what the words say, i.e. assert? This clause is a proposition: does it not 'show how things stand if it is true, and *say* that they do so stand'? That which I assent to must, as the *Tractatus* says, already have a sense; assertion cannot give it one. It is true that this sounds verbally like an agreement with Frege; but I think that what is intended here is really an attack on him. 'Already having a sense' here means: already *saying that* such-and-such is the case, and not awaiting an act of assertion in order to do so.

For the proposition is an instrument which I can use to make assertions with, just because *it* says that ... In many situations it no more depends on me that my uttering it is an assertion, than it depends on me that 'and' and 'or' are logical connectives. The instrument is there to my hand; that is why there is such a thing as *my* asserting *by its means*.

Let us then distinguish assertion as a personal act and assertion as done by propositions, sentences, themselves. Being an assertion will thus be a *logical* character of a proposition as such, because of which it is the instrument of personal assertions. Now, if we say this, we still have two connected problems on our hands. First, there is such a thing as (logical) unassertedness of a proposition; for it is correct to say that '*p*' occurs, but unasserted, in 'if *p* then *q*', though this is not an observation about what personal acts of assertion are or are not going on. But how can this be, if the proposition as such says, i.e. asserts? Second, suppose I do hear a clause 'it is raining', without knowing whether this is the whole of what is being said, and suppose hearing it does make me believe that it is raining, without committing the error of thinking I am believing what the speaker is telling his hearers — is this not in an important sense just an accident? May we not compare it to a case in which I hear the words 'Smith is clever', which in fact are being spoken in the whole sentence 'The man who taught Smith is clever' — and they similarly occasion my belief that Smith is clever? (They strike me as containing a truth which I had not realised.) If that happened, we might compare my belief to the belief in what I hear from the rabbinical 'daughter of the voice': I hear a stray phrase as I stand in a crowd, and I seize upon it, give it some personal application, and believe that, taking it as a sort of oracle or revelation. If the latter suggestion were correct, then it would be wrong to say that '*p*' occurs at all in 'if *p* then *q*'. For if I am occasioned to believe that Smith is clever by hearing the last three words of 'The man next to Smith is clever', I am occasioned to believe it by words that, where they occurred, did not constitute the proposition 'Smith is clever' at all. But this is not how it must be if I hear the last three words of 'He won't be there if it is raining' and these occasion me to believe that it is raining. In this case I *may* believe just what the 'if' clause genuinely says, not some accidental construction of my own from words which have not this application. I say 'I *may* believe', not 'I do believe', because it has to be determined whether the present tense proposition 'it is raining' really occurs there in the whole sentence. It might be future in sense and then what I believe would indeed be a re-construe on my part. There really is, however, such a thing as legitimately saying 'I believed the suggestion in the "if" clause that I heard'. So that proposition can really be said to occur, unasserted, in the 'if' clause.

This brings us back to the first problem. How can we say both that the proposition itself asserts, and that it occurs unasserted? For in both claims we are speaking of a logical character of the proposition — not of assertion with a personal subject.

The problem posed here has, I believe, been solved by my friend J.M. Rountree,[1] who offers the following definition of 'assertion in a context': An occurrence x of a proposition 'p' in a context C is an asserted occurrence of 'p' if every sentential context in C of which x is a part entails 'p'. By this definition, for example, if we take:

$$p \text{ and } q, \text{ and if } p \text{ then } r$$

as our context C, the first occurrence of p is an asserted occurrence and the second one is not. To test whether an occurrence in a context is an asserted occurrence we examine the sentential contexts containing that occurrence in order, starting with the occurrence itself. At this first stage any occurrence of a proposition will of course pass the test. And this is what justifies the claim that the proposition is in itself an assertion. Each proposition can be considered as its own context. The 'p' in '$\sim p$' entails p. So it is asserted in itself, and only unasserted in '$\sim p$'. — We next take the next narrowest context within C, in the above case 'p' and 'q' and so on up. If each one up to the whole context C entails 'p', then we say that that was an asserted occurrence.

This definition is of 'assertion in a context'. A context C is further said to be complete if no sentence connected with C yields a total context C' which does not entail C. Thus Miss Rountree. I would amplify (or clarify) by saying C is complete if no sentence connected with C, or in which C is embedded, yields a total context C' which does not entail C. The entailment in question is transitive. Hence if an occurrence of 'p' is asserted in C and C is complete, that occurrence of 'p' may be called an 'absolute' assertion of 'p'.

---

[1]   *Ed.* The person referred to is better known as Mrs Julianne Mott Jack MA, sometime Tutorial Fellow in Philosophy of Somerville College, Oxford, a younger colleague of Elizabeth Anscombe.

The assertion sign is then seen to have the function of a *signal of completeness*, not at all of a sign which imparts the assertive character to what it embraces, a character which we have seen to be mysterious, perplexing, unintelligible, as an addition to a proposition.

Rountree actually gave a definition of 'absolute' assertion: An occurrence of 'p', call it x, is an assertion of 'p' iff 'p' is entailed by every sentential content actually (or actually intended) containing x. She regards the full stop convention as one which serves the purpose of announcing that no sentence connected with C will yield a total context containing C which does not entail C. I regard the reference to intention as somewhat unsatisfactory, and the account of the full-stop convention as incorrect. This is connected with my addition (if it is an addition) of the qualification 'in which C is embedded'. I don't know whether Rountree regards 'John knows that p' as a sentence connected with 'p'. If so, my addition is mere clarification; if not, it must be added. Now a long string of propositions between full stops may occur in reported speech, thus: 'The ambassadors spoke as follows: "......."' and the prefatory phrase indicates that nothing that follows is 'complete'. The full stop convention would at best indicate completeness in the sentences so marked off as originally supposed to be said by the ambassadors.

A signal of completeness is not generally required. This can be seen from the fact that, by the definition, if 'p and q' is complete then so are 'p' and 'q' taken severally. To say this, however, leaves open the question 'Is a signal of completeness quite generally redundant?' Certainly we need to know *what is being said* to us, and therefore we need to know when we have complete contexts. We ordinarily know this without a sign whose function is to serve as a signal of completeness. That is to say, we know what is being said because we recognise completeness without a sign that signals completeness. But that is not to say that there is nothing to know here; there is something—not itself part of the proposition—of which there can be a sign. This, though not required, is thus not meaningless; and so we falsify another proposition of the *Tractatus*: 'If a sign is not *needed*, it is meaningless.'

Note that a signal of completeness is not equivalent to the phrase 'This is complete: ...'. For that could in turn go into the proposition 'If this is complete: ..., then', and in that case the proposition hypothesised as complete is not complete.

We have observed that the defeasibility theory was poorly grounded when it was taken as a *psychological* theory. Even logically it is not quite right; but it is trying to say something that is true. It is not right to say that a proposition *loses* its assertedness in some contexts. But it is right to say that a proposition in itself is an assertion and that it is not asserted in every context in which it occurs. That makes it sound as if it did lose something in contexts in which it is not asserted. But not so. 'Not asserted in the context C' is the negation of 'asserted in the context C', not yet the negation of 'asserted'. We introduce, as the basic notion of assertedness, *assertedness in a context*—which may be the proposition itself, in which context it is always an assertion— and an absolute notion of assertion has to be defined in terms of assertion in, and completeness of, a context.

The understanding of completeness may be called 'knowledge how' rather than 'knowledge that'. It is knowledge *how to take* what one learns or reads. (See *Philosophical Investigations* 527.)

I contrasted the *logical* character 'assertedness', the logical characterisation 'an assertion', with assertion with a personal subject. I wanted to insist that personal asserting is something we can do because the tools of assertion—the propositions we can construct in our language—lie ready to our hand, and it is not the personal act of asserting which confers their assertive character on the propositions.

This means that the distinction 'asserted–unasserted because only a disjunct' is a completely different one from the distinction 'asserted– unasserted because only elocution practice, or only in utterance in a play, or only a story'.

Someone hears me elocuting, and saying 'The rain in Spain falls mainly in the plains'. He says 'I wonder if that's so'. Does that mean that he didn't understand it was only elocution?

Whether something is personally asserted in a sentence that says something may in part be a psychological enquiry. 'He didn't *say* that *p*, he only said '*p*' in his sleep', we may say; or 'I wasn't *saying* that *p*, I was only repeating—with amazement—the thing I heard someone else say the other day'.

It is different if we say something is unasserted because it is a fiction. If Russell's 'A fiction is a class of lies' is inept, then it is so because a fiction is not supposed to be believed. But that means that it is asserted—only we have this strange taste for assertions that are not supposed to be believed, and such assertions we decide to say are not 'really' asserted.

IV

On Performatives: An Apparent Exception

'John knows that p', 'I know that p', 'Hitler pointed out that p' all contain p asserted. (It is often necessary to point this out for 'pointed out' when students use this expression in their essays.)

But what about the following:

> I say that p
> I declare that p
> I swear that p
> I give you my warrant that p
> I guarantee that p
> I promise that p
> I bet that p

Do not all of these forms contain 'p' asserted? And yet they do not accord with the definition. For certainly, if I say, swear, warrant, bet or promise that p, it does not follow that p is the case.

Let us distinguish between 'I say that p' as an emphatic way of saying that p, and as an observation; and again, between 'I promise that p' as a promise, and as an observation. E.g. I am reporting on the content of two reports which I am examining; one is my own, and the other someone else's. I say things like 'He says that John left before Smith began to speak, but I say that he left during Smith's speech'. If this is how 'I say that p' is being used, there neither is nor seems to be any assertion of 'p' on my part as I make the report as to my own report.

The same contrast can be made about promising. For example, I write a letter containing a promise, and indeed, using the very form 'I promise ...' to promise. At the same time I say to someone who is with me 'I am promising so-and-so that I will ...' And to this I may add 'Mind you, I haven't the faintest intention of doing it' — an appendix which would contradict the promise itself, though it does not contradict the report that I am promising.

'I promise' was usefully labelled a *performative* by J.L. Austin. Subsequently, attempts were made by him and others to extend his insight far beyond the limits within which it can be made clear and is useful. The original notion was — to offer a first, rough and approximate account — that of an expression the use of which was itself, or was itself integral to, the action which it signified. Thus in suitable circumstances, to say 'I promise that p' is to make the promise in question, so that the utterance of the words is not a report of something else that I am doing (or not doing), as is for example 'I am jumping up and down'. We can give the following rule-of-thumb method for determining whether an expression has a performative character: can you significantly attach to it the word 'hereby'? As: 'I hereby promise', 'I hereby swear', 'I hereby guarantee', 'I hereby dub thee knight'. If one says 'hereby' the question may be asked 'whereby?', i.e. *what* by? And the answer may include a gesture or act besides the words; but at least includes the words, which *may* be the sole instrument of the action.

But let us consider this case: 'I am writing on the board'. (In a lecture: this is not said out loud but written on the board.) Have we not here too a situation in which an expression is produced, and the very production of the expression is itself the action which it signifies? Suppose I attach 'hereby' to *this*; may I not do so? And yet it is certain that this case falls outside what we are trying to get at with the concept of a performative use of words. If I say 'hereby' *here* I may say it when I jump up and down and say I do so. The very meaning of 'hereby' seems to be changed, that is to say, its role: it no longer points to an *instrument* of the action signified. It is, one wants to say, not the production of the noise or mark, but the production, by whatever method, of the sense 'I promise that *p*' which, in suitable circumstances makes the utterance of the words into the action they signify. But that's no good either: what about 'I am producing the sense of *this* sentence'? We shall have to emphasise '*use*' in our first rough account and distinguish it from 'production'! But what, then, is 'use'? The case of writing on the board 'I am writing on the board' shows that the point is not whether the production of words is an account of something *else*, but whether it is an *account* of anything at all. You notice that I am asserting something in what I write on the board; and the question 'Is what I write true?' is at once answered 'Yes'. But there is no such question as 'Is what she says true?' if the message is 'I promise that *p*'. We can see this by imagining a report on what my message is — the word 'message' being sufficiently general to cover the content of a description or the fact of a promise. What's she saying now — what's the message? — That she is writing on the board. — And is she? — Yes, in fact that, namely *by* writing it, was just how the message was purveyed, that was just how she asserted that she was writing on the board. So there is at once a piece of information I give and the perception by the reporter that it is true. But if the answer to 'What's the message?' is 'I promise to pay N. five dollars' the question 'Is it true?' is senseless, unless it means 'Will she really pay?' And this is the meaning of calling 'I promise' and similar expressions 'performatives':

they don't state anything, they are not accounts of anything but they help us do the promising etc., whereas my writing, which is indeed an act in which I *do* the writing, also states *that* I do the writing. Of course what is important are the *consequences* of promising: it is those and no concomitant act which give the locution its sense.

Now here is a different sort of case. Imagine someone — a king, say — with authority to confer status. He says 'He is a free man'. He might say 'He is *hereby* a free man'. And that is the man's status forthwith, just because the one with authority said so. The 'hereby' here does point to the words as instrument. So here too we have a performative *use of words*. And anyone may make such a use of words, if he can make a gift to someone by saying 'It's yours!' But 'He is a free man' and 'It's your property' are also descriptions of states of affairs. So though these utterances are performative uses of language, they are not performative expressions: they are performative uses of descriptive expressions. It is otherwise with these first person expressions 'I promise', 'I swear', and so on.

Of 'It's yours', used performatively, we can say 'It effects what it says'. But the idea of 'a performative' is the idea of an expression the 'use' of which (filled out with a content) *is* the action it signifies; we ought not to say that it *effects* what it signifies. That is, we ought to distinguish between descriptive words used performatively, as 'It's yours' or 'He is a free man' may be, and 'performatives', by pointing to this difference: the former effect what they signify, the latter are not to be so explained.

There is indeed a temptation to explain the latter as effecting what they signify. For if (in suitable circumstances) someone says 'I promise that *p*' then has it not come about that he has promised? And was this not effected by his saying 'I promise that *p*'?

But if we do say this, don't we need to explain *what* they signify? And that we *can* do in the case of the status and the gift; but in the case of the promise or the oath we cannot. Like Hume, we will find a promise 'naturally unintelligible' — i.e. there is no act which I can explain I am doing and which I *effect* by signifying that I am doing it. The concept of actions like promising is not a concept of something independent of the existence of the signs of them, as the concept of the status of freedom is a concept of something independent of the performative use of the description 'This man is free'. The identification of an act as an act of promising — the third person or first person report use — is subsequent to the existence of the promising procedure and the concept of promising is there only if the procedure is there. Therefore, though we may subsequently say that the words 'I promise that

p' effect the act that they signify, this is not an explanation of them and would leave the act wholly mysterious. The hypothesis of anyone's giving a promise, unlike the hypothesis of his setting someone free, presupposes the grammar of acts of promising. Hence the first person 'I promise' is not to be explained as something's being true of me (even though, we grant, *made* true by my utterance) which is reported when someone says 'She promised'.

I do not mean to suggest that the performative 'I promise' is essential to there being a promise. A promise may have the verbal form of a simple future: 'I will see to that'. If the circumstances and mode of saying 'I will see to that' are sufficient for that utterance to be a promise, then the addition of the performative 'I promise' will be redundant. But it is often not redundant.

Now for 'I say'. It might seem that this is always redundant. But the most we have a right to say is that it is likely to be so. It is not redundant—i.e. it clarifies what is going on—in such a context as: 'I don't want to do more than *suggest* that the question of reinstating Smith might be reopened; that an investigation into this is perhaps opportune (at least if it would do no harm), on the grounds that justice ought to be seen to be done. And I do *say* that his dismissal was not obviously justified.' Here 'I do say' makes it clear that what follows is removed from the sphere of 'mere suggestion'.

If 'I say' is redundant, it is because my utterance 'p' is evidently the action of saying that p and it does not need to be made so by prefacing it with 'I say'. And utterance of a future indicative more often needs to be made into an act of promising by the addition of 'I promise' or some equivalent.

Now for the test of assertedness of 'p'. If I say that p it does not follow that p. So it looks as if by our definition 'I say that p' was a context in which 'p' is unasserted. But 'I say that p' cannot occur performatively in an if-clause. Put there, it at once becomes the hypothetical, descriptive 'I say'. So we have a case in which the test is inapplicable to the context C where C is 'I say that p', because when we try to apply the test, the expression 'I say' ceases to be a performative.

This suggests an inadequacy in the definition of assertedness which we have given. Not that 'I say that p' fails the test in the ordinary way, but because, the test being *inapplicable*, the definition does not cover it and similar cases. Well, what a definition does not cover it ought to exclude. But we may say: If some expression containing 'p' cannot go into an 'if' clause without changing its character, then it does apparently fail the test for 'p' asserted, but in such a manner as to merit special consideration.

A 'performative' — I now use this term as a grammatical category — does not itself say anything. When it is filled out with a proposition, we may ask what is the effect of striking it out. If our performative is 'I declare that', for example, the effect of cutting it out is quite different from when it is 'I ask whether'. For in both cases what is left is an assertion (logically speaking); but in the first case cutting out the prefatory expression does not leave the speaker with any other truth-commitment in regard to his utterance, from what he had in regard to the contained utterance before. In the second case cutting out the prefatory expression gives him a truth-commitment which he did not have before. When a prefatory expression, then, is of such a sort as to fail the test through inapplicability of the test, and is, further, of the first of the above two kinds, we can say that the proposition it prefaces occurs asserted. And we can add as a rider to the definition of assertedness that a context C containing an occurrence of a proposition 'p' is to be replaced by 'p' itself if C consists of an occurrence of 'p' and of a prefatory expression of this first type. This rule will leave the definition intact, and performative 'I say that p' will appear under it after all as an assertion of 'p' to just the extent that it naturally seems to be. For note, that though we cannot have performative 'I say p' in an if-clause, we may have it as the consequent: 'If q, then I say that p'. That this is equivalent to 'I say that if q then p' comes as no surprise.

We just observed that a performative does not say — i.e. assert — anything. That this is so results also from considering the test for assertedness. For we would try to apply the test by asking whether every context connected with performative 'I say', or 'I promise', for example, yields a total context C which entails 'I say' or 'I promise'. But we are not keeping 'I say' and 'I promise' performative in asking whether they are entailed by C. Therefore the test is once more 'inapplicable'. But just for that reason 'I say that p' is not an assertion, except indeed of 'p' itself.

V

On the Voicing of Beliefs and Thoughts

Consider

　　　　　　'I believe p'
　　　　　　'I think that p'.

If we apply our definition of assertedness, 'p' does not occur asserted in these. If there is something unconvincing about this result, that is because 'I think that p' and 'I believe that p' very, very often appear to be used just as polite and modest, or nervous, substitutes for 'p'.

'I believe' and 'I think' are not performatives. One could not put the word 'hereby' in; and there is not the peculiar difficulty, the nothingness about what they signify, that we get with performatives. We may fall into many perplexities about the state of a person which is his belief, conviction, or certitude; but we do not find the quite special oddity marking performatives: namely that there is no such thing as what they signify independent of the signs themselves in which what they signify is accomplished; so we cannot even begin to explain the signs in terms of what they signify.

Belief, and even conviction and certainty, are states of animals, human and other. 'It's no good your trying to attract his attention', I may say, 'the dog is obviously convinced that I have still got his bone'. But the non-human animals cannot e.g. assert or guarantee anything. What they cannot learn here is language itself.

So when I wonder what 'I believe' signifies, the question does not lead to an immediate impasse: 'belief' signifies a state of the believing subject. So much seems clear at first, however difficult it may be to give an account of that state.

However, it then seems very curious that 'I think that p' should ever be used as a polite or modest form of the assertion 'p' itself. With this reflection we are also in the vicinity of Moore's paradox: that 'I believe p, but not p' and 'p, but I don't believe that p' are contradictions of some sort; yet not ordinary contradictions; for 'If I believe p, but not p', for example, is not the hypothesis of a contradiction.

It then becomes tempting to say 'I believe p' is not after all about me; that it is a form of assertion of 'p', just as is 'I say that p'. Then, though 'I believe' is not a performative—for one cannot insert 'hereby' —still we ought to find a way of treating 'I believe p' somewhat as we treated 'I say that p', and explain 'I believe p, but not p' as a conjunction of a pair of contradictory assertions, just as we would readily so explain 'I say p, but not p' when this is a free-standing utterance.

This would be a mistake. We cannot explain 'I believe p, but not p' as conjoining contradictory assertions, because 'I believe p, but perhaps not p' has nothing wrong with it; whereas both 'p, but perhaps not p' and 'I say that p, but perhaps not p' are objectionable. (If 'I say that p, but perhaps not p' sounds acceptable, that is because we hear the part 'I say that p' differently in this whole context—perhaps as the frequentative and not the performative 'I say'.)

We must not make short cuts. It is admittedly a fact that 'I believe *p*' and 'I think *p*' are constantly used like assertions of '*p*'. That is to say, one could often cut out the 'I believe' or 'I think' and this would strike us as changing only the *tone* of what was said. And when someone says 'I think *p*'—e.g. 'I think Smith married Miss Jones the other day'—the reply may well treat this as the assertion 'Smith ...' For the reply may be: 'If so, he committed bigamy.'

This undoubted fact is certainly extremely interesting and demands explanation. But it can only be invoked to explain the appearance of contradiction in 'I believe it's raining but it isn't', if that is not merely *a* frequent but the *only* relevant use of 'I believe'. But suppose I am examined as to my beliefs. Suppose that the interest of the discussion is what *I* believe, not whether it is true or what follows from it. They want to assess or understand some action I have started, for example, and cannot do so without finding out what I think. So they say 'We want you to tell us what you know, or think you know, and indeed what you *think*, about ...' My reply includes statements of the form 'I believe ...' Would it not be absurd here too, if I said 'I believe *p*, but not *p*'?

My reply may indeed include a number of assertions unprefaced by 'I believe'. For if the interest is in what I believe, that interest is not left unsatisfied by my expressing my beliefs in the form of assertions of the things themselves that I do believe. Someone's utterance (or note in a diary) 'I believe *p*' is not *better* evidence that he believed *p* than unadorned '*p*' would be.

This gives us our clue. The absurdity of Moore's paradoxical sentence 'I believe *p*, but not *p*' is not to be explained by saying that 'I believe *p*' is an assertion of '*p*', which stands in contradiction to 'not *p*', but rather by saying that 'not *p*' is the (ostensible) expression of belief that not *p*, which conflicts with 'I believe *p*' because this is (ostensibly) an expression of belief that *p*.

Thus 'I say that *p*, but not *p*' (where 'I say' is performative) presents us with the combination of two contradictory *assertions*, '*p*' and 'not *p*' (in the personal sense of 'assertion'); while 'I believe that *p*, but not *p*' presents us with the combination of two contradictory *expressions of belief*.

We can see why E.J. Lemmon's example 'My trouble is, I am a homosexual but don't believe it' is no counter-example to the absurdity of Moore's paradox. For the man who says this is not professing disbelief; he is using 'I don't believe it' diagnostically. His psychoanalyst, perhaps, has told him he is a homosexual, and he accepts that when he thinks of it; but he recognises—and perhaps his psychoanalyst has pointed out to him — that his off-guard thoughts and reactions *show* that he doesn't believe this. But one does not normally diagnose one's own state of belief. When 'I believe' or 'I don't believe' is used diagnostically, Moore's sentences are not paradoxical.

If 'I don't believe' means 'I disbelieve', the two paradoxical sentences are absurd in the same way; for disbelief that p is belief that not p. But if 'I don't believe' means 'I doubt whether' without implying 'I disbelieve', then the form 'p, but I don't believe it' needs a different treatment.

'p, but I doubt whether p' combines the expression of belief and a contradictory doubt. But it is a question, what is wrong with this? For doesn't 'perhaps not p' express doubt? Yet we said that 'I believe p, but perhaps not p' was unobjectionable. To be sure 'p, but perhaps not p' will never do; but at any rate we cannot simply explain the wrongness of 'p, but I doubt whether p' just by saying that it combines expressions of belief and of a contradictory attitude (in this case doubt). For, though no one can say 'I believe p, but I doubt whether p', we *may* say 'I believe p, but I *suspect* that not p'. This is a problem that we must reserve for final comment till later;[2] for the moment, all we can say is that doubt is negation of belief, but suspicion that not p, and 'perhaps not p', are not.

We have some grounds for believing that the free-standing utterance 'I believe p' does not contain 'p' asserted. Our reason was that 'p but perhaps not p' is impossible, whereas 'I believe p, but perhaps not p' is possible. This reason may not seem entirely cogent. It takes 'p' by itself as the paradigm of assertion; why should all forms of assertion follow this paradigm? This question must wait till a later chapter.[3] But there may be another point of discontent about this argument: how is it related to what we have previously said about assertion? and to what happens when we apply the test for assertedness, and see that, by our definition, 'I believe p' is a context in which 'p' is unasserted? 'I believe p' does not pass the test; but this fact involves us in a difficult discussion.

For though 'I believe' is not a performative, yet we had to draw a distinction between 'I believe' which is called 'diagnostic' and the 'I believe' of a profession, or expression, of belief. This distinction runs parallel with the difference between the performative 'I promise' and

---

2   *Ed.* Anscombe has a footnote reference here to 'Contradictory Beliefs' and to 'Degrees of Assent'; see the initial footnote to this paper.
3   See 'Degrees of Assent'.

the report 'I am promising'. In particular, 'I believe' as expression of belief can't go into an if-clause. This makes the test inapplicable in the same way as it was inapplicable to the performative 'I say'. Can we then treat the expression 'I believe' as we proposed to treat 'I say'? Is it a prefatory expression of the sort covered by our rider to the definition of assertedness? If we cut it out, what difference will that make? We have to admit that, strictly speaking, it will make a difference; for, supposing a written text, if the author added 'but perhaps not' to what he professed belief in, we shall not have changed the text into one of the form '*p*, but perhaps not *p*'. And, if he did not put in 'but perhaps not', then unless we are to distinguish senses of 'I believe', one which will endure the addition of 'but perhaps not' while the other will not, we have still altered what he wrote from something of which we can say 'He only said he *believed* ...' to something of which we cannot say this. A man who says 'I believe' must allow *us* to say 'He only said "I believe"', even if *his* conviction would not allow him to say 'but perhaps not'.

Thus the inapplicability of the test for the assertedness of '*p*' in 'I believe *p*' is not something we could circumvent as we circumvented it for 'I say that *p*'. (And of course there we would never say 'He only said he *said* that *p*'!)

So much for the question whether '*p*' occurs asserted in 'I believe that *p*'. It does not. But neither is the whole expression 'I believe that *p*' itself an assertion *when* it is an *expression* of belief that *p*. Like 'I say that *p*' it fails the test through inapplicability of the test, and so escapes the definition of assertion.

It is easy to settle things by definition. This I do not want to do: I note this result, and it appears to me to show that the definition is a good one. But the issues that are involved are deeper than any we have yet considered in putting forward the definition.

Let us go back to the dispute, resolved by the definition, between the Frege theory and the defeasibility theory. We asked whether anything was added to a thought which was a thinking *that* ... as opposed to the mere entertaining of the idea, or framing of the thought. And we suggested that the 'mere framing of a thought' is a different thought from the 'thinking that ...' the same thing. The idea that they are the same arises from the fact that the 'content' — the thought in the non-psychological, Fregean, sense of 'thought' — is the same.

This consideration suggests that, given the expression of a thought in words, we may distinguish between the part giving the content and the part which is the sustaining framework. Let us imagine some responses to 'A penny for your thoughts!'

'N is going away.'
'I think N is going away.'
'It just crossed my mind that N is going away —
not that I actually think so.'
'I hope N is going away.'
'I'm wishing that N were going away.'
'I am very glad/angry/sad that N is going away.'

In response to the first of these responses one would never say: 'But I asked for your *thought* and you replied simply with a statement about N!' No one *discovers* that sentences express thoughts; rather, we learn to speak of a person's thought partly in connection with what he says. If someone says something, and I say 'Good heavens! Why *that* thought at *this* moment?' he cannot say 'I didn't say anything about a thought, why have you changed the subject?'

It is clear that something is — ostensibly — someone's thought, say, that N is going away *if* it is clear that he is actually saying that N is going away. Given that condition, the hypothesis that it is his thought is an hypothesis only in that it is an *hypothesis* that he is not lying. For what we do discover by experience is that sentences sometimes do *not* correspond to thoughts. We have to learn to speak of a person's lies and evasions, as well as of his thoughts, in connection with what he says.

All this holds for other sorts of expression, e.g. 'Confound all politicians', as well as for propositions. The peculiarity of the proposition, say 'N is going away', is that, in suitable circumstances, it says simply that N is going away — and yet in the same circumstances is supposedly *tells a thought*. Here the thought of the speaker is given *merely* by giving the content.

But if the thought is a mere formulation of an idea, or is a pang of fear, hope, sorrow, anger, etc. then the thought is usually not told just by the proposition giving the content. It may indeed be told by the sad or joyful tone of voice in which the proposition is uttered, or by the proposition alone given a certain context in which it is produced. (E.g. everyone is making imaginative suggestions as to what has happened.) But often further words are needed, in which the proposition is embedded, like 'It just crossed my mind that ...' or 'I am seized with the feeling of hope that ...'.

Now what is it that is *asserted*, in the personal sense of assertion, when a thought is expressed? We have already indicated that it will be whatever is asserted, in the *logical* sense, by the expression used. But now we have introduced the notion of a *thought's* being expressed, or ostensibly expressed. The sort of thought which an *assertion* (logically speaking) ostensibly expresses is a thought that ... So we are asking 'What thought *that* ...' is expressed, when a thought is expressed? Now the answer is: only, if anything at all, the *content*.

For if the expression of my thought is 'I wish N were going away', then my thought is not a thought *that* I wish N were going away: it is a wish — that N were going away. And if my thought is a toying with an idea, then the expression 'I'm toying with the idea that ...' is the expression of the toying with the idea, not of the thought that I am toying ...

So we have, first, assertion in the *logical* sense; second, *personal* assertion, i.e. use by a speaker of assertions in the first sense in such circumstances as indicate that he means to be *using* them as (logical) assertions; and, finally, we can call the latter expressions of something which it is — ostensibly — the speaker's thought is the case.

And when we ask: When a thought is told, what is asserted, i.e. expressed as something which it is the speaker's thought is the case? the answer is: Nothing — except when the thought is a thought *that* ... If such a thought is expressed purely by giving the content — say 'N is going away' — then something is asserted, namely the content itself, that proposition.

Someone may say 'But I'm toying with the idea that ...' or 'I'm seized with the feeling of hope that ...' are *propositions*, and hence assertions. Well, they certainly are free-standing utterances in propositional *form*. And in some cases they may express, not the toying with the idea or the feeling of hope, but the speaker's — perhaps horrified — realisation that he is toying with that idea or seized with the hope. And then the thought that they express is indeed a thought that ... and hence by our latest explanation they are assertions on his part. But then the speaker is telling *of* the thought which was a toying with an idea or a feeling of hope — not telling *it*, as he tells his thought that John has kept his promise if he simply says 'John has kept his promise'.

Note that sometimes there is a special linguistic form like 'If only John has kept his promise!' or 'May John have kept his promise!' associated with 'I am wishing that John has kept his promise' and 'My hope is: that John has kept his promise'. Where there is such a special linguistic form, we do not find one part of the sentence 'expressing content' and another part which is the 'sustaining framework'. And no one will ever be inclined to call such expressions assertions. Let us adopt the term 'statement' to cover both assertions and utterances in propositional form which do not express thought *that* ... Then the *statement* 'My hope is that …' will be equivalent to the non-statement 'May …!' It is no surprise that a 'statement' (which is such purely from the superficial grammatical form) here comes to the same thing as a non-statement. For the truth and falsity of the 'statement' are the same sort of truth and falsity as is found in the non-statement: they are sincerity and insincerity.

Thus, although the 'sustaining framework' gives to the whole the grammatical character of a proposition, so that we are tempted to take the utterance as an assertion and to look for what is being thought to be the case, this can be seen to be a mistake. Let us avoid this mistake and use a new term for all these first person present indicatives which form such 'sustaining frameworks' in our utterances. I will call them 'voicers' for they stand in a special relation to the *voicings* of our beliefs and our — various — thoughts. A voicer is not a performative, though it does share some of the peculiarities of a performative. In particular, no voicer is an assertion.

2

Grounds of Belief

Grounds, we think, are premises for arguments. But who argues from the characters and letters in texts that he may produce that Julius Caesar existed in ancient Rome and was killed? That it was so, and that these texts, for example, go back so-and-so far, is a piece of traditional knowledge which we acquire by being told it together with many other facts belonging to the general sketch of history. We could find no purchase for any dislodgement of the facts that Julius Caesar existed, made conquests, left accounts of them, became supreme in Rome, and was assassinated.

But *why* do we believe these things? There is nothing to say but: We were taught to do so, and in such fashion that it is part of what is called 'common knowledge'; become knowledgeable in the things spoken of as familiar facts by those who are called well informed among our people, and you will know this. — Are there then never mistakes in what belongs to the general sketch in these fields? Certainly there are: when *all* that the best informed people can tell of a period is very sketchy indeed, it may turn out that greater research reveals incoherencies, so that what was taken for historical record is reassessed as picturesque novelistic pamphleteering or something of the sort: characters or synchronies drop out as merely legendary or invented or misunderstood by an author. (Xenophon's *Gyropoedia*) Why is something rejected as untrue? Because it is incompatible with what else we have in our picture. That means: we take other things as fixed points by which we judge this ostensible record. Why do we accept *them*? — They are 'traditional knowledge' and they hang together. A story, in an ancient codex, of Julius Caesar consulting Archimedes on the construction of siege engines would be taken as a

---

piece of fanciful invention by some story teller; it would not make us think we were mistaken in our dates for their lives.

Belief on grounds which can be considered as premises for arguments presupposes belief without grounds, or at any rate without grounds that can be so considered. Hume's philosophical opinion was that these ultimate groundless grounds were sense impressions. But I say that they are such beliefs as those of which one will say 'Everyone knows that!' or 'Everyone who knows anything of such matters at all, knows that!' — But may not what 'everyone knows' be wrong? Surely it sometimes may. Remember that once 'everyone knows that' could have been said of the fixity of the globe of the earth and the motion of the spheres of the heavens around it. That will have been in all the books, will have been apparently 'common knowledge', will have apparently had the same status as what has *not* been shaken, that the earth is (roughly) a globe. One must then ask oneself, if considering something of the sort: 'How would I check it?' Now: how would *I* check that there once was such a person as Julius Caesar, who lived and died in Rome in the first century A.D. — i.e. so-and-so many years ago — had a military or political career as a prominent Roman, wrote these books? What could I call a check on it? i.e. a further way of making sure? Nothing. But what could I conceive as upsetting it? Aristarchos of Samos, who was a contemporary of Archimedes, put forward the theory that the earth was not fixed, but travelled round the sun; the sun and the stars were fixed. The theory was thought false, partly because of the lack of visible parallax: the more and less distant heavenly bodies should have been seen to pass one another as more and less distant trees do to us as we go through the country in a train. It was not realised how vast the distances were (though Aristarchus made them very vast); and in the end, *after* the theory had been accepted, parallax was detected by the most powerful telescopes.

However, the imagination readily grasps that the appearance of the sun's motion would be the same, were the earth *rotating* rather than the sun *moving in a circle* round the earth. The relative sizes and motions of the heavenly bodies must be a *theory*. The existence of Julius Caesar is not a theory to account for the phenomena. So the problem: what could I conceive as upsetting it? Is not the question: what alternative theory could I devise which would equally well account for the data? Contrast the circulation of the blood, which *is* a theory to account for the data, though so well established one can hardly imagine it upset. All the same, it makes sense to ask someone to exert his imagination to construct a different theory. The difference between the existence of Julius Caesar and the circulation of the blood is that Caesar wasn't a *theory* to explain the data. – On the other hand, if I wanted to *doubt* any historical figure, the way I'd do it would be to construct the hypothesis that he didn't exist and then see if things 'fell into place' better on this hypothesis; and if I could plausibly explain away the documents which seem to say that he did. ('Seem to say' perhaps *implicitly* as a presupposition of the belief that it looks as if we should have *if* we – broadly – believe them.)

Compare my situation with that of a man of another culture, either such as the Chinese in the time when there was little communication between the Chinese and the West, or a savage. Suppose that I, a traveller, tell each of these the story of Julius Caesar, and I add that it is *true*; that is, not invented by myself or another as people may invent tales for their own fancy. We will suppose the Chinese to be cultivated, to have some knowledge of cities and empires and their records and chronicles. If he believes me, then he believes on my testimony that the life and death of Julius Caesar is treated as a matter of chronicle and record in my civilisation. (For I may not be able to give testimony to the existence of the assumed chronicles and records – I may only know of Caesar from history lessons at school and from the way he is spoken of in our civilisation.) Contrast with this the belief of the 'savage': in supposing a 'savage' I am merely supposing a man who knows nothing of permanent records, nothing of the transmission of information from generations back even by word of mouth. A man who has no chronology even in the form of a listing of generations.

Both these men, if they believe what I say, believe it on information given – *my* information. But the Chinese presumably believes on my information not just the story but also that it derives from records which originated in the events themselves. Suppose the savage has no distinct idea of something that is handed on to him by somebody else, going back in a chain of records from many hundreds of years, to *witnesses* of the event?

What we have by transmission from the past, whether the transmission is literary or oral, may go back to witnesses or not. Compare Julius Caesar with Adam; of both we have written stories; in both cases the material has been transmitted over many generations; but in the case of Julius Caesar we believe the testimony of the records to hang upon human witnesses to the events – that is part of our idea of their being *records*; while in the case of Adam, even though a man may believe in Adam, he has, or ought to have, no such belief about the origin of the story.

The point that I want to make is that when the 'savage' derives his beliefs about what happened long ago from what has been passed down to him, the question of belief being justified by testimony deriving ultimately from observers may play no part; if raised, it may not strike him as an important one at all. So when someone tells him about Julius Caesar, he may gather that this is a story told among the other one's people, which is supposed to be true; but not that it is a matter of record. Whereas the Chinaman can ascertain that the information has the same sort of character as his information about the various Emperors of the various dynasties; that if he believes his informant, it is not a matter of his now accepting the stories told by a people as part of the wisdom of their ancestors, who were taught it heaven knows how, and perhaps by seers, soothsayers, prophets, but of his learning what must be matter of record, if it can be taken as true at all.

Let us go back to the comparison of myself with the Chinaman and the 'savage'. They believe on information given: this is a clear case, for it is *my* information. On whose information do *I* believe the thing I tell them? I really cannot cite any. That someone first told me about Julius Caesar I am sure; I infer this from my present knowledge, together with the belief that I did not come into the world knowing of Julius Caesar and could not get the information without someone's telling me. Now consider the Chinaman. If he forms an intelligent belief that Julius Caesar existed, he will believe in him *as belonging to the chronicles of the people or civilisation of his informant* (or an informer of his inform-ant)—for it doesn't belong among *his* chronicles. Even if he doesn't remember who his informant was, he must remember *that* the information came from such and such a *kind* of informant, a foreigner. As the sort of information he can identify it as being, it is connected with the informant.

Not so the savage. Someone told him this story of a great man who became powerful and was killed; having observed the story, he can forget who told it to him without detriment to the information he has derived from it. For how can he absorb it qua transmitted information from witnesses? He may have that idea in relation to some of what he is told by those who brought him up, but he is not likely to have it in relation to what happened a very long time ago. It might be he could say: My grandfather had it from his grandfather who witnessed it: but pure oral tradition *inspired by the idea of witnesses as the original source* must be short-term. Surely it can't go back reliably for thousands of years. When oral tradition is accompanied by documents and inscriptions that idea can be extended much further back, because documents and inscriptions do not alter much and the times for alteration, i.e. when they are copied, are many fewer than in an oral tradition which may be altered at any new telling.

But note that in general *we* are *also* dependent on oral tradition. Books are given us by people who tell us that these are the writings of so-and-so, and they received them from those who told *them*, and so on. A book or manuscript may be accompanied by no oral tradition; but *it* will be accepted as such and such because there is a framework for it to fit into.

How could we three, the 'savage', the Chinaman and I, stand in relation to checking? It is not clear what checking could mean for the savage, perhaps repeating the story to others who may recognise it and might amend the version of it I have given. The Chinaman could check by finding out the status of what I told him, finding out its status as a matter of 'historical knowledge' on the part of the peoples of my part of the world—by learning some of our languages, seeing some of our stores of chronicles and records and our manner of transmitting historical information, and ascertaining that what I told him has the standing that it does have among our accounts of the past. *I* can't check the story at all. Read ancient sources! you may say. But if I don't know, if I can't rely on it that Julius Caesar existed etc., how can I rely on it that Suetonius, say, is an ancient source? The state of mind, of information, is not available to me, in which I can really raise the question whether Julius Caesar existed and have it rationally settled. Someone in our society just might be in such a state: suppose some school child able enough to read Shakespeare's play for himself but not grasping that the characters were historical, never having heard mention of Julius Caesar; his family and friends never name Caesar, his reading has otherwise passed Caesar by, in history at school he only 'does modern'. And now having read Shakespeare's play he speaks of it as if it had been pure invention, of Caesar and the rest as all fictitious characters. And someone tells him Caesar was a real man in history in ancient Rome. This child can then find out that Caesar was real—he goes off to the library and looks at some history books about ancient Rome.

But *I* could not be checking that Caesar was real, by looking at such books. For I assume that the question is: *Given* that the status of statements about Caesar in relation to history books is as it is, how can I check whether Julius Caesar really existed? For of course I can't 'check' that the status of the statements is what it is; that is to say, I can at best *remind* myself that it is so. And I believe statements with that sort of status.

Why do I believe them? Can I say: Given that mankind has existed on the earth for a very long time, it is reasonable to suppose that there should be historical traditions and records, and that very broadly speaking they should be trustworthy, that various things should in this way be known about the past, i.e. about the times of our fathers, which means our fathers' fathers' fathers, *and so on*. And that a good many facts should be in such a position in our knowledge as to provide a framework into which everything else must fit; and *that* Julius Caesar existed etc. is, in our tradition, among such facts? I can indeed say that. But how do I know that mankind has existed for very many generations upon the earth? — Everything I was ever taught that had any bearing on the matter assumed or implied that it was so; any *reasoning* that anyone goes in for on historical matters is within this assumption and takes certain things as quite fixed. The assumption fits in with the treatment of what are called antiquities and of books alleged to have been composed in ancient times.

I have been given this as part of my understanding of things just as much as I have been given the idea of distant continents. Suppose someone says 'But you can *visit* distant continents!' What can I do? I can travel over water or land or clouds for a long time and find myself in places, in connection with whose names I have been told: those places are in India, Australia, America. For the fact that *these places I find myself in* are related to one another and to where I am now, as may be shown on a globe, and *are* the places named in that information by those names, I certainly rely not so much upon what I am told there as upon the *implications* of what I am told. It is true that I can obtain some experiences which, in view of what I have been taught, I shall (with certainty) call seeing the dwelling houses and public building of New Orleans, say, which is this city here on the map; and that I cannot obtain any experience which I shall call seeing the streets and houses of ancient Troy or the dwelling houses and Senate House of ancient Rome. Similarly, I can obtain an experience which, in view of what I have learned, I shall with certainty call seeing the present Pope; and not any experience I will call seeing Alexander Borgia. But that will not make me *any* better placed for the rationality of my belief that there is such a person as the present Pope, than for the rationality of my belief that there was such a person as Alexander Borgia.

My knowledge of the things among which and the places in which I live is not so much 'theory laden' as 'common-knowledge laden'. I wish to say: it is a falsification here to speak of testimony: to say, for example, that it is by testimony that I know I was born. There is something else, not testimony, though acquired by education from human

beings, which is, so to speak, *thicker* than testimony. I find that I exist
—i.e. that I live—in places which are not merely 'here' and 'there' to
me, and among people and objects which are not merely 'this one' and
'that one'.—How do I mean: I *find* this is so? In saying that, am I not
speaking as if I were a naked observer without benefit of knowledge
and assumptions, whose observation reveals that he has knowledge
and assumptions?—This 'finding' is really a reflection: I *do* exist in
places that are not merely 'here' and 'there' etc.—What would it be
like if they were? I imagine being snatched out of any familiar or
intelligible surroundings and being transported through a phantasma-
goria of scenes in which I could not act and understood nothing.

It is a fact that we mostly know where we are; e.g. we wake up
from sleep knowing where we are.

'Knowing where one is' has two meanings: it may mean perceiving
oneself to be in familiar surroundings, or it may mean, as for the
traveller, knowing how the place where he is lies in relation to where
he was before and where else he might go.

Knowing where one is in the second sense *may* involve having
ideas of no different order from knowing where one is in the bare
sense of being familiar with one's surroundings: for one may know
where one is in the second sense *from* familiarity with the surroundings and habitual traversal of the regions between these and where
one was before and where one might purpose to be.

But knowing where one is in the second sense *may* and usually
does involve ideas of a different kind. I mean that the explanation of
'where one is' may involve appeal to common knowledge of places
and their relations; in the most obvious sort of case for the present day
it may involve appeal to a *map*. I travel a long time over unknown
ground; here I am, I say, 'in Carlisle'. And where is *that*? It is
unfamiliar to me; but it is not just *here*; it is 'a city in the extreme
North-West of England'. And what is North-West and what is
England?

North-West is *this* direction. And how do I know when I am still
going in *this* direction? *I* believe it in certain circumstances; but I also
believe that this belief is justified, i.e. has the backing of surveyors and
map readers who steered by the stars or by compass.

England is the country in which I live. How do I know that, and
what do I know in knowing it? I manifest the implicit acceptance of a
host of ideas, statements, preoccupations, which have been in me since
I was first taught to use these notions at all expertly.

In the sense in which my own experience perhaps shows me e.g.
that there is a stream at the bottom of the garden of the house in which

I live, my own experience does *not* show me that I live in England. Nor does their personal experience show the same to any of the people who do live in England and know it. So it isn't that I have been told by people who knew it from experience. Presumably a decision was once made; or alternatively a practice grew up, of calling all of some region 'England'; but upon what would the specification depend? Surely upon pooled information—e.g. that Hadrian's Wall could be traced from one place to another; that this village had counted as part of such a principality and so might be agreed to lie in Wales; and so on. The work of determining England and fixing the meaning of the name *would* depend on testimony—the testimony of many different people for different parts of it. The work done, people could be taught what England was (no doubt still disputing some regions). Now those who learned thereafter can hardly be said to have knowledge by testimony. They were taught to *call* something 'England'—something indeed which could in large part only be defined for them by hearsay; and they so taught those who came after them. I am an heir of this tradition. Now, I know I live in England. But by testimony? Some would say so. But there is something queer about it. *What* do I know? That the world is divided up into countries which have names, and that the one I live in is called England and is here on the map of the globe. This involves understanding the use of the globe to represent the earth. It is rather as if I had been taught to join in *doing* something, than to believe something—but because everyone is taught to do such things, an object of belief is generated. The belief is so certainly correct (for it follows the practice) that it is knowledge; for here knowledge is no other than certainly correct belief in pursuit of a practice. But the connection with testimony is remote and indirect.

3

Motives for Beliefs of All Sorts

The idea of a motive for a belief in something sounds partly queer, and again in a way all right. 'What did you want to think a thing like that for?' one might say protestingly to someone who had mistaken one's attitudes or intentions. Or again, 'Naturally he is under a strong temptation to think such and such — if it isn't so, he loses his claim to a lot of money'. Or again: 'Out of loyalty, he sticks to the conviction that such and such.' These three examples are enough to show that the concept of motive isn't wholly dissociated from that of belief, so that it wouldn't make sense to speak of motives but only of grounds for beliefs, i.e. reasons showing or tending to show their truth. Why then is there nevertheless something a bit queer about it?

The reason is partly, I believe, that there are certain features of the concept of motive, in other connections, which it can't have in connection with belief. One of the many methods at hand in doing philosophy is to think of something which one can't say, something which makes a crazy sense (perhaps no sense, but it's a joke because a crazy sense is suggested). It is a difficult art; one might have employed the Marx brothers for it: 'I've been warned to look out for a man going around with a black moustache.' — 'Well, you wouldn't expect a black moustache to be going around by itself, would you?' It shows the sort of thing I mean by 'a crazy sense', and that is illustrated by the following: 'You beast, you thought that on purpose!' 'You thought — or believed — that on purpose' is crazy, but why? — since motives for belief aren't nonsense. Is this because belief isn't an action? No: you

---

* From an undated typescript with extensive handwritten corrections and additions by the author.

can neglect something, omit to act, on purpose, and, within limits, you can be, say, melancholy on purpose, so that doesn't seem to be the objection. Nevertheless, there is *something* in it; there is a relevant contrast here between *belief* and the *act of thinking* specifically of something, or thinking a certain thought. I will consider saying 'You thought of that on purpose' with a view to clarifying the queerness of 'You thought, i.e. believed, that on purpose'.

First, note that 'on purpose' doesn't necessarily mean on purpose to bring about something else. 'You trod on my foot on purpose, I know you did' means: 'It wasn't an accident, you meant to tread on my foot.' Or: 'He avoided the lines between the paving stones on purpose.' In the childish activity there's no further purpose.

Now one may think of something on purpose to effect something; e.g. think of something boring in order to go to sleep. But can one think of something on purpose, but not with a further purpose? Well, in the following case one can. We are doing a free association game. You say 'wait', I say 'scales'. Suppose now 'scales' is a word which has significance as a joke or something of the sort in some group to which you belong. So you ask me 'Did you think of that on purpose?' and I may say 'Of course' or 'No, I didn't remember that connection at all, it was perfectly accidental'. If I 'thought of that on purpose', though it wasn't with any further purpose, there was a wider context to which the word might have reference.

In this way an action of treading on someone's toe might be a conventional signal. Then 'Did you do that on purpose?' might be asked when it is quite clear that I trod on your toe on purpose, but not clear whether what I did had that further significance on purpose. But the question 'Did you tread on the lines between the paving stones on purpose?' may *simply* relate to treading on the lines, *not* to anything further. And in this way, 'on purpose' contrasts with 'It was a mere accident, I didn't mean that to happen', like a slip of the tongue.

Now I can't 'think of scales' like that, as it were by a slip of the mind, as I can tread on your toe by stumbling or say something by a slip of the tongue.

Now how about belief? First, it is possible, though not very common, to believe something explicitly *with* a purpose. A clear case is this: Suppose I am riding a bicycle on a tightrope. I might determinedly believe that I won't wobble and fall precisely *in order not to wobble and fall*. But believing something on purpose, as opposed to *with* a purpose, in the way in which on can *think of* something on purpose, though not with a further purpose: *this* concept has no foothold at all.

And the 'on purpose' that goes with action and doesn't go with thinking *of*, that too is excluded from belief. 'By a slip of the tongue' I wrote 'bad' when I meant 'good' — as happened to Aquinas who wrote as a title to one of his articles: 'Utrum Deus sit summum malum.' But not: 'By a slip of the thinking apparatus, I thought of Plato when I meant Aristotle', and not: 'By a slip of the believing mechanism I believed he hadn't done it when I meant to believe he had done it.' This is in one way trivial: what you meant *is* what you thought or believed. It is not trivial metaphysically, for it shows that you aren't *using an apparatus or mechanism whose action is thought or belief* in thinking something or believing something.

There is something that is not excluded from the thought *of* or from entertaining the thought *that*, but *is* excluded from belief, and that is the freakish accident. Even if it suddenly and freakishly *strikes* me that something is the case, the difference between this being a 'mere idea' and my actually accepting it isn't like the difference between *this* and *that* popping into my head.

Thus, 'on purpose' has some connections when we speak of *actions* (even in the broad sense that includes omissions), which it lacks when we speak of thoughts or beliefs. For actions 'on purpose' contrast with 'inadvertently'; not so thoughts in one way, or beliefs at all — except, of course, in connection with a *previous* intention. Now (Freud apart) actions that are done *on purpose* are just the ones we assign *motives* to. Maybe I squirted soda water at you on purpose (not by accident) though not with any *further* purpose. What was my motive? Perhaps I felt rumbustious — it was pure high spirits. Or perhaps I hadn't any motive — I just thought I would! And *this* 'I just thought I would' has no place in connection with belief. 'Why did you believe *p*?' — 'Oh, I just thought I would, I just felt like it'. One can imagine that being said as a brush-off; one can imagine it as a portrayal of silliness (a literary idea of feminine silliness, perhaps). But it can't be taken straight or as serious. One feels inclined to say: that would make belief altogether *too* voluntary. As if I could set up any proposition, or any one not evidently true or false, like 'There is a policeman at the door' and believe it at will, as I can usually stand up or sit down at will. 'Consider that proposition "There is a policeman at the door": Now believe it! Now stop believing it!' That isn't an order and counter-order that we would know how to act upon. Except on the supposition that 'Believe that' implies that the speaker is saying the thing is true, and he chooses this funny way of talking to tell me, firstly that the policeman is at the door, and then that he is no longer there.

But it's *not* that belief is *merely* involuntary. 'Faced with the necessity of making up my mind, I *decided* to accept his story.' It was perhaps open to me to accept it *or* reject it; i.e. it might be true or it might be false. 'Why did you decide the way you did?' 'Well, I *had* to decide one way or the other, and this seemed best.' Not necessarily: This seemed more likely. 'Why did you have to decide one way or the other?' An answer might be: it's not in my temperament to leave such a matter in suspense; or: it's too uncomfortable.

Here we may have someone deciding to believe this way rather than that *because it seems better*. (There may be a paradox here, but let us leave it for the moment.) That is, he is giving a reason for a decision to believe something which is *not* a reason pointing to its truth. This is a clear enough case of a *motive* as opposed to a *ground* for belief, because ground for belief means reason suggesting that it is true. Now this is a motive, namely, it is *better* to believe this than that, which seems to be one that *can* be announced by the one who has it. It is, so to speak, a *reputable* motive. Is that what makes for announceability?

But there are possible disreputable motives for belief. — Because he hated Y; because he wanted Y's job; because he got a lot of money out of doing so. *That*, we know, is a possible situation. Now, can X say: I believe this because I hate Y, because I want his job, because I'll get a lot of money out of doing so? He might diagnose himself that way: I can see I believe this because …, but can his 'I believe' be the *expression* of belief when accompanied by such a 'because'?

Now, one's first inclination is to say: no, because my hating him, or there being money in it for me, has no tendency to show that it is *true* — what I am proposing to believe. But then neither has the fact that it is *better* to accept his story than to reject it, if there can be such a fact when the evidence is equally balanced. — Why might it be *better*? Well, there might be money in it, which assimilates the cases. But it might be like this: it is rather beastly to harbour suspicion against a man if one hasn't got to. It's better — pleasanter or nobler or better general policy for the sake of human relations, if in the particular case it is not *unwise* — to think well of someone than ill, or to think well of him than to remember he may equally well deserve to be thought ill of, if one hasn't got to, so let's accept his story. Of course, it is not just a tipping of the balance one way which affects the decision to give him the benefit of the doubt. There has to be more to it than that; e.g. we then don't *dwell on* the reasons suggesting the opposite, remind ourselves of possible other interpretations when they come up and so on.

So by an announceable motive I don't mean a reputable one. A disreputable motive is *as* intelligible as a reputable one. Nevertheless, there is a contrast between belief and action in this matter of motives. Contrast: 'I do this because I hate the fellow' with 'I believe this because I hate the fellow'. The former gives a motive and in the elaboration of this we may come upon *grounds* of action — doing this will harm the one I hate, for example. But we shan't in a similar fashion come upon *grounds of belief* when we explore believing something out of hatred. For 'grounds of belief' are reasons which are supposed to show the thing is true. Where 'I believe *p* because I believe *q*' states a ground, you can rewrite 'I believe *p* because I believe *q*' as 'I believe *p*; for *q*' or say 'I believe *p*; for *q* is true, and therefore *p*'. But if 'I believe *p* because I hate X' there is no 'therefore *p*'.

'Grounds of belief' has to do with reasons which show or which one thinks show the thing is true. 'I believe it because I hate him.' 'I believe it because, if it is true, the inheritance is mine, otherwise not.' The latter at any rate seems to be an unannounceable motive. I mean, if it is said, it sounds *cynical* and one implies that the person doesn't really believe the thing. Now why is this? For if we *can* say: we will give him the benefit of the doubt, because it is better, though its being better to believe *p* has no effect on the probability of *p*, and if we can say 'I believe it because I hate him', though that too has no bearing on the probability of its truth, then the objection that 'the inheritance will be mine if this is true' has no bearing on the probability of its truth, can't *by itself* be what makes *this* motive for belief, though a very possible one, unannounceable.

Without invalidating the claim to believe one can say: 'I believe it because I hate him.' What about: 'I believe it (or I stick to the belief) because I love him, because I am his friend'? Are these two on a par? It could be an awful reproach that you had believed something about a friend if the thing wasn't true. Everyone might be excused in view of the appearances, but not you, who were his friend. Is this necessarily because of your special knowledge? No, not necessarily. The evidence may be too strong, your special knowledge not so great. But friendship makes you bet on this chance that the thing is not true. Above all, it was important not to destroy something about the friendship by having been ready to believe something that you weren't forced to believe.

Now I want to resolve the problem presented here by pointing to the difference between 'It is better *if p* is the case' and 'It is better to *believe* that *p* is the case'. It is better, more pleasing to me, *if p* is the case, gives the general form of a motive for believing *p* which does operate but is what I call unannounceable.

That is why the statement 'I believe *p* because if *p* the estate belongs to me' would make us say: I see why you want to *say p*, to *maintain* that *p*, but you are expressing cynical indifference to the truth rather than belief in saying that. You are saying, perhaps, 'Shut up about the question of truth'.

But 'I believe that because I hate him' is not impossible as an expression of belief, because believing it satisfies one's hatred. Whereas 'I believe that because if it is so, I can go on hating him' may be a truth but is not expressive of belief; in recognising that truth, one would be somewhat detached from one's belief.

But doesn't this imply that someone who believes something can give *grounds for believing* like grounds for action which aren't grounds for the belief, and that this doesn't necessarily imply non-belief?

But what about 'I believe this because I want X's job'? Do I get X's job if this is true, or simply out of *believing* it? What I am saying comes to this: it makes sense to speak of deciding to believe something, because *believing* it will get one X's job, but not of deciding to believe it because *if it is true* I shall get X's job. The motive for believing is disreputable but does not imply that the speaker *doesn't* believe the thing. This comes out in the dialogue:

A: This is a 7, I think.
B: Why do you think so?
A: Well, you see, if it is a 7 I can claim a £1000.

A: This is a 7, I think.
B: Why do you think so?
A: Well, you see, if I think it is a 7 I can claim a £1000.

Consider admiration as a motive. If 'I admire X' is itself like an outburst of admiration, then 'I believe *p* because I admire X' seems a possible profession of belief, like 'I believe *p* because I hate X'. In both cases I am thinking of the whole expression as passionate: 'I believe he did it because I hate him, the swine', where believing he did it is itself an indulgence of hatred.

Admiration, though, may work as a motive for belief more naturally where the manifestation of the admiration is *not* 'I admire him' but precisely this: the information 'He said *p*' operates on me to make me believe *p*. Here I don't *declare* my admiration, I merely show it when I say 'I believe *p* because X has said *p*'. He has only to say a thing for it to seem true to me.

The important point here is that this 'He said *p*' does not have to be mediated by 'What he said is likely to be true'. I mean: I don't have to have that opinion and to be ready to make an inference, running: 'What he said is likely to be true — He said $p — p$ is likely to be true' in order to be able to say: 'I believe it because *he* said it.'

If 'He said p' *is* so mediated, then 'He said it' becomes my ground or a ground of mine for that belief.

Let me artificially restrict 'a ground p for a belief r' to a true proposition p which (maybe in conjunction with other true propositions) proves or makes likely some believed proposition r, and 'having a ground for a belief' or 'having the ground p for a belief', to knowing or believing a ground or the ground p. But let me contrast my having the ground p with p *being* my ground or a ground of mine, even where p is my ground, in this way: p can *be* my ground for a belief r if I believe p, I think that r and I think that p proves that r or helps to make it likely. This regardless of whether p is in fact true or false.

(But I think we have *got* to distinguish between grounds for beliefs and grounds for believing. That is, I think the subject matter requires a distinction here which I formulate in that way.)

Now even if I have a ground in the sense I have given there may not be anything that is a ground of mine for the belief. For suppose I have a ground for a belief of mine p, namely: A said that p. This is a ground, if it is true and does make it likely that p. All the same, though I think p and think p *because* A said that p, perhaps I don't think that 'A said p' proves p or makes it likely: any such topics are *another theme* to me. That is how it may be if I am under an influence. He said it — that *inclines* me to believe it. But the likelihood that whatever he said (on such an occasion or topic, perhaps) should be true doesn't come into my '*because*' when I truthfully answer: I believe it because he said it.

Or again, I believed something *because* someone told me so, e.g. the way to the station, or that Princess Margaret was in the town, not with a degree of certainty proportionate to the probability that one telling me such a thing should be speaking the truth; no, I simply react with acceptance.

Should we speak of a motive here? What is a motive? It wouldn't ordinarily be called a motive; the term 'motive' tends to be restricted to passions or objects. ('What was your motive in doing that?' and 'What was your object in doing that?' may be equivalent questions.) But if by motive we mean what *prompts one*, what is one's ground for doing or omitting anything, then 'Someone told me' may well be said to give me a motive. For whether or not it gives a ground for the belief, or gives my ground for the belief, it does give my ground for doing something — namely believing. This should be called a motive. As belief isn't a sort of action, the point is a slightly awkward one to make, but the 'ground' that is here being spoken of is ground in the sense in which we speak of grounds of action and omission. But if I am right it ought to be possible to say: I believe *p*; no grounds are my grounds for that belief; though maybe I *have* some grounds (I haven't even considered whether I have, i.e. know or believe, any grounds that are grounds for *p*). But I have got a ground, i.e. motive, for believing *p*, namely that I want such and such or that so-and-so happened, which leads me to believe *p*.

What is wrong with this? Surely, that in saying 'No grounds are my grounds for that belief' I *must be considering* and that must change the situation. For *my grounds* don't have to be thought of beforehand; they can be elicited. Nothing shows them to me, I have no evidence that I know of as evidence, though maybe I would find I had grounds if I thought about it, but in any case I *believe* it and mean to go on believing it because of what I want. That may happen, but can it be explicitly professed—i.e. doesn't the profession of this sort of belief necessarily nullify itself?

Let's go back to the contrast:

> The reason why I think it's a 7 is that if it's a 7 I may get £1000.
> The reason why I think it's a 7 is that if I *think* it's a 7 I may get £1000.

Repeated in:

> The reason why I think he didn't do it is that if he did it our friendship is ruined.
> The reason why I think he didn't do it is that if I *think* he did it our friendship is ruined.

Isn't the answer that of course the *grounds (motives) for believing* (as opposed to *grounds for belief*) *cannot* be *all* I have got. Even if the likelihood of whatever he says being true is a new theme for me, it becomes a theme as soon as I start considering. And belief isn't all *that* voluntary. I cannot invent something there would be an advantage in thinking or which some passion of mine would favour belief in, and simply believe for that reason at will. And similarly, if when the belief *has* a foothold I believe out of passion, saying 'I believe the thing' involves consideration and some of the things I might make my grounds will occur to me. One may believe things for lots of motives but not quite out of the blue.

4

Thought and Existent Objects

My interest is in how thought is of its objects when the objects of thought are actual existents. I have very vaguely seen — though I would say I have not understood — the picture presented by Aristotle and adopted, perhaps with some elaboration or addition, by Aquinas. There is a productive intellect in each of us which makes the forms of material things into intelligibles and makes them exist in the passive intellect. This receives them, and *it* is what operates in our thinking of those material things. How the productive intellect makes these intelligible forms and in what way the appearances and images or mental pictures of the things play a part in its production of them I have not been able to make clear. Nor is it clear to me whether the productive or 'agent' intellect is simply the intellect in a role of concept-formation, and the 'passive' or 'acted-upon' intellect simply the intellect in a role of concept employment: I can only say I suspect that this may be a true interpretation.

However that may be, the answer to my question 'How is thought *of* its objects when the objects are actual existents?' is here restricted to the case of material things, for it is only when the objects are material things that the productive intellect makes the intelligible forms. The answer to the question in this case will be: the forms, made into intelligibles by the productive intellect, do exist in the material things whose forms they are, but as existing in matter they have not the character called 'actual intelligibility'. They are only potentially intelligibles. The material things are objects of thought in that their forms become 'actual intelligibles' by the action of the productive intellect and by its

---

* From a manuscript without title or date. Title supplied.

activation of the 'passive', i.e. the 'acted-upon intellect, with these intelligible forms. It may be that the action of the productive intellect in making the intelligibles and its action in activating the acted-on intellect are one and the same thing. The account presents us with severe problems: for example, a form existing in the intellect is not the same thing as a concept. For the general concept of a horse, say, includes general concepts of flesh and bones and blood, i.e. of stuffs, i.e. of matter, but the 'form' of a horse, however general it may be as it exists in the mind, still does not include matter. Also the question how such a form can be general has in no way been answered. One might make a parody of the Aristotelian doctrine by saying: 'In having the thought of a horse, the mind becomes a (strictly immaterial) horse.' Well, if it did, it would have become just *this* (strictly immaterial) horse and another mind would be *another* (strictly immaterial) horse. Or else, as some Arabian Aristotelians thought, there can only be one human mind, common to all mankind, otherwise the horse-in-a-mind will lack the character of generality.

These problems I only mention, I won't deal with them. For the question 'How is thought *of* its objects when its objects are actual existents?' has been answered by the contention that here an actual thought-of—thought of an oak tree, say—is the intellect active after and as having received the form of an oak, which is an actual existent. This does not make the relation to the object of thought one in which the object of thought operates on the intellect, itself impressing its form on the quasi-matter of the mind. That is how objects of sense—the carriers of sensory qualities peculiar each to a particular external sense—do act upon their appropriate sensory faculties. But an object of thought gets mapped in the intellect which is activated by the mapping; what does the mapping is the productive intellect. What then makes the thought a thought of an oak tree? The fact that it is a mapping of an oak tree. What makes it a mapping of an oak tree? The shared form. Compare how an image of a rose is 'of a rose' visibly even though the rose itself is not seen. The causality by the rose is not necessary to that. Nor is even the existence of the rose.

I have laboured the point in order to point to some restrictions and a contrast. First, the contrast, which is with the philosopher Locke. Locke is notorious—or ought to be notorious—for his account of knowledge in general.

> Since the mind in all its thoughts and reasonings hath no other
> immediate object but its own ideas, which it alone does or can

contemplate, it is evident that our knowledge is only conversant about them.[1]

Here Locke displays the fact, obvious from the earlier Books of the *Essay* — for this opens Book IV — that we can never get outside ideas to touch real existence or, as he calls it in Book III, chapter 2, 'the reality of things'. There he insists that words 'can properly and immediately signify nothing but the ideas that are in the mind of the speaker, yet they in their thoughts give them a secret reference to two other things'.[2] The first of these is to ideas in other men's minds, 'for else they should talk in vain, and could not be understood, if the sounds they apply to one idea were such as by the hearer applied to another, which is to speak two languages'.[3]

The second 'secret reference' is 'to the reality of things ... Because men would not be thought to talk barely of their own imaginations, but of things as they really are; therefore they often suppose their words to stand also for the reality of things'.[4]

Locke remarks that the second 'secret reference' relates 'more particularly to substances and their names, as perhaps the former does to simple ideas and modes'. But he regards both 'secret references' as false and illusory: 'it is a perverting the use of words, and brings unavoidable obscurity and confusion into their signification, whenever we make them stand for anything but those ideas we have in our own minds.'

Accordingly, when he comes in Book IV to write about knowledge, he tells us that it is the perception of the agreement or disagreement of two ideas. Of this there are four kinds: perception of identity and diversity, perception of relation, perception of co-existence, and finally of 'real existence'. He illustrates the four types with examples: 'Blue is not yellow', 'Two triangles upon equal bases between two parallels are equal', 'Iron is susceptible of magnetical impressions' for the first three, and 'God is' for the fourth. He has observed that the four sorts contain

all the knowledge we have or are capable of; for, all the inquiries that we can make concerning any of our ideas, all that we know or can

---

[1] John Locke, *An Essay concerning Human Understanding* (London: Tegg & Co., 1877), Book IV, Chapter I. Of Knowledge in General 1. *Our knowledge conversant about our ideas*, p.424.

[2] *Ibid.* p.324.

[3] *Ibid.*

[4] *Ibid.* p.325.

affirm concerning any of them, is, that it is or is not the same with some other; that it does or does not always co-exist with some other idea in the same subject; that it has this or that relation to some other idea; or that it has a real existence without the mind [i.e. outside the mind].[5]

Locke observes no difficulty about this last, though it is plainly inconsistent with what he has said before. For if we are to take his definition of knowledge seriously and apply it to the last of his four types, that of 'real existence', then it must be the perception of agreement or disagreement between the idea of God, say, and the *idea* of real existence, or the *idea* of an idea's having a real existence without the mind. The 'knowledge' relative to the fourth kind he characterises as 'that it has a real existence without the mind'. Not, we should note, 'that it has or has not a real existence without the mind'. But let that go: the main point to observe is that the *it* is an idea. Here then is an example of the switching senses in which Locke uses the word 'idea'; mostly it seems to be much what we would mean by 'idea', but sometimes rather to be sensation, sometimes it seems more like 'image', and occasionally 'ideas' seem to be none of these things, but rather to be something about which one can ask whether 'it is really in water', i.e. a sensible quality such as warmth. The last might just be careless writing, but the same curious use is found in our present example concerning the question whether 'it' [namely some idea] has or has not a real existence without the mind.

Noting this fault, which is hardly a mere slip of the pen, we also must notice the conflict with his earlier stricture on the 'secret reference' men illusorily make, or wish to make, to 'the reality of things'.

Hume, who in the first part of Book I of the *Treatise on Human Nature* gives for the most part a rather perfunctory rehash of some of Locke, is rather more consequent than Locke on this subject in the same book of the *Treatise*:

> Now, since nothing is ever present to the mind but perceptions, and since all ideas are deriv'd from something antecedently present to the mind, it follows, that 'tis impossible for us so much as to conceive or form an idea of anything specifically different from ideas or impressions. Let us fix our attention out of ourselves as much as possible: Let us chase our imagination to the heavens, or to the utmost limits of the universe; we never really advance a step beyond ourselves, nor can conceive any kind of existence, but those perceptions

---

5   *Ibid.* p.425.

which have appeared in that narrow compass. This is the universe of the imagination, nor have we any idea, but what is there produc'd.[6]

In the same spirit, Hume maintains the notorious proposition that 'The idea of existence ... is the very same with the idea of what we conceive to be existent', and that 'Whatever we conceive, we conceive to be existent'. These theses may indeed hang together rather well with Lockean principles; but even Hume does not stick to them: for example, he considers how we have a propensity to 'feign the continued existence of all sensible objects'; whereby he shows his own opinion that that existence is a fiction. Or again, he speaks of truth and falsehood as consisting in agreement or disagreement either to the *real* relations of ideas, or to *real* existence and matter of fact.[7]

Nevertheless, in what he says in Book I, Part II, section VI there is what Locke ought to have said given his theory of ideas, but Locke is too commonsensical.

The essential thing about such a theory of ideas as all that the mind can be conversant about and as what names stand for is that it is inappropriate to try to make the ideas reach out beyond themselves to any real existence. So what a thought is of remains simply the content of an idea. The shared form of the thought and the reality avoids this difficulty.

We have another example of this in Wittgenstein's *Tractatus*. There the shared form is that of the sentence (or any picture) and the fact which, if it exists, is the reality mapped in the sentence. The elements of the picture have a definite mutual arrangement, and this represents that things — the simple objects which are the elements in Wittgenstein's metaphysics, or the complexes formed by them — have the same mutual arrangement. The form of mapping is the possibility of the arrangement. There is an apparent feature of *link to reality* in the co-ordination of the elements of the picture with things; if the picture is a completely analysed proposition, its elements will be names of the simple objects which always exist.

But this correlation is not an initial presupposition; it only exists if the picture exists, and it exists whether the picture is true or false. The picture is a picture of the reality by presenting a possibility of existence and non-existence of elementary arrangements of objects.

---

[6]   *Treatise on Human Nature*, edited by L.A. Selby-Bigge (Oxford: Clarendon Press, 1896) Book I, Part II, section VI.
[7]   *Ibid.* Book III, Part I, section I.

The map has to have something in common with what is mapped in it. This it has whether the map is a correct or is an incorrect map of the (relevant) reality. *Then* the fact mapped will not exist but the mapping relation will still be there in the map. The thing in common Wittgenstein calls the form of mapping. 'By this conception the mapping relation, which makes the map into a map, also belongs to the map'; i.e. you do not have something which is only a map because it *correctly* corresponds in some fashion to something else. You do not have something which is a proposition only because it is true.

The contrast between Wittgenstein and Aristotle in this matter is that Wittgenstein is concerned with propositions and actual or possible facts, Aristotle with intelligibles existing in the mind and real or possible objects whose intelligible forms they are. (Whether an intelligible in the human mind can be of a merely possible object is a question I won't go into.)

Now this requires a handling of terms or concepts which seem not to fit in. Wittgenstein with a wave of the hand says 'The tacit conventions of ordinary language are enormously complicated' — if we sorted out the complications we'd get what in the end did correspond to his account.

In the Aristotelian account the analogue of this would be names that are not names of anything; at least in a sense they are not. We have a nice example of this in Anselm; not an Aristotelian, rather an Augustinian — but not a follower of Augustine in his naïf and simplistic picture of the relation of words to reality. Wittgenstein's comment on this is perfectly accurate; in the *De Magistro* Augustine really tries to make 'if' and 'nothing' into names of some sort of objects. Anselm does not follow him. In the discussion of 'nothing' (*nihil*)[8] it is treated as a name, but if it is a name of nothing there isn't anything it is a name of, so how can it be a name? The explanation given (with more elaboration than I will mention) is that it is a word meaning 'not anything': the key thought first spoken is 'perhaps there is no contradiction between signifying nothing and signifying something' — which gets the complicated explanation I have mentioned. The

---

8   *Ed.* Anselm has extensive treatment of 'nothing' in the *Monologion* but the discussion Anscombe is referring to here is in the *De Casu Diaboli* ['The Fall of the Devil'] chapter 11. The translation in the text is Anscombe's own; a full English translation of the book by Ralph McInerny can be found in *Anselm of Canterbury: The Major Works* edited by Brian Davies and Gillian Evans (Oxford: Oxford University Press, 1998) and page references for the passages Anscombe cites are to this edition.

pupil is not altogether satisfied with the explanation, since it invites saying that the 'something' that nothing signifies is the 'something' involved in 'not anything' (i.e. 'not something') just as you understand 'non-man' only if you understand 'man'. 'What I am looking for', he says, 'is what this name ("nothing") stands for, and what we understand when we hear this name: I want to know what there is. For this is what the name properly signifies, and it *is* a name just because it is significative of that, *not* because it signifies anything by negation in the way you've explained (i.e. "not anything").'[9]

The pupil thinks 'nothing' really *is* used as a name, not indirectly as a negative expression, and wants to know what of. The master (Anselm) replies that he has got a point here, but that

> Many things are spoken of according to forms [sc. of language] not according to reality. For example, we call 'to fear' an active verb where in reality it is passive. [To fear something is to be frightened by it.] And so blindness is called something according to the form of speaking, though it isn't anything in reality. We say someone has sight and sight exists in him, and in the same way that he has blindness and blindness is found in him, though this isn't something but rather not-something: blindness isn't something you have, blindness is lacking what is something. For blindness is nothing but non-sight and the absence of sight where there ought to be sight. Non-sightedness or lack of sight isn't more something where there ought to be sight than it is where there is no *ought to be sight* about it. Hence blindness is no more something in the eye just because there ought to be sight in it, than non-sight and the absence of sight is something in a stone, where you haven't got an 'ought to be' about sight. There are [he goes on] many other things that are called *something* according to the form of speaking which aren't anything, though we speak of them as we do about existent things.[10]

With this the master satisfies the pupil. I have found in Locke an illustration of what he says about the word 'nothing': 'man knows by an intuitive certainty that bare nothing can no more produce any real being than it can be equal to two right angles.' Or again in *King Lear*: 'Nothing will come of nothing.'

In modern grammars 'nothing' is listed among pronouns, not as a noun, and this holds regardless of whether the word for it has an internal structure like the English or Greek words for it (here again I illustrate Anselm's observation) or has no obvious structure, like the Latin *Nihil* or the German *Nichts*. — What it means to call it a pronoun I

---

9   *Anselm of Canterbury: The Major Works*, p.209.
10   *Ibid.* pp.209–210.

do not know. That grammatically it functions like a noun is true enough; and some scruple about calling it a noun may be all there is to calling it a pronoun. The enquiry 'What does it stand for? Nothing? Then it doesn't stand for anything, so it doesn't mean anything. It must mean something' may now be met by finding the explanation 'You can replace it with "not something"' satisfactory. But actually you can't always. 'Nothing arises out of nothing' is an example which couldn't be rendered as 'Not anything arises out of not anything', and it is fairly difficult to rewrite it. Would this do? 'Not: Something does not arise out of anything.' Hardly. Perhaps: 'For all x, if x arises, then not: For all y, x does not arise out of y', or 'Every beginning of existence is out of something', or 'There is no beginning of anything such that there is not anything out of which that beginning of existence was'.

The word 'nothing' has the feel of a name, and so do many other words like 'dark', 'silence', 'evil'. Anselm's remarks in reply to the pupil who obviously has a strong 'feel for a name' in such cases will rightly incite us to think that not all apparent names correspond to 'intelligibles' in Aristotle's sense of the Greek word νοητα. When, then, my suggested job has been done, namely, of the sharing of forms between material kinds of thing and the mind informed by those forms without matter, there are not merely severe problems to solve such as I mentioned, if we are to find the account acceptable; but a vast amount of other work needs to be done, beginning with 'merely ostensible names'.

5

Knowledge
and Essence

In the *Tractatus Logico-Philosophicus* Wittgenstein says that theory of knowledge is philosophy of psychology (4.1121). In the previous paragraph, he has spoken of psychology as a 'natural science': 'Psychology is not more akin to philosophy than any other natural science.' The remark on theory of knowledge which immediately follows is the second paragraph of the same number. So when he speaks of 'philosophy of psychology' he means the natural science of psychology and the phrase is like 'philosophy of Dynamics', as Russell speaks in *The Principles of Mathematics*.

This and some other indications (e.g. in a letter to Russell about the *Tractatus* he says it would be for psychology to find out what the constituents of thought are) show that Wittgenstein regarded psychology as a 'natural science'. On the other hand, at *Tractatus* 5.541 he gives '*A* believes that *p* is the case', '*A* is thinking *p*' as examples of 'certain forms of proposition of psychology', which, if 'psychology' is here a natural science, is rather like calling '*x* fell from a tree on to *N*'s head' a form of proposition belonging to mechanics. Later on Wittgenstein was to speak of 'psychological verbs' and that certainly did not mean verbs which belonged to the natural science of psychology. Rather, thought and belief may be matters to be investigated by psychology, but the propositions which would be instances of those 'forms of proposition' — e.g. 'Galileo believes that *the earth moves* is the case' — are ones belonging to human report at their time. This is so even though

*   Paper delivered at the Wittgenstein Symposium, Girona, 1989, and published in Josep-Maria Terricabras (ed.) *A Wittgenstein Symposium: Girona 1989* (Amsterdam – Atlanta, GA: Rodopi, 1993), pp.29–35.

my Galileo sentence is rather stilted in order to make it a substitution instance of '*A* believes that *p* is the case'. I don't think that Wittgenstein at 5.541 was saying that Russell's and Moore's theories of knowledge related to these propositions as propositions of the natural science of psychology.

Wittgenstein once answered a question of mine by saying that a lot of the works of philosophy of the recent centuries had titles which either referred to the mind in some fashion, or contained the word 'principles'. This very much characterised the philosophies, and that marked a difference between his philosophising and theirs, or so I gathered — for in this sentence I have not been quoting his actual words, but only the gist of them.

Towards the end of his life he wrote of 'the confusion and barrenness of psychology' (*Philosophical Investigations*, II, xiv). We may suppose from his letter to Russell about thirty years earlier that he then had a more hopeful view of the natural science of psychology than later on, when he said that 'In psychology there are experimental methods and *conceptual confusion*', as in certain branches of mathematics 'conceptual confusion and methods of proof'.

However it is not important for me to elucidate Wittgenstein's earlier or later opinions on experimental psychology. I have said what I have in order to avoid inaccuracy. My main aim is to point to the very great importance of the *Tractatus* thought that theory of knowledge is philosophy of psychology. The importance is to the history of philosophy in the sense of the history of philosophic thought. I don't know how much it has been noticed, but here, in this remark 'Theory of knowledge is philosophy of psychology' a break is made. For several centuries theory of knowledge had been what metaphysics had been before them. It had come to be the theory of the essence of the world, of the ultimate furniture of the universe. This tide began to come in with Descartes, if he earned the title 'the father of modern philosophy'. The waves rose to their highest with Kant's claim to have made a Copernican revolution. Copernicus' hypothesis attributed the great and obvious cosmic appearances to what was happening to their observers. The sun was not moving, the earth was carrying us observers round in rotating on its axis. So the previous powerful metaphysical convictions were to be explained by the nature of mind and reason. I hope I have not got it wrong. I have never tried to understand Kant's grand system, only the transcendental aesthetic, the analogies of experience, and the antinomies of pure reason. These three I conceived as *rami amputabiles* which could be read by themselves by anyone attracted as I was by the romance of their titles. I came to the conclusion that the antinomies of pure reason were all important for a statement of what should convince one to throw away metaphysical enquiry and argument and to embrace without its metaphor the idea of Kant's 'Copernican revolution' in philosophy.

I do not find the antinomies convincing and therefore do not embrace that idea. But the supreme position of theory of knowledge was guaranteed long before Kant and remained even among such philosophers as Bertrand Russell who abominated Kant. It was still operative in Wittgenstein in spite of his remark in the *Tractatus*. In the book he put together, which has the title *Philosophische Bemerkungen*, we find the remark: 'A proposition is a draft upon a verification.' Rather later, hearing people speak of 'the verification principle', he exclaimed 'Who is supposed to have invented that?' and when it was indicated that it was attributed to him, he said '*What*? Me?'. The remark about a proposition's being a draft of a verification may be given an *innocent* interpretation if we associate it with *Tractatus* 4.063: 'Um sagen zu konnen: '*p*' ist wahr (oder falsch) muss ich bestimmt haben, unter welchen Umständen ich '*p*' wahr nenne, und damit bestimme ich den Sinn des Satzes.' But here too we remind ourselves that explanation comes to an end and ask whether the *Bestimmung* of which he speaks is a *Bestimmung* by further propositions describing the circumstances under which I call a proposition true. We must indeed think not, for otherwise explanation will not come to an end or there will be an invocation of experience with which it does come to an end. The latter may be all right but will not consist of a description of the circumstances under which I call '*p*' true—not if that description itself has to have its sense indicated by a further description of the same sort. In the light of later thought at least, we may speak of the experience in question as that of learning language. 'How do you know what the word "red" means?' An answer might be 'I have learnt English'. We are far from 'a draft upon verification' here. Certainly it would not seem to the point to ask for a determination of the circumstances under which I call 'I have learnt English' true (or false), even though one can describe some such determination.

Forgetting about the question of characterising theory of knowledge as philosophy of psychology, if psychology is to be understood as one of the natural sciences, we may say that theory of knowledge is philosophy of psychology in a sense in which it is rather little concerned to be philosophy of experimental psychology. One of the worthwhile things to observe is that 'to know' is not what Wittgenstein called a 'psychological verb'; it is to Descartes' credit that he does not put knowledge into his list of *cogitationes*, nor yet memory, though by the twentieth century people (Broad, for example) were certainly so treating memory and there has been some uncomfortable philosophising about knowledge and belief which leans in that direction for knowledge. The interesting enquiries about knowledge, once one has given up the attempt to characterise it as a sort of belief that satisfies certain conditions, concerns what everyone, or everyone in certain cultures, can be assumed to know once grown-up and reasonably competent; and the relation of some claims of knowledge to questions like 'How do you know?'. But belief and conjecture and certainty, among which belief seems most clearly to be a psychological concept because of the lack of room for criticising a claim to believe something so long as it is reasonable to say that the something in question is something it makes sense to assert. Frege somewhere criticises someone for saying 'I define ...' with the comment that he isn't defining, anymore than he would be rising in the air by saying 'I rise in the air'. In the same manner one might criticise someone who said 'I conjecture that the world has always existed', though if he said he believed that there is no room for saying 'That's not a belief'.

We are, I think, only at the beginning of the rescue begun by Wittgenstein in this matter of theory of knowledge—which he himself seemingly began by saying 'Theory of knowledge is philosophy of psychology'. He himself in that same place raised the question whether his study of sign language didn't correspond to old philosophers' study of processes of thought. He seems not to deny that it did: 'only they mostly involved themselves in inessential psychological investigations.' He adds 'and there is an analogous danger with my method too'.—We might give as example of 'inessential psychological investigations' the consideration of inference as a performance: 'an inference is something that someone performs.' This suggests that one might say 'When someone says "therefore", we need to find out if *inferring* is really happening within him—otherwise he lies or it is an empty noise'. Is there really that mental *stepping* that has the special character of inference going on?

Let me now look at something else, a movement of thought on Wittgenstein's part which I think has hardly got through to the philosophic world. Certainly much less than the dethroning of the theory of knowledge from its supreme position—little as that has got into the heads of philosophers. What I am now speaking of is Wittgenstein's observation that essences are expressed by grammar. With this observation is hatched out the chicken that was in the egg of Frege's 'Funktion und Begriff'. There Frege makes us strongly aware of the difference between $2 \times 2^3 + 2$ and $2 \times x^3 + x$. What, he asks, is the *Inhalt*, the *Bedeutung*, of '$2 \times 2^3 + 2$' and answers: 'The same as that of '18' or '3 × 6'. Asked to explain what a function is, one is liable to get the answer: 'By a function of x there's got to be understood an arithmetical expression containing "x", a formula which included the letter "x".' According to this, for example, the expression '$2 \times x^3 + x$' would be a function of x, while '$2 \times 2^3 + 2$' would be a function of 2. This answer cannot be satisfactory, because in it form and content, sign and signified don't get distinguished, an error which is indeed 'very often encountered in mathematical writings now, even writings of authors who have made their name'.

Frege proceeds to remind us of, to draw our attention to, the fact that '$2 \times 1^3 + 1$', '$2 \times 2^3 + 2$', '$2 \times 4^3 + 4$' are all of the same pattern; they stand for different numbers—but if '$2 \times x^3 + x$' were also an arithmetical expression it would also indicate a number, though only in an indeterminate way.

The point is that in the use of such an expression as '$2 \times x^3 + x$', we get an expression of something quite different from a number. It isn't that the letter 'x' couldn't have been a numeral—it is the mode of use that shows that it is not a numeral but is used to form the expression of a function. The difference of mode of use is the difference in the *grammar* of use of letters 'x', 'y', etc., and the grammar of signs which constitutes their being numerals: a grammar that expresses the essence: natural number.

We only need to understand this opening part of Frege's great essay to be in a position to understand Wittgenstein's saying: 'Essence is expressed in grammar' (*Philosophical Investigations*, I, 371). Here two impediments have been created. One, that Wittgenstein is thought to have meant something different by the word 'grammar' from what the rest of us mean. He did not; it is only that 'grammar-school' grammar is very narrow and thin and doesn't cover, doesn't take note of, a lot of differences. Question: is 'three' an adjective in 'Three men went out to mow a meadow'? Ordinary school grammar isn't equipped to consider the question.

The second impediment is the assumption that if you speak of grammar as Wittgenstein does, it is an *arbitrary* and superficial invention which we could change at will. Well, if we change grammar in some ways, we shall change the essences that are expressed in it: I mean that we shall make it express—if it does express anything—different essences.

Some essences are indeed productions of human intelligence: thus Wittgenstein says that mathematicians produce essences. In natural philosophy (which we nowadays call 'science') there is *sometimes* a production of essences, like, for example, the essence expressed in the grammar of the term 'element'. But mostly essences are not human inventions.

In this matter too it is the same philosopher who speaks in the *Tractatus* and in the much later writings. The first speaks of structure where the second speaks of grammar. It would be a serious work to consider what here in the one is rejected by the other. Here the most important candidate is: *the general form of all propositions* — though we have to count mathematical propositions as not included and tautologies and contradictions as included only in, so to speak, a marginal way. But the general form of a proposition as such, which may be expressed using Wittgenstein's *N* operator as the general term of a formal series, may also be expressed in English as 'Such-and-such is the case'. In the *Philosophical Investigations* Wittgenstein considers this and makes a rather Kantian comparison between saying that and attributing the shape of a pair of glasses you are looking through to the objects you see with these glasses. However, it cannot be said, I think, that he has dismissed a problem successfully. In the *Tractatus* he says: 'The proposition *shows* how things are, if it is true, and *says* that they *are* so' (4.022).

How it does this is not clear at all, if it is not simply by showing how things are if it is true. On the other hand, did Wittgenstein ever work out what to say here? In the *Philosophical Investigations*, having considered these matters, he speaks of its looking as if he wanted to bargain its rigour out of logic. '*Of course*', he says, 'we can't do that; what we must do is turn our whole consideration around, but about the fixed point of our real need' (I, 108). We may think of an example of turning something round — in the *Tractatus* he thinks that the character of the logical constants issues from the nature of the proposition as such. In the *Investigations* he says that we *call* something a proposition if we operate the calculus of truth functions with it. Maybe some other examples can be found. But what in §108 did he mean by 'the fixed point of our real need'? I do not know, and I suspect that without understanding this we shall at best have a poor understanding of that book.

6

Grammar,
Structure and Essence

Reading some of a commentary by Proclus on Plato's *Parmenides*, I found Proclus saying that a name was a logical picture of its object. I mentioned this to Wittgenstein, who surprised me by saying 'I have so often had that thought'. I was surprised because in the *Tractatus Logico-Philosophicus* not the name but the proposition is called a logical picture, and not of a thing but of a possible fact; of an actual one if the proposition is true.

I was very slow to draw the right conclusion from that conversation. Namely, that it is a wrong assumption (which I inexplicitly and unwittingly made for years) that the objects, the simples, spoken of in the *Tractatus*, were uniform characterless atoms, whose arrangement alone produced the characters of familiar things, which characters indeed Wittgenstein called 'external'. The assumption was absurd — the internal characters of objects will be different if the objects are not of the same logical form (2.0233) — in fact; it looks as if their logical form and their internal character were the same thing. The possibility of a given fact must be 'prejudged' in the things that *can* occur in such a fact (2.012). This at least suggests that it is not possible for every simple object to occur in just any fact. Rather, the objects co-ordinated with names can enter into some compositions and not others according to their forms, and this holds of their names correspondingly. We cannot illustrate this with elementary propositions, as we do not know any, but we might construct analogies, using the only sorts of names we do know; we may note that 'Mount Everest chased Napoleon out

---

*   Published in *ARETÉ Revista de Filosofía*, Vol.12, No.2 (2000): 113–120.

of Cairo' does not express a possible fact—unless we change the meaning of 'Mount Everest'.

That the simple objects of the *Tractatus* are diverse in logical form is actually quite obvious. For example, we are told 'Its possibility of occurring in elemental facts (*Sachverhalte*) is the *form* of an object' (2.0141). 'Space, time and colour are forms of objects' (2.0251). These thoughts are quite near to 'Names are logical pictures of objects' if you grant the character of a name only to names of simples—even though you cannot produce an example of such a name.

This truth—that for the *Tractatus* there is a diversity of forms of objects—allows a corresponding diversity in names, even of simple objects. Such names would be the elements of a 'fully analysed' proposition—a sprinkle of names on a logical network, as Wittgenstein put it later on.

It also illumines many of the remarks in the early part of the book. Let me remind my reader:

> 2.14 A picture consists in this: its elements are related to one another in a particular kind of way.
> 2.15 The picture's elements relating to one another in a particular kind of way presents things as relating to one another in that way.
>   Let us call this connection of the elements of a picture its structure and the possibility of its structure its form of representation (*Abbildung*).
> 2.151 The form of representation is the possibility that the things are related to one another as are the elements of the picture.
> 2.1514 The representing relation consists in the co-ordination of the elements of the picture and the things.

He has said, in the immediately preceding remark (2.1513), 'According to this conception, the representing relation which makes it a picture also actually belongs to the picture'.

That means that the elements' being co-ordinated with objects is essential to the picture's being a picture—you couldn't have a picture and subsequently coordinate its elements with objects.

Applying this to the particular case of propositions having sense—i.e. ones which are neither tautologies nor contradictions nor propositions of mathematics, we are forced to realise that the names in propositional signs, or at least in 'fully analysed' propositional signs, are names iff those signs are propositional. This means that the problem of isomorphism which many—including myself—have felt about the *Tractatus* is not a problem at all. The problem was constituted by isomorphism's being two-way. If a figure x is isomorphic with a figure *y*, then equally *y* is isomorphic with *x*. So how does *x*'s isomorphism with *y* show that *x* is a picture of *y* anymore than *y* is a picture of *x*?

In some cases we must grant that which is a picture of which is not determined. If you have a simple spatial picture of another spatial arrangement, and you exhibit the correlations by lines of projection, then the second spatial arrangement is as much a projection of the first as the first is of it. Similarly with arrangements of colours. But here the forms of representation are not purely logical, but include the forms signified by the terms 'spatial' and 'coloured'. If you have a tune, with a temporal order of notes, and you see this represented by a line of musical notation which is spatial, there is no form of representation other than the logical form connecting the two things — the tune and the line of notation. (These considerations help us to understand the proposition 'Space, time and colour are forms of objects'.)

The pattern in the tune and in the line of notation is also, Wittgenstein says, in the grooves of the gramophone record of the tune and the sound waves. That need not concern us. The marks belonging to the line of notation signify the notes of the tune and not the other way round. You have, e.g. to understand such-and-such a mark *as the name of a note* in order to know what those marks are co-ordinated with. And similarly, if you wanted to say: a fact declared by a proposition was, if it really was a fact, i.e. if the proposition was true, just as much a picture of the proposition as the proposition was of the fact, you would have to call the elements of the fact names of names — for it is only as names that certain elements of the propositional sign are elements of the picture of the fact. But you could not make out what the elements of the picture were independently of its being a picture. No such difficulty arises about the elements of the fact which the picture presents. Thus the argument from isomorphism's being two-way fails, — except in cases where it is harmless and either structure may be used as a picture of the other.

Let me return to the relation between structure and form of representation. The structure of a picture is the way its elements combine, the way they relate to one another. The form of representation is both the possibility of the structure and the possibility that the objects in the reality being represented are related to one another in the same way as the elements of the picture.

How do the elements of a proposition, an elementary proposition, relate to one another? It is composed only of names of simples. They are connected together in a 'logical' arrangement.

If that is so, then the simples in the corresponding fact (if there is one, i.e. if the proposition is true) are also connected together in a 'logical' arrangement—the same logical arrangement as that of the names.

This announcement makes the connection between thought and a thinkable reality. The possibility that the things in the reality combine as they do =, i.e. is identical with, the possibility of the picture's elements combining as they do.

It is not only pictures that Wittgenstein says have 'structure'. Before coming to the pictures at 2.1 he has devoted himself to objects and *Sachverhalte*—elementary facts—in the 2.0s. *Sachverhalte* have structure. The kind of way the objects in an elementary fact hang together is its structure (2.032). And (2.033): The form is the possibility of the structure.

But we have seen that the possibility of the structure of the picture is the same as the possibility that the objects combine as the elements of the picture do. And this is called the form of representation. More than that, it is said to be what is common to the picture and the possible fact that it presents. Not that the possible fact itself has a form of representation, but that the picture's form of representation is identical with the possibility of things combining in the way its elements do. And the possibility of things combining in the way that would constitute the possible elementary fact as an actual one, i.e. the possibility of the structure of the elementary fact, is its form (2.033). Its form is thus identical with the form of representation in the picture.

A picture can represent any reality whose form it has (2.171) and any picture, whatever its form, must have logical form, the form of the reality, in order to be able to represent it at all, right or wrong. If the form of representation is the logical form, the picture is called the logical picture (2.181). And 2.182 says: Any picture is also a logical picture. This is by contrast with a picture's not having to be a spatial picture, for example.

You may have observed that I tend to say 'the reality', not 'reality', in quoting the *Tractatus*. Articles, whether in the language you are translating from or the one you are translating into, offer a severe test of understanding. I hope I have got it right.

So much for the *Tractatus*. Let us think again of Proclus' remark: 'The name is a logical picture of its object.' As the *Tractatus* lays down what 'logical picture' is to mean, that will not have been true of its names and objects. One might translate Proclus' phrase by 'logical image'—the Greek will have been εἰκὼν λογική. But whatever we do, there is something about names and their objects which is not a matter of a simple relation effected arbitrarily in the manner assumed by John Locke and John Stuart Mill. Mill said that proper names have only denotation, not connotation. Wittgenstein in his classes denounced this. 'It is a great deal of information about a word that it is a proper name, and still more, what kind of thing it is a proper name of — a man, a battle, a place, etc., etc.' In the *Tractatus*, names being restricted to simple objects, we can't say what their objects are, only give propositions describing their configurations. 'A proposition cannot say *what* a thing is, only *how* it is.' In his later work, Wittgenstein certainly gave up his simple objects. But even they had logical forms, which would come out in the propositions that could be formed out of their names — if we could in fact name them. And propositions are descriptions of elementary facts by their internal properties.

This has not simply died in the later work. Earlier, he had spoken of structure; later, he spoke of grammar, and said 'Essence is expressed in grammar'. This, we may say, was made clear in the first place by Frege in the case of the essence connected with the general notion of an arithmetical function. Of course, Frege did not produce that sentence about essence. I am inclined to say that he laid an egg, in such writings as *Funktion und Begriff* and *Was ist eine Funktion?*, which Wittgenstein hatched. In the former he pointed out the difference between, say, $2 + x^4$ and $2 + 3^4$. The former is an expression of a numerical function of which the latter is an example. The first has no numerical value, the second has one: $2 + 3^4 = 83$.

The difference of meaning between the expressions of instances of a numerical function — in this case e.g. $2 + 1^4$, $2 + 5^4$, $2 + 10^4$, etc. — and the expression of a numerical function is not an example of equivocation like 'John gave three rings' — when it is a doorbell he is described as ringing — and 'John gave three rings' when it was a present of rings for the fingers. The difference between $2 + x$ and $2 + 3$ is highly significant because the point of the former is to signify the form of such expressions as the latter. This is a grammatical difference, as can be clearly seen in the joke about the teacher who says 'Suppose there are x pounds of sugar in a box' and the pupil who puts up his hand and says 'But sir, suppose there aren't?' The pupil hasn't yet grasped the grammar of 'x' used as it is in expressions of a function for example — or he is making a cheeky joke. Even so, it would be a grammatical joke. Many such are to be found in Lewis Carroll — 'You can't believe what's impossible' said Alice. 'You can, with practice', said the White Queen. 'With practice, I can believe six impossible things before breakfast every morning.'

That essence is expressed in grammar was clear enough in the case of arithmetical functions. But it is also fairly clear in most cases of familiar concepts of substances and kinds of stuff. Examples: animal, plant, peacock, man, flea, bougainvillea, banana-tree. Also: acid, wood, metal, milk. I do not mean that we know definitions of all these things, or that it is already decided in our language whether artificial wood (if such were possible) that doesn't come from a tree, but this can't be told by test or examination, is 'really' wood.

The grammar of terms for kinds of stuff is often tied up with the notion of a pure sample. You need pure samples, or pretty pure samples, to get knowledge of the properties of the kind of stuff you are examining—that gives the grammatical connection which makes the particular grammar express the essence of the particular kind. Sometimes, though seldom, it may be discovered that what had been thought to be one kind of stuff is 'really' two—jade is a well-known example.

When we come to plants and animals the identity of an individual is of a different kind from the identity of a lump of lead, say. 'The persistence of a certain pattern in a flow of matter' comes into our account; but the notion of a pattern, as of a shape, is here special. We readily speak of the shape of a horse or human being, but we don't say that someone's shape alters when he sits down. And the term 'pattern' extends to covering 'patterns' of development over a period of life involving considerable changes, even like those from caterpillar or larva to pupa to butterfly.

I have been considering 'substantial' terms. The notion of essence is certainly not confined to these, as the example of numerical functions shows. The notion of a square in two dimensions has an essence involving that a square which is twice the area of a given square is the square on the diagonal. I once undertook to demonstrate Plato's point in the *Meno* with a nine-year-old girl who, like Plato's slave, had never learned any geometry. I began as Socrates did, drawing a rough square and asking: how long will the side be of a square twice as big? To my astonishment and pleasure she answered just as the slave did, and we proceeded just as the dialogue did, because she always said the next thing that the slave did. I became convinced that this famous bit of the dialogue was no fiction.

What did she end up knowing? One might say: *if* I drew the squares etc. quite accurately, she ended up knowing that *this* square and *this* one (the first and second guesses) weren't twice the original square but this *last* one was. But, first, I wasn't being accurate in my drawing, and, second, we could ask how she knew what we are saying she ended up knowing. Was it by the way they looked? If so, would she have any reason to suppose it would look the same another time?

You might say it would have to. But suppose another time I drew them in a different colour, and a different size. 'Oh', you might say, 'we don't mean "look the same" in those ways.' What way of 'looking the same' do we mean? 'The same in that the square on the diagonal was (and so at least roughly looked) twice the size of the original square.' But how will it look twice the size? You reply: 'By being composed of triangles, each half the size of the original square and a quarter of the new one.'

If I don't draw it so, or at least ask questions which the child answers so, then I am not asking about the geometrical proposition. (For this, accurate drawing doesn't matter.)

What I am eliciting by my questions—which are not 'leading questions' containing the wished-for answer—is an essence, part at any rate of the essence of a plane square.

Wittgenstein says in Part I of the book *Remarks on the Foundations of Mathematics*, remark 32, that mathematicians produce essences. We can see what he means in the examples: numerical functions and plane square. Functions emerged as a mathematical topic, I believe, in the seventeenth century. I didn't say Frege 'produced' such essences, but only that he showed what they were, and how to avoid confusing sign and thing signified. The square of Euclidean geometry was an essence produced many centuries before.

Mathematicians have 'produced' such essences by using a grammar; the first formulator of the geometrical notion of a square was presumably extending and adding to a grammar already in use. It is a curious thing that people can build grammar without knowing what they are doing. There is a remark something like this in the *Tractatus* at 4.002: 'Man possesses the capacity of building languages in which any sense can be expressed, without any idea how and what each word means. — As one speaks, without knowing how the individual sounds are produced.'

This may be verified, up to a point, in examples of mathematical concepts, and probably in a number of others. Committees, with a certain task or scope of authority, seem a probable example. Ostracism, in which you wrote on an ostrakos the name of someone you wanted expelled from your city, must surely have been a human invention too. That language as such was a human invention seems enormously doubtful, as does the expression 'build languages in which *any* sense can be expressed'. Languages don't fail to be languages because they need to be built on to in order to express physics in its present state. There may be in this remark about expressing *any* sense a sign of conviction that anything that is a language can say anything sayable. The later Wittgenstein, like Descartes, rather makes a comparison with an old city, the centre full of narrow twisting streets and odd corners, while the suburbs are all straight wide streets.

However, I am more interested in the similarities than the difference. And I would put it forward that 'grammar' hasn't got a special new sense, it is only more extensive than the rather thin grammar children learn at school. And grammar, as Wittgenstein considers it, corresponds to the 'structure' of pictures, of which he wrote in the *Tractatus*. In that book, maybe, we can say objects have essences, if we are allowed to say anything about objects: Wittgenstein speaks not of essences there but rather of logical forms, and there is little about them. What have essences rather are propositions and elementary facts; and this fits in well with the analogue of structure to grammar.

Part 3

Meaning, Truth and Existence

7

Private Ostensive Definition

I

In preparing to consider private ostensive definition I shall first examine Locke's *Essay on the Human Understanding*, Book II, Chapter 1, §§1–4 and 24–5, Chapter 2 together with a note based on Locke's correspondence with Stillingfleet, the Bishop of Worcester; Chapter 8, §§11–19, and Book III, Chapters 1 and 2. When I quote from Locke's *Essay* it will be in the form: II.2.1.

The notion of private ostensive definition obviously depends on those of ostensive definition and privacy. 'Ostensive definition' is a rather modern phrase, probably formulated by Bertrand Russell. 'Private ostensive definition' is a phrase devised by Wittgenstein.

It may therefore seem that Locke is an odd starting point. But in fact we shall find that the core of his doctrine is implicitly equivalent to a thesis of private ostensive definition of words standing for the most elementary or basic ideas, out of which all others are supposed to

---

* The following text is based on a manuscript and a distinct typescript which were the basis of two publications in Professor Anscombe's lifetime: a coursebook, *Private Ostensive Definition*, which she wrote for the Fernuniversität, published in 1988, with facing German translation; and a paper, 'On Private Ostensive Definition', which she delivered at the Sixth International Wittgenstein Symposium (Kirchberg/Wechsel, Austria) in August 1981, and which was published in the Proceedings of the Symposium, *Language and Ontology/Sprache und Ontologie* (Vienna: Hölder-Pichler-Tempsky, 1982), pp.212–217. I have followed the organisation of the original manuscript and not of the coursebook, and I have replaced the extensive quotations from the original German of Wittgenstein's *Philosophische Untersuchungen* in Anscombe's manuscript with her own English translation of those passages as they appear in Ludwig Wittgenstein, *Philosophical Investigations*, translated by G.E.M. Anscombe (Oxford: Basil Blackwell, 1958).

be either compounded in various ways, or devised otherwise than by composition.

Locke had devoted Book I of his *Essay* to an attack on the doctrine that some ideas are innate. Now, in the opening of Book II he says 'Let us suppose the mind to be, as we say, white paper void of all characters' — i.e. paper with nothing written on it. Elsewhere he speaks of the mind as 'an empty cabinet', i.e. it begins as an empty cabinet, and comes to be stored with a vast amount of furniture. How? In the text before us he says 'from experience' and elaborates this by saying:

> Our observation, employed either about external sensible objects, or about the internal operations of our minds, perceived and reflected on by ourselves, is that which supplies our understandings with all the materials of thinking.

These 'materials of thinking' are evidently ideas, for the very next thing he says is that 'these two are the foundation of knowledge, from whence all the ideas we have, or can naturally have, do spring' (II.1.2).

What 'two things' is he speaking of? By the text, they are (i) external sensible objects and (ii) internal operations of our minds. Now, is it just by being there or occurring that these are the sources of ideas? No, it seems it is by our observation's 'being employed about' them. In the case of external sensible objects, however, this apparently consists simply in the occurrence of sensations, for in the next paragraph (3) he says that our senses, conversant about particular sensible objects, convey into the mind several distinct perceptions of things, according to the various ways in which those objects affect them. In this way we come by the ideas we have of yellow, white, heat, cold, soft, hard, bitter, sweet and all those we call sensible qualities. He explains his phrase 'the senses convey into the mind' by saying 'they from external objects convey into the mind *what produces there* those perceptions'. (It will turn out that he means a material passage of particles and motions.) 'This great source of most of the ideas we have, depending on our senses, and derived by them to the understanding, I call "sensation"' (II.1.3).

Note 1: Locke's use of the word 'object'. It reads so as to make it natural nowadays to understand the word in that modern sense in which one may speak of *the objects to be found in someone's pockets*, or in which philosophers speak of *material objects*. In fact in the seventeenth and eighteenth centuries British philosophers show us and, I guess, effected or contributed to a development of this modern sense. But when Locke was writing the term 'object' was one that could be completed as 'object of ...': *objects* were *objects of*—e.g. objects of sense, of desire, of intention, of intellect. So that when he says 'Our observation, employed about external sensible objects', this bit of English will be understood if we as it were mentally complete it as if he had written 'external sensible objects of observation'. This he had no need to do because 'objects' would then be so understood in that sentence. And when he speaks of 'several distinct perceptions of things, according to those various ways wherein those objects do affect' the senses, 'those objects' means 'those objects of perception'.

(The terms 'object', 'objective', and 'subject', 'subjective' have undergone an extraordinary near-exchange of sense in post-Cartesian philosophy, of which we here witness a little bit. Roughly speaking, 'objective' formerly meant what 'subjective' means now, and vice versa. Formerly the *subject* was the actual thing or things, if such there were, indicated or named by the grammatical subject-term of a *proposition*.)

Note 2: Locke on 'secondary qualities'. Locke is seeking a causal account to explain the contents of human minds: the senses were affected by external things in various ways and so convey ideas into the mind. Locke gives a list of these which is actually a list only of secondary qualities, a conception deriving from Galileo and corresponding roughly to Aristotle's *idia aistheta*, i.e. objects peculiar to each of the distinct external senses. But Locke then calls sensation 'the great source of *most of the ideas we have*'.

The causal explanation is left obscure in the repeated phrase 'convey into the mind'. Later on (II.1.9) he identifies 'having ideas' with 'perception'. In Chapter 8 he speaks of the production in us of ideas of pain, whiteness, sweetness, in a way suggesting that the production of such ideas and the production of sensations are the same. The 'secondary qualities' of things are spoken of as powers in the objects to produce sensations (II.8.10), or again as powers to produce an idea or sensation (*ibid.*). He speaks (*ibid.*21) of 'being able to give an account how the same water, at the same time, may produce the idea of cold by one hand and of heat by another'. Here producing an idea and producing a sensation certainly seem to be one and the same thing, though he then immediately uses the odd phrase 'if those ideas were really in it', i.e. in the water: this must mean 'if the sensible qualities were really in the water'. The existence or occurrence of the sensible qualities here seems to be the same as the occurrence of a sensation and that the same as the production of an idea.

This identity would explain why Locke is content (as he is) just with an account of the cause of sensations. The account is a physical one. The 'primary qualities', such as shape, size and motion, are real in the things that have them, i.e. our ideas of them are resemblances of the properties of things, as our ideas of 'secondary qualities' are not. Particles get off things into our sensory apparatus and affect the minute particles of that apparatus (II.8.13, 21) and thereby convey to the brain (*ibid*.12) some motion which produces the ideas of primary qualities and in the same way (*ibid*.13) the ideas of secondary qualities, 'it being no more impossible to conceive that God should annex such *ideas* to such motions, with which they have no similitude than that he should annex the *idea* of pain to the motion of a piece of steel dividing our flesh, with which that *idea* hath no resemblance'.

I mention Locke on primary qualities because one cannot describe his causal theory of the sensation of secondary qualities without bringing in primary qualities, as the account relates to both kinds. His theory of primary qualities does not otherwise concern us, and for our purposes we can think of secondary qualities just as the sort of qualities which are objects peculiar to our sense, as colours are objects of sight and sounds of hearing.

We may note that Locke has no real explanation of how the sensations or ideas of these qualities are produced, although he wants to give a causal account; he is sure that particles can knock against particles and make them move, but lamely says that God can 'annex' an idea of yellow, say, to such a motion.

However, we are not concerned with this sort of failure on Locke's part, but rather with his conception of the two sources of our ideas: sensation and reflection.

'Reflection' is the name he gives to an inner analogue of external sense, saying it is very like and might properly enough be called 'internal sense'. It is introduced as 'the perception of the operations of our own mind within us'. These operations are such as 'perception, thinking, doubting, believing, reasoning, knowing, willing, and all the different actings of our own minds; which we being conscious of and observing in ourselves, do from these receive into our understandings as distinct ideas, as we do from bodies affecting our senses' (II.1.4).

Locke says that *all* our ideas *come from* sensation or reflection, i.e. all come from perception, as he calls it, either of objects of sense or of 'mental actings'. That is to say, in the data of perception are to be found all the 'materials of thinking'. For he does not think that all our ideas are of data of one or the other sort of perception and that we have no other ideas. For, firstly, there is another distinction of ideas: some are simple, some are complex.

He says that the qualities that affect our senses produce ideas which are 'simple and unmixed' (II.2.1). Simplicity turns out to be a surprising property of some ideas: solidity, for example, is a 'simple' idea. A 'simple' idea does not have to be an idea of an object of one sense; there are simple ideas of diverse senses, as extension, figure, rest and motion. The explanation Locke gives of simplicity is that a simple idea 'contains in it nothing but one uniform appearance or conception in the mind, and is not distinguishable into different ideas' (II.2.1). This explanation, however, is given only in connection with 'qualities that affect our senses', and it isn't clear how to apply it to ideas of reflection. Locke calls perception 'the first and simplest idea we have from reflection' (II.9.1), but I have not found him discoursing on complex ideas of reflection, characterised as such.

What he means by simplicity of ideas is probably more easily grasped by seeing what importance this conception has for him. The main thing is that simple ideas have to be data, givens. The mind can neither make nor destroy them. Once stored with simple ideas the mind has 'the power to repeat, compare, and unite them, even to an almost infinite variety; and so we can make at pleasure new complex ideas' (II.2.2).

The whole of our ideas, then, consists of the simple ideas we have and the complex ideas which are manufactured from these or with them. Can complex ideas be data, givens? Locke thinks that brutes 'take in and retain several combinations of simple *ideas*, as possibly the shape, smell, and voice of his master make up the complex *idea* a dog has of him, or rather are so many distinct marks whereby he knows him; yet I *do not* think they do of themselves ever compound them and *make complex* ideas' (II.11.7). We see a hesitation about brutes in that 'or rather'.

As for humans, so far as I have been able to detect, he thinks they do 'compound' all their complex ideas themselves. He says all complex ideas are made by combining simple ones; but that there are two other exercises of power over simple ideas. One is bringing them together without uniting them; in this way the mind gets all its ideas of relations. The other is separating them from all other ideas which accompany them in their real existence: 'thus all general ideas are made'; i.e. in this way the mind abstracts, and, as he explained in the chapter 'Of discerning', an idea 'once abstracted becomes general, and so becomes a general representative of all of the same kind'. It is obscure whether an idea, once 'abstracted', and so made from a simple idea, is to be called 'simple' or 'complex'. The important thing to notice is that the idea entering the mind from sense experience is, apparently, not general. This, in spite of Locke's saying that it is 'simple and unmixed', which sounds as if it were 'abstracted'. However, it is by no work of the mind that simple ideas enter it in disconnection from all others that 'accompany it in its real existence'.

Stillingfleet challenged Locke's assertion that all our ideas come by sensation or reflection, giving the counter-example of *substance*. Locke replied that he never said the general idea of substance came in by sensation or reflection 'or that it is a simple idea of sensation or reflection, though it be ultimately founded in them; for it is a complex idea made up of the general idea of some thing or being with the relation of a support to accidents. For general ideas come not into the mind by sensation or reflection, but are creatures or inventions of the understanding ... and as to the ideas of relation, how the mind forms them, and how they are derived from, and ultimately terminate in, ideas of sensations and reflection, I have likewise shown' (*A Letter to the Bishop of Worcester*, 19).

Stillingfleet's criticism stands. If 'general ideas ... are creatures or inventions of the understanding', it is after all not true that sensation and reflection 'when we have taken a full survey of them and their several modes, and the compositions made out of them, we shall find to contain our whole stock of ideas'. As for the ideas of relation, we have seen Locke's account of how such an idea arises through an operation of the mind on a pair of ideas which it brings together without compounding them. A relation is not (in fact or according to Locke) an operation of the mind; but he thinks that the holding of two ideas together gives the idea of a particular relation. This is all he can mean by saying that ideas of relation derive from and ultimately terminate in ideas of sensation and reflection. In the reply to Stillingfleet he also says that the mind *forms* them.

Well, relations have terms, and the terms of relations will be presented by ideas which, in the end at least, are not ideas of relations. These ideas will be, let us say, ideas of objects of sense which are actually standing in some relation. Locke's theory is that this is after all not anything actual in the reality, but involves a comparing mind for its very existence. Locke is barely intelligible on the subject, but what he has to say to Stillingfleet about a relation (of support to accidents) as one component of the complex general idea of substance is an insufficient reply to Stillingfleet's criticism. It does not stand up as an instance of his theory of relations which seems to require the presentation of the two[1] particular terms of a relation. And even if it did so stand up, the relation in question would not be one in which the ideas or their objects actually stand, but would be an idea formed by the mind holding these two ideas together; so once again it could not be said to be included in the stock furnished by our simple ideas of sensation and reflection.

His lengthy reply to Stillingfleet might be briefly summed up as 'The mind does a lot of work in constructing the idea of substance'. The mental work involved would have a logical nature which Locke's theory of ideas is unequal to covering or including. The nature of relation, he says (II.25.5), 'consists in the referring or comparing two things one to another; from which comparison one or both comes to be denominated'. That is, there are no relations if no mind is doing any comparing. This concept was no invention of Locke's; but in any case it is useless for giving an account of *substance*. Locke seems to confuse the term of a relation (here 'some thing or being') with an element in a composition; for the 'some thing or being' would be the support of accidents, i.e. would be a term of the relation *x supports y* as Locke is expounding the idea of substance.

I labour these points to show how various important ideas do not fall into line with Locke's scheme for an account of the origin of ideas. 'The mind does a lot of work on the basic ideas', he might say protestingly: it repeats the idea of *one* or *unit* to get the idea of *two*; it creates the character of generality, it compares two things and forms ideas of the relation between them.

The notion of so getting the idea *two* (II.13.1) is pathetic; it sounds as if it were based on 'twice one is two'; but if one understands that, one already has the idea *two*. Generality is a feature of any idea represented by a general term; an individual idea of a sensible property is not e.g. an individual event of a sensation of it; it is already a general idea.

II

I will not pause to discuss why in spite of these faults Locke is still read or why he is a great philosopher. Our quarry is other.

What made him say so boldly 'The understanding seems to me not to have the least glimmering of any *ideas* which it doth not receive

---

[1]   Locke seems to allow only two terms to a relation; and to insist on two distinct terms.

from these two'? And: 'These, when we have taken a full survey of them and their several modes, combinations and relations, we shall find to contain all our whole stock of *ideas* ...' (II.1.5). 'Combinations' need no explanation. 'Modes' means 'modifications' of simple ideas, e.g. by repetition or by a relation among the parts of some spatial object. Relations we have already discussed; here we should only note that Locke here talks as if relations truly existed between ideas (or sensations), which is contrary to what he tells us in the chapter 'Of Relation'. For it would appear from that that without comparing minds there would be no relations.

Locke makes a strenuous attempt to bring very many ideas into accord with his theory. This sometimes involves him in giving fairly ludicrous accounts of the formation of ideas. One may want to ask: Why has Locke been so influential?

The answer lies in the very fact that he offers so simplistic a picture, together with his insistence on being an empiricist. We get all our ideas from being given simple ideas; these we know through observation of what we experience by external or internal sense. Difficult cases will be coped with by saying 'The mind does a lot of work on the original ideas to produce those ideas which are neither simple nor compounded of simple ideas'. Putting such cases aside with a wave of the hand, we are enthralled by the basic picture of where all the contents of our minds come from. In this picture, none are innate, none are illuminations from somewhere outside nature; none involve insights into objects of pure reason; none involve any active functioning of the intellect using a machinery and ideas of its working, which machinery it has independently.

All that we have to do is to work on the details if we wish to maintain a Lockean type of philosophy.

As we have seen, Locke wished to maintain that those ideas which are neither simple nor compounded of simple ones nevertheless have simple ones as their essential material or do at least somehow involve simple ideas in the explanation of them. This was to admit that there are ideas not comprised in the two treasuries with which we begin, and the active formation of which must be an innate capacity. (Compounding would also be such, of course, but its results bring in nothing new.) That admission means: it is false that 'there is nothing in the mind which did not come in one of these two ways'. The fact that ideas which do come in one of these two ways are always *somehow* involved in the formation of those further ideas, as Locke claims, would be insufficient for the defence of the thesis of Book II, Chapter 1.

Suppose Locke had realised this, and had changed the thesis accordingly. He would then have said that we receive impressions both of sense and of reflection, and that these give us corresponding ideas. These in turn are compounded into complex ideas. But they, and the complex ideas we form, are also the material on which intellectual operations work with concepts and an innate machinery to produce ideas that do not correspond to impressions or complexes of impressions. The concepts are innate in the sense that there is an innate capacity to form them and operate with them. Some of this apparatus can be called 'logical', signs of which are the logical constants, including quantifiers and other operators, some 'formal-conceptual', signs of which are e.g. the formation of propositions, the use of terms belonging to the categories of substance and relation, and eventually the formation of those and other categorical concepts themselves.

Such a programme would have been nearer to truth than Locke's programme is. It would have retained the core of his conception of the purely empirical content and basis of a vast block of our ideas. (Or at least a conception of a *largely* empirical content.) It would have offered a much less revolutionary system. For in Locke's time it was revolutionary to reject innate ideas. It was also fairly revolutionary to—in effect—reject the intellect as a faculty distinct from the power of mental imaging. This rejection is I think not explicit, but it is implicit in much of Locke's theorising about ideas. When these are not sensations, they are imprints of sense remaining or revivable after the object of sense is no longer there. It is striking that these are all he treats of in his chapter on memory. I suppose he might have added 'combinations' of imprints, but hardly more. For the chapter is noteworthy testimony to the fact that his main enthusiasm for ideas was for those having sensory content.

Descartes' philosophy was a watershed. Down one side ran the streams of the philosophy of the 'rationalists'. Down the other, the streams of empiricism. Descartes is called the father of modern philosophy. It would probably be fair enough to call Locke the father (under Descartes) of empiricist modern philosophy. To be sure, this leaves out Hobbes; but if we are interested in strong lines of influence, as it were in genealogical trees, Locke rather than Hobbes is the ancestor after Descartes.

We have now shelled out that bit of Locke's philosophy that concerns us. I have avoided the falsification there would have been in not showing its place in his system and its importance in his influence and attraction. But now we can turn to the thing itself by itself.

How do we get those ideas Locke calls 'simple'? His answer is: By having the corresponding experiences. This is so, whether the ideas are ideas of sense or of reflection. We have seen his causal account and noted one of its faults: that he speaks of God as 'annexing' an idea of white, or pain, to some motion of particles in our brain. This fault is there by implication in the causal account of the genesis of ideas of primary qualities too. If I form the idea *square* because particles of some shape and size hit my visual apparatus and cause a motion in the brain, the brain particles don't have to form a square, nor should one think that it would be any help if they did: God will have 'annexed' the idea *square* to certain motions just as much as he annexed the ideas *sweet* and *hot*. (Locke may not have realised this; he may have thought there really would be a representation of square-ness in the brain and that *this* appropriately produced the idea.) Now, Locke says that the ideas of primary qualities are *resemblances* of the qualities in the external objects of perception. Remember, too, that ideas are in the first place sensations, so far as sensations are conceived to have content. So it is suggested that having them is (indirect) consciousness of real properties—properties they resemble if they are idea-sensations of primary qualities, and properties they don't resemble if they are secondary qualities.

An idea is often represented by a word. How does a word come by its meaning? Locke's answer is: '... words ... come to be made use of by men as the signs of their ideas; not by any natural connexion that there is between particular articulate sounds and certain ideas, for then there would be but one language amongst all men; but by a *voluntary imposition*, whereby such a word is made arbitrarily the mark of such an idea. The use then of words is to be sensible marks of ideas' which are 'their proper and immediate signification' (III.2.1).

However: 'That which words are the marks of are *the ideas of the speaker: nor can anyone apply them as marks to anything else but the ideas that he himself hath.* For this would be to make them signs of his own conceptions, and yet apply them to other ideas; which would be to make them signs and not signs of his ideas at the same time; and so in effect to have no significance at all' (*ibid*.2).

Yet in spite of this, men 'in their thoughts give them a secret reference to two other things'. Namely (1) to the ideas in other men's minds. 'They suppose their words to be marks of the ideas also of other men, with whom they would communicate; for else ... they could not be understood, if the sounds they applied to one idea were such as by the hearer were applied to another, which is to speak two languages' (*ibid*.4). And (2) to the reality of things: 'men would not be thought to talk barely of their own imaginations but of things as they really are' (*ibid*.5). But 'it is a perverting the use of words and brings unavoidable obscurity and confusion into their signification, whenever we make them stand for anything but those ideas we have in our own minds' (*ibid*.).

We have here at once a pretty explicit statement that ideas are private, since no one can signify anything but his own ideas, whatever his illusions on the subject, *and* an implication that it is possible, though unusual, for people 'to examine whether the idea they and those they discourse with have in their minds be the same'.

As to the first point, that no one can signify anything but his own ideas, this irritates one into seeking a benign interpretation; otherwise it is too absurd, implying that one cannot even speak of another's ideas. We might perhaps understand it as we would understand 'No one can breathe any breaths but his own'. That is harmless enough. But not when it leads to a picture of not being able to get outside one's own ideas in what one means. Locke's philosophy does force this picture on us, and his attempts to avoid it are unsuccessful. (To avoid it in theory, that is.)

There is something further to mention in this connection with this first point. No one can signify anything *but* his own ideas, says Locke, but does not explain how anyone can '*signify*' his own ideas. He arbitrarily makes a sound (say) to be a sign of an idea. Whence is he supposed to have got the idea of a sign? Or, if he makes sounds be signs without having any notion of a sign, *what* makes the sound into a sign? The man does, says Locke. But what is the action of making a sound into a sign? It looks as if Locke's answer had to be: he takes the word and *means* his idea by it.

As to the second point, that it is possible to examine whether the idea one has in one's own mind is the same as what someone else has, this is true enough from a commonsensical point of view. We do make such enquiries, and may find such a thing out by finding what else the other says, using the same word (say) which we can usually judge he is using in the same sense as before. This enquiry however relies on his using other words as we do. The enquiry will terminate leaving the rest of the other's words unchecked by this method.

However, at the level we are on we cannot be commonsensical. For, right or wrong, commonsense presupposes languages; and we are at present considering how words get related to ideas in the first place. At this level it is very questionable, given the assumptions of Locke's theory, whether anyone could ever so much as try to find out whether someone else meant the same 'simple' ideas as he did.

Locke says (*ibid*.6): 'There comes by constant use, to be such a connection between sounds and the ideas they stand for, that the names heard almost as readily excite certain ideas as if the objects themselves which are apt to produce them did actually affect the senses.'

There is an illicit extra assumption here, that we could rely on public objects of observation to show what someone else meant by his words. In Locke's theory, this means an assumption that public objects, together with a use of words that does not excite disagreement, constitute evidence enough that words signify the same ideas in two people's mouths. So perhaps Locke sometimes thought; nor is in itself unreasonable to think so. But has *Locke* the right to think so? Has he the right to speak at all of the idea in one mind as the same (or not) as the idea in another?

Suppose it were an image, of a circle, say. The two images would be individually different, even if we could say: They are exact replicas of one another. Of course, we can't say that; no one can see or measure the image in another's mind. — We can compare them only by exchanging descriptions — or perhaps drawings. We may find out that one is, or is not, bigger than another. But if we try to compare our *ideas* of a circle by giving descriptions, a difference will either be irrelevant or will prove we have not both got an idea of a circle. If we have, it is one idea in both our minds. The individuation of ideas by individuation of heads in which they occur is implicit in Locke. But it is mistaken, as mistaken as an individuation of numbers as the number of pebbles in my hand and the number in yours. The pebbles are different, but if I have four and you have four there is just one number of pebbles we both have. There is no question 'But are the two fours the same?' Similarly for ideas: if a relevant difference can appear, the ideas are of something different.

Locke, in some ways commonsensical, thinks of an ascertainable difference. But how could a difference of his 'simple' ideas in two heads be ascertained? This question I think he was not sufficiently aware of, but as soon as it is asked it is obviously asked justly. For no one can *mean* another's ideas as the other does, nor can he know what they are. A resolute discrepancy could arise when complex ideas are in question, if we assume common meanings for the simple terms in which complex ideas are to be expounded. But we can make no such assumption if we believe Locke: there can be no such thing as a common meaning for a word in two mouths standing for simple ideas. For Locke, the idea is the meaning and the idea is individuated by its owner, like an image.

And yet for Locke the question 'Is A's idea of *sweet* (say) the same as B's?' must be a significant one. We might say 'Someone who could look into both minds could tell whether both ideas were the same'. But how could anyone but God know such a thing? God was said by Locke to 'annex' ideas—in this place sensations—of the secondary sensible qualities to movements in the brain; so presumably God would know whether A's sensation was the same as B's, and that would be the same as knowledge whether the resultant ideas were the same, or whether the resultant ideas were fair copies of the sensations. —It does not sound much like Locke to adopt this course; but it looks as if we could push him to it, for he says: 'Everyone has so inviolable a liberty to make words stand for what ideas he pleases, that no one hath the power to make others have the same ideas in their minds that he has when they use the same words that he does' (III.2.8).

This passage suggests at once scepticism about the possibility of knowing whether someone else means the same as oneself, and belief that there is a fact of the matter.

III

If, like Humpty Dumpty in *Alice in Wonderland*, we can make our words mean what we like, it would seem that though we cannot choose what 'simple ideas' to have, we can choose among them what to mean. We also have a liberty of compounding them as we please. It follows that no one can know for sure what ideas another is expressing. This conception has taken a singular hold in respect of 'simple' ideas of colour. People who are not philosophers even will tell one that there is no knowing whether what another calls 'green' is not what oneself would call 'red'. One might reply: why do you say 'red' here and not 'middle C' or 'a giraffe'? This suggestion usually produces a blank stare; the imagination does not readily embrace it. Here we can see the point of Moritz Schlick's remark: 'One can communicate structure, not content.' The terms 'middle C' or 'a giraffe' have the wrong grammar, the wrong *logic*, as people often speak of 'the logic of' such-and-such. For example, both green and middle C are subjects of intensity of occurrence, but a giraffe is not. Also green is something seen, not heard. So it is natural to think 'you cannot know what *colour* the other sees or means', while it is an altogether outré suggestion that you cannot know what category of object he means. Hence 'one cannot communicate content, but can communicate structure'. On this Wittgenstein commented; if you can't communicate content, you can't communicate structure either. That is to say, the outer structure exhibited in the use of a term is being presumed to represent an inner structure of the inner idea or experience. But if so, why should the structure being represented be the same as the structure representing it? If you cannot know the inner content, then equally you cannot know the inner structure.

'Ostensive definition' means explanation of a word or phrase by an act of pointing which accompanies the words 'That is red' or 'This is a rhombus' or 'a dragonfly' etc., etc. We must however distinguish two different sorts of case, one of which is not definition but identification or characterisation. Wittgenstein remarks on this in the *Blue Book* page 2, saying that he wants 'to remove once and for all, the idea that the words of the ostensive definition predicate something of the defined; the confusion between the sentence "this is red", attributing the colour red to something, and the ostensive definition "this is called 'red'".'

H.H. Price used to distinguish between formal and informal ostensive definition. He remarked that formal ostensive definition is not the most usual way in which children learn what words stand for. They are in a situation, say, in which a cat is prominent and so is the word 'cat', and seeing the cat teaches them the meaning of the word.

No doubt something like this is often true, though it needs a bit more going into than Price gave it. We take a useful short cut by considering formal ostensive definition. This topic is one of the main topics in the first forty *Bemerkungen* (I shall henceforth say 'remarks', meaning numbered passages) of the *Philosophical Investigations* [*PI*] of Wittgenstein; and these forty passages, so far as they have to do with ostensive definition, should be closely studied before considering Wittgenstein's attack on the ideas of private rules, private understanding, private sense of a word, private language. But we should also read the *Blue Book*. In particular, for the topic of ostensive definition, let's say the first fifteen pages of the *Blue Book*. Or at any rate—this is the absolute minimum—the first two and a half.

Here Wittgenstein makes a very familiar distinction between two types of explanation of the meaning of a word—the 'verbal' and the 'ostensive'. 'The verbal definition as it takes us from one verbal expression to another, in a sense gets us no further. In the ostensive definition however we seem to make a much more real step towards learning the meaning' (*Blue Book*, p.1).

Wittgenstein remarks that this sort of definition is supposed to *give* the word a meaning, and proposes to explain the word 'tove' (which is not a word in the English language) by pointing to a pencil and saying 'this is a tove'. This ostensive definition can be interpreted in all sorts of ways, e.g. as meaning

'This is a pencil'.
'This is round'.
'This is wood'.
'This is one'.
'This is hard', etc., etc.

With this observation Wittgenstein has shown something of great importance: namely that ostensive definition cannot lie at the bottom, cannot be the rock-bottom foundation, of our understanding of language. For if we are to understand a formal ostensive definition rightly, don't we have to know what (logical) kind of thing is being named? See *PI*. I, 28: 'Now one can ostensively define a proper name, the name of a colour, the name of a material, a numeral, the name of a point of the compass and so on. The definition of the number two, "That is called 'two'" – pointing to two nuts – is perfectly exact. – But how can two be defined like that? The person one gives the definition to doesn't know what one wants to call "two"; he will suppose that "two" is the name given to *this* group of nuts! – He *may* suppose this; but perhaps he does not. He might make the opposite mistake; when I want to assign a name to this group of nuts, he might understand it as a numeral. And he might equally well take the name of a person, of which I give an ostensive definition, as that of a colour, or a race, or even of a point of the compass. That is to say: an ostensive definition can be variously interpreted in *every* case.'

He next, in I, 29, deals with the suggestion that the ostensive definition should mention the category (or whatever one calls it) of thing whose name is being explained: 'This *number* is called "two", this *colour* is called "red"', etc. He grants that this may avert a misunderstanding. 'But is there only one way of taking the word "colour" or "length"? – Well, they just need defining. – Defining, then, by means of other words! And what about the last definition in this chain?' Whether the word 'number' is needful in the ostensive definition depends on whether the pupil will take the explanation in an undesired way without it.

'And how he "takes" the definition is seen in the use that he makes of the word defined.'

It must already be clear what hammer-blows have been dealt to Locke's and indeed to pretty well every post-Cartesian empiricist position. We have so far not touched on 'privacy' at all. Bertrand Russell, for example, in an essay called 'Knowledge by Acquaintance and Knowledge by Description'[2] formulates the principle: *Every propo-sition which we can understand must be composed wholly of constituents with which we are acquainted.* (We must remember that Russell meant by 'propositions' not 'sentences' but rather 'meanings of (indicative) sentences'.) After restating this principle, he declares that it is merely to say that we cannot make a judgment or a supposition without knowing what we are making our judgment or supposition about. His theory of acquaintance is that he is *acquainted* with an object if he has a 'direct cognitive relation' to it. He goes on to maintain that what he has a direct cognitive relation to are, 'in a large sense', sense-data when they are particulars; otherwise they are universals. The reference to sense-data doubtless brings in privacy, but privacy is not of the essence of 'acquaintance' as he explains it. What are ordinarily counted as names, like 'Bismarck' or 'Julius Caesar' aren't really names but definite descriptions, i.e. have to be analysed for each of us who uses them into a phrase of the form 'the such-and-such'. This in turn is analysable according to Russell's famous theory of descriptions; and this analysis will be susceptible either of further analysis or of explication as consisting of names of objects of acquaintance (at least one of which is a universal) together with quantifiers and variables. This last is described by Russell as consti-tuting a difficult problem: 'the problem of the nature of the variable, i.e. of the meaning of *some, any* and *all*'.[3]

I cite this essay because it is the work of a very clever man and because it implicitly relies on an assumption that *naming*, or simply *designating*, is just one thing. Russell does not indeed speak of naming in his account of the final analysis he is indicating as a goal. That is only because of his theory of propositions as meanings, not as sentences. This enables him to say, e.g., 'All propositions, intelligible to us, whether or not they primarily concern things only known to us by descriptions, are composed wholly of constituents with which we are acquainted, for a constituent with which we are not acquainted is unintelligible to us'.[4] That end bit is surely one of Russell's frequent and easily corrigible bits of slapdash writing. He must mean 'for we could not understand a sentence containing a genuine name of some-thing with which we were not acquainted'. We can understand

[2]   *Proceedings of the Aristotelian Society,* 11 (1910/11); also in Bertrand Russell, *Mysticism and Logic* (London: Allen & Unwin, 1963), pp.152–167.
[3]   *Mysticism and Logic,* p.166.
[4]   *Ibid.,* p.167.

sentences containing what are commonly called names, or containing definite descriptions of objects we are not acquainted with, just because a complete analysis of them would give us sentences the *names* in which are all names of objects we are acquainted with. These objects would be of different kinds, some particulars, some universals, and among the universals some would be relations of various polyadicities.

There is lurking in this enquiry an unquestioned assumption that the barely mentioned relation of name-to-object-named is unproblematic. Russell does speak of 'proper names, i.e. of words which do not assign a property to an object, but merely and solely name it' adding that he would hold that in this sense there are only two words which are strictly proper names of particulars, namely 'I' and 'this'. Later in the same paper he says 'A man's name is what he is called, but however much Scott had been called the author of *Waverley*, that would not have made him to be the author; it was necessary for him actually to write *Waverley*'.[5]

We know, in fact, that Russell's curious theory of knowledge, expounded in this essay, would involve him in denying that 'Scott' was a genuine name of Scott, except possibly for Scott himself, if he did call himself 'Scott'. Would Russell have counted e.g. Scott's signing his name as his calling himself 'Scott'? That seems uncertain, going by what Russell says about Bismarck: 'Assuming that there is such a thing as direct acquaintance with oneself, Bismarck himself might have used his name directly to designate the particular person with whom he was acquainted. In this case, if he made a judgment about himself, he himself might be a constituent of the judgment.' It looks as if Russell thought of the purpose of names as merely to be constituents of sentences expressing judgment or suppositions.[6]

Can we answer the question 'What is it "merely and solely to name" an object of acquaintance?' We know what is being excluded here—attributing anything to the object, for that is mentioned to exclude it from what proper names (in a strict sense) do. But what is it then that they positively do? They designate—he might have been willing to say—their objects.

Wittgenstein imagines someone saying: 'We name things and then we can talk about them: can refer to them in talk' and he comments: 'As if what we did next were given with the mere act of naming. As if

---

5   *Ibid.*, p.163.
6   *Ibid.*, p.157.

there were only one thing called 'talking about a thing'. Whereas in fact we do the most various things with our sentences.

'Think of exclamations alone, with their completely different functions' (PI. I, 27). He gives examples like 'Water!', 'Help!', 'Fine!' and of course need not have confined himself to exclamations: we have already seen how the example of signing one's name does not seem quite to fit Russell's conception of what one does with a name. It doesn't actually seem even to be an example of 'talking about a thing'.

Wittgenstein, recalling Mill's dictum that proper names have only denotation, not connotation—i.e. they *simply* stand for their objects and contain no information about them, they have so to speak no content, remarked that it is a great deal of information about a word that it *is* a proper name, and more if one knows of what kind of thing. To this we could add that knowing 'of what kind of thing' is mostly necessary if e.g. we are to understand the sentences in which a particular proper name occurs. There is of course more to say on this point, but I will not say it here; examples proving the truth of Wittgenstein's remark are easy to invent. We do not have to know who or what individual is named by a proper name, at least in general, in order to construe the sentences in which it occurs properly; that is not the kind of understanding that is in question.

A reading of the remarks 1–40 of the *Investigations* should have the effect on one's mind that one no longer thinks of naming so simplistically as one was inclined to do before. Here, when I speak of naming, I am not confining myself to uses of proper names. In modern English and American philosophy there has been a strong tendency to restrict the term 'name' to meaning 'proper name', so much so that it almost seems a novelty to remind people that there are common names too, and that there is nothing wrong with saying that 'red' is the name of a colour, 'coal' the name of a kind of stuff, 'pain' the name of a lot of sensations, 'East' a name of a direction of the compass, and so on. Indeed such talk is perfectly familiar; the only puzzle is why it should be forgotten in some discussions of theory of meaning.

What should be clear after Wittgenstein is that we cannot say: *naming* is just one thing and the differences lie in the *different kinds of things that are named*. If we say this, we'll have to admit that the 'different kinds' aren't just different like 'different kinds' of fruit: apples, pears, cherries, tomatoes. Or indeed, like the different kinds of pain: a stabbing pain in the guts, a burning pain in the skin, a sting, a stitch, soreness, muscular rheumatism, and so on. One wants to say: the variety of things that we name is *logical variety*. And that means that just conferring the status of a name on a word does not yet tell us how the word is going to be used: how, for example, one is going to be able to use the notion of identity in connection with the name. We saw something of this in Locke's confused dicta about *the same idea*. The word 'idea' is a name, let us say, of something in people's minds. A knife cutting your finger, says Locke, gives you a sensation, which produces (or is the same as?) an idea of pain. Someone might say to Locke: I already had the idea of pain; you are misusing the word 'pain' if you say that cutting my finger produces the idea of pain in me; and you are misusing the word 'idea' too. The fact that both 'pain' and 'idea' are names does not determine what is the right way to use them here.

J.M. Barrie's *Peter Pan*, and various other fairy tales, deliberately offend against the grammar of the word 'shadow'; one might equally say 'against the logic of the idea *shadow*'. A child who was being bought a railway engine and a train in a toy shop, and was asking for a railway accident as well as railway signals to complete the gift, would show that he had not grasped the grammar of 'a railway accident'. At least he might be showing this. The case of the shadows in the fairy tales, and the popular sayings about rainbows, warn us of the possibilities of metaphor or sinister meaning or grammatical jest in dealing with words.

The principal lessons from Wittgenstein's remarks relating to ostensive definition in the *Investigations* are:

(1) Ostensive definition is a perfectly o.k. way of telling someone the meaning of a word.

(2) Ostensive definition is no more conceptually than it is genetically the basis of our understanding of language. It can only take place effectively where the learner already has a certain amount of language and can ask for a name.

(3) Prior to this there can be 'ostensive teaching' where the child is shown things and talked to about them. (See *PI*, 6.) This is usual.

(4) Being shown something and given a name N for it does not teach how to use the name N, it does not teach what else is N or when what was called N is still N. For that, a technique of use of the name N has to be learned, either from scratch or by analogy with words of a similar logical type which have already been learned.

It is of course possible to have a table, like a sheet of samples, to show what colours the names of a range of paints mean. But understanding this is based on grasping a technique of connecting names in a certain spatial relation to coloured rectangles (say) with the colours shown in the rectangles, and this in turn with the colours to be expected of paint in pots bearing those names. What is actually done with words, that is, the practice into which a use of words is woven, lies at the bottom of the learning of one's first language. This sort of practice, with the words woven into it, Wittgenstein called a 'language-game'. He extended this idea from his first introduction of it, about which he speaks of his 'clear and simple' invented language-games as 'objects of comparison' (see *PI*, 7 and 130)—to an apparent claim that all proper use of language *is* playing language-games. If this is so, then one ought not to speak of 'the language-game with the word ...' unless one can describe the 'game'. Indeed at *PI* 486 he says 'Describe language-games!' immediately after asking the question 'How is the word "justification" used?' and at 654 in connection with a queer case of being guided in one's path by a 'map' that is not a map, he says: 'Our mistake is to look for an explanation where we ought to look at what happens as a "proto-phenomenon"'... (655): 'The question is not one of explaining a language-game by means of our experiences, but of noting a language-game.' In 486 we could reconcile the order to describe language-games with the description of his 'clear and simple language-games' as 'objects of comparison'; but hardly the remarks 654, 655.—I am inclined to say: it can be useful to describe the activity with words interwoven into it, which constitutes the use, or part of the use, of various words. But it is worse than useless to utter the words 'the language-game with ...' as it were with a wave of the hand.

Let us now turn towards our goal in this exposition. We can be given a rule like the house-painter's colour chart. But we have to learn how to use the rule. A rule by itself, or even with an interpretation appended, 'hangs in the air'; interpretations can themselves be variously interpreted, just as the original rule could receive more than one interpretation. So giving an interpretation does not give us a theoretically satisfactory answer to the question how a rule can determine what we are to do in following it. (See *PI*, 85–6, 143–51, 185–7, 198–202.) There is something else that shows what the rule means, and that is: what is actually done by those who are counted as following the rule.

One cannot secure just one way of going on with the development of a series, for example, by saying 'You must go on *in the same way*'. For the question is: what *same* do you want? And that can only be shown by a practice, and by acceptance and agreement in the practice.

Now these considerations together make clear why the picture presented by Locke and the picture widely accepted by philosophers, of how we understand language, will not do at all.

First, it assumes that simple possession of a sample and using it to define a word can fix the use of that word for the future as correct if it is used *of the same* as what was used to define it. But what same is meant is not given by e.g. pointing to something.

Second, it assumes that the grammar or logic of a word can be fixed by pointing to something and saying 'That is N'. But how could seeing something, say, tell one the grammar of a word which is connected with it just by the pointing gesture and by the utterance 'That is ...' followed by the word?

Somehow children learning their native language learn the use of words in great diversity. As we have remarked, 'ostensive teaching', as Wittgenstein calls it, plays some part in this; in 'ostensive teaching' one says e.g. 'Look! This is a kitten'; but Wittgenstein says he will not call it ostensive definition because the child can't yet ask what a thing's name is. In this brief clause he touches on the fact that the very idea of naming has somehow to be got hold of. We have seen how Locke in the *Essay on the Human Understanding* and Russell in 'Knowledge by Acquaintance and Knowledge by Description' seem to assume that this does not need any learning, any account, but is one simple and obvious thing.

Russell indeed gets as near as he can to making it so in the case of giving a proper name to a particular, but, as we have seen, he characterises a proper name as a word that does not 'assign a property to an object', but simply and solely *names* it. What *naming* is he assumes anybody will know. No doubt his readers would think they knew; but are children born with this knowledge? Locke at least would be outraged by the suggestion; but the same question must arise in his case: men arbitrarily 'impose' words as signs of their ideas.

The two assumptions that I have spelled out, about the foundationally instructive character of ostensive definition, relate to ostensive definition conceived as a teaching activity by which children learn the 'categorematic' terms for familiar things. As to the 'syncategorematic' words, they are left to one side, perhaps as a difficult problem, as we see Russell doing.

Locke and Russell are not actually concerned with teaching children language, at least not in the texts we have been considering. But ostensive definition, if it is supposed to be a way of acquiring words, is essentially a concept connected with teaching. It is those who teach the child who are supposed to give it knowledge of meanings of words ostensively. My observations on the two assumptions involved therefore apply to ostensive definition as an activity of a teacher; they apply to *public* ostensive definition.

That does not mean, however, that they do not apply to the notions of having words for objects of 'perception' which we find in Locke and Russell, where the objects are private, being 'ideas' in Locke and 'sense-data' (in a very broad sense) for Russell. My account of the two assumptions fits the thought of Locke and presumably of Russell in 1911, though he is not so much concerned with the source or acquisition of ideas as Locke is, and indeed opposes the view that words stand for ideas rather than e.g. for particulars and universals. That, however, does not make the two assumptions irrelevant to Russell. In reading them one should only think of the 'pointing' that is mentioned as a purely mental 'pointing', carried on by one who is considering how he has these meanings for his words.

The conception of ostensive definition as absolutely basic in one's explanation both of the meanings of one's sentences and the content of one's knowledge is — or was — a very natural thing. This I can testify to on my own account. As a teenager captivated by some philosophical problems, among them 'What do I know? And how?', and not even knowing that this sort of enquiry was called 'philosophy', and never having heard the words 'ostensive definition', I formulated some such account: I knew what some words meant by verbal definition, until I came to ones that stood for things I could point to. Sensible qualities were easy, but I worried a lot about cats and cups. When I later heard the word 'ostensive definition' I immediately responded to it as expressing a familiar idea; I had been giving myself ostensive definitions by way of illustrating my theory of knowledge for a year or two; if I had got into conversation with anyone about it (which I do not remember doing) I would have pointed to things or mentioned them as familiar objects of experience. How such a raw teenager picked up from the powerful underground influences of a great philosopher she had probably barely heard of, I don't know. But for what it is worth, my testimony is that thinking on these lines was entirely natural.

The privacy of sensation and thought is something else; but from some people's propensity to say: 'You never can tell whether someone else sees the same colours as you, even though he uses the same words and applies them to the same things. Of course he calls English pillar boxes "red", but perhaps the colour he experiences is green' — from the fact that it would not be startling to be told this by one's neighbour at a dinner party, I infer that the philosophical stress on the privacy of one's sensation and idea of 'red' is something that a lot of people find natural too. I myself found it annoying rather than attractive when I came to it as a young university student; but I could not deny the apparent force of it.

Wittgenstein gives full expression to the idea in many places; we should start out from the discussion of obeying a rule in the early two hundreds of *PI*, I, which I have already cited. At first he seems to be writing especially about continuing progressions; but it quickly becomes clear that it equally applies to how one goes on with the use of the word 'blue' or 'red', for example. At 225 he has said: 'The use of the word "rule" and the use of the word "same" are interwoven.' This is indeed obvious: in applying a rule you must 'do the same as before'. But what same is in question? This may be answered by saying 'the same that consists in following the rule'. But what that was, was just the question. — Similarly: 'You must use "red" always for the same colour.' But what is the same colour? 'It's the same colour if it is red.' Only if you know how to go on applying 'red' do you know what 'same colour' means in the explanation of 'red' — and remember that there are applications of 'same colour' which would actually be wrong — too restrictive — as a rule for what you could call 'red'.

The essential thing about private experience, Wittgenstein observes at 272, isn't each person's having his own, but that no one can know whether other people have the same or not. 'The assumption would thus be possible — though unverifiable — that one section of mankind had one sensation of red and another section another.' This indeed is obvious and precisely it is what is apparently acceptable to the people I mentioned, who will tell you 'Of course no one can tell ...'. A certain frivolity here is just what they enjoy. For their opinion does not appear to have any consequences at all. If you remark that there are tests for various different kinds of colour-blindness, and your interlocutor has a certain degree of philosophical sophistication, they will construct the case where all possible tests make two people's colour vision come out the same — their powers of discriminating are the same — but still 'you can't know'. Here they steer for the notion of the ineluctably private and untestable, with positive appetite.

'What am I to say about the word "red"? (Wittgenstein remarks at 273) — that it means something 'confronting us all' and that everyone should really have another word, besides this one, to mean his *own* sensation of red? Or is it like this: the word "red" means something known to everyone; and in addition, for each person, it means something known only to him? (Or perhaps rather: it *refers* to something known only to him.)'

In the next remark, he says that of course such expedients don't do anything for us in the way of helping us to grasp the functioning of 'red'; rather, they express a particular experience 'in doing philosophy. It is as if when I uttered the word I cast a sidelong glance at the private sensation, as it were, in order to say to myself: I know all right what I mean by it' (274).

Sensations and concepts of 'inner' acts and states are approached under the general heading of obeying rules in the *Investigations*. We have seen how this is quite correct, since an example of a sensible quality – a sample in the visual case – with a name set over against it is a sort of rule. But there is a peculiarity of sensation and other psychological concepts: namely, what is called 'privacy'.

Something may be private because it is not shared. So my toothbrush is private – I hope. But what goes on 'in my mind' and the contents of the sensations that I experience and my 'mental images' – these are private in a far stronger sense. Another *cannot*, not merely does not, share them. In *PI*, II, xi, p.222 Wittgenstein imagines an expression for this which is very vivid: he puts it in quotation marks, which is a sign that he imagines someone saying this: "A man's thinking goes on within his consciousness in a seclusion in comparison with which any physical seclusion is an exhibition to public view." Someone who thought that might have the same thought about mental images and even about sensory contents.

At I, 243 Wittgenstein reflects on the possibility of imagining humans who speak only in monologue, with which they accompany their activities; and then asks: 'But could we also imagine a language in which a person could write down or give vocal expression to his inner experiences – his feelings, moods, and the rest – for his private use? – Well, can't we do so in our ordinary language? – But that is not what I mean. The individual words of this language are to refer to what can only be known to the person speaking; to his immediate private sensations. So another person cannot understand the language.'

After a certain number of remarks on how words refer to sensations – especially the word 'pain', and the absurdity of speaking of oneself as 'knowing' one is in pain, together with the observation at 248: 'The proposition "Sensations are private" is comparable to: "One plays patience by oneself"', and some more general observations, Wittgenstein returns to the theme of 243 at 258. He imagines wanting to keep a diary about the recurrence of a certain sensation: he associates the sign 'S' with it, and writes 'S' in a calendar for each day on which he has the sensation. 'I will remark first of all that a definition of the sign cannot be formulated.' Here one might agree: the fact that one has made a certain mark in a calendar for every day on which a certain sensation—or anything else—happens does not offer any information on the basis of which one could produce a definition of the mark. It could serve as enabling a record of the recurrences without being susceptible of definition—merely because one knows one made that mark according to the rule. An *association* of a mark with something is insufficient ground for asking for a definition of the mark. However, Wittgenstein has got this remark in the context of discussing the possibility of 'giving a name to a sensation'. In 257 he remarks that when one speaks of this 'one forgets that a great deal of stage-setting in the language is presupposed if the mere act of naming is to make sense. And when we speak of someone's having given a name to pain, what is presupposed is the existence of the grammar of the word "pain"; it shows the post where the new word is stationed.'

Thus in the next remark, 258, he is elaborating this point by trying to imagine someone conferring a name on a sensation without such a 'stage-setting'. He doesn't even call it a name, he only calls it a 'sign' or mark. The remark about its not being susceptible of definition provokes, in the dialogue which so much of his writing is, a reaction from someone who wants to conceive 'S' as a name, and thinks that all that is necessary has been provided—the association with a sensation, and the recurrent sensation itself. So he replies 'But still I can give myself a kind of ostensive definition!' That is, he *can* give it (a definition) to himself, as a kind of ostensive definition. 'How? Can I point to the sensation?' asks Wittgenstein, and his alter ego replies: 'Not in the ordinary sense. But I speak, or write the sign down, and at the same time I concentrate my attention on the sensation—and so, as it were, point to it inwardly.' Wittgenstein asks how this can be anything but a mere ceremony, it can't fix the meaning of a sign, which is what a definition is supposed to do. The reply is that this happens through the concentration of attention, which has impressed the connection of the sign and sensation on me. Wittgenstein's comment is that this talk of impressing the connection on me can only mean: 'this process brings it about that I remember the connection *right* in the future. But in the present case I have no criterion of correctness.'

This observation is of course based on the lack of a 'stage-setting' in the shape of a grammar of the word that is supposed to be being defined. No grammar, no sense for 'the same' because no rules of application of the concept of identity in this case.

Wittgenstein might well have terminated this numbered remark here, for the point has been made. In his zeal for capturing the particular sentiment that operates on a philosopher defending the position he is attacking—who is indeed his own alter ego—he does not stop, but adds: 'One would like to say: whatever is going to seem right to me is right.' Here, it seems to me, Wittgenstein makes his alter ego sell himself into Wittgenstein's hands by saying: *whatever* seems right *is* right. I would rather express the same sentiment by saying: 'Seeming right is going to be good enough! I shan't be able to be wrong!'

However that may be — I mean however Wittgenstein has made his alter ego lay himself open to the final crack, he presumably will have done so even if he puts it as I suggest. If there is no such possibility as being wrong, what sense is there in a claim to be right here?

Wittgenstein simply replies to his version of the reply: 'That only means that here we can't talk about "right".'

IV

Let us as it were step back and consider our topic afresh.[7] What is at stake? It is the question whether there are private objects — whether we have logically private objects of knowledge, are acquainted with them, proceed somehow from them to the construction of an 'outer' world. It is hard to give up the idea of private objects.

If a word stands for a private object, it must have a private ostensive definition. And the converse also holds: if a word needs a private ostensive definition, it stands for a private object. Private objects are therefore at stake in the question whether we give ourselves private ostensive definitions.

The whole business concerns experiencing, wherever the content of experience can be thought of as an object. In some contexts we might rather speak of a private state of affairs; but I will confine myself to contexts where it is natural to speak of an object. That *experiencing* is what is in question comes out if we consider what is meant here by a 'private' object. Think of the explanation: 'It's something which some-one else — logically — can't have'. — Is one's body a private object then? — No, *that's* not the sort of having. — What then? — It's the sort of having there is in having an experience. When I have an experience I have something which someone else can't have, and that's the private object. 'Have' something here means 'experience' something.

And when I walk, don't I do something no one else can? For no one else can do *that* walking.

---

7   *Ed.* What follows is a version, with slight modifications by the author, of Anscombe's 1981 paper 'On Private Ostensive Definition' referred to in the initial editorial footnote.

But that's obviously a purely verbal point, it's just surface grammar. The walking you mean isn't identified, hasn't got an identity as *this* walking, except as the walking you do then.

Well, when you have an experience, pain perhaps, or a mental image, or a particular experience of sound, is what you speak of as that pain etc. to be identified otherwise than as one, of such a kind, that *you* are having then? Has one any better right to say 'No one else can have *this?*' than I had to say 'No one else can do *this* walking?'

'Yes! and that is precisely why there is the private object in the one case and not the other. For the object isn't just a grammatical object. Not a cognate accusative like the walk that you walk. I grant the *experiencing* is to be identified like the walking only as the experiencing that I am doing at a certain time. But it gives me, shows me, an object. Such an object is the first kind of existent that I get hold of; such objects are my sole direct cognitive connection with the world. If it is a pain, for example, it acquaints me indirectly with my body; it itself is an object of direct acquaintance. "There's something there!" I want to say.'

'Such objects are not independent of the experiencing subject, but given that they are being experienced, they exist. Just what their relation is to independently existing objects is for correct philosophical analysis to tell us; but of one thing I can be sure, namely that all my knowledge of empirical reality depends on my having these objects. When I define a word by such an object, I guarantee that word's non-emptiness *and* its significance in a single blow.'

What about the difficulty that no one else can know what you mean if your meaning depends on the experience of objects which they can't experience?—'Oh, that's something that will be taken care of somehow or other.' There is certainly a public aspect to my use of the words I use in communication with others. I make an assumption —and isn't it a fair one?—that they have the same private objects as I do; but in any case, there is agreement on the application in public circumstances. The suggestion that we might all have quite different private objects as our meanings for words which we have in common —e.g. that you 'get' what I'd call middle C, or an impression of a giraffe, when I speak of red or when your eyes are directed upon a pillar box—that is too bizarre to entertain. There may even be arguments to show that this cannot be so. Somehow this difficulty can be got rid of, whether by arguments from analogy or probability or the connection of the private object with a certain logical structure. We can happily disregard any suggestion that this difficulty is fatal to the private object: we *know* there are private objects, and no such problem will persuade us to give them up.

If we do really know this, that could be a reasonable attitude. But it may be rather an excuse for not thinking, where we ought to be thinking. Certain considerations show that the supposed knowledge is an illusion we have produced in ourselves. The illusion is however a mis‧ understanding of certain facts which are not illusions.

Suppose I concentrate on something and say 'This is sof', intending thereby to fix the meaning of the word. Or, if it should be a word of my language, seeking to guarantee to myself that I know its meaning. —But knowing that implies knowing how it is generally understood. There would have to be the additional judgment 'This would be called "sof" by anyone who knows the regular meaning of the word.' True: so if I am trying to assure myself that I know the meaning I also make that judgment. But even without it I may think I have a guarantee that I *have* a meaning for the word. This is my absolute certainty. I can call it the Cartesian guarantee because for this purpose it would not matter even if the object was, say, an optical illusion.

It is tempting to think that this procedure, or the possibility of it, lies at the bottom of our understanding of words. Or, if not of all words, at least of some, for we might hesitate about 'logical' words like 'or' and 'all'; or we might even be sure that the account only applied to 'categorematic' words, and not to ones whose sole function is to show how others are connected into a sentence. Or again, we may think that our procedure can only apply to 'pure' experience words, the names of secondary qualities and other simple sensation contents like 'itch', 'tingle' or 'sting'.

Some such motive lies at the back of the opinion that many non-technical terms are nevertheless 'theory-laden'. 'Theory' contrasts with 'givenness in experience'.

If my word 'sof' meant e.g. 'table', or 'pre-Raphaelite', or 'shadow', or 'paralysis', or 'smell of burning', or 'insect bite', I would not be likely to picture myself as having a guarantee of meaning by concentrating on something which I then call by such a name. This is for more than one reason. First, although all those things may be perceived, there is an element of hypothesis about all of them. There is more to one's perception's being 'of a table', for example, than is exhibited in momentary perception. Further, though a table may be only an appearance, and so may the brown colour of an object in a certain light, still 'table' is not a 'sensible-property' concept; whereas even the false appearance of brown does present the colour brown to the sight. —Again, all of those terms are either already complex verbal expressions, or susceptible of definition as if abbreviations of such expressions. — Now, if 'sof' had one of *those* meanings, all these reasons would make it unnatural to think that one had a guarantee of meaning in one's here-and-now experience, and to suppose that it would *not* be fatal to this if others disagreed with one's application of the word. — Once a small child called some drainpipes 'cookhouse doors'.[8] Presumably what others called 'cookhouse doors' didn't matter to him: this was *his* word for something then. But if it was actually his word FOR *a drainpipe* the mere seeing of drainpipes then and there could not enable him to make it so — could not *present* him with the content of a concept of that type. Previous experience, acquaintance with the names of *such* objects, familiarity with the expectations of other impressions even if only hypothetical, would be essential, would as it were supply the template for constructing a new name of the kind.

Now with a word for a sensible quality or for a sensation such as pain the situation is quite different. The terms are unhypothetical. The whole of the quality here answering to the name is presented to sense. The simple terms that stand for such things cannot be thought of as abbreviations of complex definitions. These terms don't hang together with the idea of confirmation by further experience.

Some philosophers (e.g. Ayer, in *Language, Truth and Logic*) have thought the 'ostensive' application ('*This* is white') even of such terms was pretty hypothetical because it involved a judgment that *what* one was calling something was the same as one had called that before. But with one cavil, these are the objects that seem apt for giving words meaning when the words are used to express the experience of a sensible quality. It does feel overwhelmingly convincing to fix my eye on a blue expanse, and alluding to that colour, to say 'That's blue'. Admittedly, I may get into one or two small difficulties if I say I have shown myself what 'blue' means. To take Ayer's point: do I know I am using the word as I have used it before? — Well, I am *sure*. But what's the use of that if there's no conceivable check on whether I am right? But it doesn't matter: here and now I am meaning *this* by 'blue', and so I have attached a meaning to the word, even if it is a new meaning. That also takes care of the remote possibility that taking it as a public word someone else might not agree. It is *Spitzfindigkeit* to insist on that

---

8   There is an English soldiers' song with the refrain: 'Come to the cookhouse door, boys/ Come to the cookhouse door.'

possibility; but if anyone does so, I fall back on the claim that *I, now,* have a meaning for it. 'What is meant by it is presented to me.'

Another difficulty might be raised about the range that my word 'sof' is supposed to have. The colour words, for example, that we all easily remember, have rather wide ranges. 'Pain' stands for something very various. So how different could what I concentrated on have been and still served to *give the same meaning* to 'sof'? — Well, once again this is something it should be possible to take care of. We might restrict our term so that e.g. it covered no range of a property, but only a quite particular place on its scale or spectrum. Or we might say that there is a focal point — say the midpoint of a range — such that everything to which the term could apply is referred to that point, and this essence was what I got hold of.

Nevertheless, in offering these escape routes, we already introduce something rather more difficult to brush aside. What sort of a word is 'sof' at all? My concentration on a *this* cannot tell me the grammar of the word I am associating with it, or the grammar of the sentence 'This is sof'. The sentence is supposed to be a definition, of course; but is the defined word to be understood e.g. as a proper name or as a predicable?

How could experiencing something fix the grammar of a word? And this word must surely have a grammar.

How could experiencing something fix whether anything in another encounter, or whether anything else, and if so *what* else, is to be called something that this is being called?

Here Ayer might say 'You see, it was no use circumventing my point by making a new definition in face of the *present* object. For you'll want to use the word again — otherwise why define it? And any later use will involve the assumption that you are using it for the same. The assumption may always be false, and therefore there are no ostensive certainties.'

But what we have to consider first is not the possibility of scepticism. For we can be sceptical only where we know what we are doubting, i.e. where we do understand the sense of it.

Let us first take this point: any later use will involve the assumption that you are using it for the same. If I meet someone, learn his name, 'Jack' say, and use it of someone in a later meeting, meaning it as the name of that man that I learnt it for before, *then* indeed I am making an assumption: I am taking this man to be the same as that one. But when I merely mean 'Jack' as that man's name, it can't be said that I must be making a like assumption, or reidentifying something as

Jack. It is easy to see this, as I might have to remember Jack *in order* to make any such reidentification.

Thus we must distinguish between 'using it for the same', in the sense of using it in the same meaning, and 'using it for the same' where this means *also* applying it to something that *is* the same: 'Jack' for a man *here* presented for example, or newly described. Here there *is* an assumption or belief.

Only where we have a distinction between these two senses can that assumption be involved in a later use of a word once learned. We don't *assume* we are using the word "than" or "perhaps" 'for the same' or as before, any more that we normally *assume* we are talking or speaking English. With those words, indeed, there's no temptation to think we identify anything to ourselves in using them. Where such temptation arises, because a word is wrongly construed as a name, or we want to call it a 'referring expression', we get spurious problems of reidentification. Such problems surround the word 'I', for example, as I have argued elsewhere.

But we must also take care in another way how we speak of 'using a word *for*' something. If I say 'This paper is magenta' I am not using the word 'magenta' as a name either of the paper or of anything else. I am applying it to the paper; and if I say I call the paper magenta because it's the same as what I called 'magenta' before, 'calling' has the sense 'asserting of' and 'being the same' relates to predicates. For if a is φ and b is φ we may say in this sense that they are the same — there is something that they both are.

When, however, I say 'This colour is magenta' I am using 'magenta' as a name. The character of a name gets imposed *ad hoc* on a word by the syntax of some sentences it occurs in and of some questions which it answers. The fact that the word occurs as a name, however, is no proof that we are dealing with an object. It is true that name and object are correlative; but that only means that if we construct a name (syntactically speaking), we also construct either an object, syntactically speaking, or a relation to some actual object. For a sign may be connected with something without being its name: it may merely be attached to that object, or we may learn to associate them. Think of the signs '+' and '−' which stand by the pins of an electric plug, and are also associated for us with different wires in a flex according to the colours of their coverings. Similarly two signs 'in' and 'out' may be memorised in connection with trays identified by position on an office desk. The answer 'in' may be given to the question 'Which tray is this?' and so the question and answer may import a use of the sign 'in' as if it were a *name* of a *tray*. But the question 'Which sign goes with this tray?' does not do that, though it has just the same point. Considered as names in answer to *that* question, the signs 'in' and 'out' are names of themselves.

The establishment and memorising of the connections is for the sake of an application of the signs — wiring electric plugs, dealing with incoming and outgoing mail. With their *application* they acquire *real* significance. We might say: Only now have they meaning — and their meaning is not like that of names. Thus a name-like character conferred by the syntax of some sentences in which a sign occurs, is insufficient to make it out as the name of some object; either the supposed object itself, as an object, or the relation as if of name to an actual object, is pure syntactical construction.

In short, Frege is wrong in his view (if it really was his view) that an object is the correlate of a name in such wise that you prove that numbers are objects by showing that numerals are (indispensable) names. We can of course *call* the supposed correlates of words that have a name-like character 'objects', and it may be a convenient way of talking, making it easier, perhaps making it possible, to say much that we want to say. And so we say as a matter of course that 'two' is the name of a number, 'red' the name of a colour, 'pain' the name of a sensation, 'West' the name of a direction; and we would speak of the 'objects' in question. Many people hold and have held that if a true proposition has a name as subject and cannot be restated so as not to include such a subject, then we must hold that the subject has an object corresponding to it. Thus they derive a metaphysical conviction from the formal character of a true proposition. Or rather, from its formal character together with its truth. But also, from its epistemological status; for that has a great deal to do with possibilities of analysis. And that is one reason why the simple sensible qualities are treated, in their particular occurrences, as *object encountered*. *Their* names *must* be fixable by ostension! And a certain course of reasoning leads one to think that the most basic ostension is private.

However, our considerations show that this *can't* be so. Public ostensive definition is all right if you know or can pick up what kind of word is being defined — a proper name of a dog, the name of a colour, of an architectural style, of a taste, of a step in a dance. Knowing that means knowing the answer to our question 'What's the grammar of the word? What sort of reapplication is it to have?' *Mere* utterance of a sign, a sound, say, while experiencing something, can't be given the role of fixing the sound as a sign with a certain character. Something *else* must give it that role. I utter a sound, what makes it a *name*? You feel as if *meaning that thing* by that sound would do it. And that may be so, *if* you already know how to use a sign in a particular grammatical way. But the thing you are attending to can't teach you the way.

And this is what makes the idea of private ostensive *definition* into a *fraud*, which we are universally tempted to perpetrate.

Giving a definition: Someone *gives* a definition *to* someone. If the recipient learns from it, the giver knew: the recipient *was* ignorant. So: If *I* can show *myself* something, then *I* already knew. If I can teach myself then I do not need teaching. I cannot be divided into the knowing self that teaches and the ignorant self that is taught.

'But can't I *fix* the meaning?' How? – 'By saying to myself: "*This* is A".' But once more, when have I A again, or when again am I to call something 'A'? – 'When it is like *this*.' Like this, in what way? 'In the respect I mean when I call *this* "A".' But how did I fix *that*? 'I feel sure I know it, I know what I meant.' That's no answer. You are so regarding it, that it makes sense for you to be wrong, and at the same time there's nothing that being wrong – or right – consists in.

If I can take *my meaning* as fixed by *this*, then I'll be justified in thinking that *this* has fixed *a* meaning for 'A'. But I only *fancy* I can because I attach *what* I mean by 'A' to the way I understand '*this*'. So the meaning of 'A' is given, fixed, by the meaning of 'A'. The same objection holds if I try to explain what I'll rightly call 'A' again by 'the same as this'. *What* same? If the application of 'A' is not yet determined, neither is the relevant application of 'the same as this'. I have yet to fix what I call 'the same' in 'the same as this'. Or, what to call recognising A again.

Once more, I must have a way, a technique, of using 'A'. Something *else* is, or isn't, to be called 'A'. Nothing else, if A is a particular soap bubble which explodes at once, and 'A' is its proper name. Something else, if 'A' is the name of a sound. How long, how loud, whether one can observe it in the dark, whether it can be imitated – these are just a few of the things that go with the meaning of 'A'. How can *this* that I am attending to tell me all that or determine any of it? 'First I see it as *this* and then I call it such-and-such.' *This*? What? There has to be an answer to that, and that is why the answers to the questions are already determined, as many of them are, in my approach to the object; and that is why it is a fraud to think that the object, uncharacterised by such determination, can fix them. I already know. So I am not fixing what I mean by 'A'. Or if I *am* fixing it, it's just the *last* point that I am fixing. 'A', say, it to be a name of a piece in a game – *that* I know, and now I say it is *this* piece. When I think I am reassuring myself by giving myself a private ostensive definition, I am dwelling on, attending to, an A; I already know what an A is, or what sort of thing is to be called an 'A'. I am not reverting to the justification of the meaning of the word.

That I can 'simply attend' to something and dwell on it is noteworthy, remarkable. If it is a simple sensible quality I can absorb it, drink it in, get hold of the whole of what the name here names. That one can 'sensibly attend' to an object is one of the things that characterise the important concept of an object of experience. A human expression, yes, that is such an object; a coefficient of expansion, no. A Blake painting, yes, a speed limit, no. A colour in a surrounding, yes, the principles of perspective, no. 'Objects of experience' do not indeed have to be 'elementary data'. Indeed, it's not at all clear that there *is* such a thing as an elementary datum according to the old empiricist conception—the given that fixes the meaning of a word without grammar—so that one wants to *mean* it by squeaking at it, as Wittgenstein once put it. What is true is that there *is* this inclination, that it is strongly connected with the idea of 'I'—what *I* have, what it takes being *I* to have—and, more reasonably, that the expressions of experience which mention simple sensible qualities are in an important sense unhypothetical.

8

Kripke on Rules and Private Language

When I first heard Saul Kripke lecture on Wittgenstein (London, Ontario in 1976) it made a different impression on me from what the printed text tells me. My then impression was that the idea of a 'new sceptical question' — explicitly compared to Hume's question and solution about causality — was a by-thought that Wittgenstein stimulated in Kripke; an 'as if' thought or as it were a pair of spectacles which Kripke suggested one might find useful in considering certain extraordinary arguments in the *Philosophical Investigations*: 'See them as the arguments of a wild sceptic who doubts one's claim to have meant "plus" by the plus sign in previously doing sums' (my quotes).

Furthermore, he wasn't claiming to give an exposition of Wittgenstein, but of what he, Kripke, got out of Wittgenstein — which included this idea of a new sceptical problem; and at some point the suggestion appeared that one might take the sceptical problem seriously.

There is a vestige of all this in the Preface and the 'Introductory' (Chapter 1) of the present volume. 'I can be read ... as almost like an attorney presenting a major philosophical argument as it struck me' (ix). And 'So the present paper should be thought of as expounding neither "Wittgenstein's" argument nor "Kripke's"; rather

---

* Critical Notice of Saul A. Kripke, *Wittgenstein on Rules and Private Language* (Cambridge, MA; Harvard University Press, 1982) published in the *Canadian Journal of Philosophy*, Vol.13, no.1 (March 1985): 103–109. This is the second review of Kripke's book published by Anscombe in 1985. The other, originally published in *Ethics*, 95 (January 1985): 342–352, is reprinted in *From Plato to Wittgenstein: Essays by G.E.M. Anscombe*, edited by Mary Geach and Luke Gormally (Exeter, UK & Charlottesville, VA, USA: Imprint Academic, 2011), pp.231–246.

Wittgenstein's argument as it struck Kripke, as it presented a problem for him' (5).

But the first of these two sentences is followed by: 'If the work has a main thesis of its own it is that *Wittgenstein's sceptical problem and argument* are important, deserving serious consideration' (my italics). Throughout Chapter 2 ('The Wittgensteinian Paradox') Kripke expounds the paradox as scepticism about whether in computing $68 + 57$ as 125 one is not making a mistake about what one has previously meant by '+'. (I remember that in giving the lecture he emphasised that this was *not* a doubt whether $68 + 57 = 125$—if you wanted to ask anyone whether *that* was so, you could go to grade school and ask there.)

The 'bizarre sceptic' who suggests that as one previously meant '+' the answer should have been 5 is explicitly Kripke's invention, a legitimate one for expounding how he made 'the paradox' significant to himself. I have a further memory, namely that his remark 'Wittgenstein could be seen as having discovered a new sceptical problem', came rather late in the lecture, as did the comparison with Hume on causality. This may be inaccurate, disprovable by a transcript. However that may be, in Chapter 2 of the book Kripke is speaking of 'Wittgenstein's sceptic', indeed by page 21 he is saying 'This'—i.e. the problem about one's past meaning—'is the sceptical paradox' and on page 17 he says 'Here of course I am expounding Wittgenstein's well-known remarks about "a rule for interpreting a rule"'. What he has just been speaking of is 'the sceptic's smiling reply' to one's claim about one's past intentions. It is, I suppose, *a* kind of use of Wittgenstein's 'well-known remarks' about interpreting rules, though those do not concern claims about what one previously meant. By pages 51 and 52 Kripke is speaking of 'Wittgenstein's sceptical argument'.

Wittgenstein's 'well-known' remarks are as follows:

> 84. I said that the application of a word is not everywhere bounded by rules. But what does a game look like that is everywhere bounded by rules? whose rules never let a doubt creep in, but stop up all the cracks where it might?—Can't we imagine a rule determining the application of a rule, and a doubt which *it* removes—and so on?
>
>   But that is not to say that we are in doubt because it is possible for us to *imagine* a doubt. I can easily imagine someone always doubting before he opened his front door whether an abyss did not yawn behind it, and making sure about it before he went through the door (and he might on some occasion prove to be right)—but that does not make me doubt in the same case.

85. A rule stands there like a sign-post. — Does the sign-post leave no doubt open about the way I have to go? Does it show which direction I am to take when I have passed it; whether along the road or the foot-path or cross-country? But where is it said which way I am to follow it; whether in the direction of its finger or (e.g.) in the opposite one? — And if there were, not a single post, but a chain of adjacent ones or chalk marks on the ground — is there only one way of interpreting them? — So I can say, the sign post does after all leave no room for doubt. Or rather: it sometimes leaves room for doubt and sometimes not. And this is no longer a philosophical proposition but an empirical one.

86. Imagine a language-game like (2) played with the help of a table. The signs given to B by A are now written ones. B has a table; in the first column are the signs used in the game, in the second pictures of building stones. A shows B such a written sign; B looks it up in the table, looks at the picture opposite, and so on. So the table is a rule which he follows in executing orders. — One learns to look the picture up in the table by receiving training, and part of this training consists perhaps in the pupil's learning to pass with his finger horizontally from left to right; and so, as it were, to draw a series of horizontal lines on the table.

Suppose different ways of reading a table were now introduced; one time, as above, according to the schema:

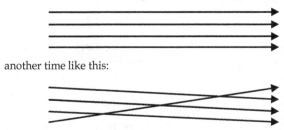

another time like this:

or in some other way. — Such a schema is supplied with the table as the rule for its use.

Can we not now imagine further rules to explain *this* one? And, on the other hand, was that first table incomplete without the schema of arrows? And are other tables incomplete without their schemata?[1]

It is obvious that Wittgenstein was not writing these remarks with sceptical intent. He was opposing scepticism. Not, indeed, by pur-porting to disprove every imaginable doubt about what a rule means

---

[1] Ludwig Wittgenstein, *Philosophical Investigations,* translated by G.E.M. Anscombe (Oxford: Basil Blackwell and New York: Macmillan, 1953), pp.39–40.

— so that the rule with its meaning is sealed for ever as if in an impermeable block of transparent plastic. He did it by (a) pointing to the always imaginable *new* doubt about a rule introduced to defeat a previously imagined doubt and (b) asking whether a table is incomplete without a key of interpretation. The answer to this question is that it *may* be — e.g. we look at the beginning of a dictionary to learn rules of interpretation for signs and arrangements found in the body of the book. But it may *not* be: we do not look for a key for relating names and samples on a paint manufacturer's chart.

I think that Kripke is at least inclined to believe in the mental fact of meaning as providing the impermeable transparent container, and that *therefore* he regards (a) as a description of a new and powerful scepticism. I use the adjective 'powerful' because of his insistence that the 'new sceptical problem' deserves to be taken seriously.

Certainly we should take the arguments of §§ 84–86 seriously. In the first place, the doubts of a sceptic are here dealt with partly by raising doubts about the doubts. I mean: first we imagine a doubt about how to take an arrow as a directive; then we imagine a diagram which is to serve as a rule for how to take the arrow as a directive. And now we can imagine a doubt about how to take the diagram as a directive. This process has in it to go on *ad inf.* — that is to say, it does not terminate in an answer about which it is impossible to contrive a doubt.

I take a 'sceptic' to be one who doubts on principle where a doubt is imaginable. Thus a doubter who doubts how to take a particular arrow which points vertically upwards in an airport is probably not a sceptic. Unless the arrow is a piece of practical stupidity, his doubt can be resolved by a rule of interpretation about which he feels no doubt. But the sceptic has embarked on an infinite series of doubts. Objectionable infinite series are of two kinds: one kind ought never to be allowed to begin because an alleged solution to a problem raises the same problem over again, whose solution raises it in turn about itself ... The other kind can be allowed to begin, but ought to stop somewhere and doesn't because it is persisted with; it is this feature that makes it viciously 'infinite'.

In §84 the 'sceptical' doubt is imagined and is characterised as infinite: the sign of this is the phrase 'and so on'. Wittgenstein then observes that this is not to say that we are in doubt because we can imagine a doubt. In §85 the imagined interpretations of a sign-post are observed not to do the job implicitly imagined for them — namely, that of clearing up the totality of imaginable doubts about what the sign-post means; and the distinction between an actually doubtful sign-post and one that is not doubtful, which remains, is an empirical distinction. In §86 we have at first not interpretations of interpretations, but different schemas of interpretation for a table. If we answer the questions comprising the last paragraph of §86 (one should always answer the questions in Wittgenstein) the correct answers will be: Yes. No. Perhaps.

Thus we have a rejection of scepticism. But Kripke uses the remarks about 'further rules to interpret rules' to present himself and us with a sceptical problem. Everything *you* say to prove what you formerly meant by '+', the 'bizarre sceptic' reinterprets so as to make it accord with what *he* says you formerly meant. Or, rather, with what he is arguing you can't prove you didn't mean. With what right does Kripke do this?

What we see is his inner conviction – modestly expressed, or hinted at from time to time – that the ever and again imaginable new doubts are something whose conceivable truth is incompatible with the truth about knowledge of the meaning of a rule for an operation, or for the future application of a word.

The matter comes up again:

> *Investigations* §201: Our paradox was this: a rule could not determine any way of going on, because *any* way of going on can be brought into accordance with the rule.

Here Wittgenstein is talking about the man described at §143 as receiving a normal training in the sequence of numerals in the decimal system; and at §185 as being further taught to write down series starting from 0 on getting orders of the form +*n*. When asked to go on beyond a 1000, however, his behaviour becomes strange: he has written the +2 series normally up to there, but now he writes 1000, 1004, 1008, 1012. When we say 'Look what you're doing!' he doesn't understand. It simply seems right to him to go on like that. He thinks it *is* doing the same as what he was doing before. In such a case, Wittgenstein says, we might say, e.g.: 'This human being naturally understands that order ['+2'], with our explanation, as *we* would understand the order "Add 2 up to 1000, 4 up to 2000, 6 up to 3000, etc.".'

At §198 Wittgenstein's interlocutor says 'How can a rule tell me what I have to do at *this* place? Whatever I do can, after all, be made to agree with an interpretation of the rule'. 'No', Wittgenstein replies: 'That's not what you should say. Rather: Any interpretation, together with what it interprets, hangs in the air; it cannot serve as a support for what it interprets. Interpretations by themselves do not determine meaning.'

This then is the back reference for 'Our paradox was this' at §201. But note how §201 continues, after saying '*any* way of going on can be brought into agreement with the rule'. It says 'The answer was: if every way of going on can be brought into agreement with the rule, then it can also be brought into conflict with it. Hence there would be neither agreement nor conflict'.

He goes on to say 'That there is a misunderstanding here comes out in the way we supply one interpretation after another in this course of thought; as if each interpretation quieted us at least for a moment, until we think of an interpretation that in turn lies behind this one. For in this way we show that there is a way of taking a rule which is *not* an interpretation; rather, it is manifested from case to case of applying the rule: in what we call going by the rule and what going against it.'

Now Kripke says 'Each new application we make is a leap in the dark; any present intention could be interpreted so as to accord with anything we may choose to do. So there can be neither accord, nor conflict. This is what Wittgenstein said in §201' (§202 in Kripke's text, but this is evidently a misprint).

Here (55) Kripke is still describing 'the sceptical argument', which, he says, 'remains unanswered'. He does not notice (apparently) that 'there can be neither accord nor conflict' is *not* presented by Wittgenstein as part of a troublesome *problem* — the problem of how a rule can determine what one is to do at any particular place — but as part of an *answer* to the complaint 'anything I do can be brought into accord with the rule'. The argument purporting to show this is 'a misunderstanding', says Wittgenstein. It is empty, just *because* it would equally show that everything I might do could be made to conflict with the rule. The proper conclusion to draw is that the rule, with its interpretation, 'hangs in the air'.

Kripke's line, hardly concealed, is to say that the way I *meant* the rule (or the way I *understood* the formula) is in truth decisive. Thus for him 'There would be neither accord nor conflict' presents itself, in spite of the text, as *still* part of the new, terrific, sceptical argument.

Wrongness of exegesis, especially when exegesis is disclaimed, is not so grave a charge — even if Kripke somewhat belies the disclaimers.

What Kripke claims — namely that there is a serious sceptical argument — *that* is what is interesting, and it is one thing we should be grateful to him for. It is Kripke's argument—I mean, he is its mother, even if it was begotten in him by Wittgenstein.

The doubt is: did Kripke really mean plus by '+' in the past? If someone tells him he didn't, but rather meant a different function by that symbol, he can't show that he did mean plus. Anything he cares to mention about his past—whether his thoughts or written or spoken calculations, could have occurred just as they did, while all the time he used '+' he meant a different function (call it 'quus'), coinciding with plus in its results over all the examples that he ever worked out or met. But now with a sum (quum?) to do which he has never done before, the difference between plus and quus makes its appearance. And he does it *wrong*, he does it as if '+' meant plus; he is in a funny mental state and absurdly thinks he always meant plus. Associated concepts like 'addition', 'independence', etc. he equally misremembers when he really had the corresponding ones for 'quus' — *quaddition* is what he used to do. Nothing that happened in the past is denied; but nothing that happened proves he meant plus. For meaning plus is not an event that happens, like saying the word 'plus' in one's head.

How can he answer the sceptic? He can challenge him about how *he* can know that S.K. meant quus. But how can he, S.K., *prove* that he did mean plus? So how does he know he is not under an illusion in thinking that he did?

9

Truth, Sense and Assertion

1. The Greek philosopher Protagoras, who wrote a treatise on truth, made a contract with a pupil to whom he was teaching the art of rhetoric for fighting legal cases. The contract was half the fee straight away, and the other half of it if—but only if—the pupil won his first case. The pupil engaged in no case. So after a while Protagoras sued him for the remaining half fee. 'If I win', argued the pupil, 'then by the decision of the court I don't have to pay; if I lose, then by our contract I don't have to pay.' Protagoras argued in parallel. How the court decided isn't on record. I haven't any doubt the whole thing was fixed up between them in advance.

2. Protagoras was one of the tribe called Sophists—the first European inventors of logical puzzles. He didn't believe there was any such thing as false opinion—anything anyone thinks is true, it's like perception, it's how things appear to him. The Sophists invented an argument that there can't be false thinking: 'He who thinks what is false thinks what is not; but what is not isn't anything; so he who thinks what is false isn't thinking *anything*, but if he isn't thinking anything, he isn't thinking.' Plato tried to solve the problem by saying that one who thinks what is not is thinking something *different* from what is, and so, after all, is thinking. This doesn't work unless, explaining 'not so' as 'different from so' I also insist that 'different

* From the typescript of the Lovejoy Lecture, The Johns Hopkins University, April 1987. The first half of Elizabeth Anscombe, 'Truth, Sense and Assertion, or: What Plato should have told the Sophists', in Ewa Żarnecka-Bialy (ed.), *Logic Counts* (Dordrecht: Kluwer Academic Publishers, 1990), pp.43–46 recapitulates in concise form the argument of the Lovejoy lecture.

from so' implies 'not so'. Otherwise, things might be both *so* and *different from so.*

3. The question—rather in the form 'How is it that a false proposition makes sense?'—came to interest the Cambridge philosophers Russell, Moore and Wittgenstein in the first quarter of this century. But other waters had rolled under the bridge in the interval.

4. St Augustine had produced an argument that truth must be eternal: for if it had a beginning, then before that it was true that there was no truth; and if it will have an end, then after that it will be true that there is no truth. Both are absurd. You could construct a parallel argument for the eternity of falsehood. So far as I know, St Augustine didn't consider the point.

5. The truth and falsehood of propositions of kinds that may be true *or* false—that for *such* propositions truth and falsehood are twins, was perceived in the eleventh century by St Anselm. It comes in his *De Veritate*,[1] a dialogue between a teacher and a pupil. What is truth in a true proposition, a true 'enuntiation'?[2] Is it the thing enuntiated? No, says the pupil, the thing it enuntiates is not its truth but the *cause* of its truth.—Is it the utterance itself, its signification, or anything belonging to the definition of the proposition? No, says the pupil, for if it were any of those things, the proposition would always be true; for all those are the same whether what it enuntiates is the case or is not the case. — Well, what is it? I can't think of anything to say, says the pupil, except that when it signifies the being so of what is so, there's truth in it and it's true. The teacher then asks him what affirmation is *for*—what it has been created for—and he says it is for signifying the being so of what is so. This, then, the teacher says, is what affirmation ought to be doing; and when it is signifying what it ought, then it is signifying rightly. We, the readers, should note that this rightness of an action of signifying, performed by an action of affirming that something is so, is explained with the same words as those offered by the pupil as 'all he can say' when asked for his positive account of *the truth of a proposition.* —The teacher briefly adds that the same holds when the proposition signifies the not being so of what is not so.

6. Now the pupil, who is no stooge, asks: 'What am I to reply, if someone says that even when an utterance signifies as being so what

---

[1]   *De Veritate*, c.2.
[2]   I intentionally keep to the Latinate spelling.

is not so, it signifies what it ought? For it's been equally given it to signify as being so both what *is* and what is *not* so. For if it hadn't been given it to signify as being so even what is not so, it wouldn't signify *that* being so. Then even when what it signifies is not so, it is signifying what it ought. But then the utterance *is right and true* even when it enunciates, as being the case, what is *not* the case.'

7. This point the teacher does not deny. It is indeed, he says, not usual to call a proposition true when it signifies as being the case what is not the case—all the same it does have rightness and truth, because it is doing what it ought—i.e. signifying what's been given it to signify. But when it signifies the being so of what *is* so, there are *two* ways in which it does what it ought: first, it does its job of signifying what it does signify; and second it signifies what it was created for ... It 'more ought to do what it was given its signification for than what it was not given it for'. For why was it only given it to signify the being so of something when it isn't so or the not-being so when it is so? Precisely because it *couldn't* be given it to signify something's being the case solely when it is the case, or not being the case solely when it isn't the case. So there's one kind of rightness which consists in its signifying what it does—and that is a constant property—and another kind which consists in its signifying what it was given its signification for. This rightness is variable and depends on one's use of it. If I say 'It's daylight' so that it signifies what actually *is* the case, I am using the signification of 'it's daylight' *rightly* ... But when I use the same utterance to signify its being so when it is not so, I am not using it rightly: it was not made for that.

8. Note that here we have two things: one, a *teleology* of the kind of proposition in question, and here there is an argument—a proposition (if it's the kind to be true or false) is *for* being true because the other possibility for it is ancillary. The second is what affirmation was created for—namely the right use of the proposition according to what it itself is for.

9. St Anselm in this brief stretch of dialogue shows, first of all, that by a proposition he understands a sentence, vocally uttered or written or signed with the fingers in deaf and dumb language, etc. He doesn't mean what we nowadays call an 'abstract proposition'. He does regard propositions as liable to have multiple occurrences. In consequence he regards propositions that may be true or false as changing from true to false or false to true as things change. In this he contrasts with almost all modern logicians, who regard it as a different propo-

sition if it changes from being true to being false—the *time* at which it is uttered is a perhaps unmentioned part of it, or of its sense. And so, 'It's daylight' said at different times would be as many different propositions.

10. Anselm speaks separately of affirmation and denial of, or in, propositions. This was quite traditional, but from his saying 'The argument will work for denial too' we can assume that he would accept the blanket term 'assertion'—the denial of a proposition being the assertion of its negation. Assertion presumably has a personal subject, so we can see that Anselm says *both* that the proposition signifies things' being thus and so, *and* that the person using the proposition does so. However, he seems not to notice that a proposition can occur as a subordinate clause, an *if*-clause, for example, and then *there is nothing wrong* with its being false. We might correct him, then, by saying that a proposition, true or false, performs the task of signifying what it does, and the person who asserts it also uses it to signify what it does, but there is a further duty, on the part of one asserting, of signifying as being the case only what is the case. He can use the proposition so, because if it is the complete thing that is said, that is properly what it is for. It is of course possible that Anselm would only *call* something a proposition if it was a complete one—i.e. one that is not part of another.

11. The most signal thing that he does in this stretch of dialogue is to note a certain parity of truth and falsehood in connection with the sort of proposition he is talking about. 'It's been given to the proposition equally to signify something's being so when it is so, and when it is not so' and 'it couldn't be given to it to signify something's being so only when it is so'. With this observation we find ourselves in the company of Frege and Wittgenstein. Frege thought that so long as a sentence was well-formed and did not contain any proper names that did not stand for anything, the sentence was itself a complex name either of truth or of falsehood. He did not restrict his consideration to propositions that might be either true or false, but neither did he exclude such propositions from it. His conception of 'the true' and 'the false', or truth and falsehood, as objects, is as wild as it seems, and has one noteworthy objection to it: why should one aim at believing, judging, asserting, only the true? As Michael Dummett has observed, this is rather like describing a game in which there is winning and losing without there being anything to show that the object of a player is to win. Frege misses the teleological points that are so important in Anselm.

12. Wittgenstein does not think that sentences are complex names at all and explicitly accused Frege of error in this. But he is with Frege, and with Anselm, in thinking that the sense of a proposition is independent of the facts. With this reference to 'facts' he shows that he is speaking of propositions which logically may be true or may be false: the sense, then, is independent of what Frege taught us to call the truth value of a proposition, i.e. of whether the proposition is true or false.

13. Hardly anyone would *deny* that the sense of a proposition, one that may be true or false, is independent of its truth value. Wittgenstein's observation in fact is: 'If we don't remember that the sense is independent of the facts, it is easy for us to think of truth and false-hood as equally justified relations between signs and what they signify.' So evidently he *denies* that truth and falsehood are equally justified relations, and he warns against thinking that, given a proposition p and its negation, $\sim p$, 'p', say, signifies in the true way what '$\sim p$' signifies in the false way. We are reminded of Anselm saying: it couldn't be given to a proposition to signify that something is so, only when it *is*, i.e. without its being able to signify that that thing is so, when it *isn't*. *Why* couldn't it? Because the thing it is to signify is the same in the two cases, both when it is so and when it isn't. So mightn't one think that it signifies, *through* that signifying of the same in the two cases, what actually *is* the case, but sometimes in a peculiar way called 'the false way'? Anselm makes no such suggestion, and Wittgenstein warns against it. But Wittgenstein goes on to imagine something further: Could we communicate with false propositions, as hitherto with true ones — so long as it was understood that they were 'meant wrong', i.e. meant as false? He replies 'No! For if we use 'p' to say that not p and things *are* as we mean they are, the 'p' in the new way of taking it will be true, *not* false'.

14. Here he has put his finger on two nerves in the matter. The first is, that you could have a code in which every sentence was to be under-stood as the negation of itself in non-code use. That this is possible is very striking. It would not be possible for example to have a code in which every adjective was to be interpreted as meaning 'pink'. You'd be severely restricted in what adjectives of the non-code language you used. But the negation code is a possibility. It has even been used — Joan of Arc used it in communicating with her generals, and signalled that she was doing so by having a little cross put at the top of the page. This brings us to the second nerve. *Which* of the two opposite senses, that of a proposition and that of its contradictory, is actually being

asserted is what fixes that aspect of the sense. And this would not be possible if it were not for the parity between truth and the corresponding (contradicting) falsehood which Anselm's pupil maintains and which Anselm accepts. The dialogue in fact emphasises and insists on the parity. It could not be given to the proposition to say what it says is the case only when it *is* the case. Anselm indeed does not seem to notice that this means you could use the negation-code. (He is a very succinct writer who might have noticed this without remarking on it.) At any rate if either he or Wittgenstein had been witnesses at Joan of Arc's trial, where she was accused of blasphemously signalling lies with a cross, they could have declared 'These were not lies — or if they were, not for the reason you think'.

15. Anselm, the teacher, explains the truth of propositions by a teleological account of — as I will now say — assertion. Assertion is *for* signifying *as* being so what *is* so; so asserting what is not so is a wrong use of assertion, and truth is explained as rightness of assertion precisely as assertion. This could be the explanation of Wittgenstein's warning against regarding truth and falsehood as equally justified relations between signs and what they signify. There is no doubt the German says that, though English translators have funked so translating it. On the other hand, it is notorious that Wittgenstein criticised the 'assertion sign' used by both Frege and Russell. It is logically meaningless, i.e. it lacks logical meaning, he says, it merely shows that the authors believe the propositions they mark with it.

16. He also remarked that affirmation can't give propositions their sense — what is affirmed must already have a sense; and the same holds of denial. So we are left wondering — is the falsehood of a proposition something bad about *it* — as Anselm seems to think; for, using his word for a proposition, he talks about the two different ways of being true, one, having the sense that it has, and the other, doing what it's *for*. Also, we remember that the pupil said that the truth of a true proposition couldn't be the *thing* enuntiated: that must be the *cause* of its truth. Well, is there a thing enuntiated when the proposition is *false*? At one point the pupil seems to imply that there *is*: 'But if it is right and true by signifying what it ought, as you have shown, an utterance is true even when it enuntiates as being so what isn't so.' Protagoras might say: no *enuntiatum*, so no *enuntiatio*.

17. Well, we have seen that Wittgenstein in fact concedes to assertion a role in determining sense. He does this in his reason for denying that we could communicate with false propositions as hitherto with true

ones, so long as it's understood that they're meant to be false. We couldn't, because if we are using '*p*' to say that not *p*, and what we mean actually *is* the case, '*p*' is true, not false, in the new way of taking it. So assertion, i.e. what you are asserting, does determine which is which of the two opposite senses, those of '*p*' and '~*p*'. '*p*' and '~*p*', he goes on to say, have opposite senses, but there corresponds to these one and the same reality. What reality? we want to know. The answer must be, that being the case which one of them says is the case. Which it is is not given us in their senses. And which sense each has is a matter of what *we mean to assert* in using them.

18. This account, however, still seems to leave open the possibility of saying that one of them is related 'in the true way' to just what the other is related to 'in the false way'. Now if that is supposed to characterise their *senses*, it can't be right—precisely because their senses are independent of the fact, that is: are independent of which either of them is, true or false. If it is not supposed to characterise their senses, it is a harmless way of speaking.

19. I have remarked that Anselm is at variance with the majority of modern logicians in treating the sort of proposition we are talking about as variable in truth-value. Russell wrote in severe criticism of a logician who took this line, giving as an example 'Mrs Brown is not at home'. 'Here', Russell says, 'it is plain that what is variable primarily is the meaning of the form of words. What is expressed by the form of words at any given instant is not itself variable, but at another instant something else, itself equally invariable, is expressed by the same form of words.' He makes a comparison with 'He is a barrister', which expresses a truth in some contexts and a falsehood in others. 'Thus the variability involved is primarily in the meaning of a form of words.' That 'thus' is very significant. What Russell says is all right about 'He is a barrister' if the point is that the *he* will likely be a different person on different occasions of the use of that sentence. In order to make 'Mrs Brown is not at home' analogous, Russell says 'we know the time at which this is said, and therefore we know what is meant'. Well, we might *not* 'know the time'; and if one says 'it means: Mrs Brown is not at home *now*', one has to say, if one wants to follow Russell, that 'now' means a time, and a different time each different time it is said. But 'now' is no more the name of a time than 'today' is a date. We can conclude that Russell's explanations are not real, and the real thought lies precisely in that 'Thus'. A certain sentence 'expresses a truth in some contexts and a falsehood in others. *Thus* the variability involved is primarily in the meaning of the form of words.' The whole reason

lies in the sentence's expressing a truth in some contexts and a false-hood in others. But that is the very thing that raises the question: must it be a different proposition really, because of that? Is it like a proper name's being a different name, though equiform, if it names a different thing?

20. Anselm, together with Wittgenstein who has further elaborations on the theme, seems satisfactory except for the unanswered question I have mentioned: is there an 'enuntiated thing' when the proposition is *false*? He made no objection when the pupil said that the 'thing enuntiated' was the cause of the truth of the proposition. But neither did he object to the expression 'what it enuntiates' used by the pupil of a supposedly *false* proposition. Again, this may only be an instance of Anselm's undistractability when his eye is on a target. The significance —the sense—of the proposition is the same whether it is true or false. What about 'what is enuntiated'? Will it too be the same when the proposition is false as when it is true? Is enuntiation the same as signification?

21. This question should elicit from us the last bit, the keystone of the arch representing the relations of truth, sense and assertion. There is *no* 'thing enuntiated' by a false proposition. A true proposition tells one something if one believes it. A false proposition believed still tells its believer nothing. A *person* may tell one a falsehood; but, just as we say that a proposition as well as a person *says* such-and-such, so we may also say that a proposition believed *tells* its believer something. — But only if it is true. For then it reflects the being so of what *is* so. But the analogue of this, for a false proposition, would be that it reflects the being so of what is not so. And there is *no* such thing as either. A paradox, on the other hand, does not say *anything*. There is no solution to the question whom the court should find right in Protagoras' suit.

22. Where the Sophists were right is reached in my present formulation: the false proposition, while it does *say something*, does not, being believed, *tell* its believers anything. So: he who thinks what is false thinks what is not; he thinks something which tells him nothing; but that does not mean he thinks nothing, i.e. does not think anything.

23. I will end by speaking again of the paradoxes, and in particular of the one that a librarian in Oxford gave to Russell. He knocked on his door, handed him a piece of paper and went away. On the piece of paper was written 'What's on the other side is true'; Russell turned it over and found 'What's on the other side is false'. Let's call the first

one (the one with 'true' in it) *a*, and the other *b*. If *a* is true *b* is true —
for that's what *a* says. But if *b* is true *a* is false — for that's what *b* says.
So if *a* is true *a* is false. But if *a* is false *b* is false, for *a* says *b* is true. But
if *b* is false *a* is true, for *b* says that *a* is false. So each of them if true is
false and if false is true. I conclude that neither says anything. But, you
may say, your argument was partly from what they *did* say. True, it
was; but I would now insert 'if *a* says anything' after 'that's what *a*
says', and similarly for 'that's what *b* says'. Note that if *b* had been
something else, like '2 x 2 = 4', there'd be no question, *a* would then
say something. One has to argue it out. Things can turn out not to say
anything because of certain extraneous facts. However, the paradoxical character is a tip-off. I applaud Russell's desire to exclude paradoxical propositions, but not his desire to have a general principle by
which he does it. The matter needs arguing in the particular case.
Indeed, in the case of that piece of paper, the paradoxical character,
which of course was what interested Russell, is in fact a distraction.
Suppose that 'What's on the other side is true' had been written on
both sides. It would quickly be evident that nothing was said — one
can't find out *what* is being said to be true. (Similarly for 'What's on
the other side is false', written on both sides.) And that should be
enough to damn the paradoxical case of the same thing. But each
paradox (or kind of paradox) needs excluding ad hoc, on its merits.
Russell perhaps does this, but he has a sort of formula. He gives a list
of words: 'truth', 'falsehood', 'function', 'property', 'class', 'relation',
'cardinal', 'ordinal', 'name', 'definition', and says: 'Any such word, if
its typical ambiguity is overlooked, will apparently generate a totality
containing members defined in terms of itself and will thus give rise to
vicious circle paradoxes.'

That sounds as if he meant that a totality containing members
defined in terms of itself was always illegitimate and a possible source
of paradoxes. But perhaps not so: for he says: 'The appearance of
contradiction is always due to the presence of words embodying a
concealed typical ambiguity and the solution of the apparent contradiction lies in bringing the concealed ambiguity to light.'

So it is not just the totality containing members defined in terms of
itself that is 'illegitimate', but the fact that the totality is generated by
means of a word ambiguous in logical type.

Russell is therefore not refuted by the perfect legitimacy of my
making a list of all the lists kept in my office, which will include itself
if it is kept in my office. Or even a list of all the lists kept in my office
which do not include themselves — so long as I *don't* keep it in my
office. But what about a list of all the lists in the world that don't

include themselves? That seems to generate a characteristic Russellian paradox—but what is the ambiguity of logical type involved in constructing this description?

10

'Making True'

If you are told or otherwise believe an *either-or* proposition, the question may easily arise what makes it true. 'The potato crop in Ruritania was halved by blight in 1928' — 'Well then, either the expected, planned for crop was in excess of the people's needs, or there was a shortage of potatoes that year, or a lot were imported ...' That seems a fair deduction, and we may ask which was true. If only one was, then we'd say it made the disjunction true. If all were, then all of them did.

Similarly, if it is said that some elements have a certain property, the question may arise which do. Suppose someone says that iodine and chlorine do. He purports to have told us what makes the 'some' proposition true. He wouldn't be contradicted by someone who gave other ones, but not iodine and chlorine.

Thus though an *either-or* proposition or a *some* proposition, if true, must be made true by the truth of some such other proposition, in general none of these *must* be true if the original proposition is. This shows that explanation by means of truth conditions does not provide an analysis in these cases. By an 'analysis' I mean something that is at least an equivalent proposition. For an *either-or* proposition neither the conjunction of all its elements nor one of its elements nor the conjunction of any subset of its elements up to the totality of them all is a proposition equivalent to the *either-or* proposition — though any subset up to the totality will make the *either-or* proposition true. And similarly for 'some' propositions.

* Paper read to the Oxford Philosophical Society in 1982. Published in Roger Teichmann (ed.) *Logic, Cause and Action: Essays in honour of Elizabeth Anscombe* (Cambridge: Cambridge University Press, 2000), pp.1–8. © The Royal Institute of Philosophy. Reprinted with the permission of Cambridge University Press.

'The proposition is explained by giving the totality of sets of elements whose conjunction (when there is more than one) makes it true.' Or: 'It is explained by giving the totality of rows in the truth-table for its elements, for each of which it is true.' Perhaps: but the explanation gives us no equivalent. Only if you form a disjunction of the whole set will you have an equivalent. But what's the good of that, when it was the sense of a disjunction that you wanted to explain? You could go on forever in that way.

Disjunctions and propositions with 'some' are somewhat favourable examples for a concept of what makes true. In finite cases giving the totality of sets of truth-conditions gives rather precise and unexceptionable information about the sense of a proposition of this sort. If it's a 'some' proposition there is a qualification to add: the case being finite, there can be a list, and when one says 'some' one is referring to the totality of sets of truth-conditions that are constructible using the list. One doesn't have to know the items which are members of the list. Neither all of them nor any of them.

However, to repeat, when one asserts a disjunction or a 'some' proposition, the question what *does* make it true is not a question about its sense. At best it may be a question about what one has in mind, a 'How do you mean?' question. But one need not have anything in mind in that way. One may declare that someone has broken into one's desk, and have no one in mind. Similarly one may say, 'Jack or Tom or Jim did it', and not have it in mind that, e.g. Jack and Tom did it.

If a disjunction is true because more than one of its elements is true, then more than one makes it true. Is this like more than one man hauling on a rope in the same direction? Each is strong enough to haul the weight that is hauled; so either they haul it quicker than either would alone, or they each have to do less work, the labour being shared. Perhaps we can answer questions about who really does the work or how much each does. But it can't be like that with two elements of a disjunction, both true. This warns us against the idea of a work done, or a force exerted, in making true. I shall return to this.

First, however, there are also other ways of making true besides the kind I have mentioned. One is to be seen in the question 'What makes *that* the French flag?' with the answer 'That it's three vertical stripes, that sort of width, of red, white and blue — only, by the way, it's upside down.' 'How *can* it be?' 'Sorry, I mean it's the wrong way round.' 'But then *it* isn't the French flag.'

This exchange brings out facts about flags—that you may describe them (if they aren't symmetrical about an axis parallel to the flag pole), going from the flagpole outwards.

'What makes this the French flag' is here understood to be the formal cause. But there is also a question whose answer is an historical account of the proceedings by which the French shifted from the Fleur de Lys to the tricolour. This gives us an efficient cause of this being the French flag.

There is another way of making true which is neither formal cause nor efficient cause nor fulfilment of a truth-condition. For example, the way assertions of hypocrisy are made true. I advance various facts about someone's actions, offering them as reason to call that person a hypocrite. This—taking it to be correct—is not a matter of formal cause; rather, I recount events and imply an interpretation of them apparently amounting to a description of hypocrisy. This description would be of a formal cause—but if it in turn amounts to an efficient cause, then this efficient cause will be a cause by way of habit, not of the alleged hypocrisy, but rather of future similar hypocritical behaviour.

It isn't a formal cause because there is a step between. Hypocrisy is pretending you are virtuous in ways you are not, or pretending you lack vices which you have. Lofty condemnation by A, say, of someone for a vice is implicitly a claim not to have that vice; that is the intermediate step here. Or perhaps one should rather say: Lofty condemnation of someone for e.g., not caring for the accuracy of what he says about someone else is implicitly a claim not to go in for that sort of thing oneself.—'Ah, but it might just be a fit of temper.' Certainly—at least certainly it can very well be a fit of temper; but the *lofty* tone of condemnation makes it not *just* a fit of temper but also a stance of righteousness. 'Well, it's all a matter of interpretation.'—That is true; but so must be any accusation of hypocrisy; and can't the interpretation be right?—'There might be some other account to give if you knew more facts.' Possibly; but one would like that illustrated, taking the description I have started with, and applying more facts which I might reasonably be supposed ignorant of. For example, the 'lofty condemnation' was a joke, or a deliberate attempt to annoy; i.e. A was only *pretending* to have the righteous stance. Or again it was a pre-arranged signal for some non-apparent purpose. 'If I write a letter with a snarl like that in it, that's to mean that your involvement in such-and-such a fraud has been discovered and you'd better get out of the country.'

Thus we can't say we have here a 'making true' which is a matter of the formal cause. Identifying these circumstances as making the statement about hypocrisy true is identifying them as falling under a description which in turn brings citing them under the description 'giving a formal cause'. That is, it does so in, or given, the circumstances and on the assumption that these are all the relevant circumstances. We could say: Here, if things are what they seem, we have proceedings which make it true that A is 'rather a hypocrite'.

There are many statements which are made true in such and similar ways. A related expression is: 'true in virtue of'. This has to be understood in the right way, not, e.g., as referring to something that *brings it about* that something is true, e.g., 'The statement was true in virtue of a verbal alteration'. Similarly it might be said that someone paid in virtue of his resolute determination to discharge all debts. But since there is no such thing as pure acts of paying, if someone paid, then he did it in virtue of, e.g., handing over some coins, and there must always be some particular way in which he did it.

Here someone might say that 'He paid in virtue of ...' (understood in the right way) and '"He paid" was true in virtue of ...' are different. And similarly for another expression, namely, 'consisted in'. 'His paying *consisted in* his handing over some coins then' contrasts with 'The truth of "he paid" consisted in his handing over some coins then'. For the latter talks about a bit of language and the former does not. Then what about 'Its being true that he paid consisted in ...'? Now I think I need not concern myself with the *oratio recta* form—I at least would translate it into a foreign language altogether, unless there was some particular purpose for which I needed to leave the quoted bits in English. I take Q, 'Q is true', 'it is true that Q' all to be equivalent.

There is just one point to be made here, though. I might be taught to utter a sentence and told that it means such-and-such, which I hold to be true, but have forgotten everything except how to utter the sentence and that it does mean something which I hold to be true. Then I can say 'Q is true' or even 'it is true that Q' and this not be meaningless in my mouth, though Q would be. This can be explained as follows: I am saying: For some p, Q says that p, and p.

If we ask what *that* consists in, or in virtue of what it is true, or what makes it true, it seems clear that an answer would depend on what Q was—for *ex hypothesi* my utterance 'It is true that Q' can only be translated into another language leaving Q as it is. And similarly if I say 'Q is true'. For the rest, my remarks about 'some' propositions apply—even up to the possibility that there is more than one p such that: Q says that p, and p. The question falls apart: what makes it the case that *Q* says something? and given that it says something, i.e., that for some *p* it says *p*, what makes it the case that we can add *and p*? The first question could be answered in a rather vague way, given the information that *Q* was a bit of Arabic, say: for those who know Arabic it has a *use* such that for some *p* it says *p*; but we can go further only by giving (imaginary) illustrative examples, or by saying something that *Q* *does* say. This last would be like mentioning an element that did have a certain property. The second half of the question can really only be asked without total vagueness when we have got our *p* specified, and the questions 'what makes it the case that etc.?' about this will depend for their answer on what this *p* is. I may seem to have jumped a gap here—when the *p* is specified, what makes it the case that the bit of Arabic said *that*? But that wasn't our question; our question was: what made it the case that there was something said? — and that was adequately answered by giving something that *was* said.

There is, then, that amount of reason to distinguish between saying that *Q* and saying that *Q* was true, or that it was true that *Q*. It depends on a quite particular situation. But if one can say that ..., it is all one to do so and to say that ... is true. (I leave on one side the case where '"*Q*" is true' is false, not because '*Q*' is false, but because it lacks a truth-value because it contains a vacuous name.)

It is sometimes said that the equivalence—i.e. between *p* and *it is true that p*—can't be combined with a truth-condition account of meaning. The argument for this might be represented as follows:

> What is the meaning of a proposition; say *p*?
> Its meaning is given by a comprehensive account of the conditions on which it is true.
> But what does '*p* is true' mean?
> It means the same as *p*.
> But that's what I wanted to know in the first place, that is, what *p* *does* mean.

In short, if *p* and *it is true that p* are equivalent and you tell me conditions on which it is true that *p*, I don't know what you've given me conditions of, if I don't *already* know what it means to say that *p*.—This argument is based on a misunderstanding. You don't know till told them perhaps, either the conditions on which it is true that *p*, or the conditions given which, *p*—but they are the same. It is correct to say that, not knowing these conditions, you don't know what 'it is true that *p*' means (except in the sense that it, I mean *p*, says something which *is* so). But to say you don't know what 'it is true that *p*' means is the same as to say you don't know what it comes to to assert *p*. What you perhaps do know, or at least what is the presupposition of your question, is that there is something it comes to, and that that is the same as it comes to to assert '*p* is true', and if you know the latter you know the former.

'Truth-conditions' is just a convenient locution. So 'truth-conditions of *p*' = 'conditions of *p*', that is to say: what is, or what is the range of possibility of what is, when *p*. Of this, there *may* be an explanation of the various kinds I've been considering—and there may not.

But in the particular case we may ask: 'What does it consist in, that …?'. What does it consist in, that *p*?—in this case? or ever?

There are plenty of cases where we know there must be an answer to the first question, and plenty where we can give some 'for example' answers to the second, though it is obvious that there isn't a complete list of possible answers which could tell what it might consist in.

But there are also cases where there doesn't seem to be an answer. For example, 'believing that there was a step there'. One has stumbled, perhaps, or nearly stumbled, at any rate trodden oddly, and one says 'I thought there was a step there'. *When* did one think that? Obviously when one was making that step, and stepped wrong. Now does *that* mean: stepped as if for a step up, or a step down, when there wasn't one? Possibly; but has anyone ever investigated? One's reason for saying one or the other is precisely that one 'thought there was a step there', and would be able to say whether the step one thought was there was a step up or a step down. We believe that in such a case one *did* step as if for a step up, or for a step down, because it is part of one's verbal reaction (or mental description, if one merely thinks it) that one thought there was a step, and it was (say) *down*.—If one considers just what happened at the moment, inasmuch as one 'thought there was a step there', one can find nothing except being set to step down. But *that* of course will have been present at the other steps down if one was going down some steps. And that leaves out the fact that 'I thought there was a step there!' is a reaction characteristic of mis-stepping. But not just of *any* mis-stepping. We might say: that it is a characteristic reaction *defines* the special sort of mis-stepping that is in question. The reaction—the verbal reaction—doesn't have to occur; but it can still be used to define the mis-stepping. In what, then, did it consist, that 'one thought there was a step there'? We ought not to go on looking once we have realised the facts of this sort of case. That one 'thought there was a step there' belongs to a (particular) kind of mis-stepping. That is to say, the sense of it that we are considering does so. It is for example quite unlike *this* case: one passes by a narrow passage-way, and says 'I thought there was a step there but I see there isn't'.

Nor is it like the case where it looks to one as if there was a step, when there isn't, as one realises by keeping on looking. For in that case one has had the thought, or impression, 'there's a step'. But in our case one has mis-stepped, and it was *that sort* of mis-stepping and not another sort. — If one can say what deceived one, what presented the *appearance*, like a trompe l'oeil doorway, then one had the belief after the presentation. But just that is lacking in the case of simple mis-stepping, when one exclaims 'I thought there was a step there!' It was no doubt this feature that led Russell to call this a minimal case, which furnished the minimal definition of belief as 'muscular preparedness for action'.

If what makes something true is something else — that is to say, the truth of a proposition which is not equivalent to the first — then it looks as if we had to say: 'This can't go on for ever: we must come at last to the case where what makes '*p*' true is just that *p*.' Now I want to say that this is not right. If making true were like hauling, we might reasonably consider that there it must come to something that hauls without being hauled by something else — though even there we would not suppose it to haul itself, but simply to be an unhauled hauler. And the analogue would be that what makes true must itself be made true by something else, until we come to something that makes true without being made true. But making true isn't exercising a sort of force; we saw we couldn't speak of a division of labour when a disjunction was made true by the truth of all its elements. We can't ask which really does the work, or whether the disjunction is made truer, like an object being moved more quickly or further. Therefore we can't reason analogously to the argument that there must be an unhauled hauler, which is *the* hauling source of all this hauling force that is exercised. Nor is it any defence of the analogy to say that there may be more than one ultimate hauler, because, if there is, the force of each can be lessened or the hauling is done more quickly or a greater load is hauled.

If we did pursue the analogy while forgetting this point of contrast, then when we ascribed the truth-making to something that makes true without being made true, we should be forgetting about the other elements of the disjunction we are considering. If the truth of *p* consists in the truth of *q* or *q* makes it true that *p*, then how will we be able to accommodate the fact that it is also made true by *r*'s being true — *r* being sufficient, and independent of *p*? Well, we *can* do so precisely because *q* has not done a work which must not be usurped, and can't be shared, by r. But that means that the argument to the first truth-maker is not like an argument to the first, i.e., unhauled, hauler in a series of haulers each of which is hauled by its predecessor till we come to an object which hauls without being hauled.

Nevertheless, any making true must come to an end, or to several ends: a relation of making true cannot be supposed to be repeated *ad infinitum*. For if it runs in a circle, then p will be made true by q as much as it makes q true. And if it doesn't run in a circle then there never is a completed series of terms of the series. But unless we *finish* somewhere, and so indicate a finite series of terms if it doesn't run in a circle, we don't reckon to have given what makes true except in a partial way: for if r is made true by q and q by p and we simply stop at p while admitting that no doubt something else makes p true, then we have only given an incomplete account of *this* way in which r is made true. So we not merely must stop at some p, but there must be some p stopping at which finishes that particular account.

Since this is so, we must allow the termination in a proposition that makes true without being made true by something else—I mean by the truth of a non-equivalent proposition. This however does not yet give us the idea of a proposition whose truth makes true without itself being made true; for unlike hauling 'making p true' might be done by p itself. So we would have our terminus when we came to what is made true, but not by the truth of any *other* proposition. However, a proposition can't make itself true: we have to gloss the statement and say 'p is made true by the *fact that p*'. If we have a Tractatus-like metaphysics of facts this would be possible: we would have reached an elementary proposition, made true by the existence of an atomic fact. But without such a metaphysic we are only saying p is made true by its being the case that p, or by its being true! That is an empty statement, with only a false air of explanation.

And so in the end we'd have to accept as termini propositions which are true without being made true. If this seems shocking, that is because of a deep metaphysical prejudice. If we take 'making true' in any of the senses that I have mentioned for it, there is no reason to be shocked. A disjunction is made true by the truth of any of its elements; but *they* don't have to be disjunctions in their turn and usually aren't. When they aren't we've got to the terminus *for that sort of making true*. There is a formal cause of this being the French flag, namely the arrangement of vertical stripes of certain colours and proportions; there may be a formal cause of each vertical but it is unlikely that it too will have a formal cause in its turn. And so the termination of truths being made true by other truths, in truths not made true in any sense that has been introduced, is not so bad after all; in fact it is altogether to be expected, or rather it is inevitable. The general principle, that what is true must be made true by something, can't be rebutted by calling in question *any* idea of 'making true', but it is rebutted if we demand that the particular manner of making true always be given for the question that is being asked when one says what, if anything, makes a certain proposition true.

11

Existence and Truth

I

One of the remarkable things Frege did was to assimilate concepts to arithmetical functions. He begins[1] this process by adding such signs as =, >, < to the familiar signs serving to form expressions for functions like + and –. So he 'can speak of the function $x^2 = 1$'. The values of this function for different arguments are not numbers, but are truth and falsehood, which he now calls 'truth-values'. A functional expression, say x^4, when completed with an argument means (*bedeutet*) a number: '2^4' means 16. Equally then, '$1^2 = 1$' means truth; '$2^2 = 1$' means falsehood. Further '$2^2 = 4$' and '$2 > 1$' mean the same thing, namely truth. (We might prefer to say: are different designations of the same thing, truth.) So $(2^2 = 4) = (2 > 1)$ is a correct equation.

Frege considers the objection that '$2^2 = 4$' and '$2 > 1$' say different things, express different thoughts. He replies that so do '$2^4 = 4^2$' and '$4 \times 4 = 4^2$'. All the same one can replace '2^4' with '4×4' because these two expressions mean the same. This holds also of the pair '$2^4 = 4^2$' and '$4 \times 4 = 4^2$'. In the former case the two signs mean the same number, in the latter the same 'truth-value'; the term 'truth-value' is introduced to us in this context. Identity of thing meant does not have identity of thought as a consequence. One has to distinguish sense and meaning: '2^4' and '4×4' have the same meaning, being proper names of the same number, but they have not the same sense. Just for that reason '$2^4 = 4^2$' and '$4 \times 4 = 4^2$' have the same meaning but not the same sense: they do not contain the same thought. What Frege here calls 'thoughts' is the sense of a designation of a truth-value.

He concludes that we have as much right to write

---

*   Presidential Address to the Aristotelian Society, 12 October 1987. Published in *The Proceedings of the Aristotelian Society New Series* — Vol.LXXXVIII (1987/88), pp.1–12. Reprinted by courtesy of the Editor of the Aristotelian Society: © 1988.
[1]   'Funktion und Begriff', *Kleine Schriften* (Hildesheim, 1967), p.131.

$(2^2 = 4) = (2 > 1)$
as
$2^4 = 4 \times 4.$

To what purpose all this? It facilitates the broadening of the language of arithmetic into that of logic. This is exemplified in the case in hand. Consider that the value of $x^2 = 1$ for -1 as argument is truth, and this can be expressed by saying '-1 falls under the concept: square root of 1'. From this we see that we can say: a concept is a function whose value is always a truth-value. This is no less exemplified by the function (as we may now call it)

$(x + 1)^2 = 2(x + 1).$

Here we get truth for the argument -1 and we can express this as follows: '-1 is a number smaller by 1 than a number whose square is equal to its double.'

Frege does not *argue* in 'Funktion und Begriff' that he can take =, > and < as signs serving to form expressions for functions. He simply says he will do it. This involves treating $x^2 = 4$ as having a value for any argument. We need not cavil at calling such a value a truth-value. (I will not dwell here on the fact that 'any argument' is to be taken strictly, so that the moon is a possible argument. Frege can handle that without falsifying what I have just said.)

An expression for a numerical function, completed with a numerical argument, not only has a numerical value: it means or designates a number. Frege boldly embraces the consequences for his new functional expressions. In fact it would be difficult to see what could be signified by adding them to the signs that serve to form expressions of functions, if it did not signify that. So he says that e.g. '$2 > 1$' not only has a truth value but means truth.

There is a bit of argument in the text: because '2^4' and '4×4' are expressions meaning the same you can substitute one for the other, and it followed from this that '$2^4 = 4^2$' and '$4 \times 4 = 4^2$' have the same meaning, though they don't have the same sense. About this we can say that it follows provided = is a sign, like + and –, for forming the expression of a function. It follows just as much as the 'identity of meaning' between '$2^4 - 4^2$' and '$4 \times 4 - 4^2$'. There is more but to my mind not more successful argument to the point in 'Sinn und Bedeutung'. I would say that taking =, > and < as signs for forming function-expressions on the model of +, – and exponentiation already demanded that e.g. '$4^2 = 16$' not only have a value, but stand for it. That the value is a truth-value, once suggested, seems incontrovertible. The only alternative that might readily come to mind is that the sentence means its sense. To this we can think of several objections; a sufficient one here and now is that there is something the same between '$4^2 = 16$' and '$2^4 = 16$', but the senses are different. It is what is the same that is the 'value'. Unless, then, we find something intermediate between sense and truth-value, we are stuck with the truth-value as the 'value' we are looking for. Accepting the truth-value as the value our expression stands for, we are at once landed with the correctness of the equation:

$$(4^2 = 16) = (2 > 1).$$

In short, the ground was already won with Frege's adding =, > and < to the signs serving to form expressions of functions.

Welcome consequences of Frege's doctrine include the following:

(1) The connection with reality is given by sentences being complex names of the true and the false. This is secured by their not containing any empty names and being well-formed. Sentences containing empty names have only sense, not meaning.

Students of the philosophy of Locke and Hume will remember the ineffectual and inconsistent struggles of the former to give an account of knowledge in his philosophy, and the bold insistence of the latter that it is impossible by any reach of the mind to get beyond sensation and ideas.

(2) The question what is the bearer of the predicates 'true' and 'false' does not arise if true and false are objects, being the values of functional expressions completed into sentences.

(3) On the other hand, if the functional expression has been completed with the name of an object, saying that the resultant expression is a name of truth is equivalent to saying that the object falls under the concept designated by the functional expression. Saying it is a name of the false is saying it does not fall under the concept in question.

(4) Although the considerations are perforce largely about expressions, names and sentences, neither concepts nor objects nor senses, nor those senses he calls thoughts, are linguistic. Nor are values of expressions, unless indeed we speak of a linguistic value —e.g. a sentence itself might be called a linguistic value of a linguistic function.

Frege's enquiries of course go a great deal further than anything I have touched on. I have only needed to speak of what is most simple and elementary in order to make my claim that that first move, of counting =, > and < as signs that serve to form expressions for functions, is one which has great import for philosophy.

If we dwell on the conception that the true and the false are objects, we may well be put off, especially by falsehood's being called an object. This is mitigated by the consideration that to say that, for a given a, fa = the false is no more than to say that a is not f. Truth and falsehood are twins; you can always negate a proposition.

On the other hand, the conception of sentences as names of objects —an immediate consequence of Frege's additions to the signs that form expressions of functions—does stick in one's craw. How strange that you can turn a name of one object into a name of another by e.g. prefixing the negation sign! This is related to the property of duality which marks propositions. Every proposition has a dual, which is its contradictory. The dual is not just to be constructed by prefixing the sign of negation; we can ask for the duals of 'and', 'or', 'some' and 'all', and negate predicates. Thus the dual of the sentence 'All Englishmen are either white or black can be given as 'Some Englishmen are neither white nor black'.

I imagine that these facts about propositions would not give a twinge of conscience to a man who was willing to add =, > and < to + etc. as signs for forming functional expressions. Nevertheless it is a serious objection. The objection is not to complex names as complex — '4^2' is a complex name; but it has no negation, it is not an instance in which we can exhibit de Morgan's laws. No, it is to that very thing which I numbered (1) among a list of advantages.

It is noticeable that although our logical talk is strongly affected by Frege—we talk of truth-values and of part of a schematic sentence 'fa' which expresses a function—no one, so far as I know, speaks of sentences as names of the true and the false. But when we examine Frege's taking =, > and < as signs for forming expressions of functions, we see three things: (1) that it was pretty inevitable that he should invent the notion of truth-values; (2) that when an embedded sentence expresses a 'complete thought', substitution within it of a different name for the same object would have to leave the truth-value of the containing sentence unaffected; (3) that he would have to regard the embedding of such a sentence in another as necessarily truth-functional. He therefore has to examine various cases where there is apparently an embedded sentence whose truth or falsehood does not matter for the truth-value of the whole. This leads us to his well-known treatment of indirect speech constructions.

Arthur Prior objected to this,[2] wanting to say that 'John believes that grass is pink' is as much a function of 'Grass is pink' as is 'Grass is not pink', and is directly about grass. But he was here forgetting the possibility, within belief contexts, of exchanging even simple proper names of the same thing, and changing the truth-value of the whole containing sentences by doing so. This makes it difficult to say that such a sentence gives us a function of the embedded sentence, which is left with its customary meaning.

Frege's reasons for adding to the arithmetical functions involves a great assimilation to them. He persuades us in the first place with new functions like $x^2 = 2x$ and $2^4 = 4^2$ (the latter, of course, being a function, say $2^x = x^2$, completed with an argument), where any operation on one of the complex items must be repeated on the other one in the equation to retain truth. It is interesting that his enterprise was so successful, when applications to other kinds of sentences would not seem obvious at all.

In direct speech reports we have words meaning words; in indirect speech constructions the words mean their 'customary sense'. But this is not the only sort of example one has to consider. There are several other types of case, discussed in 'Sinn und Bedeutung', e.g.

(a) Whoever discovered the elliptical form of the planetary orbits died in misery.

(b) If a number is less than 1 and greater than 0, its square is less than 1 and greater than 0.

(c) After Schleswig-Holstein was separated from Denmark, Prussia and Austria quarrelled.

(d) Because ice is less dense than water it floats on water.

(e) Bebel mistakenly supposes that the return of Alsace-Lorraine would appease France's desire for revenge.

Frege deals with the subordinate clauses in these sentences in various ways: the upshot is usually that at least the subordinate clause does not simply express a 'complete thought'. In (c) it expresses, so to speak, a thought and a half. In (e), he says, the subordinate clause has to be taken twice over, once as having its customary meaning, and then also as meaning its customary sense.

---

2   In the posthumous book *Objects of Thought* edited by P.T. Geach and A.J.P. Kenny (Oxford: Oxford University Press, 1971), p.52: 'Truth-functions and belief-functions ... are functions of the same arguments.'

An important type of example he does not deal with is sentences of the form 'p because of q'.

He thinks he has shown with sufficient probability that cases where one can't replace a subordinate clause with one of the same truth-value *salva veritate* do not disprove his view that a truth-value is what a sentence means, when it has a thought as its sense.[3]

Nevertheless, with the example of 'Odysseus landed at Ithaca' Frege observes that we aren't concerned with anything but the sense, as 'Odysseus' is an empty name. This too is in 'Sinn und Bedeutung'. He says:

> The fact that we concern ourselves at all with what is meant by a *part* of the sentence indicates that we generally recognise and expect a meaning for the sentence itself.

He next asks: 'Why is the thought not enough for us?' and gives the answer 'Because, and to the extent that, we are concerned with its truth-value ... It is the striving for truth that drives us always to advance from the sense to the thing meant'. Here we are to understand by 'the thing meant' the thing meant by e.g. the proper name 'Odysseus'.

But now Frege says in a separate paragraph: 'We have seen that the meaning of a sentence may always be sought, whenever the meaning of its components is involved; and that this is the case when and only when we are inquiring after the truth-value.' Here I fear we must say we have seen no such thing as that 'the meaning of a sentence may always be sought'. The most he has a right to say so far is 'We have seen that something *other than the sense* may be sought, and this is the case when and only when we are inquiring after the truth-value'. This weakens the transition to his next sentence, which begins another new paragraph:

> 'We are therefore driven into accepting the truth-value of a sentence as constituting what it means.' And further on: 'Every assertoric sentence concerned with what its words mean [i.e. what they designate] is therefore to be regarded as a proper name, and its meaning, if it has one, is either the True or the False.'

It is apparent that Frege was not perfectly satisfied with his argument for this as he presents it at first. For he resumes the topic and quotes Leibniz: '*Eadem sunt quorum unum alteri substitui potest salva veritate*' —

---

3   'Sinn und Bedeutung', final page.

'Those are sames of which one can be replaced by the other without loss of truth'. Of course this sentence is a bit notorious—for what do we substitute for what? Not the things names are names of, but the *names*, which will not be 'sames'. Let's rewrite: 'You've got sames, or rather the *same*, designated, if you can always replace one designation by another and what you say is still true.' You are 'keeping truth', note, not 'keeping the truth-value'. We must therefore suppose a conditional: *if* the first thing you said was true, the second, containing the substitution, will be true. Frege's analogy with numerical functions, which has introduced the notion of a *truth-value*, makes him think that what is needed is preservation of *truth-value*, not of truth. Here we may see the seed of Prior's suspicion that Frege (whom he greatly admired) was the villain of the 'extensionalist' piece, by his very introduction of that notion of *truth-value*.

However, let's stay for the moment with Frege's use of Leibniz precisely to bolster up his idea that sentences are designations or names. You've got sames if you can always replace one designation with another, and what you say is still true. Well, take a whole sentence. What you may still have got for sure, if you replace it by another which has the same truth-value? Why, obviously the truth-value. *So* two sentences with the same truth-value are the same! At least, they aren't (probably) the same sentence, but you've got a same presented, designated, meant. So we can say: '2 x 2 = 4 and Descartes tutored the queen of Sweden are the same' just as much as we can say 'The President and the Commander-in-Chief of the armed forces are the same'.

The arguments in 'Sinn und Bedeutung' look like strivings to catch something, to reach it, which get near but do not get hold of their object.

It is a question how much logicians are consciously or unconsciously dependent on the powerful influence of Frege for their extensionalism, as Arthur Prior called the thesis that the only functions of sentences are truth-functions. I don't know the answer to this question, and will leave it.

II

We are enormously indebted to Frege for quantification theory and—essentially—its notation, though his actual notation is not in use. The debt got mediated by Bertrand Russell, who dogmatically proclaimed that what got called the existential quantifier gives us the only sense of 'exists'. I do not know any similar claims by Frege.

Following Frege, we can accept the explanation of 'F exists' or 'There is such a thing as an F' as equivalent to '"F" is not an empty term'. It is preferable to read '(∃x) Fx' as 'Something is F'.

Now this expression is not tensed. This at once informs us that Russell was wrong: there is a sense of 'existence' not captured by this quantifier. It is the sense in which we speak of something's coming into existence, existing for a long or short time, ceasing to exist, or existing for ever. When something F ceases to exist it does not cease to be an instance in '(∃x) Fx' is verified.

With this is connected the following: there are properties of things whose subjects do not need to exist in order to have them. That is, they do not have to exist at the times at which they have such a property. They may for example have ceased to exist. No great-grandfather of mine was alive at any time at which I have been alive. They all became great-grandfathers of me after they had died. Or, if saying that assumes something which some would want to deny and which involves rather profound questions — as it does — then I will take another example, say the great-great- ... grandfathers of a chimpanzee.

Another such property is that of being famous. Protagoras' treatise on truth is fairly famous but not extant. Perhaps it is not merely not extant but does not exist at all in any copy anywhere in the world. But it is famous. So a thing doesn't have to exist in order to be famous.

In order to make this point we have to insist on the difference between being fictitious and having ceased to exist. What never existed at all has not ceased to exist as I am now speaking of cessation of existence. People wonder whether once there was a land, Atlantis, as spoken of in the tale of it, or whether 'Atlantis', in that use of it, is an empty name. Some people will speak of the existence or non-existence of characters in fiction. Mrs Harris is a famous non-existent character in a fiction: that is, it is part of the fiction that Mrs Harris (truly) was a non-existent person, a second-order fiction as some would like to put it. In another way the Chinese shoe salesman in *Tom Sawyer* is a non-existent character in that fiction, I mean there is no such character in that fiction, not even in a capacity of non-existence like Mrs Harris. This Chinese shoe salesman is not famous but with sufficient philosophical discussion might become infamous. Now I do not want to get into this sort of topic at all. I do not deny the existence of Mrs Harris as a famous non-existent character in a fiction, who was dreamed up by an existent character in the fiction. But I don't now want to speak either of such existence or of such non-existence. I put a fence between me and such matters. The things I mean that have real properties when they do not exist are not fictitious things, and both examples that I have given are things that did exist and acquired properties (or still had them) when they had ceased to exist. If something has a name, its ceasing to exist does not make that name become empty. Ceasing to exist does not imply that it is not a possible verifier of a proposition: 'For some x Fx' — for the name can go into the argument place. It can replace the x in the open sentence 'Fx'. To avoid special problems let 'For some x Fx' be 'For some x, x was born on a camel's back in front of the Sphinx in Egypt'. Let's say I assert this, and when you ask me 'who or what?' I don't reply that I don't know though having reason to make my assertion; no, I say I do know one such case; a rabbit I knew, it was called Woofy; dead now as it happens. So Woofy is a rabbit that was born on a camel's back in front of the Sphinx in Egypt. No one would dream of saying that can't be said if Woofy is no more. Obviously one can think of such examples very readily.

It may be an embarrassment to confess the truth, namely that this is a fictitious case. We can all produce non-fictitious cases, e.g. For some x, x is a horse which was struck by lightning when galloping across a hillside with some other horses in the 1960s. This I can testify to. I hope I have said enough to show that I mean to speak of existence and ceasing to exist, not in any fictitious or Pickwickian sense. So when I say there are properties which things can have when they do not exist I do not mean anything that would be verified in the heroine of *Pride and Prejudice*.

Here it is very natural to say: we can accept this so long as the things in question *have* existed, as is implied when I speak of ceasing to exist.

There are those who would say: no, past existence is not necessary, future existence will do. And indeed if being famous after death or destruction is an instance of having a property when you don't exist, then why not 'being predicted' or 'being provided for in someone's will'? Here there is one thing that can be said very briefly: such properties are attributable only to what*ever* will turn out to verify them or who*ever* they are verified in in the future (assuming they aren't verified in present or past existents).

Suppose a prediction by someone: 'There will be two young ravens, call them A and B, in this room at this time on this date in ten years time. One will have a white stripe on one wing, the other will not.' Ten years later we all crowd into the room to see if the prediction comes true. There are just two ravens here, obviously pretty young, and one has a white stripe on one wing. The prophet is there but rejects congratulations, saying 'I was wrong. It's B that has the stripe and I meant A when I said one of them would'. Well, if 'call them "A" and "B"' was all there was to naming them A and B, then

> If to think it out you try
> It doesn't really signify.

The same of course is true of a pair of arbitrary names laid down now in a similar way as names of past things. Only if you use names previously and severally given to individuals does being wrong about which was which become possible. For that, however, the individuals have to have existed.

I have mentioned this point because it speaks for the thesis that things can have properties when they don't actually exist. But this thesis may all the more seem acceptable only with the proviso that it must be limited to 'things that don't exist' only because they have ceased to exist. They at least must *have* existed. Counter-examples will be explained away or receive some special logical classification.

Suppose that Hume's 'missing shade of blue' were a reasonable suggestion—suppose it were not to be limited to one man's experience and the not-missing shades could be presented in an orderly array with a gap which we couldn't fill. We would be able nevertheless to make some comments characterising the missing shade. It has for example a touch of green in it, because the adjacent members in the colour spectrum in which its place is a gap do both have a touch of green in them. So here would be a non-existent thing with a certain property. If it were a useful supposition, I would expect that we would give it some special classification to do with having a place in a system. So presumably it is with 'non-existent chemical compounds'. Such examples do not disturb us.

I now come to an example which if right upsets the substantive restriction to things that have existed. In Wittgenstein's *Philosophical Investigations* the following passage occurs. It begins with some remarks enclosed in quotation marks—this means that they are put forward for consideration, formulated, not asserted.

"What the names in language signify must be indestructible; for it must be possible to describe the state of affairs in which everything destructible is destroyed. And this description will contain words; and what corresponds to these cannot then be destroyed, for otherwise the words would have no meaning." I must not saw off the branch on which I am sitting.

One might object, he adds, that this description would have to except *itself* from the destruction.

Now I have an objection to this objection. Someone says: 'Let us suppose a time of the non-existence of everything destructible.' Would it be reasonable to reply: 'You will have to except *your supposition* from this?' Or if he says 'Let us suppose a time when this description held true: nothing destructible existed'. Would it be reasonable to say 'You will have to except that *description* from the generalization about what didn't exist'?

No. A description, a proposition, a sentence – these are sets of signs intended in a certain signification. Why should such things not have a property when they do not exist? E.g. the property of truth. Truth is a property the *bearer* of which – be it proposition or opinion or Fregean 'thought', if I may so miscall that – does not have to exist at the time when the property holds of it.

If this if right, then the non-existent bearer may not *have* existed either. It may indeed never be going to exist; for no one may ever formulate the proposition or hold the opinion.

In the seventeenth century it began to be true that planets move in elliptical orbits if and only if planets began to move in elliptical orbits in the seventeenth century.

12

Existence and the Existential Quantifier

Mainly following Frege we can explain the existence of an F quite generally as the non-emptiness of the concept F. That is to say, a statement that there exists an F is a statement about the concept, namely that something falls under it. Similarly, a statement of number is a statement about a concept. 'There is a ...' and 'There are seven ...' express second-level concepts, under which fall first-level concepts, the expressions for which would go where I have put dots. Unity or oneness isn't in general an extra feature of one F, as if we could say: When you have one F, there is an F and it is *one*. That *there is one* F again means merely that the concept F is not empty, that something falls under it. So it doesn't add anything to there being an F. That there is *only* one F means that for some x, x is F, and for all y, if y is F, y is the same F as x. And equally we can say 'There are several Fs' says, not that something has a character of multitude, πληθος, but that for some number n, there are an x_1, and an x_2 and so on up to x_n such that x_1, x_2 and so on up to x_n are Fs and are different Fs. (I have made a small variation on Frege in speaking of x's being the same F as y, etc., and not merely being the same as y.)

There is plenty more to say about numbers but this is all we need for present purposes to understand the most usual sort of statement about how many such-and-such's there are.

'I believe in one god' in practice means not just 'I believe in a deity' but 'I believe in only one'.

---

*   From a manuscript without date or title; title supplied.

But is there no such thing as ascribing unity to something, or denying it, where unity is a feature or character? As when we say that a play lacks unity.

And is there no other sense of 'existence'? That unity and existence and number do hang together like this is a thoroughly useful and clarifying bit of logical theory. But when Russell tells us that existence is expressed by the existential quantifier and that's an end of the matter — there is no other sense — we may doubt.

In this sense of existence it is impossible for anything to cease to exist. Abraham Lincoln is dead but he still falls under the concept 'sometime President of the U.S.A.' Protagoras wrote a book *On Truth*. It is no longer extant. But it still falls under the concept 'treatise written by Protagoras'.

If we are symmetrists about time we ought also to say that if Russell is right about existence it is impossible for anything to begin to exist.

If you are an asymmetrist about time you may have a problem about the future truth of a proposition: '($\exists x$) at present Fx' unless it is to be verified by something that already exists now or else has existed. You will have such a problem if you think that the question 'Namely?' must in principle have an answer when someone has truly asserted, for example, that there are hills older than the Himalayas, or that some people survive being swallowed by a whale.

I will not delay on this, but press on with the fact that there is coming into existence and passing away, and that this existence is *not* expressed by the existential quantifier. This sense of 'existence' is like that of 'life'; indeed life is a form of existence.

It is a question whether in *this* sense of 'existence' numbers and forms exist, have existence apart from other things being numbered or in-formed. Plato thought they did: that they were eternal and unchangeable substances (οὐσίαι). (This sense of 'existence' is not one in which what has existence must be capable of *passing away*, or it must have been possible that it *came into existence*.)

Was Plato wrong? Is the existence of a number or of a form of things nothing but what is expressed by the existential quantifier?

We can ask 'Is there a number which is a sum of two cubes in five different ways?' This is much like 'Is there such a thing as a cross between a Kodiak and a Polar bear?' In both cases we can explain the question as meaning 'Is this an empty concept?'

But for numbers there is no justified assumption of a realm of individuals whose inhabitants we're, as it were, finding the natural history of. Contrast *bears.* 'That sounds quite possible' we may say. But do we know it's really possible before we've got such a cross?

I deprecate the term 'existential quantifier' and the reading of '$(\exists x)$ ...' as 'There exists an x such that ...'. I call it rather the 'particular quantifier' and would read it 'For some x'.

If we read it 'There exists an x such that ...' it looks as if we could point to a contradiction in '$(\exists x)$ x no longer exists'. If this is read as 'For some x x no longer exists', what we are doing corresponds to the fact that something does not cease to fall under any concepts by dying or otherwise ceasing to exist. The question, 'Namely, for example?' is easy to answer truly: 'Bucephalus' (Alexander's horse) or 'The crown of Edward the Confessor'. It is quite different to be dead or destroyed and to be fictitious or mythical or imaginary.

A number can sometimes be taken in by eye, touch or hearing. Then it *can* be called a property — mentioned in a perceptual judgment — of a collection of individuals that have the role of the units making up the number of the collection of *those* units.

The kind-name of the units gives the concept under which the counting is proceeding — e.g. dots, squares that are not within larger squares, horses.

'But the procedure of counting can also be applied to numbers! — or to colours!' Yes, but there is an important difference. There is no sense to the question 'What makes the unity of a number?' It is a number, and *numbers* are what you happen to be counting.

Whereas there is sense to the question what makes the unity of a spot or other mark. We must distinguish two questions:

1. What is the criterion for *this* being another specimen of the unit whose kind-name gives you the concept under which you are counting?
2. What is the unity of *this* unit?

If the second question is different from the first it means 'What is the unity of an X' where Xs are the units you are counting.

There are terms for which question 2 makes no distinct sense, no sense different from that of 1. Numbers, colours, and forms generally are such. And there are terms for which 2 has a distinct sense.

Where the question about unity has no distinct sense, the numerals used in counting, and the word 'multiplicity' don't signify any feature in the objects. Unless you call it a feature that they 'fall under a concept which itself falls under the second-level concept signified by

"There are several ..."' Nor does 'one' here ever add anything to the existence which is expressed by the particular quantifier.

Where there *is* a distinct question, the numeral terms may refer to whatever makes *another* φ possible, where 'φ' is the expression of the concept.

Here for example belongs the idea of matter as principle of individuation. Contrast counting stamps on a sheet of 25p stamps, and counting *patterns* of 25p stamps.

Consider a heading 'substances' and under it the terms 'living thing' and 'alive'. 'Living thing' is a classificatory term, 'alive' is not. It is like 'extant' and 'current', which we might write down under 'alive'.

Answering to 'living thing' we might then put the *wider* term '(substantial) entity'. Although it may belong to the essence of something to be a living thing or a substantial entity, that is not to say it must be alive or extant. This we see from the fact that substantial entities may cease to exist, and living things may die.

It is an opinion which some people hold with a surprising emphasis that a dead man—a human corpse—is a man. One who thinks this has missed the fact that, for a living thing, existing (in the sense in which existence can stop) is being alive. A human corpse may be called 'a man', you may count how many dead men there are in a cellar after a shoot-out, but that does not mean that what you are counting in counting dead men is men: you are counting ex-men.

How can we choose between symmetrism and asymmetrism about past and future? The smoothness of the logical system with quantification over times is an insufficient argument. Besides, it seems to make it impossible to know that there are no men with naturally green beards, if future men perhaps have naturally green hairs on their chins. However, asymmetrism has its problems: how do you *avoid* significantly tensing the existential quantifier? Should we say: temporal things are not appropriately dealt with using these formalisms?

There is one argument that I know of that can be offered in favour of asymmetry. I base it on an observation of Arthur Prior's, from which I produce the following story. Suppose I say: Ten years hence, on this date and at this time, there will be two birds in this room, call them A and B. One of them will have a white stripe on its wing. The time comes, and some of us gather here to see if I was right. Sure enough there are two birds here, and one of them has a white stripe. You all congratulate me and I say 'Oh! but I wasn't right! It's the wrong bird that has the stripe, it should have been the other one!'

Now what I said in making the prediction was *true*. So I *was* right, and without elaboration I can't claim to have been wrong.

The case is like the difference between truth and knowledge pointed out by Gettier. If I say 'A Russian politician was assassinated yesterday' and it turns out that Gorbachev was shot yesterday in Minsk, what I said was true. It wasn't knowledge if my reason for saying it was my belief that Andropov had been stabbed to death in Moscow, which did *not* happen. The future is not accessible to knowledge (short of prophetical utterance). That is, it is not accessible to knowledge as the past is because of a set of connections from the event to the belief. Knowledge of the future is indeed possible by inference from the past and present; but the reason why the story about the birds is so comical is that it makes the prediction sound as if it were meant to be a bit of knowledge with identification of this bird and that; i.e. my saying 'Oh! I was wrong!' is introduced in the story as if it were on a par with my saying 'Oh! I was wrong!' even though *what I said* was true: a Russian politician was assassinated; I was wrong about who and how and where, so what I said did not express knowledge.

We are standardly taught that the existential quantifier is tenseless. Remember that modern quantification theory was invented by Frege, who was pretty exclusively interested in the foundations of arithmetic. Arithmetic is tenseless, so you will have tenses neither in the readings for quantifiers nor in the functional part of quantified propositions. Russell extended his interest over temporal things and so you have straight away the problems about tenses not merely in the quantifiers but in the functional expressions. I've mentioned one problem about the quantifiers: if you say 'There's no human being with a green beard' or 'No human being has a green beard', are you including all future human beings in the compass of your declaration? The inclination to do so inclines you also to be a symmetrist about time. But there is also that tense in 'has a green beard'. You may be instructed to deal with tense by introducing quantification over times, thus: 'For no x, for no time t, is x a human being at t with a beard at t' and to regard that 'is' as tenseless like the 'is' of number theory. Your quantifier is to range over past, present and future objects and you keep tense out of the functional part of your proposition by also quantifying over times. This, which is standardly taught in many places, introduces a metaphysical principle of symmetry between past and future into what is learned and taught as formal logic.

13

On a Queer
Pattern of Argument

The pattern to which my title refers is:

1°	If p, then q.
2°	If r, then not (if p then q).
3°	If not p then r.
∴	p and q.

We get 'not r' from the first two premises and then 'p' from 'not r' and the third; with the first one again this gives us the conclusion.

ARGUMENT A

Now consider the following instance of the pattern; I will call it argument A.

1'	If that tree falls down, it will block the road for a long time.
2'	That's not true if there's a tree-clearing machine working.
3'	If the tree doesn't fall, there will be a tree-clearing machine working.
∴	The tree will fall and the road will be blocked for a long time.

The argument is formally valid and its premises are mutually compatible. They can all be true together just in the case where the tree

---

*   From *Peter Geach: Philosophical Encounters* edited by Harry A. Lewis (Dordrecht: Kluwer Academic Publishers, 1991), pp.121–135.

falls and blocks the road for a long time. How is it then that there is obviously something screwy about this argument?

The answer seems to arise from a consideration of the subject-matter. In order actually to 'come to the conclusion' you would have to hold the premises true. But, one would say: how can you be confident of 1', if 2' is true and is also *as* pertinent as the truth of 3' makes it? How can you believe that the tree will block the road for a long time if it falls, if you grant that this won't be true if there's a tree clearing machine operating? You might, indeed, if you were quite certain that there was no question of there being a tree-clearing machine. But you accept that if the tree doesn't fall there will be one. So, unless you *already* believe that the tree will fall, how can you be sure that there won't be a machine working? Of course, if you are sure that the tree will fall, we can understand how you might be in a position to accept the truth of those other propositions too. You may have some reason to think that if the tree does fall, no tree-clearing machine will be working. So you judge that none will be working, and hence that (2') casts no doubt on (1'). But in that case, the validity of argument A notwithstanding, it by no means tells us the real grounds of your conclusion. You believe that the tree will fall, and that if it falls the road *will* be blocked. Those are the real grounds for believing that it will fall and the road be blocked. You *assent* indeed to those other two propositions, and from them and the hypothetical that you do have as a real ground, the same conclusion follows. But the premises as given could not be the grounds of belief in the conclusion, even though they are all assented to and the conclusion does follow from them.

(There is an exception we must make in order to be quite accurate. If one took the three hypotheticals as true on someone's authority, one could use them as premises and believe the conclusion on the strength of them. Here the premises really would be one's grounds. But a question arises about the authority. If it were simply someone making judgments on the situation, the argument of the last paragraph would apply to it.)

If all this is right, we have here a rather interesting case of a set of propositions which entail a conclusion but are impossible grounds for coming to that conclusion, and that not in any trivial or obvious fashion. (Trivial cases are easy to construct; any circular argument is one, for example.)

The peculiarity of our case is that there doesn't seem to be any difficulty about reasonably judging any of the three premises to be true without having already judged the conclusion or part of it to be true. The difficulty lies in combining them in knowledge, or in a reasonable judgment, unless part of the conclusion is part of the ground for accepting the combination. One wants to say: that you can get this conclusion out of these three propositions is ground for doubting the conjunction of them! But the reason is not that the conclusion is itself false, let alone absurd. It is a perfectly possible proposition, and is objected to only as a conclusion from perfectly possible propositions, which are mutually compatible and from which it does follow.

The reason for objecting seems not to be anything peculiar to our example, but to reside in a fairly general character of the first two premises when the first one does not state any 'necessary truth', i.e. when q does not *follow* from p. The general character seems to be this: one can usually accept instances of 1° and 2° together, when q doesn't follow from p, only when one is independently confident that not r. The circumstances are rare in which one thinks if p then q, and just because of that, it being clear that if r, then not (if p then q), and one can deduce that not r. Notice that when one judges 'If p then q' it is easy to invent propositions 'If r, then not (if p then q)' which one will accept without the slightest perturbation of one's belief that if p then q. E.g. in the example in hand, make the second proposition: 'If an angel will dive down and pick up any tree that falls, it's not true that if that tree falls it will block the road.' Or: 'If the tree will evaporate as soon as it falls ...' Our actual example is disquieting just because 'If there's a tree-clearing machine it's not true that ...', though compatible with the first proposition, nevertheless seems to cast doubt on it. Is this a matter of form or content? One answers 'content', because of the compatibility. On the other hand, the *point* of producing a remark of that form, if someone has said 'If p then q', *is* in general to cast doubt on the hypothetical. Whether it actually does so is not just a matter of the content, but of the particular circumstances. There are circumstances in which it would be as silly to say 'Not if there's a tree-clearing machine working' as to say 'Not if there's an angel ...'. It might be wondered how we can discuss the matter outside any particular context; but we have a perfectly possible third premise, and if it is accepted as true, that at once means that the second premise *is* highly pertinent. It couldn't be true that if the tree didn't fall there'd be a tree-clearing machine, unless tree-clearing machines were a practical likelihood. (Of course our hypotheticals are not material hypotheticals.)

So the point is that the truth *and pertinence* of the second proposition must throw doubt on the first one except for someone with special information that there *won't* be a tree-clearing machine at work. And this point we can generalise. If we judge that if *p*, then *q*, and a true proposition 'if *r*, then not (if *p* then *q*)' is presented to our attention, that is liable to cast doubt on our first judgment. What casts doubt will not be the truth alone of the second proposition, but its truth combined with the impossibility of just dismissing it because we don't have to take its antecedent seriously.

There are large numbers of hypothetical judgments that are like this. It is an interesting and important observation that there is a whole class of judgments such that when we make them we are not implicitly dismissing as false everything that would falsify them. In contrast, when I make a categorical statement with appropriate confidence, it is very often the case that I can straightway rule out as false what would falsify it—just because I know that *it* is true.

Then we have perhaps discovered the special character of (theoretical) hypotheticals whose consequents don't follow logically from their antecedents. We might call this character 'essential defeasibility'. This will be the reason why, even though 'not *r*' follows from 'if *p* then *q* and if *r*, then not (if *p* then *q*)', still it may be highly unreasonable to deduce 'not *r*' from that conjunction.

But is this character quite general? Is there no such thing as an indefeasible sort of 'if *p* then *q*', where '*q*' doesn't follow from '*p*'? Or, rather, a sort of case where the judgment 'if *p* then *q*' has it in it to be indefeasible?—I mean, if one has judged it soundly, it could itself be used to reject '*r*' in 'if *r*, then not (if *p* then *q*)'. If this is possible, we can have a case where we come to the conclusion '*p* and *q*' from the three hypothetical premises 1°, 2°, 3°.

ARGUMENT B

I believe that there are such cases. Here is one: we have a bank of coloured lights operated by an apparatus of circuits, switches, etc. behind them. There are, among others, a red and a green light and there is a green inhibitor which, when it is on, prevents the green from coming on. The main way it does this is by changing a circuit which otherwise runs from red through green. Now let us suppose that we have our pattern of argument in this material. I will call it argument B:

1″	If the red light is on so is the green.
2″	If the green inhibitor is on, it's not true that if the red light is on so is the green.
3″	If the red light is not on the green inhibitor is on.
∴	The red light is on and so is the green.

The whole apparatus must either be actually working, with current turned on, lights flashing, etc., or else the description 'The red light is on' means 'The arrangement is such that, given the current, the red light shines' etc. It doesn't matter which way we take it, so long as we stick to one way at a time.

1″ is said because the red-green circuit is intact — and the bulbs with their attachments in good working order.

2″ is said because the green-inhibitor is such as to break the red–green circuit when turned on. It switches the path of any possible current so as to by-pass green.

3″ is said because the red switch, in its off position for red, is so connected with the green-inhibitor as to turn it on.

The conclusion follows, whichever way we take it. Either the display is working, and then the conclusion is that the red and green light are actually shining, or, if it is not currently working, present adjustment of the mechanism is such as to make it show red and green lights if there is current.

Here, then, is a case where an argument in this pattern is undisturbing. The reason is that there is no difficulty about concluding from 1″ and 2″ together that the green-inhibitor is off. And the reason for that is that 1″ is true because of a particular set-up, so that we could be satisfied that it was true, enough to respond to 2″ by saying 'Well, the green-inhibitor is off, then'.

At this point I ought to confess that I have found electrical engineers and other experts recalcitrant to the argument. They have not been willing to grant that 'red on, green on, and green-inhibitor off' is the only situation consistent with the three hypotheticals. But I think the reason is that the hypotheticals are not standard descriptions of machines. In particular, the second one is apt to puzzle an engineer. If we make an array showing the off-on possibilities for red, green and the green-inhibitor, we cannot say that any row verifies any of the hypotheticals; we can say that some rows are incompatible with the first and the third, but can't say even as much as that about the second. We may strike out, as incompatible with the conjunction of all three, any row that is incompatible with any one of them. Putting a tick for 'on', a cross for 'off', 'F' for 'incompatible', and 'PT' for 'possibly true', we can construct a compatibility table as follows:

	Red	Green	Green-inhibitor	Propositions		
				1″	2″	3″
a	✓	✓	✓	PT	PT	PT
b	✗	✓	✓	PT	PT	PT
c	✓	✗	✓	F	PT	PT
d	✗	✗	✓	PT	PT	PT
e	✓	✓	✗	PT	PT	PT
f	✗	✓	✗	PT	PT	F
g	✓	✗	✗	F	PT	PT
h	✗	✗	✗	PT	PT	F

Only four lines (c, f, g, h) are ruled out as incompatible with one or other of the propositions. But we can delete the first two lines on the ground that from the data about the green-inhibitor, we know that it can't be on with green on too. This leaves us with d and e as compatible with each of our hypotheticals, and the engineer is apt to say: 'So, you see, there are two states compatible with these specifications, and you are wrong to say that red and green must be on. We can have red and green off and the green-inhibitor on.' He says this because — except for the exclusion of *green and green-inhibitor both on* — he demands that the matter be decided by what is excluded and what allowed by the hypothetical propositions considered severally. Of course he can accommodate the point about green and the green-inhibitor to his way of looking at the matter: it's really a fourth hypothetical: 'If the green-inhibitor is on, green is off', which ought to be put into the specifications. This will lead to the exclusion of the first two rows in the same way as the others are excluded. He makes nothing of the second proposition: 'If the green-inhibitor is on, it is not true that if red is on green is on.' By the methods we have just been applying, it has no consequences, and he is apt to conclude that it imposes no constraints on the construction or state of the apparatus.

However, we ought to have excluded all the first four rows. The reason is that although all but one of those rows are compatible with each of the three hypotheticals, *none* of them is compatible with the first two *taken together*; for this conjunction requires that the green-inhibitor be off. Thus row d is excluded after all, and row e alone is compatible with the three hypotheticals taken together.

So argument B is a case where the conclusion may be reached as a genuine deduction from those premises. The thing that is most characteristic, relative to this possibility, is that each of the hypothetical propositions is based on, is even descriptive of, a *quite particular* set-up. The more an hypothetical proposition approaches to being in effect a description of an arrangement or of the properties of an object or region, the more it will be possible to use it, if true, to reject the antecedent of a related proposition of the form 2°. One may wonder how a 'generic' proposition[1] of the form 2° could be known, in a case where its antecedent is regularly false. Our example gives a way. The green-inhibitor is not operative, it remains in the off position but its construction shows us how it is apt to operate. And, of course, it merely remains in the off position so long as the first hypothetical is true. Switching red off will at once activate the green-inhibitor and make the first hypothetical false. But, again, we may know that the first hypothetical is then false, not because sometimes red is on and green not, but because the red-green circuit is broken. Not that the matter *has* to stand so, for we have not stipulated whether the *status quo* will be restored by merely switching red on again; if it is not, then the falsehood of 'If red is on green is on' will appear also in our now getting red without green. But if switching red on does restore the *status quo*, we shall not have red sometimes on without green, even when 'If red is on green is on' is false. To repeat, these hypotheticals are not truth-functional. And, further, we have a case of non-collapse of 'if p, then if p then q' to 'if p then q'.

ARGUMENT C

This is perhaps best embedded in a story. It runs:

1‴   If NN. decides at four o'clock to leave at five, he will leave at five.

2‴   If the doors are locked at four fifty, it's not true that if NN. decides at four to leave at five, he will leave at five.

3‴   If NN. does not decide at four o'clock to leave at five, the doors will be locked at four fifty.

∴   NN. will decide at four to leave at five and will do so.

I will make NN. Napoleon's son, the King of Rome; the time will be when he was living at Schönbrunn. I will suppose (this is mere imagination on my part) that the usual practice at the palace is to have guards, who are supposed to prevent the prince from leaving, posted

---

[1]   Here, contrary to the practice of Russell, Church, etc., I speak of a proposition as capable of being now true, now false; von Wright calls a proposition so conceived 'generic'.

at all exits, except when they are locked up, and that they are regularly locked up at four fifty in the afternoon. The locking makes it impossible for the prince to get out so long as they are all locked up. However, on this particular day an Arch-duchess has been visiting. She is due to make her farewells inside the palace at four o'clock, and this is the moment at which, there is some suggestion, the prince might decide to leave with her. At four forty five she will descend with her lady-in-waiting, her jewel boxes, her maids, her guards; she will leave the palace and be ensconced in her carriage to the accompaniment of ceremonious salutes; at five she will drive away.

The prince has a tutor, perhaps new to the task, with some sense of his charge's princely dignity and power of decision; we may suppose that our first proposition: 'If the Prince decides at four that he will leave at five, then he will leave at five' is this tutor's indignant response to someone whom he hears laughing at the suggestion that the young man is thinking of leaving with the Arch-duchess. The second statement 'if the doors are locked at four fifty, it's not true that if the Prince decides at four to leave at five, he will leave at five' is made by a courtier who knows the usual practice with respect to the locking of the doors, and also knows that the Prince will not be able (for some reason) to come down to get out of the palace *before* four fifty. The final remark is a contribution of the Emperor's secretary: he knows that the Emperor has given orders that if the Prince makes no decision at four to depart with the Arch-duchess, the doors are to be locked as usual at four fifty—though nothing has been said about what is to be done if the Prince does make such an arrangement.

The tutor, we will suppose, does not doubt the truth of either contribution from the other two; but, convinced of the royal dignity of his pupil, he reiterates that if the Prince arranges—decides—at four to leave at five, he will do so. The argument then leads to the conclusion that the Prince will decide to leave and will leave. But this is even madder than the argument about the tree.

It is not much to the point to remark that the tutor is wrong in his belief in the first proposition. *He* believes it; if he believes the other two observations, he ought to be able to draw the conclusion which follows from the three propositions. We may ask how he can believe the second proposition if he is so sure of the first; but he might do so because he knows enough of the palace practice to know that once the doors have been locked at their regular time, it is a complicated procedure to get them unlocked; it takes too long; he knows the Arch-duchess is unconditionally to set off at five, and the business of getting a door unlocked would delay the Prince's exit from the palace far too long, if he tries to emerge after the doors have been locked. Clearly the tutor's willingness to accept the second proposition without being shaken in his belief in the first is determined by a further belief, namely:

> X   If NN. decides at four o'clock to leave at five, the doors will not be locked at four fifty.

But while the addition of this to the tutor's beliefs makes us understand why he is not bothered by the second proposition, it doesn't make any difference to the reasonableness of drawing the conclusion.

Notice that the third proposition doesn't work (as in our construe of the tree case) to ensure the pertinence of the possibility that the doors will be locked. In the tree case, we said 'How can one believe the first proposition if the second is as pertinent as the truth of the third shows it to be?' But the Emperor's order would be rather reassuring than otherwise to the tutor; to be sure, the doors may be locked, but his only information on whether they will be or not is that they will be if the Prince doesn't decide to leave — and their being locked in that case doesn't matter.

Except that the tutor can apparently *derive* from the first two propositions that the doors will *not* be locked! Our question now must be: how can he hold both propositions, when their conjunction implies a proposition whose falsehood he is perfectly prepared to entertain — so long as it's false only if his pupil does not arrange to leave? There must be something wrong with, or misinterpreted about, his belief in the first two propositions, if they are to license him to conclude that the doors absolutely will *not* be locked.

He holds these three propositions:

> 1'''   If the Prince decides at four to leave at five, he will leave at five.
>
> 2'''   If the doors are locked at four fifty, it's not true that if the Prince decides at four to leave at five he will leave at five.
>
> X   If the Prince decides at four to leave at five, the doors will *not* be locked at four fifty.

and his belief in the third one explains his equanimity in face of the suggestion that the doors *will* be locked. But what use is it to say that? It still follows from the first two, taken together, that the doors will not be locked at four fifty; and it still seems unreasonable to believe that on the ground of the first two. All the more because by taking this conclusion together with the third proposition, 3''', the tutor will be able to deduce the Prince's actual choice and action. *That* is completely preposterous.

Since it is preposterous to draw the conclusion, the tutor, if he recognises this, cannot after all believe the first two propositions together. Suppose he firmly adheres to the first one. What is he to say to the second? He must say that *it* is true only if the Prince does not decide to leave. That is, he withholds assent from it and replaces it by:

> (i) 'If the Prince does decide at four to leave at five, then it is *not* true that if the doors are locked at four fifty, it is not true that if he decides at four to leave at five he will leave at five.'

This might be called a somewhat mystical conviction, but it enables him to escape the absurd deduction. Can he grant that the second proposition is true *if* (not just *only if*) the Prince does *not* decide to leave? i.e. can he say:

> (ii) 'If the Prince does not decide at four to leave at five, then, if the doors are locked at four fifty it is *not* true that if he decides at four to leave at five he will leave at five'?

He surely can't grant that. He insists that if the Prince decides at four to leave at five, he will leave at five; to grant that, in the case where he does not so decide, this is false if the doors are locked, would be very strange. Why? Because by proposition 3''' the doors *are* locked if he does not make that decision – so, if he does not make that decision it is *not* still true that if he does make it he will leave; but it *is* true (*ex hypothesi*) that if he does make it he will leave; and so by *modus tollens* he *must* make the decision after all, and once more we have a preposterous deduction. Thus the tutor must assert (i) and refuse assent to the original second proposition (2'''), if he is to adhere to the first one and not be drawn into a fantastic deduction that the doors will not be locked (and so, via the third proposition, that the prince will decide to leave and will leave). If he cannot but grant the second proposition and is nevertheless unwilling to infer that the doors will not be locked, he must allow the second proposition to cast doubt upon the first. That is, he must do so in the circumstances, because it is evidently quite on the cards for the doors to be locked.

ARGUMENT D

Argument A (about the tree) might occur, crazily, as follows: the three propositions are statements made by three different people talking together, and a fourth straightway says he believes them all and draws the conclusion! This is crazy because, in the absence of any indication from the first one, he should not be assumed still to believe what he said at first. It is not of course ruled out that he still does think the same. For it may be a mere fragment of his thought—he may be already convinced that the tree will fall *and* will block the road. Then he has given vent to this thought only in a partial form when he says 'If that tree falls, it will block the road'. In this way one who is too timid to assert what he knows or believes, especially about the future, may come out with such an 'If ...'.

This leads on to the fourth embodiment of the pattern, argument D. It might be produced by a less evasive and tortuous Johannes de Silentio picturing Isaac in the interval in which he has realised that *he* is the intended sacrifice, and before Abraham's hand is stayed. Isaac reasons:

1''''   If God has promised my father that he will be the father of a great nation through me, then my father will be.

2''''   If my father kills me, it's not true that if God has promised him he will be the father of a great nation through me, then he will be.

(*Therefore he is not going to kill me.*)

3''''   If God has not promised my father that he will be the father of a great nation through me, my father is going to kill me.

∴   God has promised that to my father and it will be fulfilled.

This argument differs from all the others in that in the first proposition the consequent necessarily follows from the antecedent. The question is: why should Isaac believe the second proposition? Many children have been murdered by their parents. Upon the belief 'What God has promised, he will perform' neither this fact nor the present threat of such a death has any bearing at all. 1'''' 'If God has promised my father that through me he will be the father of a great nation, then he will be' is true in the way the generality is. We must suppose Isaac's thought to be not a mere statement of something obvious—and irrelevant—but only the tip of an iceberg. In reality, Isaac's belief is that God has promised Abraham that. That is what he will have been brought up to believe. So the first proposition has for him the significance rather of 'Since God has promised my father that, my father will etc.', and not only the significance of the necessary hypothetical. This would also explain why Isaac should think of the second proposition. There has been this promise. If his father kills him, the necessary hypothetical itself, the irrefragable 'What God promises, he will perform' will be falsified. The third proposition states something that must have been dreadfully obvious to Isaac—if his belief in the existence of that promise is wrong, it is all up with him. It *looks* as if it were all up with him. But it cannot be, because God performs his promises, and if Isaac is killed God doesn't perform his promises. So it isn't true, it cannot be true, that this is his end. If that's not true, then since clearly 3'''' *is* true its antecedent is false. Of course we made Isaac assume that already, in explaining why he might believe 2'''', but if, believing 1'''' and 2'''', he manages to believe he will not be killed, the evident truth of 3'''' strongly reinforces his belief in the promise.

Note that there is an alternative possibility for Isaac, which does not involve his drawing the conclusion that Abraham will not kill him. He might reject 2'''' and replace it by:

> If God has made that promise, it is not true that if my father kills me it is not true that if God has promised that through me my father will be the father of a great nation, he will be.

This is parallel to the proposition (i) by which we described the tutor as replacing 2''' in argument C. I suggested it was a somewhat mystical conviction: the tutor is so sure of his pupil's royal dignity and independence, that he brushes aside the evidence on the consequences of the door's being locked—if the Prince once makes that decision, he'll carry it out no matter what. The suggestion was pretty absurd and was only made to evade the preposterous conclusion. In fact of course the tutor should abandon the first proposition rather than the second as soon as he sees the consequences of accepting all three. (Still, there is something about this case that remains obscure and intensely puzzling.)

The parallel proposition for Isaac is not in the same position as the tutor's proposition (i). It is essentially the thought that even if Abraham kills him, God can raise him up and still fulfil the promise. And, as with the original proposition 2'''', Isaac's only reason for believing it would be his belief in the promise. (There is not in his case the odd problem of avoiding a preposterous conclusion out of the three hypotheticals.) Of course no germane conclusion now follows from the three propositions. Proposition 3'''', which suggests the doubt that must threaten Isaac, would now be amplified as 'If God has not made that promise, my father is going to kill me and that *will* be the end of me'. But the propositions have fallen apart and are not combined in any argument.

We can easily parallel argument D in more familiar matter. Let the propositions be: 'If they've published the award, they'll give me the money', 'Not if there's no money in the kitty', and 'If they haven't published the award, there's no money in the kitty'. Instead of Isaac, we have an anxious young woman who has *heard* that they've published the award, but who has some rather good evidence that there'll be no money in the kitty. There are differences: the first proposition not being necessarily true, it's not too puzzling why she should accept the second; she might after all take it as casting doubt on the first. So we have to put in that the standing of the 'they' is such as to make it seem out of the question that they should publish the award and not give the money. If that *is* out of the question, then why should she accept the second proposition—unless (and here is a close parallel with Isaac) she believes they have published? No money in the kitty means no payment will be made—just as no Isaac means no descent of a nation through him. Harmless, *unless they have published*—but she *thinks* they have. If she's really convinced of that and of 'their' probity, she may reject the threatening evidence of no money in the kitty. Perhaps she quite sees that (in the circumstances) if they *haven't* published, it means there's no money in the kitty; for not merely has she heard that they've published, but (we will suppose) they ought to have done so—*unless* they have no money to pay the award. So if she is sure about their having published, and firm in her confidence in them, she infers that there must be money there, and her belief that they have published is reinforced, for only if there isn't money will they *not* have done so.

In these cases the argument does not function to establish the conclusion *p* & *q*, for it operates because the person deploying it already believes that *p*. But it's not like the tree case, where the second and third propositions did no work that we could see, once we found out that the believer in the first proposition believed that *p*. In argument D the logical relations of the three propositions give us a structure of confidence, probable anxiety and doubt, clinging to or abandoning conviction, which is worth examining. A man who believes an instance of *p, if p then q, and if r then not (if p then q)* may have to bet on *r*'s *not* being the case, though any evidence that antecedently seems germane to whether *r* is the case or not speaks *for* *r*. That is, the things you would enquire into in order to find out whether *r* held all suggest it does hold. He may have to make some grave decision (our young woman can easily be made an instance of this); he may even have to bet his life. And yet the grounds for believing the proposition 'if *p* then *q*' may not themselves tend to make *r* improbable. As we saw in examining the engineers' objections to argument B, the propositions which severally allow a case, may exclude it when combined, and the grounds for believing the separate propositions may have very little to do with one another.

CONCLUSION

In discussing this pattern of argument, I have raised a problem rather than clarified anything. It is quite easy to go on constructing further arguments on the same pattern. E.g. 'If that dog's got rabies, that man is a goner; that's not so if the man takes such-and-such a course of injections; if the dog's not got rabies, the man will take those injections: *ergo*, the dog's got rabies and the man is a goner'! And so on. The arguments are often quite crazy. But aren't they valid? And aren't both premises and conclusions quite possible – given, for each case, a suitable story? (The third premise usually needs a story. But stories are easily supplied.) It is possible that minute scrutiny of the case would always yield reason to say the premises would not be jointly believed. But why does one know in advance that one wants to find something of the kind? Am I wrong – against the engineers – to think argument B is all right? Is there usually some lurking ambiguity? For the *form* is surely valid. And the use of such an argument to reinforce conviction in threatening circumstances, as in the D arguments, is as sound as the convictions themselves.

Several people have suggested that what would really be meant by the second premises would be, schematically, 'If *r*, then if *p* then not *q*'. But that is too strong. 'Not (if *p* then *q*)' means that *p*'s being the case doesn't involve *q*'s being the case, not that it involves *q*'s not being the case.

Index

Printed in the USA
CPSIA information can be obtained
at www.ICGtesting.com
CBHW020752111124
17203CB00041B/188